Methods
That Matter

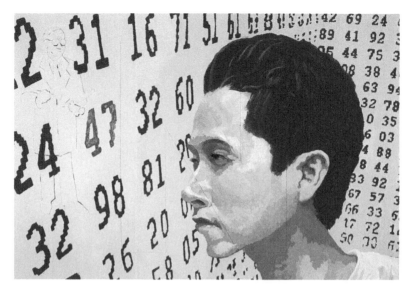

Beyond N by Robert Mullenix.

Methods That Matter

*Integrating Mixed Methods for More
Effective Social Science Research*

EDITED BY M. CAMERON HAY

The University of Chicago Press   Chicago and London

M. CAMERON HAY is associate professor of anthropology, coordinator of Global Health Studies, and director of the Global Health Research Innovation Center at Miami University, as well as associate research anthropologist in the Center for Culture and Health at the University of California, Los Angeles. She is the author of *Remembering to Live*.

The University of Chicago Press, Chicago 60637
The University of Chicago Press, Ltd., London
© 2016 by The University of Chicago
All rights reserved. Published 2016.
Printed in the United States of America

25 24 23 22 21 20 19 18 17 16   1 2 3 4 5

ISBN-13: 978-0-226-32852-2 (cloth)
ISBN-13: 978-0-226-32866-9 (paper)
ISBN-13: 978-0-226-32883-6 (e-book)
DOI: 10.7208/chicago/9780226328836.001.0001

Library of Congress Cataloging-in-Publication Data
Names: Hay, M. Cameron, 1965–
Title: Methods that matter : integrating mixed methods for more
   effective social science research / edited by M. Cameron Hay.
Description: Chicago ; London : The University of Chicago Press,
   2016. | Includes index.
Identifiers: LCCN 2015036868 | ISBN 9780226328522
   (cloth : alk. paper) | ISBN 9780226328669 (pbk. : alk. paper) |
   ISBN 9780226328836 (e-book)
Subjects: LCSH: Social sciences—Methodology.
Classification: LCC H61 .M492644 2016 | DDC 300.72—dc23
   LC record available at http://lccn.loc.gov/2015036868

♾ This paper meets the requirements of ANSI/NISO Z39.48–1992
(Permanence of Paper).

For Tom,

mentor, friend, and

champion of mixed methods

Contents

Preface: Applying Methods That Matter

This book is about the insights, joys, and challenges of mixed methods research. It is written by social scientists and for social scientists, whether novices thinking about their first research project or seasoned researchers who secretly sense that they are missing some crucial piece of the puzzle. It is also for people who want to partner with others or do research on topics that directly matter for people's lives and well-being.

Social scientists do research to answer compelling questions typically framed within the scholarly conversations of our fields. We write books or journal articles. We make presentations at conferences. We stay abreast of the scholarship in our fields. All of these practices tend to occur within disciplinary silos. Anthropologists write for and talk to other anthropologists. Psychologists write for and talk to other psychologists. Through the pragmatics of communication and academic advancement, we have refined our methodologies and our abilities to speak among ourselves—and also limited our engagement across disciplines.

Most researchers, within and beyond academia, have a discipline-specific methodology comfort zone. For people trained in psychology or sociology, the methodological bias tends to be for standardized surveys and controlled experiments that yield numbers, quantitative data. Thus the research questions addressed in quantitatively oriented disciplines are those that can be explored deductively with predetermined ranges of topics, choices, and possible outcomes. For people trained in anthropology, the methodological bias tends to be for participant observations and interviews in naturally occurring contexts that yield ethnographic qualitative data. Thus the research questions addressed in qualitatively oriented disciplines are those that can be explored inductively, allowing the participants themselves to define the salient topics, choices, and outcomes as they go about their everyday lives. As a result, this methodological division has consequences on the types of research questions one can ask, and on who will read one's answers.

A mixed methods approach offers a different vision: (1) allows the research problem itself to guide the methodology; (2) uses a mix of quantitative and qualitative methodologies to examine that problem both deductively and inductively so that findings will be explainable; (3) produces results that engage scholarly conversations across disciplines as well as speak to policymakers.

The costs of not being part of the same conversation are significant. Using singular methodological perspectives can result in expensive research projects that fail to offer explanations for findings (as discussed in Harkness and Super, chapter 8). *Beyond N*, the painting by Robert Mullenix on the frontispiece of this volume, illustrates potential shortcomings of single-methods research. The researcher with his clipboard and long coat is etched in the paint, so embedded in the medium of his work that he can see his subject only through a screen of numbers. From his point of view, the subject is just one among many who together make up the "N" of his research. The N, embossed in the canvas itself, symbolizes the number of participants in a research project: the larger the N, the greater the "power" or probability that the research will detect an effect. The importance of the numbers that fill the canvas is unquestionable: they are an essential tool for doing research and communicating with researchers. The subject seems almost squinting, trying to see through the screen of numbers to the researcher. This subject is richly painted and appears to be young—a teenager or young adult perhaps—but the face and hair are rather androgynous, and the ethnic background of the subject is also unclear. This is a face with a story and perspective that might change the course of the research if only the researcher could see beyond the screen of numbers. The title suggests a need for research to move *Beyond N*, beyond numbers alone, to incorporate the nuances of subjects' lived experiences. Likewise, the painting insists that the viewer cannot just pay attention to the painted subject—the numbers and the ability to communicate with the researcher are also crucial. Ultimately, *Beyond N* challenges the viewer to see the value of both perspectives and invites the viewer to imagine a world beyond the dichotomies of the two.

Mixed methods research, if used by individual or collaborating researchers, enables the collection of generalizable and contextualized data simultaneously. Is it worth the effort it takes to go past our methodological comfort zones? The authors in this book answer with a resounding Yes! In their chapters, they demonstrate that mixed methods is more than worth the effort—it can lead to more interesting findings than either qualitative or quantitative methodologies alone.

This book is an invitation to explore the benefits of mixed methods. It opens with LeVine's historical overview of methods in the social sciences, discussing how many early social scientists were interdisciplinarians but disciplinary politics gradually made claims to validity through particular methods, splitting methods into two camps and fragmenting the social sciences in the process. In the next chapter, Worthman outlines a theoretical framework for conceiving of human behaviors, biologies, and psychologies as shaped by the material, social, and cultural worlds that humans themselves create. Part II consists of three chapters detailing personal accounts of intellectual journeys venturing outside the different methodology camps of cultural anthropology (Hay), psychology (Fuligni), and education (Gallimore). The chapters in part III explore cultural values and concepts, including how misusing methods can be deeply problematic, particularly for understanding cultural values (Shweder), how mixed methods can be successfully used to explore cross-cultural assumptions regarding infants (Keller) and child development (Harkness and Super), and how American theories about poverty are cultural products that do not reflect the experiences of people living in poverty (Lowe). Part IV groups chapters that are focused on the methods and research tools that facilitate collaborative research, specifically examining emerging literacy among immigrant children (Lieber), the experiences of parents of adults with autism (Daley), and how clinical decision making could utilize local knowledge as evidence alongside the published, evidence-based medical literature (Hay, Weisner, and Subramanian). The unique insights of longitudinal research, particularly when combined with mixed methods strategies, is the subject of the chapters in part V, focusing on sibling relationships and their impact on child development (Maynard), community relationships and their consequences for child maltreatment (Korbin), social relationships and their importance in the maintenance of gangs (Vigil), and family relationships as families struggle to make accommodations for their children with developmental delays (Bernheimer, Gallimore, and Keogh). The chapters in part VI highlight research designed to address problems through interventions or policy, including: the benefits of comparative research in studies of antipoverty policies (Huston, Duncan, and Yoshikawa), the integration of basic science knowledge with studies of educational practice to address policy for early childhood education (Edwards), and the challenges of conducting research among and creating an intervention for a hidden community, in this case in order to reduce the risk-taking behavior of the clients of transgender sex workers (Wilcox). Part VI consists of a single concluding chapter by Weisner discussing why mixed methods produces findings that matter—a chapter that can be used to bolster mixed methods grant proposals and publications, and encourage mixed methods researchers to stand firm against methodocentric critiques.

Ideas on How to Use and Teach This Book

There are multiple ways to read this book. *Methods That Matter* is a conversation among colleagues from different disciplines and it invites the reader who wants to join our conversation to read it cover to cover. The cover-to-cover reader will leave the book with a sense of the history and theory of mixed methods research, its nuances and possibilities in answering a variety of research questions from a diverse range of fields, while learning about the particularities of cutting-edge research on a wide range of topics that matter in the real world, including: human development and education, health and medicine, immigration and social groups, poverty and policy. The chapters of this book are linked in multiple ways, and readers are invited to join the conversation of the volume as it fits their particular interests.

All of the chapters are intentionally written to be approachable for undergraduates, so in many ways, chapters could be read in any combination. Undergraduate students may find it useful to begin their exploration of mixed methods with LeVine's chapter on its history and the chapters by Hay, Fuligni, and Gallimore—each a narrative about a personal journey into mixed methods research.

Also, the book can be read as a way of venturing into mixed methods with tour guides from particular methodological camps and disciplines. Starting with chapters by authors from familiar backgrounds may make it easier to imagine the usefulness of mixed methods in one's own work. By perusing the biographies of authors (in the appendix), readers can begin with those authors from familiar fields including anthropology, criminology, economics, education, human development, law, pediatrics, psychology, and public health. I encourage any reader who chooses to start reading the book this way to continue by reading authors from a different disciplinary background. One of the great surprises of this volume is how similar the chapters are in writing style and data presentation; mixed methods research really is a way to break down disciplinary barriers and facilitate broader conversations.

The book can be read to gather insight on designing research. Researchers will likely want to start with the chapters by LeVine, Worthman, and Weisner to understand the arguments and theory that support mixed methods research, and then could further explore the book for ideas to address particular kinds of research problems. For researchers striving to study that which is palpable but difficult to measure or study, in addition to the chapters specifically focused on understanding culture in part III, they might also want to examine Lieber; Hay, Weisner, and Subramanian; Korbin; Vigil; and Wilcox for ideas to examine particular types of research questions or populations. For example, Vigil and Wilcox both discuss ways to work with difficult-to-reach communities, problems that they were able to solve with creative mixed methods designs. Readers who want to do collaborative research may wish to start with the chapters in part IV and move on to the chapters by Gallimore; Keller; Harkness and Super; Bernheimer, Gallimore, and Keogh; Huston, Duncan, and Yoshikawa; and Wilcox, all of which discuss collaborative research endeavors. Furthermore, for those planning large-scale comparative projects, Shweder; Keller; Harkness and Super; Huston, Duncan, and Yoshikawa; and Edwards all speak to both the difficulties and successful strategies for doing this kind of large-scale science. Someone planning a longitudinal research project may want to start with chapters in part V and also pay attention to chapters by Fuligni; Gallimore; Keller; Harkness and Super; Daley; Edwards; and Weisner, who discuss research that spans multiple projects and decades, using findings from initial projects to shift focus in subsequent ones. Readers striving to design research that speaks directly to policy may want to read the chapters by Gallimore, Lowe, Lieber, Korbin, and Vigil in addition to the chapters in part VI.

In doing research that crosses disciplinary boundaries, integrating perspectives and methods, the authors in this volume illustrate the advantages of a restored social science, one that has come of age by doing the kind of integrative, holistic, and often collaborative research our social scientist ancestors originally envisioned. We invite you to join our conversation.

Acknowledgments

Methods That Matter is an invitation to join a scholarly conversation and is itself the product of many deeply satisfying discussions. Those discussions began over dinners and flourished during a special Methods That Matter conference, generously funded by a donation from Robert Lemelson in collaboration with the Society for Psychological Anthropology and hosted by Miami University. I am grateful to the Society for Psychological Anthropology for its support of this endeavor, and also for sponsoring roundtable and keynote panels on the topic at national and biennial meetings. In his scholarship, Rob Lemelson has set a high standard for bringing together scholars from diverse disciplines to expand conversations and scientific insight; it is my hope that this volume meets those standards and contributes to the kind of expansive science his leadership has encouraged. In the spirit of Lemelson's work, all royalties derived from this book will be donated to the Society for Psychological Anthropology to support future mixed methods endeavors.

Others also have contributed significantly to this project. I am grateful to the authors, who were uniformly enthusiastic about the project, provided original chapters to the volume, and have each been a pleasure to work with throughout the process. I owe special thanks to Jill Korbin and Hal Odden for their unwavering encouragement. Miami University generously contributed to the support and organization of the Methods That Matter conference in September 2013 in Oxford, Ohio. I especially thank Kathy Erbaugh for her marvelous logistic skills, and my wonderful colleagues at Miami University, particularly John Cinnamon, Yvette Harris, Neringa Klumbyte, Linda Marchant, Leighton Peterson, Mark Peterson, and Vaishali Raval. My students are a continuing source of motivation and insight, and I trust they will find this volume useful in their own research. This volume benefited from the efforts of two anonymous readers who generously provided comments on an earlier draft, the skills of Nora Devlin, Louise Kertesz, and Ryo Yamaguchi in the publishing process, and from the keen support of our editor Elizabeth Branch Dyson at the University of Chicago Press. A final word of gratitude is owed to Tom Weisner for introducing me to the world of mixed methods, and to my family—Rob, Turner, and Sydney Rollins—for reminding me why in work, as in everything else, it is important to focus on what matters.

PART ONE

Methods and Theory for More Holistic Human Sciences

Repairing the Fractured Social Sciences: An Introduction from a Historical Point of View

ROBERT A. LEVINE

The social sciences today are divided into research communities that cherish their separation from each other. They resemble the Tower of Babel more than a mature science with complementary inquiries strengthening a common body of knowledge. The disciplines and subdisciplinary research communities are not at war but are simply turned inward to such a degree that they do not recognize each other's contributions as knowledge worth considering in their own research. Researchers do not cite the works of other research communities and often examine the same topics without reference to each other's works. Their differences are largely methodological or epistemological, i.e., each research community is organized around a particular set of methods taken to generate knowledge; research findings from the use of other methods are ignored or dismissed as being irrelevant to knowledge generation. Thus the boundaries between disciplines, or in some cases between method-based research communities within disciplines, are wide and deep. It wasn't always this way.

Far from the Omniscience Ideal

How different this is from the ideal formulated in 1969 by my old friend and collaborator Donald T. Campbell (1969) in his "fish-scale model of omniscience"! He envisioned the social sciences as scales on a fish in which each specialty was unique but overlapping its neighboring specialties, so that the mutual relatedness of topics and data was mediated through shared boundaries, guaranteeing that specialists could use knowledge generated by adjacent specialties, resulting in "omniscience" if not literal omniscience. Campbell was quite aware that this ideal was not being met when he formulated it, at a time when there were fewer journals policing the boundaries than there are now. He was in effect attacking the increasing specialization of his time, and the haughty pride—he called it the "ethnocentrism of disciplines"— that maintained it, which has only worsened since then.

This divisive tendency presents obstacles to interdisciplinary research, which is often marginalized in the academic world of the social sciences. Fields like psychological anthropology and human geography that attempt to bring together perspectives from several fields using varied methods are often regarded as lacking the core or coherence needed to conduct research and train students. The low regard in which these interdisciplinary fields are held has its origins before 1920 but has strengthened greatly since the middle decades of the twentieth century, when the social sciences as a whole were smaller and contained fewer research communities than they do now. And sixty years ago, there was more contact and communication between colleagues in adjoining disciplines like sociology and social anthropology. Campbell liked to tell the story of how around 1951, when he was teaching at the University of Chicago, he submitted a paper to *American Anthropologist*, then edited by Sol Tax at Chicago, and to his surprise it appeared in *The American Journal of Sociology*, edited by Everett C. Hughes down the hall. Tax had decided it wasn't anthropological enough and sent it to his colleague, who promptly published it. That kind of collegiality across social science disciplines may be rare nowadays, particularly among journal editors, but Tax's action showed how even then policing the boundaries was important to him as a midcentury journal editor.

When the social sciences emerged from philosophy in the late nineteenth and early twentieth centuries, many of the pioneering figures were interdisciplinarians, especially in connecting psychological and social thinking in their work. Prominent examples are the psychologists Wilhelm Wundt, James Mark Baldwin, F. C. Bartlett, and L. S. Vygotsky; the sociologists Max Weber and W. I. Thomas (of the Chicago School of Sociology); the anthropologists W. H. R. Rivers, Bronislaw Malinowski, and Edward Sapir; and (outside of academia) the psychoanalysts Sigmund Freud, Otto Rank, Abram Kardiner, and Harry Stack Sullivan.

Even Emile Durkheim, though sharply distinguishing social from psychological facts, was actually quite psychological in much of his theorizing ("social sentiments"). He also combined qualitative with quantitative methods, notably in *Suicide* (Durkheim, 1897, 1951), relating an ethnographic description with a numerical frequency, what Alex Inkeles (1959) would later call the correlation of a "state" and a "rate."

"Social psychology" became a recognized field within sociology as well as in psychology during the first half of the twentieth century. There were interdisciplinary "movements" like the Frankfurt School in sociology and the culture and personality movement in American anthropology.

Many of these interdisciplinary trends dwindled as the academic disciplines expanded and were bureaucratized in universities and professional associations, especially during the great expansion of the American universities in the 1960s. Disciplinary orthodoxies hardened, not only in doctrine but also in the institutionalization of departments and journals with sharp boundaries and vested interests.

Methods That Came to Define Science

Yet in competing for scarce resources the social science disciplines and research communities were not simply an unordered collection of specialties; they made claims for recognition as science based largely on the degree to which their canonical methods seemed to resemble those of the natural sciences. Those using mathematics, controlled experiments, formal assessments, exact measurements, statistical analysis, and methods linked to physical growth, physiological reactions, or brain images—gained credibility as scientific, while others using more exploratory or observational approaches in uncontrolled settings came under pressure to justify themselves in scientific terms. The highest ranks were awarded to academic disciplines that had become highly mathematical, like economics, or that conducted experiments, like psychology; others survived in the wide and ramified world of US academia, but were marginalized to some degree.

The ranking of social science research specialties was often legitimized by taking physics as the model for all sciences. The logical positivist philosophy of science that rose to prominence in the 1930s and 1940s provided recipes for formalizing social research to make it resemble physics: first, derive testable propositions from a general theory; second, define concepts formally and operationally; third, verify or falsify hypotheses through quantitative (preferably experimental) research. Scientific knowledge would consist exclusively of propositions that survived this process. Later, historians of science would show this to be an idealized account of how physicists work, which was rarely so tidy (Kuhn 1971; Latour and Woolgar 1986), but in the 1950s and 1960s many social scientists were attracted to it, and some journals continue to follow its mandates.

American anthropology was not one of the disciplines most influenced by this conception, or misconception, of physics. Since early in the twentieth century, in the United States (unlike Britain, France, or Germany) anthropology has consisted of four distinct fields—physical or biological anthropology, prehistoric archeology, linguistic anthropology, and social or cultural anthropology—fields sharing a commitment to field research that expands knowledge through comparative and historical analysis of an increasing number of well-documented variants, rather than through controlled experiments in the laboratory. However it might reduce the scientific prestige of anthropology, field research for comparative and historical understanding is well established as a method of choice in the life sciences. Anthropology in this respect resembles Darwin's field observations of plants and animals in all their diverse forms—a model appropriate to the building of knowledge about the social behavior of humans.

Biology once had a sharp division between experimentalists and field researchers, but this was resolved during the twentieth century, first by the "neo-Darwinian synthesis" incorporating genetics into evolutionary theory, and more recently with the integration of molecular findings from DNA research into biology at all levels. This success story could be read as demonstrating that even after the advent of molecular genetics there is still an important place for field studies in the new unified biology, but some take a different lesson from it, supporting the priority and urgency of grounding human behavior in the brain; hence the growing interest of psychologists and psychiatrists in "neuroscience," reducing behavior to its biological underpinnings. Meanwhile, the need for integrating the social sciences—or at least reducing their dissonance and mutual ignorance—received less attention.

Glimmers of Interdisciplinarity in the Darkness
of Disciplinary Divides

John Whiting and Beatrice Whiting at Harvard nonetheless conducted research and trained students, myself and others, some of whom are in this volume, in interdisciplinary research designing and conducting ambitious research projects (e.g., the Six Cultures Study and the East African studies) on child rearing and development in different cultures. Much has been published from and about these projects, but certain aspects deserve emphasis in the present context: the Whitings assumed that quantitative and qualitative methods were equally necessary to describe, analyze, and interpret childhood around the world (J. Whiting 1994; B. Whiting and Edwards 1988). At the time I began working with them in 1954, this assumption was not widespread among social scientists, especially psychologists, and was in fact going out of style. The strains that eventually led to the breakup of the Harvard Department of Social Relations in 1970 were already evident. But the Whitings' continued pursuit of interdisciplinary research was based on their experience in the 1930s at Yale's Institute of Human Relations (IHR) with teachers like Edward Sapir and John Dollard. Focused on psychocultural processes of child development, the Whitings kept the multiple-methods candle lit in a period of increasing interdisciplinary darkness.

For John Whiting, Dollard had probably been the key guide. The only important pioneer of the culture and personality movement who has not been the subject of a biography, Dollard had been trained as a quantitative sociologist at Chicago, where he met Sapir. On Sapir's recommendation, he went to Berlin for training at the psychoanalytic institute there. Sapir then brought him to Yale, and he carried out field research in Mississippi for *Caste and Class in a Southern Town* (1937) and (with Allison Davis) for *Children of Bondage* (1940). Later Dollard radically changed his interests to the "learning theory" of Clark Hull (then the senior psychologist at the IHR), which led to a terminal break with Sapir and to his collaboration with the psychologist Neal Miller, with whom he wrote the influential books *Social Learning and Imitation* (1941) and *Personality and Psychotherapy* (1950). After John Whiting's return from fieldwork in New Guinea, Dollard, along with Bronislaw Malinowski, supervised his postdoctoral work translating his dissertation into a book, *Becoming a Kwoma* (1941), a case study analyzing the child-rearing practices of a particular community in terms of Hullian behavior theory. From Whiting's point of view, Dollard's qualitative field study of a community and the Miller-Dollard combination of experimental child psychology and psychoanalysis constituted models for his own future research and that of his students. It is no exaggeration to say that in pursuing this combined model, Whiting ignored the decline of interdisciplinary work in American social science during much of his career. Beatrice Blyth Whiting added the influence of Sapir and other approaches from both anthropology and psychology. The Whitings' collaboration was the most exciting example of psychocultural research extant. In my encomium for the Whitings in 1989, when they received the Society for Psychological Anthropology's first Career Contributions Award, I likened their role to that of the monks who kept classical learning alive during Europe's Dark Ages after the fall of the Roman Empire. (Not a perfect analogy, but it captures the importance of their place in our history.)

Mixed Methods and Interdisciplinary Training: Keys to Repairing Fractures

Psychocultural research survived its darkest age in the third quarter of the twentieth century (roughly 1950–1970). Its revival thereafter—particularly in Southern California but also in a few other places, and in our scholarly journal (*Ethos*, begun in 1973) and our association (Society for Psychological Anthropology, 1977)—gives hope that interdisciplinary research will rise again to lead the social sciences out of the fragmented condition I described in the opening of this chapter. This happened in the biological sciences when the traditional university departments proved a poor match for the boundary-crossing research activity in which biologists were actually engaged. In social science, this hope can be realized only if disciplines begin speaking the same language or at least recognizing as knowledge the evidence from varied sources as they go about their research. That is why the "mixed methods" movement—recognizing the mutual importance of both quantitative and qualitative findings in establishing validity—is not only a major step in that direction, it is also the essential basis for building substantive connections across disciplines.

Another indispensable condition for the integration of the social sciences is interdisciplinary training. This means that in attacking problems in border regions, a social scientist should have the knowledge and skills of the several disciplines involved and be able (and willing) to publish articles in their journals. As an anthropologist operating in the child development field, for example, Tom Weisner brings developmental psychology to bear on those problems. His devastating critique (in a psychological journal, Weisner, 2005) of the Bowlby-Ainsworth attachment theory for its exclusive focus on the mother-child dyad and its neglect of distributed care and social networks is that of an insider as well as outsider. Without this kind of skillful boundary-crossing, the study of child development—which was originally conceived as an interdisciplinary field but has often devolved into an inward-looking developmental psychology—will fail to progress in building a body of scientific knowledge.

Psychocultural researchers interested in child development were fortunate to have the Whitings as our role models, but that does not mean that the Whitings simply transmitted that distinctive blend of behaviorism and psychoanalysis that had been constructed by Miller and Dollard or that the Whitings' students—including Ruth and Lee Munroe, Tom Weisner, Rick Shweder, Carolyn Edwards, Susan Seymour, Gerald Erchak, and me—became their disciples. In the child-development field of the twentieth century, there was a profusion of theories we now consider false starts, blind alleys, or just plain wrong—ranging from G. Stanley Hall's recapitulationism through behaviorism in its several manifestations to Piaget's cognitive stages, etc. Wedded to its scientific aspirations (and pretensions), child development research was nonetheless vulnerable to paradigm shifts and sectarian theoretical loyalties. The Whitings' students attempted to shed empirical light from multiple perspectives on fundamental problems of development, as in the following examples.

Thomas Weisner trained local observers in western Kenya to make quantifiable home observations, enabling him to identify sibling care as a high-frequency aspect of infant environments, first in East Africa and then in many other parts of the world, raising basic questions about early relationships in child development (Weisner and Gallimore 1977). Also in western Kenya, Ruth and Lee Munroe (1971) devised the method of spot observations for assessing infant care, based on contextual evidence that daytime caregiving in East Africa occurred largely in outside settings that permitted a local fieldworker to observe unobtrusively (and thus more validly than interviewing the mother). The observations could be repeated over time and aggregated for quantitative analysis. In our Gusii Infant Study my colleagues and I used the

Munroes' spot observation method to assess continuities and changes in infant care over the first thirty months among Gusii infants in southwestern Kenya (LeVine et al. 1994). Earlier, in Nigeria, we had replicated a number of Piaget's early studies, asking what if Piaget had begun his interviews with children among the Hausa of northwestern Nigeria instead of in Geneva in French-speaking Switzerland? Our quantitative studies, grounded in ethnographic fieldwork among the Hausa, found grounds to challenge Piaget's claims for universal trends in cognitive development as assessed through concepts of kinship (LeVine and Price-Williams 1974) and dreams (Shweder and LeVine 1975). More recently, my research group at Harvard completed a four-country study of women's school-based literacy (LeVine et al. 2012), using quantitative and ethnographic data to compare samples of mothers in Mexico, Nepal, Venezuela, and Zambia. As students of the Whitings, we combine the contextual understanding of ethnography with questions of frequency across ages, persons, and cultures; this is central to our methodology.

As we carry forward the banner of interdisciplinary research and mixed methods into hostile (or at least resistant) territory, we should keep in mind that there are distinguished antecedents for this cause. One was Franz Boas, whom we used to think of mainly as a cultural relativist and the teacher of Margaret Mead, Ruth Benedict, Edward Sapir, and A. L. Kroeber. But long after Boas's death in 1942, the late George Stocking (1968, 1974) and others revealed a more complicated Franz Boas, whose radical positivist scruples kept him from proposing an overall theory but who clearly had his own mixed methods approach. Boas was a statistical pioneer, who met Francis Galton, corresponded with Karl Pearson about correlation coefficients, devised his own versions of analysis of variance and factor analysis in analyzing his large-scale study of immigrants' physical growth in 1911, and required his doctoral students at Columbia to take a course in statistics—taught by Boas himself. He is now regarded as part of the "statistical turn in American social science," most of which took place at Columbia during World War I (Camic and Xie 1994). Yet there is no doubt that he also focused on cultural distinctiveness in his teaching and encouraged Mead and Benedict, up to a point. Boas avoided speculation and never overtly approved of psychoanalysis (though he attended Freud's 1909 lectures at Clark), the culture and personality movement started by his students, or the psychometric approach of Cattell, his colleague at Columbia. His recognition of culture as in part a mental phenomenon was not accompanied by the adoption of a method he could trust for studying it. Malinowski's ethnographic method eventually became the approach adopted in the English-speaking world, and for many anthropologists that meant leaving out quantification. The Whitings worked to restore a balance between qualitative description and statistics, and their students have carried on this work in several interdisciplinary arenas. By offering mixed methods as a general approach, the authors in this volume are helping to repair our fractured social sciences and restore the integrity lost in the last century.

References

Camic, Charles, and Yu Xie. 1994. "The Statistical Turn in American Social Science: Columbia University, 1890–1915." *American Sociological Review* 59: 773–805.

Campbell, Donald T. 1969. "Ethnocentrism of Disciplines and the Fish-Scale Model of Omniscience." In *Interdisciplinary Relationships in the Social Sciences*, edited by Muzafer Sherif and Carolyn W. Sherif, 328–48. Hawthorne, NY: Aldine.

Davis, Allison, and John Dollard. 1940. *Children of Bondage: The Personality Development of Negro Youth in the Urban South*. Washington, DC: American Council on Education.

Dollard, John. 1937. *Caste and Class in a Southern Town*. New Haven: Yale University Press.

Dollard, John, and Neal Miller. 1950. *Personality and Psychotherapy*. New York: McGraw Hill.

Durkheim, Emile. 1897/1951. *Suicide*. New York: Free Press.

Inkeles, Alex. 1959. "Personality and Social Structure." In *Sociology Today*, edited by Robert K. Merton, 249–56. New York: Basic Books.

Kuhn, Thomas S. 1971. "The Relations between History and History of Science." *Daedalus* 100 (2): 271–304.

Latour, Bruno, and Steve Woolgar. 1986. *Laboratory Life*. Princeton: Princeton University Press.

LeVine, Robert A., and Douglas R. Price-Williams. 1974. "Children's Kinship Concepts: Cognitive Development and Early Experience among the Hausa." *Ethnology* 13 (1): 25–44.

LeVine, Robert A., Sarah LeVine, Beatrice Schnell-Anzola, Meredith L. Rowe, and Emily Dexter. 2012. *Literacy and Mothering: How Women's Schooling Changes the Lives of the World's Children*. Oxford: Oxford University Press.

LeVine, Robert A., Suzanne Dixon, Sarah LeVine, Amy Richman, P. Herbert Leiderman, Constance H. Keefer, and T. Berry Brazelton. 1994. *Childcare and Culture: Lessons from Africa*. New York: Cambridge University Press.

Miller, Neal E., and John Dollard. 1941. *Social Learning and Imitation*. New Haven: Yale University Press.

Munroe, Ruth H., and Munroe, Robert L. 1971. "Household Density and Infant Care in an East African Society." *The Journal of Social Psychology* 83 (1): 3–13.

Shweder, Richard A., and Robert A. LeVine. 1975. "Dream Concepts of Hausa Children." *Ethos* 3 (2): 209–30.

Stocking, George. 1968. *Race, Culture, and Evolution: Essays in the History of Anthropology.* New York: Free Press.

Stocking, George. 1974. *A Franz Boas Reader: The Shaping of American Anthropology 1883–1911.* New York: Basic Books.

Weisner, Thomas S. 2005. "Attachment as a Cultural and Ecological Problem with Pluralistic Solutions." *Human Development* 48 (1–2): 89–94.

Weisner, Thomas S., and Ronald Gallimore. 1977. "My Brother's Keeper: Child and Sibling Caretaking." *Current Anthropology* 18 (2):169–90.

Whiting, Beatrice, and Carolyn P. Edwards. 1988. *Children of Different Worlds: The Formation of Social Behavior.* Cambridge: Harvard University Press.

Whiting, John. 1941. *Becoming a Kwoma.* New Haven: Yale University Press.

Whiting, John. 1994. *Culture and Human Development: The Selected Papers of John Whiting.* Edited by E. H. Chasdi. New York: Cambridge University Press.

TWO

Ecocultural Theory: Foundations and Applications

CAROL M. WORTHMAN

Ecocultural theory characterizes the role of cultural ecology in psychosocial development and has evolved in anthropology as a powerful tool for understanding and investigating the sources of human diversity. In its relatively short history, anthropological theory initially treated human differences as products of innate conditions but was swiftly converted by the concept of culture to regarding them as mainly a cultural product. The insight was a dual one. Through culture, humans largely create the circumstances in which they live, in material, social, and experiential terms. The resultant cultural ecology, in turn, strongly shapes the physical, behavioral, and mental attributes of the members of a culture. The question remains of just how such linkages are forged. Many answers to this question appear to lie in human development.

This chapter traces anthropology's ecological understanding of culture and its relationship to the dynamics of human development and outlines the foundations, evolution, and application of ecocultural theory. A series of examples are presented to illustrate the power of this theory to generate hypotheses and fresh insights into the sources not only of human difference but also of differential well-being. Extensive work links culturally mandated parenting practices such as infant feeding, daily routines, or punishment to child functioning, including emotion regulation, attention and learning, or relationships. Such effects are much more than skin deep and have been linked to patterns of stress responsivity, immune activity, and physical and mental health. As such, the framework has come to inform other social and biological sciences, as well as policy and clinical applications.

Evolving modes of inquiry play crucial roles in this project. Plumbing the depth and breadth of human diversity has demanded new methods that speak to emerging, diverse, and morphing understandings of what it is to be human. Among the many lines of inquiry dedicated to this domain, research grounded in ecocultural approaches necessarily has involved mixed methods. It follows logically, then, that investigators in this tradition have provided exemplars demonstrating the value of mixed methods and spearheaded their integration in the social sciences and beyond. The following essay traces this inquiry-charged journey.

Early Foundations

A young discipline, anthropology emerged in the late nineteenth century from a mixed trajectory of observation/description and theory to document and account for human diversity in all its forms (Stocking 1989–1999). This project was fueled by three great innovations, two conceptual and one methodological. First, the concept of culture was recast in relativistic, pluralistic (cultures) terms, against entrenched humanist traditions regarding culture as progressive—a single evolutionary gradient from "primate" to "advanced." Although anthropology did and still does define culture as the system of beliefs, values, practices, and material artifacts shared by members of society, the dynamic, experiential, and ecological bases of culture were recognized early on. Franz Boas, a founder of the field, framed culture as the "thousand activities and modes of thought that constitute our daily life," "activities and modes of which we are never even conscious" that are transmitted "because they constitute the whole series of well-established habits according to which the necessary actions of every-day life are performed" (Stocking 1966, 8).

Second—and related to the reframing of the culture concept—was recognition of experience and context as key determinants of human behavior and thus as prime agents in human diversity. Differences in mental functions and capacities were the first order of concern, but the path toward a relativist view ran through physical differences. Boas tackled the patent quantitative differences among groups by examining correlates of variation in head shape among seven European immigrant groups in New York City, and discovered it was sensitive to environmental influences (Boas 1912). That so "typological" a feature as cranial form was subject to small but real environmental effects undercut the notion of fixed racial taxonomy (Gravlee, Bernard, and Leonard 2003a, 2003b). This paved the way for muscular cultural determinism, which argued that the great preponderance of meaningful human variation is a product of culture, since cognitive and behavioral differences are largely learned, engrained through cultural processes shaping experience (Geertz 1973). And because culture gets under the skin, it may account for physical differences as well. But more on that later. Meanwhile, notice that a pioneering feature of this work was to use quantitative physical measures to elucidate social determinants of human psychobehavioral diversity.

Third was the commitment to "being there." Systematic participant observation as the core mode of ethnographic inquiry was a methodological innovation that applied to humans the formal field approaches drawn from naturalists. Thus anthropological research was grounded in everyday settings of individuals, households, and communities (Atkinson and Hammersley 1994), commencing at the turn of the twentieth century and including British anthropologists such as W. H. R. Rivers, Malinowski, and Evans-Pritchard along with Boas and his many American students (Kroeber, Sapir, and later Mead). Participant observation remained the dominant mode of ethnographic inquiry when, in the later twentieth century, the entire field grappled with the limits of ethnographic methods in terms of subjectivity, history and social change, sampling bias, politics of representation, and other epistemological and ethical concerns (Clifford and Marcus 1986).

Allied to these three innovations was comparative method, which rests uneasily between anthropology's commitments to universalism and relativism, the dual assertions of a shared humanity alongside inherent diversity. Claims by early theorists that the comparative method was both central to anthropology (Evans-Pritchard 1963; Radcliffe-Brown 1951) and essentially impossible (Evans-Pritchard, recalled in Needham 1973) reflect ongoing tensions in the field. Boas early recognized that limitations of comparative method—especially problems of sampling, nonindependence (Galton's problem), inferring shared causes from shared outcomes—preclude construction of a grand unifying theory of culture variation and change, but he emphasized that nonetheless, comparative work could discover the dynamics underlying cultural diversity (Boas 1896). Recent investigators have supported his emphasis on studying culture change where the events are independent (Mace and Pagel 1994). Effective recent moves in comparative method include use of simulations (Nunn et al. 2010) and renewed multisited research on human variation in relation to culture rather than cultural variation or culture change per se (Bowles et al. 2010). Thus anthropologists are beginning to address the giant gap in understanding of human cognition (e.g., decision making, cooperation) left by psychology's almost exclusive focus on western populations (Henrich et al. 2004; Henrich, Heine, and Norenzayan 2010), to examine how culture influences mind and behavior through effects on processes of cognition and emotion. Such advances have been spurred by an expanding methodological portfolio that integrates ethnographic inquiry, deploys game theory and cognitive testing, and builds on quantitative and qualitative data from multisited studies.

Anthropology and Ecology

As the innovations highlighted above matured in anthropological theory and practice, the discipline established strengths in common with the most powerful theory to emerge from nineteenth-century life sciences: evolution. Both culture and evolution currently are conceived as nonprogressive and deterministic. Evolution is about a process whose outcome is indeterminate albeit constrained by many forces, as is culture. The problem of continuity through time (intergenerational and enculturation, respectively) and emphasis on the power of place (natural selection and cultural ecology, respectively) are common concerns for each. Competing theories of cultural transmission and change are widely debated in anthropology (Gupta and Ferguson 1992; Sperber 1996; Steward 1955), even including dual inheritance theory, which aims to integrate culture and biology in an evolutionary account (McElreath and Henrich 2007; Richerson and Boyd 2005). Our concern here is with the latter emphasis, on ecology and the power of place.

Clarification of what is meant by "ecology" and its use in anthropology will be helpful here. One of its founders, Ernst Haeckel, defined ecology as "the whole science of the relations of the organism to the environment including, in the broad sense, all the 'conditions of existence'" (Stauffer 1957, 140). Although this definition would seem so broad as to be vacuous, its empirical grip comes from the processes of evolution. By identifying key roles for natural selection and adaptation, evolutionary theory placed ecology at the heart of organic diversity and design. Ecology is where the rubber of organic design meets the road of real life and its inherent vicissitudes: through processes of natural selection, the design or inbuilt capacities and structures of organisms are evolutionary products honed to work in the expectable environments the organism inhabits. One of the great insights of biology over the last thirty years has been the extent to which organisms rely, by design, on the environment to instruct their functioning. Such insights have reshaped concepts of adaptation not only by identifying a range of mechanisms by which plasticity is achieved (Stearns and Koella 1986) but also by highlighting development as a nexus where dynamics between design and ecology play out (West-Eberhard 2003). More on this later.

The historical links to natural history and engagement with human diversity on a global scale made ecology congenial to anthropology. Roots for the emphasis on proximal conditions are reflected in Boas's work on cranial form mentioned earlier, where accounts for human variation seriously consider effects of the conditions of everyday life. Ecology also resonated with commitments to comparative method and an integrated theory of culture variation and change. Early work in cultural ecology sought ecological constraints responsible for culture and culture change, as reflected in cross-cultural regularities. Here, the field disagreed sharply over views of cultural history as unilineal evolution (White 1959) or diffusely unpredictable (Steward 1955), and furthermore over the importance of materialist-adaptationist factors for understanding culture as such (Harris 1979).

Ecocultural theory also had grounds in cultural evolution, but before turning to this line of work, other powerful anthropological streams of ecological thought must be acknowledged. These include reproductive ecology, which examines effects and mediators of culturally informed behaviors (e.g., workload, breast-feeding) on reproductive functioning and outcomes; behavioral ecology, which tests the relationships of evolutionary principles and adaptive design to human behavior (especially foraging and food distribution, reproductive behavior) and cognition (including decision making or jealousy); developmental ecology, which tracks developmental sensitivities to context in human growth and function (Kuzawa 2008; McDade and Worthman 1999; Worthman 2009). Then there is ecological or environmental anthropology, which examines human-environment interactions, often in relation to culture and adaptation. Prominent examples include yam growing in a highland New Guinea society, examined through a systems theoretical approach (Rappaport 1968), Balinese water temples in cultural practices regulating rice farming (Lansing and Fox 2011; Lansing 2006), and behaviorist-archeological accounts of the origins of agriculture (Kennett and Winterhalder 2006).

The complexity of the questions pursued in these lines of research stimulated dramatic expansions in the portfolio of mixed methods for research. Studies cited in the previous paragraph, for instance, have involved GIS and mapping, production metrics, biomarkers, genetics, standardized interviewing, anthropometry, and ethnography. Working with "real people in the real world" imposes on methods both ethical and practical constraints that had been overlooked by the human sciences, which had been limited largely to laboratory settings and/or Western postindustrial populations (Henrich, Heine, and Norenzayan 2010). Meeting these constraints has demanded creative method development that, reciprocally, opened the way for other investigators to use mixed methods in population-based research. Furthermore, inquiry-driven integration of new methods has enabled investigators to operationalize ever more complex problems with effective and feasible study designs. Chapters in this volume contain examples that illustrate this galvanic effect.

Foundations of Ecocultural Theory

Ecology provided a vantage from which the assumption of human unity could be preserved while accounting for variability. The logic that emerged was as follows: through culture, humans both participate in and produce the conditions of everyday life, in material, social, and mental terms. Consequently the primary source of human variation is culture, and an important approach through which to view the effects of culture on humans was through cultural ecology. Thus the ecological perspective in anthropology proceeds from the assumption that human thought and behavior, grounded in culture, are the prime agents shaping the conditions in which humans live and thus, the human condition (Geertz 1973). These conditions are not only physical, but also social, emotional, and cognitive. Although anthropologists came to disagree profoundly over the primacy of culture in human diversity and the degree to which what humans bring to the table in the form of "human nature" is important, such logic informed psychological anthropology, inspired in part by Freudian theory and the rise of psychology from William James onward.

Although it would seem obvious that understanding human variation and its relationship to culture might best be advanced by examining the process of becoming a competent member of a society, human development has claimed a narrow space in anthropology. Child development and rearing form the bottleneck through which culture passes from one generation to the next. A thread of work on human development ran from Boas to his students, particularly Mead, whose ethnographic studies of childhood and adolescence in New Guinea, Samoa, and Bali stimulated broad popular appreciation that developmental pathways were influenced by culture: psychobehavioral differences among societies were due in part to enculturation during the process of growing up (Mead 1928, 1930; Mead and Macgregor 1951). The manifest learning capacities and malleability of young minds were taken for granted as routes through which culture got under the skin. The question of how it did so was asked in societal terms (rituals, attitudes, and practices of enculturation) rather than in terms of the child's dispositions or capacities.

The theoretical stakes were raised when, after similar ethnographic beginnings in Samoa (Whiting 1941), John Whiting went on to build theory and programs of research to map systematically the relationships between culture and mind, as they play out during child development (Whiting and Child 1953). At first the project was a comparative cultural ecological one (Whiting 1954; Whiting and Child 1953). Later, in conjunction with Beatrice Whiting, it included one that asked how deep and how wide the cultural differences in human mind can be, and probed the role of the cultural ecology of early childhood in the formation of psychobehavioral outcomes.

Again, mixed methods played a key role in the enterprise. An important early innovation was the emphasis on linking theory with generation of testable hypotheses about the relationships of culture with behavior and psychology. Another was use of theory-driven protocols for data collection in multisited studies of psychobehavioral development; the most famous of these was the Six Cultures Study of Socialization begun in the 1950s, followed by a similar one on adolescents in the 1980s. These studies attempted to advance cross-cultural research by surmounting a major barrier to comparative analysis, by using shared protocols to gather data collected in a rigorously comparable manner.

A field manual guided data collection on child care, settings, and child behavior at each site in the Six Cultures Study (Whiting et al. 1966). The hallmarks of this pathbreaking enterprise were intense collaboration, replication across multiple cultures, extended fieldwork, model production and hypothesis testing, use of quantitative (structured interview and observation) and qualitative ethnographic methods, and multiauthor publication. All these were, and still are, uncommon in cultural anthropology.

Before turning to the emergence of ecocultural theory and research, another influential stream of work integrating mind, culture, and ecology must be included here. Gregory Bateson moved on from ethnographic fieldwork in New Guinea and Bali with an increasingly developmental focus to formulate a cybernetic, systems-theoretical approach to interactions of social and mental phenomena. The focus was almost entirely on identification of psychic dynamics built into social life that animate and propel human behavior. In his work on initiation ritual, he coined the enduring term "ethos" to capture meaning-making and motivating emotional elements of normative behaviors, emphasized the multivalent and multidetermined nature of human experience and action, and attempted to link structures of social behavior with patterns of thought (Bateson 1958; but see his own insightful critique of this concept in a later essay, Bateson 1987a). Importantly, Bateson identified the conditions for and mechanics of schismogenesis, a concept that he and others elaborated and applied to understand mutually reinforcing or regressive processes in conflict or cooperation. Later essays, particularly work on schizophrenia, aimed to further locate human cognition (and dysfunction) in social dynamics, and specified the dynamics involved in "double bind" conditions (Bateson 1987b).

A powerful integrative thinker, Bateson drew together multiple streams convergent in ecocultural theory. Trained in evolutionary biology and critical of classic approaches to variation in comparative anatomy, he sought to fuse empirical observation with insight into the relationships among phenomena that reflect underlying design constraints on form interacting with function *in context*. This approach reflected work in developmental biology on the importance of biomechanical constraints in organic design at every level of organization, from molecular to cellular to systemic to organismic (Thompson 1942). Bateson extended the approach in two ways, first, by proceeding beyond the organismic level to behavior, social relations, and culture, and second, by including information as a fundamental design constraint. Inclusion of information opened the door to fresh ecological perspectives in long-standing issues of inheritance (information transmission) in biology as well as in cognition, communication, and coordination at play in human experience and social life (Worthman 2009). His applications of this ecological design-oriented approach to problems such as schismogenesis or schizophrenia suggested its value for understanding function and dysfunction at the individual, interpersonal, community, and societal level.

By Nature Nurtured

The Whiting Model neatly bridged the nature-nurture problem by proposing that it is human nature to be nurtured (see Worthman 2010a for detailed review). Thence it follows that relationships between cultures and the psychology and behavior of their members are dynamic, formed largely through the conditions of early child rearing. The model posited that adult psyche (motives, needs), capacities, and behaviors are products of the interplay between constitutional psychobiobehavioral processes of human development and the contexts in which they unfold. Because these contexts are populated by adult members of the society and shaped by culturally constituted material and structural conditions, cultural ecology was operationalized vis-à-vis child development in terms of the proximal conditions of rearing. This view gave primacy to dynamics on the ground, in the child's everyday experience, rather than to cultural abstractions or population-level characteristics. Hence the model aimed to generate hypotheses about the significant forces in early experience and their relationship to child outcomes, with the possibility of thereby explaining cultural differences. Note that this approach resonates with Boas's observation that the comparative method does best in identifying the *processes* that underlie similarities and differences, rather than the forms and contents themselves (Boas 1896). Recall also that the approach inherently relied on mixed methods.

This model proved to be powerful. It informed decades of theoretical and empirical advances by Whiting himself, his students, the field of psychological anthropology, and arguably psychology as well (Bronfenbrenner 1979; Edwards and Weisner 2010; Weisner and Edwards 2001; Whiting and Edwards 1988; Whiting and Chasdi 1994). The reasons it is useful are instructive. First, resolution of the invidious nature-nurture split opened new work that targeted the interactions between them. Second, development turned out to be an arena where these dynamics are particularly evident and accessible to study. Third, the model proved to tap more accurately into how human development works, as attested by recent decades of findings in developmental science (Bornstein 2009; Boyce, Sokolowski, and Robinson 2012; Gluckman et al. 2009; Worthman et al. 2010). From conception, the developing organism relies on inputs from the environment to inform the processes of development. In the case of humans, much of this information is communicated socially (as needed for language acquisition) or through the conditions produced by human action informed by culture (as needed for sensory and cognitive development, also development of immune function or gut flora).

Fourth, a focus on the proximal environment of child learning strategically narrowed the scope of study from all agents or cultural features that might affect child development to the proximal envelope of contexts and experiences that children in a culture likely would encounter. The shape of this envelope furthermore was couched in probabilistic terms, by gender, age, social status, and so forth. Fifth, the emphasis on the concrete—on tasks and practices, companions and actors, social and material resources, physical and social demands—facilitated direct engagement with infant and child experience. The commitment to study social development bottom-up rather than solely top-down brought culture down to earth, as it operates in the child's lived experience. While the emphasis was on cross-cultural comparison, the model also was tuned to the intracultural variation that accommodates contemporary concerns for diversity, power and social marginalization, disparities in opportunities and outcomes, and other structural and demographic conditions. Sixth, use of multidimensional models permitted informed selection of a rich range of methods determined by the question at hand rather than the reverse.

Finally and importantly, the model did not focus on outcomes or human variation per se. Rather, it emphasized dynamics behind such variation and identification of key variables that drive them. In this case, the focus was the cultural ecology of early child experience, as it related to development and formation of psychobehavioral outcomes such as helping behavior or aggression. Given the above-summarized history of anthropology's struggle to navigate between the Scylla of reductionist cultural evolutionism and the Charybdis of relativist cultural constructivism, this was a major advance. Anthropology's models and methods can and do discover important generalizable insights into conditions and consequences attending the varieties of human lifeways and experience, but they do so best when the conceptual focus is on *how* things work rather than *what* should happen.

Ecocultural Theories Today

The lines of thought and research tracked here are being glossed as ecocultural theory because they form a coherent stream in anthropology. However the term "ecocultural theory" was used first by Weisner, a student of the Whitings, in an important yet specific conceptual contribution that merits further framing before being discussed. Among the many contributions by the Whitings and their students, an important conceptual advance by Harkness and Super (Harkness and Super 1994; Super and Harkness 1986) was the codification of the developmental niche, the daily experiences of a child living in a particular time and place, produced by two interacting aspects. One is a trio of interacting microsystems of customary practices, physical and social settings, and caregivers; the other is the child, an active agent shaping her/his microenvironment who embodies those lived experiences. This universally applicable model permits comparative cross-cultural studies about formation of, dynamics within, and correlates of developmental niches. Using the developmental niche model, Harkness and Super as well as their collaborators have been uniquely successful in the conduct of multisited comparative cross-cultural field research in the Whiting tradition (Harkness and Super 2000, 2005; Super et al. 2008). With a focus on cultural forces that shape caregivers, they have shown how parental ethnotheories guide parenting and relate to cultural differences in child socioemotional development (Harkness et al. 2007a; Harkness, Super, and Mavridis 2011).

Weisner's formulation of ecocultural theory identifies the child's participation in activities within culturally constituted and coherent settings as universally the single most important environmental influence on its development (Weisner 1996, 1997). He emphasizes family routines as a key feature of family functioning of central importance in the well-being of the entire household, children included (Weisner 2002), insofar as sustainable routines represent the bedrock for meaningful accommodations by households/families to their daily life circumstances or ecocultural niche (Gallimore et al. 1989). When they work well, family routines can create predictability with flexibility and promote valued and meaningful life agendas while also managing within available resources and minimizing conflicts (Weisner 2010). From this it follows that a hallmark of family functioning is the ability to sustain a daily routine, a novel hypothesis about an issue of central concern as the nature of households and family shifts rapidly (Weisner et al. 2005). As with the developmental niche, daily household routines offer a universally applicable construct related to observable phenomena from which to pursue multisited research.

Measures of daily routines have been applied to explore intracultural diversity both in typical families (Spagnola and Fiese 2007) and those facing challenges such as conditions of poverty (Duncan, Huston, and Weisner 2007; Lowe et al. 2005), minority status (Budescu and Taylor 2013; East and Weisner 2009), illness (Fiese, 2006) or child disability (Marquenie et al. 2011; Skinner and Weisner 2007). In these western settings, mealtime and bedtime routines have been found to be particularly important for child well-being, as have competing time demands overall (time famine). Child routines also have been assessed in a cross-cultural study of six western countries (Harkness et al. 2011) that combined daily diaries with debriefing of parents for meanings attached to each activity. Both similarities (time for meals, TV, grooming, travel) and substantial differences (family, school, enrichment, play) in child routines and time allocation were identified. This mixed methods design found that central themes of family, play, school/child development, and meals varied by prevalence in parents' talk across societies, but that meals were least salient in all six.

We also have used activity records and debriefing in studies of families in the United States (DeCaro and Worthman 2007) and Egypt (Worthman and Brown 2007) and found that the combination of a daily diary approach with debriefing interviews of participants to extract meanings and trade-offs reflected in the recorded activities and schedules represents an especially powerful approach for gaining insight into the dynamics of daily life. Indeed, in the case of the Egyptian study of sleep behaviors, such diary debriefing was critical to the insight that sleep is a social behavior (Worthman 2011a). This initially counterintuitive hypothesis is being swiftly taken up and tested at a time of epidemic sleep problems that have resisted amelioration (El-Sheikh 2011; El-Sheikh, Kelly, and Rauer 2013). As Harkness and colleagues put it: "qualities can be counted and quantities can be described" (Harkness et al. 2011, 811) to yield an especially clear, richly informative picture of how everyday behavior is related to cognition (intentions, values, meanings) and emotion (mood, stress, conflict, locus of control) as situated in their cultural and physical settings.

Embodiment

Concomitant with any encultured mind is an encultured physical being. Whiting's insight that it is human nature to be nurtured proved correct. Overwhelming evidence indicates the environment-expectancy of human development, and many lines of research document pathways and mechanisms by which this occurs (see reviews in Worthman et al. 2010). Babies arrive prepared to engage eagerly with the social worlds into which they are born (Hrdy 2009). That said, the body is not merely an adjunct for the mind, but the two sustain an intimate, mutually informative conversation throughout life. Socio-emotional and cognitive development are shaped by early environments of rearing, as is physical development. Thus the developmental effects of cultural ecology on mental and social life are allied with developmental effects on brain and body. Putting it strongly, the body is as anchored in culture as is mind. Anthropologists have fitfully recognized this relationship but have been slow to probe thoroughly its implications and consequences.

Hence, culture becomes embodied through the natural process of nurturing, as the structure and functions of the body incorporate experiences in social-cultural conditions that inform the course of adaptive development. The evolving concept of embodiment in anthropology (Seligman and Brown 2010) finds parallels in Bourdieu's notion of *habitus* as social capital and competence for specific social milieu ingrained through daily experience (Bourdieu 1977). In health and population sciences, embodiment is termed "biological embedding," recently recognized and characterized as occurring "when experience gets under the skin and alters human biological and developmental processes; when systematic differences in experience in different social environments in society lead to systematically different biological and developmental states; when these differences are stable and long term; and, finally, when they have the capacity to influence health, well-being, learning, or behavior over the life course" (Hertzman 2012, 17160).

The flood of recent evidence for embodiment or biological embedding has galvanized a paradigm shift in the study of human development and health (Boyce, Sokolowski, and Robinson 2012; Keating 2009), a shift that over a century's work in anthropology helped to catalyze. Specifically with regard to ecocultural theory, this work proceeded with Boas's data on context and cranial form, through the Whiting Model and John Whiting's empirical and cross-cultural work on the long-term effects of early stress (Gunders and Whiting 1968; Landauer and Whiting 1981), and on to the work of developmental anthropologists such as LeVine, Weisner, Super and Harkness, Konner, and many others, evolving ecocultural theories and accumulating evidence. The focus of ecocultural theory on the cultural ecology of affect and affect regulation as they drive psychobehavioral development, social competence, and well-being has maintained space for physical correlates as well.

Consequently, ecocultural studies including biomeasures routinely discover linkages among cultural practices, stress physiology, and emotion regulation (Worthman 2009). For example, lower cultural consonance, or the extent to which an individual's beliefs and behaviors match widely shared views (Dressler et al. 2005), has been associated with worse physical and mental health outcomes (elevated blood pressure and depression) in American and Brazilian populations (Dressler et al. 2007). The related phenomenon of status incongruity, or mismatch between actual socioeconomic status and attainment of culturally valued goods, is associated with similar effects. For instance, incongruity between attainment of conflicting traditional versus westernized status markers and the extent to which one valued such markers was related to an immune biomarker of stress among Samoan adolescents (McDade 2001). Similarly, elevated blood pressure among urban African American adolescents in Chicago was related to incongruity between consumption of high-status goods and family socioeconomic status (Sweet 2010). Such research firmly demonstrates the relationship of structural and economic inequalities with well-being (Gravlee 2009). Additionally disruptions of early rearing environment, even for culturally valued purposes, can exert long-term physical and emotional effects. A dramatic example is the evacuation of Finnish children and temporary separation from their families (average 1.8 years) in World War II, which resulted in greater adult depression and cardiovascular morbidity and mortality among evacuees than those who remained at home in the war (Alastalo et al. 2012; Pesonen et al. 2007). As ecocultural theory predicts, culturally normative "best practices" also leave an enduring stamp.

Ecocultural Theory in Method and Application

If successful development is about becoming competent in the world as it is, how might success be defined and attained in a world of globalization, rapid social change, and contextual instability? The ethnographic traditions surveyed above scrupulously dissociated participant research from intervention, both on ethical and methodological grounds. Yet the value of inquiry is its impact in human thought and action, and the streams of ecocultural theory and its precursors discussed here have aimed for such impact. For instance, Boas applied his work to issues of racism (Boas 1906 [reprinted 1982]), Mead tackled norms of sexuality, Bateson applied analysis of schizophrenia to treatment (Bateson 1987b), and Whiting advocated that anthropology open more effective routes to positive social change, particularly via early child care (Whiting and Child 1953).

Indeed, right at the outset, Weisner and colleagues' formulation of ecocultural theory explicitly aimed to inform the design of intervention aimed at families with challenged children (Bernheimer, Gallimore, and Weisner 1990). In their view, daily routines offer constraints and opportunities crucial to design of effective intervention to support what works or leverage positive change (Bernheimer and Weisner 2007). Importantly the proposition is both grounded in theory and allied with distinctive methodological orientations that place the locus of research in daily lives, attend to people's narratives of their lives and the meanings ascribed to them while also tapping quantitative or material features, and commit to be in place as an unobtrusive observant participant for a while. In the arena of challenged children, for example, this approach has informed interventions to develop family-specific problem solving for children at developmental risk (Chao et al. 2006) and to build family accommodation for children with disabilities (Harkness et al. 2007b; Steiner et al. 2012). Policy also is intervention, and ecocultural theory has been applied successfully to evaluate an intervention in support of families subject to national back-to-work policy (Duncan, Huston, and Weisner 2007), examining the impact of child-care subsidies on daily routines of low-income families (Lowe and Weisner 2004). This ecocultural study identified the reasons for differential efficacy of the intervention and directly addresses national policy discussions (Weisner 2011).

Moving to a global scale, anthropologists in the ecocultural tradition writ large have mobilized to proffer fresh integrative models and frameworks aimed explicitly to inform global policy and discourse for advancing family and child welfare (Britto, Engle, and Super 2013). The matter is urgent. If humanity is forged in the crucible of care, then major impacts may be expected from dramatic ongoing shifts in early-rearing environments (Hrdy 2009). Such shifts relate to trends regarded as positive aspects of "development" (changes in parental labor participation and shifted child care, universal schooling, or displacement through urbanization, labor, or family migration) as well as to trends recognized as problematic (increasing resource inequities, persistent scarcity, and orphanhood, displacement, and family disruption from conflict or diseases such as HIV AIDS).

Thus the evidence that social ecology is the main determinant of child development and health disparities has been used to seek the points for effective intervention in social ecologies of child development (Panter-Brick, Lende, and Kohrt 2012). Harkness and colleagues have shown how the developmental niche can be applied in diverse cultural settings in forming policy and enhancing intervention efficacy, and nicely delineate the tensions among the developmental agendas of young children, the cultural agendas forming the developmental niche, and the goals of intervention (Harkness et al. 2013). Gaps in the logics of macro development policy have been identified that directly affect human development, and alternatives proposed (Worthman 2011b). Global development theory posited a direct link between education and the economic development of societies, resulting in ongoing global transformations of cultural models of the life course and ideals for the "good life." But the model presumed that introduction of universal education would fuel development without a clear mechanism for how the rate of employment creation would match the production of graduates. The consequent suffering at individual, familial, and societal levels has been evident and dramatic. Further, this logic discounted competing cultural values and diversity in life-course models, generating resistance and conflict as the limitations of the model have become apparent. A compelling positive exemplar of such resistance and assertion of alternate models and values is Bhutan's national policy of Gross Domestic Happiness that envisions "an educated and enlightened society . . . at peace with itself, at peace with the world, built and sustained by the idealism and the creative enterprise of our citizens" (Education Monitoring and Support Services Division 2013, v). Ecocultural models also have been applied to help explain how global transitions (in vital rates, education, nutrition and disease, and politics, economics, and ecology) are affecting child well-being worldwide, and their pragmatic value illustrated through interventions to promote child well-being that are congruent with these models and supported by evidence (Stevenson and Worthman 2014).

The tide of global policy discourse is turning toward realizing child developmental potential, and none too soon (Worthman 2010b). Armed with ecocultural theory, methods, and an array of comparative evidence, anthropologists stand ready to advance this turn. In line with such leadership, they are fielding more multisited, collaborative research, prompting a re-engagement with comparative method as "the link between field-based ethnography and society-based issues" (Peacock 2002, 67). Moreover, as chapters in this volume exemplify, the models and mixed methods developed and deployed in this tradition have stimulated and scaffolded work in many disparate fields beyond anthropology, including psychology, economics, social policy, public health, and biomedicine. Widespread recognition among academics, policymakers, and a growing public that "culture gets under the skin" has opened opportunities for partnership with psychologists, physicians, biologists, educators, economists, policymakers, and civil society to apply insights from robust evidence-based theory to create novel, culturally sensitive approaches with the shared goal to promote the welfare of families, children, and adults in societies large and small. This project is urgent and will require every bit of human creativity and capacity for self transformation and cooperation to address the tremendous ecoculturally generated challenges we now confront.

References

Alastalo, Hanna, Katri Raikkonen, Anu-Katriina Pesonen, Clive Osmond, David J. Barker, Kati Heinonen, Eero Kajantie, and Johan G. Eriksson. 2012. "Cardiovascular Morbidity and Mortality in Finnish Men and Women Separated Temporarily from Their Parents in Childhood—A Life Course Study." *Psychosomatic Medicine* 74 (6): 583–87.

Atkinson, Paul, and Martyn Hammersley. 1994. "Ethnography and Participant Observation." In *Handbook of Qualitative Research*, edited by Norman K. Denzin and Yvonna S. Lincoln, 248–61. Thousand Oaks, CA: Sage Publications.

Bateson, Gregory. 1958. *Naven, a Survey of the Problems Suggested by a Composite Picture of the Culture of a New Guinea Tribe Drawn from Three Points of View* (2nd ed.). Stanford: Stanford University Press.

———. 1987a. "Experiments in Thinking about Observed Ethnological Material." In *Steps to an Ecology of Mind: Collected Essays in Anthropology, Psychiatry, Evolution, and Epistemology*, edited by Gregory Bateson, 73–87, Northvale, NJ: Aronson.

———. 1987b. *Steps to an Ecology of Mind: Collected Essays in Anthropology, Psychiatry, Evolution, and Epistemology*. Northvale, NJ: Aronson.

Bernheimer, Lucinda P., Ronald Gallimore, and Thomas S. Weisner. 1990. "Ecocultural Theory as a Context for the Individual Family Service Plan." *Journal of Early Intervention* 14 (3): 219–33.

Bernheimer, Lucinda P., and Thomas S. Weisner. 2007. "'Let Me Just Tell You What I Do All Day . . .': The Family Story at the Center of Intervention Research and Practice." *Infants and Young Children* 20 (3):192–201.

Boas, Franz. 1896. "Limitations of the Comparative Method of Anthropology." *Science* 4: 901–08.

———. 1906 (reprinted 1982). "The Outlook for the American Negro." In *A Franz Boas Reader: The Shaping of American Anthropology 1883–1911*, edited by George W. Stocking, 310–16. Chicago: University of Chicago Press.

———. 1912. Changes in the Bodily Form of Descendants of Immigrants. *American Anthropologist* 14: 530–62.

Bornstein, Marc H. 2009. *Handbook of Cross-Cultural Developmental Science.* Mahwah, NJ: Lawrence Erlbaum.

Bourdieu, Pierre. 1977. *Outline of a Theory of Practice.* Cambridge: Cambridge University.

Bowles, Samuel, Eric A. Smith, and Monique B. Mulder. 2010. "The Emergence and Persistence of Inequality in Premodern Societies: Introduction to the Special Section." *Current Anthropology* 51 (1):7–17.

Boyce, W. Thomas, Marla B. Sokolowski, and Gene E. Robinson. 2012. "Toward a New Biology of Social Adversity." *Proceedings of the National Academy of Sciences of the United States of America* 109 Suppl. 2: 17143–48.

Britto, Pia Rebello, Patrice L. Engle, and Charles M. Super. 2013. *Handbook of Early Childhood Development Research and Its Impact on Global Policy.* New York: Oxford.

Bronfenbrenner, Urie. 1979. *The Ecology of Human Development: Experiments by Nature and Design.* Cambridge, MA: Harvard University Press.

Budescu, Mia, and Ronald D. Taylor. 2013. "Order in the Home: Family Routines Moderate the Impact of Financial Hardship." *Journal of Applied Developmental Psychology* 34 (2):63–72.

Chao, Pen-Chiang, Tanis Bryan, Karen Burstein, and Cevriye Ergul. 2006. "Family-Centered Intervention for Young Children At-Risk for Language and Behavior Problems." *Early Childhood Education Journal* 34 (2): 147–53.

Clifford, James, and George E. Marcus. 1986. *Writing Culture: the Poetics and Politics of Ethnography.* Berkeley, CA: University of California Press.

DeCaro, Jason A., and Carol M. Worthman. 2007. "Cultural Models, Parent Behavior, and Young Child Experience in Working American Families." *Parenting: Science and Practice* 7: 177–203.

Dressler, William W., Mauro C. Balieiro, Rosane P. Ribeiro, and José Ernesto Dos Santos. 2007. "Cultural Consonance and Psychological Distress: Examining the Associations in Multiple Cultural Domains." *Culture, Medicine and Psychiatry* 31 (2):195–224.

Dressler, William W., Camila D. Borges, Mauro C. Balieiro, and José Ernesto Dos

Santos. 2005. "Measuring Cultural Consonance: Examples with Special Reference to Measurement Theory in Anthropology." *Field Methods* 17: 331–55.

Duncan, Greg, Aletha Huston, and Thomas S. Weisner. 2007. *Higher Ground: New Hope for the Working Poor and Their Children.* New York: Russell Sage Foundation.

East, Patricia L., and Thomas S. Weisner. 2009. "Mexican American Adolescents' Family Caregiving: Selection Effects and Longitudinal Associations with Adjustment." *Family Relations* 58 (5): 562–77.

Education Monitoring and Support Services Division, Ministry of Education. 2013. *Educating for Gross National Happiness: A Training Manual.* Thimpu, Bhutan: Phama.

Edwards, Carolyn P., and Thomas S. Weisner. 2010. "Special Issue in Honor of Beatrice Whiting." *Journal of Cross-Cultural Psychology* 41 (4): 483–632.

El-Sheikh, Mona, ed. 2011. *Sleep and Development: Familial and Socio-Cultural Considerations.* Oxford: Oxford University Press.

El-Sheikh, Mona, Ryan Kelly, and Amy Rauer. 2013. "Quick to Berate, Slow to Sleep: Interpartner Psychological Conflict, Mental Health, and Sleep." *Health Psychology* 32 (10): 1057–66

Evans-Pritchard, Edward Evan. 1963. *The Comparative Method in Social Anthropology.* London: Atholone Press.

Fiese, Barbara H. 2006. *Family Routines and Rituals.* New Haven, CT: Yale University Press.

Gallimore, Ronald, Thomas S. Weisner, Sandra Z. Kaufman, and Lucinda P. Bernheimer. 1989. "The Social Construction of Ecocultural Niches: Family Accommodation of Developmentally Delayed Children." *American Journal of Mental Retardation* 94 (3): 216–30.

Geertz, Clifford. 1973. *The Interpretation of Cultures: Selected Essays.* New York: Basic Books.

Gluckman, Peter D., Mark A. Hanson, Patrick Bateson, Alan S. Beedle, Catherine M. Law, Zulfigar A. Bhutta, Konstantin V. Anokhin, Pierre Bougnères, Giriraj Ratan Chandak, Partha Dasgupta, George Davey Smith, Peter T. Ellison, Terrence Forrester, Scott F. Gilbert, Eva Jablonka, Hillard Kaplan, Andrew M. Prentice, Stephen J. Simpson, Ricardo Uauy, and Mary Jane West-Eberhard. 2009. "Towards a New Developmental Synthesis: Adaptive Developmental Plasticity and Human Disease." *Lancet* 373 (9675):1654–57.

Gravlee, Clarence C. 2009. "How Race Becomes Biology: Embodiment of Social Inequality." *American Journal of Physical Anthropology* 139 (1): 47–57.

Gravlee, Clarence. C., H. Russell Bernard, and William R. Leonard. 2003a. "Boas's Changes in Bodily Form: The Immigrant Study, Cranial Plasticity, and Boas's Physical Anthropology." *American Anthropologist* 105 (2): 326–32.

———. 2003b. "Heredity, Environment, and Cranial Form: A Reanalysis Of Boas's Immigrant Data." *American Anthropologist* 105: 125–38.

Gunders, Shulamith M., and John W. M. Whiting. 1968. "Mother-Infant Separation and Physical Growth." *Ethnology* 7: 196–206.

Gupta, Akhil, and James Ferguson. 1992. "Beyond 'Culture': Space, Identity, and the Politics of Difference." *Cultural Anthropology* 7: 6–23.

Harkness, Sara, and Charles M. Super. 1994. "The Developmental Niche: A Theoretical Framework for Analyzing the Household Production of Health." *Social Science and Medicine* 38: 218–26.

———. 2000. "Culture and Psychopathology." In *Handbook of Developmental Psychopathology* (2nd ed.), edited by Arnold J. Sameroff and Michael Lewis, 197–214. New York: Kluwer Academic/Plenum Publishers.

———. 2005. "Themes and Variations: Parental Ethnotheories in Western Cultures." In *Parental Beliefs, Parenting, and Child Development in Cross-Cultural Perspective*, edited by Kenneth Rubin and Ock Boon Chung, 61–79. New York: Psychology Press.

Harkness, Sara, Charles M. Super, and Caroline Johnston Mavridis. 2011. "Parental Ethnotheories about Children's Socioemotional Development." In *Socioemotional Development in Cultural Context*, edited by Xinyin Chen and Kenneth H. Rubin, 73–98. New York: Guilford Press.

Harkness, Sara, Charles M. Super, Caroline Johnston Barry Mavridis, and Marian Oumar Zeitlin. 2013. "Culture and Early Childhood Development: Implications for Policy and Programs." In *Handbook of Early Childhood Development Research and Its Impact on Global Policy*, edited by Pia Rebello Britto, Patrice L. Engle, and Charles M. Super, 142–60. New York: Oxford University Press.

Harkness, Sara, Charles M. Super, Ughetta Moscardino, Jong-Hay Rha, Marjolijn J. M. Blom, Blanca Huitrón., Caroline Johnston, Mary A. Sutherland, On-Kang Hyun, Giovanna Axia, and Jesús Palacios. 2007a. "Cultural Models and Developmental Agendas: Implications for Arousal and Self-Regulation in Early Infancy." *Journal of Developmental Processes* 1 (2): 5–39.

Harkness, Sara, Charles M. Super, Mary A. Sutherland, Marjolijn J. M. Blom, Ughetta Moscardino, Caroline J. Mavridis, and Giovanna Axia. 2007b. "Culture and the Construction of Habits in Daily Life: Implications for the Successful Development of Children with Disabilities." *OTJR: Occupation, Participation and Health* 27: 33S–40S.

Harkness, Sara, Piotr Olaf Zylicz, Charles M.Super, Barbara Welles-Nyström, Moisés Ríos Bermúdez, Sabrina Bonichini, Ughetta Moscardino, and Caroline Johnston Mavridis. 2011. "Children's Activities and Their Meanings for Parents: A Mixed-Methods Study in Six Western Cultures." *Journal of Family Psychology* 25 (6): 799–813.

Harris, Marvin. 1979. *Cultural Materialism: The Struggle for a Science of Culture.* New York: Random House.

Henrich, Joseph, Robert Boyd, Samuel Bowles, Colin Camerer, Ernst Fehr, and Herbert Gintis. 2004. *Foundations of Human Sociality: Economic Experiments and Ethnographic Evidence from Fifteen Small-Scale Societies*. Oxford: Oxford University Press.

Henrich, Joseph, Steven J. Heine, and Ara Norenzayan. 2010. "The Weirdest People in the World?" *Behavioral and Brain Sciences* 33 (2–3): 61–83.

Hertzman, Clyde. 2012. "Putting the Concept of Biological Embedding in Historical Perspective." *Proceedings of the National Academy of Sciences of the United States of America*, 109 Suppl. 2, 17160–67.

Hrdy, Sarah B. 2009. *Mothers and Others: The Evolutionary Origins of Mutual Understanding*. Cambridge, MA: Harvard University Press.

Keating, Daniel P. 2009. "Social Interactions in Human Development: Pathways to Health and Capabilities." In *Successful Societies: How Institutions and Culture Affect Health*, edited by Peter A. Hall and Michèle Lamont, 53–81. New York: Cambridge University Press.

Kennett, Douglas J., and Bruce Winterhalder. 2006. *Behavioral Ecology and the Transition to Agriculture*. Berkeley: University of California Press.

Kuzawa, Christopher W. 2008. "The Developmental Origins of Adult Health: Intergenerational Inertia in Adaptation and Disease." In *Evolution and Health*, edited by Wenda Trevathan, E. O. Smith, and James J. McKenna, 325–49. Oxford: Oxford University Press.

Landauer, Thomas K., and John W. M. Whiting. 1981. "Correlates and Consequences of Stress in Infancy." In *Handbook of Cross-Cultural Research in Human Development*, edited by Ruth Munroe, Robert Munroe, and Beatrice Whiting, 355–75. New York: Garland Press.

Lansing, J. Stephen. 2006. *Perfect Order: Recognizing Complexity in Bali*. Princeton: Princeton University Press.

Lansing, J. Stephen, and Karyn M. Fox. 2011. "Niche Construction on Bali: The Gods of the Countryside." *Philosophical Transactions of the Royal Society—Series B: Biological Sciences* 366 (1566): 927–34.

Lowe, Edward D., Thomas S. Weisner, Sonya Geis, and Aletha C. Huston. 2005. "Child Care Instability and the Effort to Sustain a Working Daily Routine: Evidence from the New Hope Ethnographic Study of Low-Income Families." In *Developmental Pathways through Middle Childhood: Rethinking Contexts and Diversity as Resources*, edited by Catherine R. Cooper, Cynthia T. Garcia Coll, W. Todd Bartko, Helen Davis, and Celina Chatman, 121–44. Mahwah, NJ: Lawrence Erlbaum.

Lowe, Edward D., and Thomas S. Weisner. 2004. "'You Have to Push It—Who's Gonna Raise Your Kids?': Situating Child Care and Child Care Subsidy Use in the Daily Routines of Lower Income Families." *Children and Youth Services Review* 26 (2): 143–71.

Mace, Ruth, and Mark Pagel. 1994. "The Comparative Method in Anthropology." *Current Anthropology* 35 (5): 549–64.

Marquenie, Kylie, Sylvia Rodger, Kim Mangohig, and Anne Cronin. 2011. "Dinnertime and Bedtime Routines and Rituals in Families with a Young

Child with an Autism Spectrum Disorder." *Australian Occupational Therapy Journal* 58 (3):145–54.

McDade, Thomas W. 2001. "Lifestyle Incongruity, Social Integration, and Immune Function in Samoan Adolescents." *Social Science and Medicine* 53: 1351–62.

McDade, Thomas W., and Carol M. Worthman. 1999. "Evolutionary Process and the Ecology of Human Immune Function." *American Journal of Human Biology* 11: 705–17.

McElreath, Richard, and Joseph Henrich. 2007. "Dual Inheritance Theory: The Evolution of Human Cultural Capacities and Cultural Evolution." In *Oxford Handbook of Evolutionary Psychology*, edited by Robin Dunbar and Louise Barrett-Connor, 555–70. Oxford: Oxford University Press.

Mead, Margaret. 1928. *Coming of Age in Samoa: A Psychological Study of Primitive Youth for Western Civilization.* New York: W. Morrow.

———. 1930. *Growing Up in New Guinea: A Comparative Study of Primitive Education.* New York: W. Morrow.

Mead, Margaret, and Frances Cooke Macgregor. 1951. *Growth and Culture; A Photographic Study of Balinese Childhood.* New York: Putnam.

Needham, Rodney. 1973. *Right and Left: Essays on Dual Symbolic Classification.* Chicago: University of Chicago Press.

Nunn, Charles L., Christian Arnold, Luke Matthews, and Monique Borgerhoff Mulder. 2010. "Simulating Trait Evolution for Cross-Cultural Comparison." *Philosophical Transactions of the Royal Society of London—Series B: Biological Sciences* 365 (1559): 3807–19.

Panter-Brick, Catherine, Daniel Lende, and Brandon Kohrt. 2012. "Children in Global Adversity: Physical Health, Mental Health, Behavioral Health, and Symbolic Health." In *The Oxford Handbook of Poverty and Child Development*, edited by Valerie Maholmes and Rosalind B. King, 603–21. New York: Oxford University Press.

Peacock, James. 2002. "Action Comparison: Efforts towards a Global and Comparative Yet Local and Active Anthropology." In *Anthropology, by Comparison*, edited by Richard G. Fox and Andre Gingrich, 44–69. New York: Routledge.

Pesonen, Anu-Katriina, Katri Raikkonen, Kati Heinonen, Eero Kajantie, Tom Forsen, and Johan G. Eriksson. 2007. "Depressive Symptoms in Adults Separated from Their Parents as Children: A Natural Experiment During World War II." *American Journal of Epidemiology* 166 (10):1126–33.

Radcliffe-Brown, Alfred Reginald. 1951. "The Comparative Method in Social Anthropology." *Royal Anthropological Institute of Great Britain and Ireland Journal* 81 (1/2): 15–22.

Rappaport, Roy. 1968. *Pigs for the Ancestors: Ritual in the Ecology of a New Guinea People.* New Haven: Yale University Press.

Richerson, Peter J., and Robert Boyd. 2005. *Not By Genes Alone: How Culture Transformed Human Evolution.* Chicago: University of Chicago Press.

Seligman, Rebecca, and Ryan A. Brown. 2010. "Theory and Method at the

Intersection of Anthropology and Cultural Neuroscience." *Social Cognitive and Affective Neuroscience* 5 (2–3):130–37.

Skinner, Debra, and Thomas S. Weisner. 2007. "Sociocultural Studies of Families of Children with Intellectual Disabilities." *Mental Retardation and Developmental Disabilities Research Reviews* 13 (4): 302–12.

Spagnola, Mary, and Barbara H. Fiese. 2007. "Family Routines and Rituals: A Context for Development in the Lives of Young Children." *Infants & Young Children* 20 (4): 284–99.

Sperber, Dan.1996. *Explaining Culture: A Naturalistic Approach*. Oxford: Blackwell.

Stauffer, John. 1957. "Haeckel, Darwin, and Ecology." *Quarterly Review of Biology* 32: 138–44.

Stearns, Stephen C., and Jacob C. Koella. 1986. "The Evolution of Phenotypic Plasticity in Life-History Traits: Prediction of Reaction Norms for Age and Size at Maturity." *Quarterly Review of Biology* 40 (5): 893–10.

Steiner, Amanda M., Lynn K. Koegel, Robert L. Koegel, and Whitney A. Ence. 2012. "Issues and Theoretical Constructs Regarding Parent Education for Autism Spectrum Disorders." *Journal of Autism and Developmental Disorders* 42 (6): 1218–27.

Stevenson, Edward G. J., and Carol M. Worthman. 2014. "Child Well-Being: Anthropological Perspectives." In *Handbook of Child Well-Being: Theories, Methods, and Policies in Global Perspective*, edited by Asher Ben-Arieh, Ferran Casas, Ivar Frones, and Jill E. Korbin, 485–512. Dordrecht: Springer.

Steward, Julian Haynes. 1955. *Theory of Culture Change: The Methodology of Multilinear Evolution*. Urbana: University of Illinois Press.

Stocking, George W. 1966. "Franz Boas and the Culture Concept in Historical Perspective." *American Anthropologist* 68: 867–82.

———. ed. 1989–1999. *History of Anthropology Series*. Madison: University of Wisconsin Press.

Super, Charles M., and Sara Harkness. 1986. "The Developmental Niche: A Conceptualization at the Interface of Child and Culture." *International Journal of Behavioral Development* 9: 545–69.

Super, Charles M., Giovanna Axia, Sara Harkness, Barbara Welles-Nyström, Piotr Olaf Zylicz, Parminder Parmar, Sabrina Bonichini, Moisés Rios Bermúdez, Ughetta Moscardino, Violet Kolar, Jesús Palacios, Andrzej Eliasz, and Harry McGurk. 2008. "Culture, Temperament, and the 'Difficult Child': A Study of Seven Western Cultures." *European Journal of Developmental Science* 2 (1–2): 136–57.

Sweet, Elizabeth. 2010. "'If Your Shoes Are Raggedy You Get Talked About': Symbolic and Material Dimensions of Adolescent Social Status and Health." *Social Science and Medicine* 70 (12): 2029–35.

Thompson, D'Arcy Wentworth. 1942. *On Growth and Form* (2nd ed.). Cambridge: Cambridge University Press.

Weisner, Thomas S. 1996. "Why Ethnography Should Be the Most Important Method in the Study of Human Development." In *Ethnography and Human*

Development: Context and Meaning in Social Inquiry, edited by Richard Jessor, Anne Colby, and Richard Shweder, 305–24. Chicago: University of Chicago Press.

———. 1997. "The Ecocultural Project of Human Development: Why Ethnography and Its Findings Matter." *Ethos* 25 (2): 177–90.

———. 2002. "Ecocultural Understanding of Children's Developmental Pathways." *Human Development* 45: 275–81.

———. 2010. "Well-Being, Chaos, and Culture: Sustaining a Meaningful Daily Routine." In *Chaos and Its Influence on Children's Development: An Ecological Perspective*, edited by Gary W. Evans and Theodore D. Wachs, 211–24. Washington, DC: American Psychological Association.

———. 2011. "'If You Work in This Country You Should Not Be Poor, and Your Kids Should Be Doing Better': Bringing Mixed Methods and Theory in Psychological Anthropology to Improve Research in Policy and Practice." *Ethos* 39 (4): 455–76.

Weisner, Thomas S., and Carolyn P. Edwards. 2001. "Special Issue in Honor of Beatrice Whiting." *Ethos* 29 (3): 239–389.

Weisner, Thomas S., Catherine Matheson, Jennifer Coots, and Lucinda P. Bernheimer. 2005. "Sustainability of Daily Routines as a Family Outcome." In *The Psychology of Learning in Cultural Context: Family, Peers, and School*, eds. Ashley Maynard and Mary Martini, 41–73. New York: Kluwer/Plenum.

West-Eberhard, Mary Jane. 2003. *Developmental Plasticity and Evolution*. New York: Oxford University Press.

White, Leslie A. 1959. *The Evolution of Culture: The Development of Civilization to the Fall of Rome*. New York: McGraw-Hill.

Whiting, Beatrice Blyth, and Carolyn Pope Edwards. 1988. *Children of Different Worlds: The Formation of Social Behavior*. Cambridge: Harvard University Press.

Whiting, John W. M., and Eleanor H. Chasdi. 1994. *Culture and Human Development: The Selected Papers of John Whiting*. Cambridge: Cambridge University Press.

Whiting, John W. M. 1954. "The Cross-Cultural Method." In *Handbook of Social Psychology*, vol. 2, edited by Garner Lindzey, 523–31. Cambridge, MA: Addison-Wesley.

Whiting, John W. M., and Irvin L. Child. 1953. *Child Training and Personality: A Cross-Cultural Study*. New York: Yale University Press.

Whiting, John W. M., Irvin L. Child, William W. Lambert, Ann M. Fischer, John L. Fischer, Corinne N. Nydegger, William F. Nydegger, Helen Maretzki, Thomas W. Maretzki, Leigh Minturn, A. Kimball Romney, and Romaine Romney. 1966. *Field Guide for a Study of Socialization*. New York: John Wiley.

Whiting, John W. M. 1941. *Becoming a Kwoma*. New Haven: Yale University Press.

Worthman, Carol M. 2009. "Habits of the Heart: Life History and the Developmental Neuroendocrinology of Emotion." *American Journal of Human Biology* 211: 772–81.

———. 2010a. "The Ecology of Human Development: Evolving Models for Cultural Psychology." *Journal for Cross-Cultural Psychology* 41: 546–62.

———.2010b. "Child Survival and Health." In *Handbook of Cross-Cultural Developmental Science*, edited by Marc Bornstein, 41–79. Mahwah, NJ: Erlbaum.

———. 2011a. "Developmental Cultural Ecology of Human Sleep." In *Sleep and Development: Familial and Socio-Cultural Considerations*, edited by Mona El-Sheikh, 167–94. Oxford: Oxford University Press.

———.2011b. "Inside/Out or Outside/In? Global Development Theory, Policy, and Youth." *Ethos* 39 (4): 432–51.

Worthman, Carol M., and Ryan A. Brown. 2007. "Companionable Sleep: Social Regulation of Sleep and Co-Sleeping in Egyptian Families." *Journal of Family Psychology* 21: 124–35.

Worthman, Carol M., Paul M. Plotsky, Daniel S. Schechter, and Constance Cummings, eds. 2010. *Formative Experiences: The Interaction of Caregiving, Culture, and Developmental Psychobiology.* Cambridge: Cambridge University Press.

PART TWO

Discovering Mixed Methods

Ethnography in Need of Numbers: Mixing Methods to Build Partnerships and Understand Tigers

M. CAMERON HAY

Ethnography is what drew me to anthropology. Ethnography, with its contextualized stories and descriptions of complex ways of being in the world—that were simultaneously different and familiar—entranced me. I wanted to be an ethnographer, and as my favorite ethnographic books had no numbers beyond estimates of population size or cultivated hectares, I was committed to the idea that I didn't need numbers to do good anthropological research.

As a student, I was increasingly interested in issues of identity: how did individuals and social groups craft identities that enabled them to cope with life's challenges? I wanted to listen to people's stories and watch how they told stories about themselves for themselves and for others in order to make meaningful lives within their families and communities. I wanted to crawl into other people's skin as much as possible and walk around for a while to understand their world as they understood it. So on the one hand, I was motivated to get at, as Bronislaw Malinowski put it at the beginning of the twentieth century, "the native's point of view" (Malinowski [1922]1984). On the other hand, I was coming of age in a time of anthropological angst, prompted by the postmodern turn in anthropology, in which people questioned whether we could ever really know anything about the other, limited as we are by our own perceptions, interpretations, and experiences, much less get at anything like other people's perspectives on their worlds. Could using the classic method of ethnographic participant observation—living with and like other people, striving to understand how they interpreted the world—still be successful? Answering this question would require theorizing and redefining "culture" with the rest of anthropology at the time, and doing so while in the midst of ethnographic fieldwork. I had enough on my plate without worrying about numbers.

So I petitioned to be exempt from the standard departmental requirement to take statistics in graduate school. I argued that I had had one course in statistics as an undergraduate, so I understood the fundamentals. I had nothing against mathematics, but what interested me was not numbers, and for the kind of research I wanted to do, I didn't need numbers (or so I thought). I needed the wonderful, get-your-feet-dirty kind of fieldwork that would yield rich, contextualized ethnographic data. So my department let me off the statistics hook. And I was grateful. It took me a decade to regret both the request and the decision.

Numbers as Justification and the Surprises of Qualitative Data

In the interim, as anthropologists say, I went "to the field." For me, that meant twenty-two months living on the lower slopes of an active volcano in a community of 800 people. I lived in a house with a family of twelve in a space the size of a typical American elementary classroom. At the time, the only plumbing available was in the form of streams winding their way through rice fields. The only electricity was at the mayor's house who had hijacked the electrical line so that he could put the only television in the area on his front porch, where crowds would gather to watch *Dynasty* reruns, commenting on the wealth of Americans (I was clearly an anomaly, for they could tell I had nothing like the wealth they observed on the television). Gradually my research topic shifted, as topics are wont to do in anthropology. What is so well reasoned in our minds and our grant proposals within the ivory tower often disintegrates when confronted with the everyday realities of lives lived without safety nets. And because I gradually became aware that the Sasak people I lived with cared not a whit about their identity—they knew exactly who they were, it was the rest of the world that was out of whack with the best way of doing things—I started paying attention to what they paid attention to, namely how to deal with a life that is precarious, lasting "only a day and a night." In the end, I paid some attention to numbers; for example, I counted the number of burials I attended (42), the number of women who gave birth while I was in the field (36) as well as the number I watched helplessly as they died in childbirth (3), and I reviewed the reproductive life history data I had gathered over glasses of bitter coffee. I converted these contextualized numbers into statistics—showing a crude death rate of 26.3/1,000, a one-in-twelve chance of dying in childbirth, and a forty to fifty percent infant and child mortality rate—that I documented in my resulting ethnography to legitimate a focus on ethnomedicine, the local ideologies and practices people used to cope with illness (Hay 1999, 2001). So for me at the time, numbers were useful to help justify a particular focus but were not themselves insightful.

Instead what I found intriguing was the compelling qualitative data that in this community medical knowledge was egalitarian. In most societies in the world, medical practice and the associated knowledge to heal illness is mastered by a few people. We call them doctors, nurses, or health care practitioners. In other parts of the world, they may be referred to as shamans or healers. In all places, they are specialists, whose medical knowledge is distinct from that of the rest of the community. Thus, seemingly by definition, medical knowledge is hierarchical—those who do not have access to it are dependent on those who do.

Anthropology, or at least the kind of anthropology I do, is a naturalistic science. We design methods much as a fisherman weaves his net—to catch whatever happens to be in local waters. We may have a sense of the range of what we will likely find—it is more likely to be a fish than a marsupial—but every now and then we will pull up something that takes us utterly by surprise, like a fisherman that pulls in a swimming tiger.

In the field, for a long time, I kept throwing the tiger back, thinking that, to carry the analogy a bit further, it was some kind of large striped fish, not a tiger at all. Because of course the Sasak did have people who specialized in healing: shamans and midwives. But the more I watched and listened, the more I realized that it was a tiger after all. Everyone over the age of about five had access to healing knowledge that could potentially treat a particular person's illness; the only difference between the specialists and the rest of society was that specialists had amassed more healing knowledge than everyone else. It was a matter of quantity, not quality. Here was a society in which medical knowledge was essentially egalitarian.

I came home, wrote up my findings, and, when I came up to breathe again, noticed that whenever I turned on the television, or went to the doctor, I was increasingly bombarded with the message that "knowledge is power" and to be a good patient, I needed to be an informed one. The Internet was potentially changing what had been, since Talcott Parsons's description of it in the 1950s (Parsons 1951), a hierarchical medical system into an egalitarian one, in which, according to the advertisements on television and in magazines, paid for by pharmaceutical and insurance companies, patients should be "informed" so that they could make their own health decisions and advocate for certain medications and procedures. The increasing availability of medical knowledge on the Internet potentially gave everyone access to medical knowledge. Would online health information make biomedicine in the United States egalitarian along the lines of the Sasak medical tradition?

Similar Questions, Different Context, and Needing Different Methods

With generous funding from the National Science Foundation and a new research position at the UCLA Center for Culture and Health, I began seeking physicians to partner with—physicians who would allow me to interview their patients and record their interactions with them in order to understand whether patients were indeed using online health information and if so, how and to what end. Rheumatologists at UCLA, and later neurologists too, opened their doors to me, interested in the research question and thus in partnering on research. But when they asked about my planned methods—interviews and conversational analysis of doctor-patient interactions—they were clearly bewildered: what kind of research was this? What about standardized instruments, whose findings they relied upon? Wasn't I using the MOS-36? What about the SDAI? How would I know what I had found? Would I use a logistic regression or a T-test? It was my turn to be flummoxed. They were clearly using English, but it might as well have been Greek for all I understood.

Seeking support for my position as a qualitative researcher, I knocked on the door of Tom Weisner, the head of the Center for Culture and

Health, and asked for advice. How was I to convince these physicians of the virtues of qualitative research methods? Tom, insightfully, turned the question back to me, saying in essence, "Why wouldn't you want to do research that makes sense to the people you want to work with?" And thus began my education in mixed methods.

I read medical journal articles in rheumatology and neurology to better understand how researchers in those fields typically looked at questions of patient knowledge and experience. I worked with local mixed methods researchers like Tom Weisner (chapter 20), Ted Lowe (chapter 9), and Eli Lieber (chapter 10), knocking on their doors to discuss research design issues. I spent hours in the library, researching different standardized instruments (which I learned were surveys that had been validated statistically to reliably measure a particular variable), and identifying which ones were directly relevant to the larger research questions: yes to a pain scale at each appointment (Wong and Baker 1988), and at second appointments, a helplessness scale (Nicassio et al. 1985), and the MOS-36 (Medical Outcomes Study-36, Hayes, Sherbourne, and Mazel 1993), a self-report questionnaire measuring current physical and psychological function, used across a wide range of disease populations. But I answered no to the Simplified Disease Activity Index (SDAI), a physician score of biological disease activity appropriate only for some rheumatological populations (Smolen et al. 2003). Later, Lieber would patiently walk me through how to score and analyze these data, and he'd have to do so repeatedly because thinking through quantitative analysis was just such a foreign process to me—what is the difference between continuous and discrete variables again? What is a null-hypothesis? I was learning from scratch a new way of thinking about collecting data, a new way of being as alien to me initially as moving into a house with twelve other people in a community that lacked electricity and indoor plumbing. That statistics course I had forgone so many years ago would have come in very handy.

I had added numbers to a primarily qualitative research project in order to partner with physicians and make my research comprehensible to them. I didn't expect the numbers to yield anything interesting. The scales and numbers would simply allow me to demonstrate that I had learned the language of quantative data, the currency of medical research. I would be able to describe the study population in ways that made them comparable to other populations in the published medical literature. I did not imagine at the time that learning the language of numbers had started me on a pathway into mixed methods.

Another Surprise Yielding a Mixed Methods Convert

And then I pulled up another tiger. Overall, 62.5 percent of rheumatology patients had walked into their first appointment having researched online their suspected disease, and patients in that 62.5 percent were significantly more likely to report higher levels of pain. But only twenty percent of patients overall spoke with their physicians about the information they had found online (see Hay, Strathmann et al. 2008; Hay, Cadigan et al. 2008). Were these the patients in more pain? Not necessarily. Patients who reported higher levels of pain at the first appointment were both more likely to have gone online for health information and less likely to mention that information in the appointment. What? I redid the statistics. The statistics were correct and pointed to something I hadn't expected. Here was another tiger.

So I went back to the qualitative postappointment interviews in which I had asked patients about the appointment and whether they had talked with their physician about the information they had found online, why or why not. Many had not given reasons, but of those who did, hesitancy to be perceived as confrontational, as a difficult patient, was a primary concern: as one patient put it, "You know, with doctors, it's difficult. Because they don't like it when patients come in and tell them that they want this or that." Patients feared stepping on a physician's toes—"Maybe he thinks I'm too involved in my therapy"—and imagined that their health care could suffer in consequence. This was a surprise both to me and to my physician-partners, who work conscientiously to provide the best possible care to patients under all circumstances.

The statistics had pointed to a finding that otherwise would not have come to light. And to make sense of the statistics, to try to understand what they meant, we needed the qualitative data. Using mixed methods led to more interesting findings and importantly to findings that were relevant to my clinical partners and in the interests of the population being studied, that is, the patients—offering a fuller understanding of their situations and perceptions.

Moreover the quantitative findings provided a scaffold upon which the qualitative findings made sense to a medical audience, enabling us to publish collaboratively in medical journals, thus gaining a much larger audience for the study, and one in a position to do something to improve patient care.

I started the project needing numbers in order to build partnerships with physicians. In the process, I learned a new language. A language as difficult to learn as the Sasak language had been, and as important to master if I wanted to understand and be able to communicate in a world of medicine. I had thought I was just mastering a language for pragmatic reasons, but learned that my ethnographic insight was greater with numbers. Numbers enabled me to explore a story of pain and fear as inhibiting communication that I would not have seen in my qualitative data if the statistics had not pulled up a tiger.

Acknowledgments

The research described in Indonesia and in the United States was supported by the National Science Foundation (SBR-93139; ADVANCE-0137921) with additional funding from the National Multiple Sclerosis Foundation (0137921). I also thank the people in Lombok and in the United States who patiently encouraged me to expand my methodological toolkit, with special thanks to the UCLA Center for Culture and Health.

References

Hay, M. Cameron. 1999. "Dying Mothers: Maternal Mortality in Rural Indonesia." *Medical Anthropology* 18 (3): 243–79.

———. 2001. *Remembering to Live: Illness at the Intersection of Anxiety and Knowledge in Rural Indonesia.* Edited by David Chandler and Rita Smith Kipp. *Southeast Asia: Politics, Meaning, and Memory.* Ann Arbor: University of Michigan Press.

Hay, M. Cameron, R. Jean Cadigan, Dinesh Khanna, Cynthia Strathmann, Eli Lieber, Roy Altman, Maureen McMahon, Morris Kokhab, and Daniel E. Furst. 2008. "Prepared Patients : Internet Information Seeking by New Rheumatology Patients." *Arthritis Care and Research* 59 (4): 575–82.

Hay, M. Cameron, Cynthia Strathmann, Eli Lieber, Kimberly Wick, and Barbara Giesser. 2008. "Why Patients Go Online: Multiple Sclerosis, the Internet, and Physician-Patient Communication." *The Neurologist* 14 (6) (November): 374–81.

Hayes, R. D., C. D. Sherbourne, and R. M. Mazel. 1993. "The RAND 36-Item Health Survey 1.0." *Health Economics* 2: 217–27.

Malinowski, Bronislaw. 1984. *Argonauts of the Western Pacific.* Prospect Heights, IL: Waveland Press.

Nicassio, Perry, K. A. Wallston, L. F. Callahan, and T. Pincus. 1985. "The

Measurement of Helplessness in Rheumatoid Arthritis: The Development of the Arthritis Helplessness Index." *Journal of Rheumatology* 12: 462–67.

Parsons, Talcott. 1951. "Illness and the Role of the Physician: A Sociological Perspective." American Journal of Orthopsychiatry 21: 452–60.

Smolen, J. S., F. C. Breedveld, M. H. Schiff, J. R. Kalden, P. Emery, G. Eberl, P. L. van Riel, and P. Tugwell. 2003. "A Simplified Disease Activity Index for Rheumatoid Arthritis for Use in Clinical Practice." *Rheumatology* 42 (2): 244–57.

Wong, D., and C. Baker. 1988. "Pain in Children: Comparison of Assessment Scales." *Pediatric Nursing* 14: 9–17.

FOUR

Crunching Numbers, Listening to Voices, and Looking at the Brain to Understand Family Relationships among Immigrant Families

ANDREW J. FULIGNI

My training as a developmental psychologist in graduate school was strictly quantitative in nature. Virtually all of the empirical articles assigned in my courses were based on experimental or other quantitative-based methods such as cognitive testing, questionnaires, and the enumeration of observed behavior. Similarly I apprenticed on research projects that focused on educational assessment and established inventories of parenting and child development. I enjoyed the focus on quantitative methods, particularly the variety of statistical techniques that could be used to analyze the data. I eagerly enrolled in advanced statistical courses beyond those required for my degree, learning about cutting-edge modeling of longitudinal, multi-informant, and multilevel quantitative data. By the time I completed my coursework and embarked on my dissertation, I believed that I was well prepared to conduct sophisticated research on the development and adaptation of adolescents from diverse ethnic and cultural backgrounds.

At that time, little did I know that my focus on a single method provided me with a limited view of the developmental processes of these populations. It was only with the introduction of additional, more qualitative methods that my colleagues and I were able to more fully understand the key issues at play in the adaptation of Asian, Latin American, and immigrant teenagers. In particular, the use of mixed methods has provided three key insights into the dynamics of family relationships among these families: the importance of the larger family unit beyond the individual members; a sense of family obligation as a source of academic motivation; and the meaningfulness of family obligation and assistance. As described below, combining both qualitative and quantitative methods has allowed us to gain these insights at multiple levels of analysis, from the cultural to the biological.

The Importance of the Larger Family Unit

I was stumped. Despite having a good command of prior research, well-formed hypotheses endorsed by my committee, appropriately designed measures and a sufficient sample size, the results of my dissertation did not come out as expected. My study focused on the transition to adolescence among teenagers from Asian backgrounds in the United States. Existing research on the transition to adolescence demonstrated disruptions in parent-child interactions that were attributable to the push for autonomy on the part of the increasingly mature child. Given that child autonomy and parental authority differ as a developmental imperative between Eastern and Western cultures, I hypothesized that the increases in conflict and declines in closeness previously observed among parent-adolescent dyads in European American families would be less evident among Asian American families. I selected well-established, reliable, and valid measures of family interactions and beliefs about autonomy and authority. I then traveled from Michigan to the San Francisco Bay area and administered questionnaires to large numbers of adolescents from Asian and European backgrounds.

Consistent with cultural theory and prior research, adolescents from Asian backgrounds indeed endorsed the importance of individual autonomy less and believed in the legitimacy of parental authority more than their peers from European backgrounds. Yet no matter how many different statistical analyses I performed, I could not find any ethnic differences in the nature of parent-adolescent relationships. Asian and European American youth reported the same levels and developmental changes in dyadic conflict and emotional closeness with their mothers and fathers. Disappointed, I nevertheless wrote up the results. I speculated that the ethnic similarity in dyadic relationships in the face of ethnic differences in beliefs about autonomy and authority might be attributable to the difficulty for Asian families to put their cultural beliefs into practice in the face of the powerful influence of the broader American social context (Fuligni 1998). Not an unreasonable idea, but one born from the failure of finding support for my earlier hypotheses.

Disappointed as I was about not finding what I expected, I went back to the drawing board to consider the implications of the findings. I could not believe, despite the lack of ethnic differences in the data, that relationships within Asian and European American families were essentially the same. So I decided to conduct my first focus groups. Being trained as a strictly quantitatively oriented developmental psychologist, it was not without trepidation that I and my graduate students at New York University gathered groups of two to five adolescents from Chinese American families in New York City to simply talk about their family relationships. These groups were not run according to the most systematic principles, but I consulted a few colleagues and read several articles on how to promote discussion and gain insights using this method.

The focus groups were revealing. Consistent with the findings of my dissertation, the Chinese American adolescents talked about their dyadic relationships with their mothers and fathers in ways that were no different from the typical European American adolescent. They liked and appreciated their parents, but they expressed the same frustrations, points of disagreement, and moderate level of emotional distancing as those one hears from their European American peers. If anything, the Chinese American teenagers suggested that they felt that their relationships with their parents might be less close than those of their friends from European American backgrounds. Had I conducted such focus groups before I began my dissertation, I suspect that my hypotheses would have been very different.

More importantly, a theme emerged from these discussions that would generate a line of research that I have continued for almost twenty years. The focus group participants referred to their individual parents and their larger family in very different ways. Even with the typical difficulties they had with their mothers or fathers, the Chinese American adolescents expressed a strong connection to their larger family as a unit. They felt that being part of the family was a signifi-cant part of who they were, what they did, and how they planned for the future. Regardless of how well they got along with their parents and siblings as individuals, they defined themselves in terms of their family membership and often expressed a sense of obligation to support, as-sist, and take into account the needs and wishes of the family. It should be noted that this sense of obligation did not immediately jump out of the conversation. Instead, it was referenced in a rather nonchalant manner. The adolescents seemed to consider this obligation as such an obvious part of their everyday life that it did not need to be remarked upon, but it was such a consistent theme that we began asking about it more directly in our conversations.

At the same time as conducting the focus groups, I began to read more broadly on adolescents from immigrant families. I was particu-larly struck by ethnographic studies of immigrant Asian and Latin American communities that highlighted adolescents' strong connec-tion to the family as manifested in a sense of obligation to support, assist, and respect the family (Suárez-Orozco and Suárez-Orozco 1995; Zhou 1997). This obligation to the family did not seem to depend on how emotionally close adolescents felt to their individual family mem-bers. Although parent-child relationships at times appeared fairly dis-tant and formal, the teenagers felt a keen sense of duty to the family.

Together, these ethnographies, my dissertation findings, and the fo-cus groups suggested that there was an important difference between closeness in dyadic parent-child relationships and a sense of connec-tion to the larger family group. This connection to the family group may be what is most distinctive about relationships with families from Asian, Latin American, and perhaps other cultural backgrounds as compared to those from European backgrounds in the United States. This connection is perhaps most clearly manifested in the importance placed on family obligation.

Therefore, my students and I decided to create a multiple-item ques-tionnaire measure of this sense of obligation to support, assist, and re-spect the family that could capture this distinctiveness and yet still be relevant for adolescents from multiple backgrounds, including Euro-pean American teenagers. Our focus group discussions played a major role in the creation of our measures, leading us to design them with multiple goals in mind. First and foremost, we wished the scales to be meaningful for adolescents. Many of the existing scales tapping col-lectivism or similar attitudes tended to be inventories of abstract values and attitudes that were relevant for adults and had little basis in the everyday lives of teenagers. We also wished to keep the focus on the adolescents' own family, as opposed to attitudes or values in regard to a larger, depersonalized and abstract other group (e.g., "people" or "elders"). Therefore, we focused on specific types of assistance and respect toward specific family members, such as "taking care of your brothers and sisters" or "spending time with your grandparents." We believed that such an approach would be the most effective way to construct questions that would be meaningful for the teenagers to answer because they took into account activities typical of their daily lives.

When constructing items, we kept in mind an additional goal of minimizing any positive or negative valance attached to obligations. Prior work on parentification—a term used in a body of research that examined children taking on parental roles in the family—suggested that when youth take on family obligations in distressed families there are negative ramifications, and scales of parentification typically make reference to family assistance and burden within the same item (Godsall et al. 2004). Given our interests, we wanted a measure with the flexibility to test whether family obligations had negative or positive implications for youth. Therefore, none of the items in our family obligation measure address whether adolescents feel that their family obligations are difficult, stressful, or burdensome (nor whether they are rewarding, satisfying, or enjoyable). Rather, we simply ask teenagers whether they felt that they should provide assistance or respect the authority of the family.

Finally, it was important to create a measure that was not biased in favor of females by focusing exclusively on gender-typed activities such as cooking and child care. Instead, we aimed for an inventory of items that allowed for the expression of family obligation by both male and female adolescents. Our goal was not to create a measure that would artificially create gender equality when it did not exist in the real world, but we did attempt to include items that assess the ways that male adolescents may express family obligation in their everyday lives (e.g., providing financial assistance to the family).

The measure has been a success. Informed by our qualitative focus groups and ethnographic research published by others, we designed a quantitative instrument that has consistently demonstrated significant differences between ethnic and cultural groups. In the first use of the measure, tenth- and twelfth-grade students from Mexican, Central and South American, Filipino, and East Asian backgrounds in the San Francisco area placed a greater emphasis on the three aspects of family obligation than did their peers from European backgrounds

(Fuligni, Tseng, and Lam 1999). Differences were quite large, sometimes reaching a magnitude of more than one standard deviation. Ethnic variations were replicated in a study conducted in Los Angeles, with ninth-grade students from Chinese and Mexican immigrant families endorsing all three aspects of family obligation more strongly than those from European backgrounds (Hardway and Fuligni 2006). Finally, in a study of college students in the northeast, Tseng (Tseng 2004) found that students from Asian backgrounds more strongly endorsed family obligation than did those from European backgrounds. Interestingly, we have replicated the findings of my dissertation study suggesting few ethnic differences in dyadic relationships (i.e., conflict and cohesion between adolescents and their parents; Chung, Flook, and Fuligni 2009; Hardway and Fuligni 2006), providing further support that the most significant ethnic differences lie in adolescents' connection and identification with the large family unit.

Family Obligation as a Source of Academic Motivation

Convinced about the value of mixed methods, I began to integrate qualitative and quantitative methods into my ongoing research. It was at this point that my group became influenced by Tom Weisner and his Ecocultural Family Interview, an invaluable approach to examine how cultural meaning is embedded in the everyday activities of families (Weisner 1997). Consulting with Weisner, I and my team regularly conducted in-depth, qualitative interviews of subsamples of youth who participated in larger studies in which we administered quantitative questionnaires and collected grades and test scores from official school records. The cross-talk and walking back and forth between the interview transcripts and the statistical analyses of the quantitative data were invaluable.

A theme that began to emerge from the personal discussions with the youth was the extent to which they believed trying hard to do well in school and go to college was part of their sense of obligation to the family. This linkage also was evident in ethnographic research done by other scholars of immigrant families (Gibson and Bhachu 1991; Suárez-Orozco and Suárez-Orozco 1995; Zhou 1997). Intrigued, we began examining the statistical associations between our quantitative scales of family obligation and other measures of academic motivation and educational aspirations. The associations were quite clear. Consistent with what the youth were telling us in their personal interviews, adolescents who possessed a greater sense of obligation to support, assist, and respect the authority of the family reported more academic motivation and had higher aspirations to attend and graduate from college (Fuligni and Tseng 1999).

The importance of this family-based motivation became even clearer with additional analyses that we conducted with our quantitative data, again stimulated by an in-depth reading of the transcripts from these interviews. Motivational theorists often identify different types of motivation, and one type of motivation important for adolescent achievement is the utility motivation placed on education—that is, the extent to which education is seen as an important and useful endeavor for the future (Eccles 1983). The youths' narratives seemed to reflect this type of motivation. In particular, those from Asian and Latin American backgrounds appeared to believe that going to college and getting a good job was a key way that they could help their families. Fortunately, we had quantitative measures of exactly this type of motivation and were able to show that a sense of family obligation uniquely predicted a utility value of education as opposed to other types of motivation (Fuligni 2001). And, just as importantly, complex statistical analyses suggested that a sense of family obligation was a key source of the higher level of motivation that those from Asian and Latin American backgrounds needed to attain the same level of academic success as their peers from European backgrounds, given the many challenges faced by the ethnic minority teenagers.

Nevertheless, a sense of duty to support and assist the family can present both challenges and opportunities. The same sense of obligation that fuels a desire to do well in school also can create the very real need to help the family in ways that ironically get in the way of completing schoolwork and studying sufficiently for exams. We and others have observed this in our quantitative analyses, with students who spend more time helping the family and providing financial support to the family having more difficulty getting good grades in high school and persisting toward a postsecondary degree in college (Fuligni and Witkow 2004; Telzer and Fuligni 2009b; Tseng 2004).

The same double-edged sword of family obligation has been evident in our qualitative data. In describing the difficulty of balancing family assistance and schoolwork, a ninth-grade girl from a Mexican immigrant family said: "Sometimes I get irritated and frustrated about the fact that I have to sit late at night. Sometimes during the weekday, they [her parents] would go late at night to Wal-Mart or something, or to the market because they wouldn't have time during the day. So, she [her mother] leaves it up to me to watch my little brother or sister. Sometimes I have a lot of homework so I tell her I have homework and she says, 'Oh, you have to watch your brother and sisters.' I wind up staying up really late or sometimes I wind up finishing it in class." (Fuligni 2011, 111). It is important to note that despite the need to take care of her younger siblings, this student still tries to find a way to get her homework done. Nevertheless, one can imagine how it may be difficult to maintain a high level of academic performance if these family demands continue at a high level for a long period of time.

It appears that the way in which the double-edged sword cuts for these youth depends in large part on the economic circumstances of the family. In a series of case studies of some of the participants whom we followed from high school into young adulthood, the extent to which the family-based motivation to pursue education actually leads to college depended on the immediate needs of the family (Fuligni, Rivera, and Leininger, 2007).

Ernest's parents came to the United States from Mexico with a third-grade level of education before he was born. His parents both worked at multiple custodial and cleaning jobs, including nights and weekends, earning around $20,000 per year. Although he saw receiving a college degree as a key family obligation, the family's finances led him to instead take a job as a forklift operator immediately after graduation. Trying to save money, he began to take part-time courses at a local community college while still working at his job. Ernest saw doing this on his own as a key way to pay back the family: "I made a decision that I wanted to do this on my own . . . I want to do this on my own 'cause they've [his parents] already helped out enough as it is in my life and other people's lives so that I really said, I've gotta take care of this on my own . . . They offered many times to help me out but I said, you know, it's cool, I'll take care of this on my own. You've done so much as it is, it's the very least I can do to help myself and to help you." Although the motivation is there, Ernest's road to a college degree is steep and long, given that he is attending part-time and that the dropout rate is high for students like him.

In contrast, May's parents came to the United States from Hong Kong when May was five years old and they recently moved back there after her younger brother completed high school and entered college. Unlike Ernest, May came from a family with more than ample economic resources and with a father who had received graduate-level education. May's father ran a successful business in Hong Kong, one that she reported brings the family over $100,000 per year in income and allowed her mother to not have to work. With her good grades, financial resources, and college-educated parents, attending a prestigious four-year residential university was never in question for May: "When we were growing up they actually never told us to study, like they never ever told us, 'You have to get A plusses,' or 'You have to excel in school.' . . . But somehow us four we just, you know, tried to do well in school and maybe it's just a personal, like, personal, like, face issue or whatever." The "face" to which May referred is another aspect of her family obligation. Her family had the means to send her to an elite college, so it was her duty to fulfill that obligation: "I guess after a while like uhm . . . I was fine with the idea of listening to my parents, like, 'Oh yeah, go to Berkeley' . . . But yeah there was just that pressure and then, so I went anyways, you know, met a lot of the close friends I have now from there, so I have no regrets about choosing Berkeley."

Together, the cases of Ernest and May highlight three essential points about the link between family obligation and academic motivation that has been apparent in both our qualitative and quantitative data. First, the sense that doing well in school and wanting to go to college as key obligations of youth in immigrant families exists regardless of the families' ethnic and economic backgrounds. Second, the extent to which that family-based educational motivation can be realized depends to a great extent on the financial resources of the family. Finally, fulfilling the obligation can be challenging for all youth, whether because, like Ernest, they have difficulty affording college or because, like May, their parents may have very specific ideas about how their children should fulfill that obligation, regardless of whether those ideas coincide with their children's ideas.

The Meaningfulness of Family Obligation and Assistance

The connection between family obligation and academic motivation discussed above highlights the more general importance and meaningfulness of family obligation and assistance for adolescents from Asian, Latin American, and immigrant families. Assisting the family, whether directly by helping out at home or working at a job or indirectly by trying hard at school, is more than just an activity or goal. It reflects a larger identification with the family and one's cultural background, as well as a desire to be considered a "good" and contributing member of that important social group. As a Vietnamese adolescent told Zhou, "To be an American, you may be able to do whatever you want. But to be a Vietnamese, you must think of your family first" (Zhou 1997, 166).

Together, our in-depth discussions with youth and the more quantitative data we have collected consistently emphasized this meaningfulness and connection to identity. As such, we developed the idea that family membership served as a social identity for youth from Asian, Latin American, and immigrant backgrounds (Fuligni and Flook 2005). As traditionally defined, a social identity is "the individual's knowledge that he belongs to social groups together with some emotional or value significance to him of his group membership" (Tajfel 1972, 292). Usually applied to larger social categories such as gender or ethnicity, social identity has rarely been applied to the family. Yet we feel that considering family membership as a social identity captures the sense of "weness" of the family that goes beyond dyadic relationships in the family. We believe that it has best captured the essence of the youths' discussion of their obligations to their families—that above and beyond how well they get along with their mothers and fathers, they have a sense of obligation to the larger family unit because it is a critical part of how they define themselves and provides meaning to their lives (Fuligni and Fuligni 2007).

The meaningfulness of family obligation and assistance—that overarching sense that we obtained from reviewing the interview transcripts of our open-ended discussions with youths participating in our larger studies—gradually became a stronger focus of our research. We wished to examine how actual family assistance was associated with psychological well-being. Employing a daily diary checklist method, we asked adolescents to complete a report of their activities and experiences every night before going to bed for two weeks. The report included a list of behaviors related to helping the family, including taking care of siblings and household chores. Consistent with the idea of the challenges and benefits of family assistance discussed earlier, we found that family assistance was related to both a greater sense of burden and a higher level of happiness among youth (Telzer and Fuligni 2009a). Most importantly, we also observed that the link between helping the family and happiness was largely due to the role fulfillment the adolescents experienced from helping the family. That is, helping the family led to a greater sense of feeling like a good son or daughter and good brother or sister, which in turn led to a higher level of happiness. Importantly for our theory about family identity, role fulfillment is a key dynamic of social identity—a key motivation for those who identify with a social group is to be a "good" member of that group (Hogg 2003).

The importance of role fulfillment—which we noted both in our qualitative interviews and in our quantitative analyses—became even more evident as we moved to incorporate biology and neuroscience into our work. We specifically wondered whether we could capture the meaningfulness of this everyday activity of helping the family within the developing biology and brains of the adolescents in our study. We were excited about the possibility of seeing evidence of cultural norms and values being represented within developing teenagers.

We began by examining how helping the family on a daily basis might influence stress biology and immune functioning. Continued high levels of stress and challenge over time can compromise immune functioning by making it difficult for the body to control inflammation (Miller, Cohen, and Ritchey 2002). Inflammatory processes are critical for fighting infections and wounds, but they can create wear and tear and compromise normal biological functioning if they are not controlled, leading to chronic adult health conditions such as cardiovascular disease (Hamer and Steptoe 2009). Therefore we examined the link between time spent helping the family on a daily basis and c-reactive protein (CRP), a key marker of chronic inflammation. Consistent with the demanding nature of helping the family, we found that 18-year-olds who engaged in high levels of assistance also had elevated circulating levels of CRP (Fuligni et al. 2009). However, this depended in part on the extent to which the youth obtained a sense of role fulfillment from assisting the family. Those for whom helping the family was a key source of feeling like a good member of the family actually had lower levels of CRP when compared to youth who engaged in the same levels of assistance who did not obtain a sense of role fulfillment. In summary, the meaning for the youth of helping the family actually shaped how the act of helping impacted a key marker of health and immune function.

Intrigued, we next examined whether helping behavior was also associated with particular neural activation among youth while they were actually helping the family. We recruited a group of participants from our ongoing studies, all of whom we had scored two years previously on their degree of role fulfillment from helping their family. We had them now play a version of the "dictator game" while in an fMRI scanner. Specifically, the youth were presented with a series of financial offers that included whether they and their parents would gain or lose money. We were interested in two particular types of offers. The first was called a "sacrificial donation" in which the parents gained money (e.g., + $5) and the participants themselves lost money (e.g., −$2). The second offer was a "reward" in which the participants gained money (e.g., + \$4) and their parents did not lose anything (i.e., \$0). Participants then pushed a button in the fMRI scanner to indicate whether they would either accept or reject the offers. The offers and the stakes were real and the participants received actual cash at the end of the study, and their parents were mailed cash directly to their homes.

The fMRI scans of the participants' brains showed a link between the role fulfillment the participants obtained from helping their family two years earlier when they were eighteen years old and neural activation when they made decisions to donate money to the parents. Specifically, those with greater role fulfillment showed greater activation in reward-related regions such as the ventral and dorsal striatum and the ventral tegmental area when they made sacrificial donations to the family as opposed to when they received cash rewards themselves (Telzer et al. 2010). Additionally Latino youth, who generally place a stronger value on assisting the family, showed greater activation in these areas when making donations to the family as compared to those from European backgrounds. Together, these two findings highlight how the social and cultural meaning of family assistance can be observed within the brain when individuals are making family-relevant decisions.

Why Mixed Methods Mattered

It has been almost twenty years since I was a quantitatively trained developmental psychologist leaving graduate school and embarking on a program of research that took me from crunching numbers to listening to the voices of adolescents from Asian, Latin American, and immigrant backgrounds. Hearing the youth in their own words has made me reinterpret my data, revise my hypothesis, and pursue new questions. Using mixed methods has provided insights that led me to even more methods and techniques that allow us to look within the developing biology and brains of our research participants. Doing so has yielded great fruit that enriches our understanding of the family relationships of these ethnic minority youth, who represent the fastest-growing segments of the American population. Beyond adolescents' relationships with their individual parents and siblings, there exists an identification with the family as a larger social group, and membership in that group has consequences for development at multiple levels, from the cultural to the biological.

References

Chung, Grace H., Lisa Flook., and Andrew J. Fuligni. 2009. "Daily Family Conflict and Emotional Distress among Adolescents from Latin American, Asian, and European Backgrounds." *Developmental Psychology* 45 (5): 1406–15.

Eccles, Jacquelynne S. 1983. "Expectancies, Values, and Academic Behaviors." In *Achievement and Achievement Motivation*, edited by Janet T. Spence, 75–146. San Francisco: Freeman.

Fuligni, Andrew J. 1998. "Parental Authority, Adolescent Autonomy, and Parent-Adolescent Relationships: A Study of Adolescents from Mexican, Chinese, Filipino, and European Backgrounds." *Developmental Psychology* 34: 782–92.

———. 2001. "Family Obligation and the Academic Motivation of Adolescents from Asian, Latin American, and European Backgrounds." In *Family Obligation and Assistance during Adolescence: Contextual Variations and Developmental Implications, (New Directions in Child and Adolescent Development Monograph)*, edited by Andrew Fuligni, 61–76. San Francisco: Jossey-Bass.

———. 2011. "Social Identity, Motivation, and Well Being among Adolescents from Asian and Latin American Backgrounds." In *Health Disparities in Youth and Families: Research and Applications*, vol. 57, edited by Gustavo Carlo, Lisa J. Crockett, and Miguel Carranza, 97–120. New York: Springer.

Fuligni, Andrew J., and Lisa Flook. 2005. "A Social Identity Approach to Ethnic Differences in Family Relationships during Adolescence." In *Advances in Child Development and Behavior*, edited by Robert V. Kail, 125–52. New York: Academic Press.

Fuligni, Andrew J., and Allison S. Fuligni. 2007. "Immigrant Families and the Educational Development of Their Children." In *Immigrant Families in Contemporary Society (Duke Series in Child Development and Public Policy)*, edited by Jennifer E. Lansford, Kirby Deater-Deckard, and Marc H. Bornstein, 231–49. New York: Guilford Press.

Fuligni, Andrew J., Gwendelyn J. Rivera, and April Leininger. 2007. "Family Identity and the Educational Progress of Adolescents from Asian and Latin American Backgrounds." In *Contesting Stereotypes and Creating Identities: Social Categories, Social Identities, and Educational Participation*, edited by Andrew J. Fuligni, 239–64. New York: Russell Sage Foundation Press.

Fuligni, Andrew J., Eve H. Telzer, Julienne Bower, Michael R. Irwin, Lisa Kiang, and Steven W. Cole. 2009. "Daily Family Assistance and Inflammation among Adolescents from Latin American and European Backgrounds." *Brain Behavior and Immunity* 23 (6): 803–09.

Fuligni, Andrew J., and Vivian Tseng. 1999. "Family Obligations and the Achievement Motivation of Children from Immigrant and American-Born Families." In *Advances in Motivation and Achievement*, edited by Stuart Karabenick and Timothy C. Urdan, 159–84. Stamford, CT: JAI Press, Inc.

Fuligni, Andrew J., Vivian Tseng, and May Lam. 1999. "Attitudes toward Family Obligations among American Adolescents from Asian, Latin American, and European Backgrounds." *Child Development* 70 (4): 1030–40.

Fuligni, Andrew J., and Melissa Witkow. 2004. "The Postsecondary Educational Progress of Youth from Immigrant Families." *Journal of Research on Adolescence* 14 (2): 159–83.

Gibson, Margaret A., and Parminder K. Bhachu. 1991. "The Dynamics of Educational Decision Making: A Comparative Study of Sikhs in Britain and the United States." In *Minority Status and Schooling: A Comparative Study of Immigrant and Involuntary Minorities*, edited by Margaret A. Gibson and John U. Ogbu, 63–96. New York: Garland.

Godsall, Robert E., Gregory J. Jurkovic, James Emshoff, Louis Anderson, and Douglas Stanwyck. 2004. "Why Some Kids Do Well in Bad Situations: Relation of Parental Alcohol Misuse and Parentification to Children's Self Concept." *Substance Use and Misuse* 39 (5): 789–809.

Hamer, Mark, and Andrew Steptoe. 2009. "Prospective Study of Physical Fitness, Adiposity, and Inflammatory Markers in Healthy Middle-Aged Men and Women." *American Journal of Clinical Nutrition* 89 (1): 85–89.

Hardway, Christina, and Andrew J. Fuligni. 2006. "Dimensions of Family Connectedness among Adolescents with Mexican, Chinese, and European Backgrounds." *Developmental Psychology*, 42 (6): 1246–58.

Hogg, Michael. A. 2003. "Social Identity." In *Handbook of Self and Identity*, edited by Mark R. Leary and June Price Tangney, 462–79. New York: Guilford Press.

Miller, Gregory E., Sheldon Cohen, and A. Kim Ritchey. 2002. "Chronic Psychological Stress and the Regulation of Pro-Inflammatory Cytokines: A Glucocorticoid-Resistance Model." *Health Psychology* 21 (6): 531–41.

Suárez-Orozco, Carola, and Marcelo Suárez-Orozco. 1995. *Transformations: Immigration, Family Life, and Achievement Motivation among Latino Adolescents*. Stanford: Stanford University Press.

Tajfel, Henri. 1972. "Social Categorization." In *Introduction à la psychologie sociale*, vol. 1, edited by S. Moscovici, 272–302. Paris: Larousse.

Telzer, Eva. H., and Andrew J. Fuligni. 2009a. "Daily Family Assistance and the Psychological Well-Being of Adolescents from Latin American, Asian, and European Backgrounds." *Developmental Psychology* 45 (4): 1177–89.

———. 2009b. "A Longitudinal Daily Diary Study of Family Assistance and Academic Achievement among Adolescents from Mexican, Chinese, and European Backgrounds." *Journal of Youth Adolescence* 38 (4): 560–71.

Telzer, Eva H., Carrie L. Masten, Elliot T. Berkman, Matthew D. Lieberman, and Andrew J. Fuligni. 2010. "Gaining While Giving: An fMRI Study of the Rewards of Family Assistance among White and Latino Youth." *Social Neuroscience* 5 (5–6): 508–18.

Tseng, Vivian. 2004. "Family Interdependence and Academic Adjustment in

College: Youth from Immigrant and U.S.-Born Families." *Child Development* 75 (3): 966–83.

Weisner, Thomas S. 1997. "The Ecocultural Project of Human Development: Why Ethnography and Its Findings Matter." *Ethos* 25 (2): 177–90.

Zhou, Min. 1997. "Growing Up American: The Challenge Confronting Immigrant Children and Children of Immigrants." *Annual Review of Sociology* 23: 63–95.

FIVE

"It Depends": The First Law of Education Research and Development

RONALD GALLIMORE

In a half century of trying to improve classroom instruction through research and development, "it depends" is the conclusion some of us came to, reluctantly so at first, and then gladly, because we could stop blaming ourselves for the failure of our interventions to generalize and scale. When our interventions succeeded, sometimes we couldn't always figure out why. In general when education reforms and innovations work, the magnitude of effect is modest at best, but why should that be the case? If proper instruction is provided, children should learn, shouldn't they? The story told here is of how I got into mixed methods education research and development (R&D), when, where, and why educational innovations work, and why educational outcomes often depend on local context.

Hula Dancing and Fieldwork

No way. I'm not making a fool of myself.

"Well, that's kinda' the point, Ron," my new anthropologist colleague Alan warned. "If you don't, they'll think you're 'high-nose,' local for da 'kine stuck-up mainland guy, a coast haole. Come on, you read about this stuff.

Some cultures test out a newcomer with a humiliation ritual. You gotta' let them know you are a good sport before they'll trust you."

Actually, I didn't know a thing about researching culture. I never took an anthropology class. Not one, not as an Arizona undergrad, not in Northwestern's clinical psychology PhD program. Like many psychologists trained in the early sixties I had been conditioned to distrust the traditional methods of anthropology: ethnography, participant observation, and other methods that relied on a human observer as scientific instrument. Oh no, no reputable psychologist trusts these methods—they're not reliable, objective, standardized, or scientific. I don't remember jokes made at the expense of anthropologists, but as a discipline, many experimentally minded, objective psychologists treated it as one.

Smugly comfortable with the research methods I knew, my confidence began to crack a little when I volunteered with a Long Beach, California, community association. It was 1964, my first year as assistant psychology professor at Cal State, Long Beach. JFK had been murdered a year before. Lyndon Johnson, riding high in the polls, was pushing civil rights and Head Start legislation.

After the community association got use of an abandoned church in west Long Beach, I helped refit it for after-school tutoring programs and one of the first Head Start programs funded in California. Over the months I worked there, I regularly interacted with African American children helping renovate the old church.

Without realizing, I was doing participant observation. It was a turning point, but I didn't know it yet. I didn't even know I was employing a fundamental research method of anthropology. But I did it well enough to stumble over a paradox that made me realize the limitations of the only research methods I had learned in psychology. Hanging around the old church as it was being renovated, I watched African American children exhibit remarkable competencies––attentive and focused, verbally adept, socially cooperative, quick to learn basic carpentry and painting skills.

When these same youngsters came for tutoring, they were grade-levels behind in school achievement, bored or confused by the work tutors assigned, inattentive, sometimes unruly. To investigate the paradox, I tried some standard psychological methods, including learning trials and aptitude and personality inventories. As in the tutoring sessions, the youngsters struggled, scoring below age norms.

But these trusted and refined assessments did not erase my observations over many weeks of the youngsters' evident competencies working on the old building. I was perplexed. How could I advise the tutors and public school teachers? I had no idea how in the classroom they might access the evident competencies the children displayed outside of school. Nothing I had learned in a clinical psychology program and several years' clinical experience had much to offer.

I took this paradox to my graduate school advisor Lee Sechrest, an early advocate of mixed methods, who had recently completed a year of fieldwork in the Philippines, and was now spending a year at the East-West Center at the University of Hawai'i. He agreed that for me to get anywhere working on this paradox, I needed to add more arrows to my methodological quiver. Lee arranged for me to visit Honolulu to meet anthropologist Alan Howard, who had just started the Nanakuli research project and needed a psychologist collaborator.

Three months later, I found myself on stage dancing the hula in Nanakuli, a Native Hawai'ian community about as distant from Waikiki as it is possible to drive without plunging into the Pacific. Socially and economically, it was even further from the cool rooms in the basement of my new department. I was now Research Psychologist in the Department of Anthropology at the Princess Bernice Pauahi Bishop Museum.

You Can Observe a Lot by Watching

Learning to gain acceptance in a different culture did not hasten my acquisition of fieldwork methods. For a long time, I was a resistant learner. I couldn't shake my suspicions that ethnography and participant observation were unreliable methods, susceptible to the unreasonable power of compelling anecdotes. My anthropology colleagues must have despaired at having a slow learner join the project. But they did not give up on me.

An epiphany was prompted by confusion. Mine. I spent nearly a year interviewing forty Hawai'ian mothers, using a standardized protocol developed by a legendary developmental psychologist. Focused on early socialization practices, it had been used in other cultures as well as in the USA, and fit the then-prevailing assumption that children's early weaning and toilet training experiences were proxy measures of their parents' child-rearing practices and predictive of later development.

I was puzzled by some of the mothers. When asked about early milestones like toilet training and when their three-year-old had attained them, more than a few said "sistah' did 'em," or something equivalent.

The standardized coding scheme that came with the interview protocol did not include a category for "sistah' did 'em," and a whole lot others. The standardized recourse was marking them "uncodable." To my dismay, uncodable responses mounted, putting at risk the interview study. Hoping for publishable results, I was in despair.

And then, my epiphany: anthropologists JoAnn Boggs and Cathie Jordan began pointing out the obvious. "Sistah' did 'em" was the mothers' way of describing the extensive use of sibling caretaking practiced by Hawai'ian families. Even six- and seven-year-olds were changing diapers and filling bottles to feed their infant and toddler siblings.

Belatedly, I began informally chatting with mothers, learning they took sibling care for granted, some offering up value rationales that caring for little ones teaches the older ones responsibility. Once opened, the mind can see the obvious. Yogi Berra was right: "You can observe a lot by just watching."

There is no more convinced practitioner of a method than a new convert. Once I saw how the qualitative methods of my anthropology pals could augment, supplement, and save from disaster a quantitative study like the standardized coding of the psychology interview project, I became a true believer, if not a competent practitioner. My schooling by anthropologists was not yet complete. I had finished an elementary course, but I was about to enter a more exacting one taught by Tom Weisner.

I can fix the point when it happened. Weisner proposed and we wrote a review and interpretation of the sibling and child caretaking literature that was ultimately published in *Current Anthropology* (Weisner and Gallimore 1977). When we began I thought of sibling caretaking as a packed variable, something Hawai'ians did, and other groups perhaps not, or not so much. Weisner was having none of this. He pushed for unpacking variables like "sibcare[1]" into constituent elements, never taking for granted that people with the same social address—Native Hawai'ian, for instance—were invariant in their beliefs and practices. I learned from Tom to look at the everyday routines of families, and look for instances of sibling caretaking. Then identify compromises needed to sustain sibling caretaking that families had to make between what is possible (ecological affordances and constraints) and what is desirable (cultural values and schema). Multimethods were required to piece all this together.

When we met, I had finished the Nanakuli fieldwork, and with Roland Tharp launched a new project, this one with an explicitly applied purpose and mission. But first, some background before returning to researching sibcare.

The Princess's Lab School

In 1972, the year I met Tom, the Kamehameha Project or KEEP began operating a k–3rd lab school in urban Honolulu. KEEP was funded by The Kamehameha Schools/Bishop Estate, a trust created in the nineteenth century by the sole surviving heir of King Kamehameha I—the Princess Bernice Pauahi Bishop. The purpose of KEEP and the lab school was to provide the Kamehameha Schools a knowledge base for the effective education of Hawai'ian students.

KEEP's first project was development of an effective program of instruction that capitalized on the natal culture of its Native Hawai'ian students (Tharp and Gallimore 1988). We wanted to identify the minimal alterations or "least change" the public school programs needed for student success—for example, could class size be kept at public school levels (thirty to one at the time)? Each year we recruited a class of kindergarteners living in a low-income, blue-collar area of Honolulu, so that lab school students were representative of the population of public schools where achievement was extremely low.

These self-imposed conditions were intended to make KEEP evolve as a credible model for the public schools. We hoped this would increase the likelihood our research-based programs would be more easily adopted and sustained over time with ordinary public funding levels.

The principle of least change was also consistent with the assumption that Hawai'ian children were capable of learning as well as any group. If Hawai'ian children were not, as we argued, deficient, then we should be able to find ways to teach them well without radical changes.

It took five years of R&D to evolve an effective reading instruction program. As a group, children taught with the KEEP program achieved on standardized reading tests at or above national norms, while comparable groups of students continued to score below average. Quantitative internal and external evaluations of the program (Tharp and Gallimore 1988) indicated the program worked both at the KEEP lab school and in public school classrooms. Eventually, the KEEP program was implemented in more than forty public school classrooms in Hawai'i.

Did Hawai'ian Sibcare Research Help Improve Child Learning in the Lab School?

When R&D started at the lab school, we assumed Hawai'ian children's familiarity with sibcare was a cultural strength that could be capitalized on during classroom instruction. In Nanakuli, Hawai'ian families were, on average, large and related households often living in close proximity, so that children were reared in an atmosphere of interdependence and shared work, even if there were no older siblings. Our ethnographic observations and my psychological interview study had suggested that from infancy on, children were folded into the sibling group for care, instruction, and shared responsibility for household chores. The sib group was given autonomy to complete assigned chores and held accountable as a group. If a child did not complete a chore, the sib group as a whole might be sanctioned, giving every member a stake in monitoring the performance of their brothers and sisters. Child care, housework, cooking, laundry, and yard maintenance were among the most frequent chores observed (Gallimore and Howard 1968; Gallimore, Boggs, and Jordan 1974; Jordan 1985; 1978; Weisner, Gallimore, and Tharp 1982).

A caveat. We never confirmed these descriptions by counting frequencies of observed instances of sibcare in Nanakuli. We fell into the easy generalization that sibcare was invariant, pervasive, and common experience for Hawai'ian children. Given this, we were confident that the KEEP ought to include peer learning centers as part of the program because we believed that Hawai'ian youngsters would find collaborating with peers comfortable and familiar.

Another plus—peer learning centers were not a radical departure from conventional practice. By the early 1970s, they had begun to be used on the mainland as well as in Hawai'i public elementary schools. Peer learning centers were hardly in wide use yet, but because they were on the radar of most educators we thought them a good candidate, given our "least changes" strategy. We also assumed that to make them more culturally accommodating we might have to make some tweaks.

In the KEEP version of peer learning centers, four to six students shared a table to work on assignments while the teacher taught a lesson to another small group. When instruction began in the morning, each child retrieved a folder from a personal shelf to learn his or her assignments and which of several centers to rotate through. One of the centers they rotated through was the one that met for twenty minutes with the teacher for a lesson, e.g., a reading comprehension session. After twenty minutes, the teacher, or a child assigned the duty, signaled time to rotate. Children in the peer centers were permitted to help each other, so long as each completed individual work that the teacher monitored daily to hold each individual accountable.

Cathie Jordan, KEEP's chief anthropologist, documented that in the centers an act of peer assistance occurred every three minutes in kindergarten and every 2.5 minutes in first grade (Jordan 1985, 1978). There was a wide range of assistance, including modeling and direct instruction, and a frequent shifting between teacher and learner roles. Researchers and teachers alike believed the students responded well to the learning centers—a judgment seemingly confirmed by standardized testing, indicating the KEEP reading program was working well.

But the centers were part of a complex, multielement program, so it was impossible to attribute specific benefit to them. Did centers work because they were culturally more compatible? Or was access to peer learning opportunities simply a generally good instructional practice?

The limitations of our sibcare research were now revealed. We knew that in general sibcare occurred in the Nanakuli households we observed; but we knew little about the subtle aspects of its function, and more specifically exactly how it did or did not assist the learning of younger children. We needed to "unpack" sibcare practices to get a more fine-grained picture of how it might influence children. For full details on the unpacking effort, see Weisner, Gallimore, and Jordan (1988), from which the following summary is adapted.

We began unpacking sibcare by interviewing fifty-six mothers with children in the lab school (grades two and three). The mothers were asked if they used sibcare, their reasons, rules for its use, sibcare goals and values, etc. As ecocultural theory predicted, larger families (six-plus members) and mothers with a heavy workload were more likely to report sibling caretaking, if they had children of the appropriate ages in their households. Families without available older children did utilize occasional child care provided by kin living in other households, but they did not have regularly available child caretakers, and reported less overall sibcare.

Even mothers without opportunities to practice sibcare valued it in general, and predictably those who could encourage sibcare were more likely to report positive aspects of it. Yet these mothers with sibs available were also more likely to mention that sibcare created short-term conflicts, and a few had abandoned its use because a sib did poor caretaking. Although sibcare played a significant role in many families and was regarded as acceptable child-care practice, it was not perceived to be culturally mandated. If a family chose not to employ sibs as caretakers, even if available, there were no community or extended kin sanctions or reproofs.

Thus these fifty-six KEEP mothers from a dense urban area confirmed some findings of the Nanakuli study of semirural families. Sibcare was practiced and valued, but there was a variability in the practice that we failed to note in Nanakuli. The Nanakuli mothers likely might have told us much the same, except we never conducted the kind of interview we did with the KEEP mothers. I had been beguiled by the unreasonable power of anecdotal observations into an overgeneralization.

The mothers' report of variability in the practice of sibcare challenged an assumption I made when we started creating version one of the KEEP reading program: all the Hawai'ian students entered the lab school with lots of sibcare experience and would need or benefit from something akin to sibcare in the classroom.

To assess individual sibcare experiences, we followed up the KEEP mother interviews with spot observations of KEEP children at home and after school (see Weisner, Gallimore, and Jordan 1988). Eight children were randomly selected, one boy and one girl from each of the four KEEP classrooms (k–third). Seven were observed on twenty different days and one on sixteen different days. Each child was observed after school for approximately thirty minutes on each visit. One hundred and fifty-four different observations were completed.

·   On thirty percent of visits, eight target children (TC) were judged to be in the care of no one.
·   On forty-seven percent of visits, TCs were in the care of a parent.
·   On twenty-three percent of visits, a TC was being cared for by an older child, not always a sib.

Bottom line: sibcaretaking occurs but is not an invariant and pervasive practice.

In addition, children's experience of sibcare varied day to day. Even if a child had no sibcare one day or another, he or she was often in proximity of sibcare experienced by others. Sibcare was part of the social landscape, seemed familiar to all, and was experienced by most at least some of the time, but it was an inconsistent and intermittent individual experience.

It had been an overgeneralization to assume every Hawai'ian child entered formal schooling unprepared for an environment lacking some approximation of sibcare, or that a setting heavily adult-directed might be culturally incompatible. Pointing to sibcare-like features in learning centers was beginning to seem a thin reed on which to hang claims about the KEEP program's cultural accommodations.

So we asked, besides some sibcare-like features, were any aspects of natal practices reflected in KEEP's learning centers? Something more subtle than the affordance of learning by peer availability?

The spot observation study offered a wider lens to capture natal practices that might affect classroom instruction. These included children's language use, evidence of direct teaching or instruction in the home and community, and other evidence of literacy-related activity (such as reading, doing homework, etc.). Personnel present were examined (adults, siblings, other children), as well as tasks and interaction scripts. During spot observations, we recorded instances of adult-child and child-child interactions, child activities and speech within dyads (mother-child, older boy-younger girl, etc.). All were rated and supplemented with observational notes for each of the 154 home visits.

These data indicated children frequently participated in joint social and verbal interactions. They shaped their interaction styles, communication, and language use with parents, siblings, and peers. Activities prompting language and literacy behaviors involved child-generated tasks and largely child-assisted teaching and learning. These were activities not directly tied to cultural institutions such as sibcare, but were related to the presence of peers and multi-age play groups of children in home settings.

A revised hypothesis based on our accumulating knowledge from these multiple studies using multiple methods (ethnographic observations, interviews, spot observations) suggested that classroom settings that afford literacy-related behavior in child-generated activities and mutual assistance might be a key accommodation to children's home experiences.

Differences and Similarities between Natal Settings and KEEP Learning Centers

In terms of personnel present and types of tasks, there was limited overlap between home settings and the peer learning centers. An obvious difference was the age mix of available peers in learning centers that was more restricted than in home settings. But in terms of peer teaching and learning, this seemed not to matter.

Cathie Jordan identified a phenomenon in KEEP classrooms she called "scanning." There were two varieties: children scanning the classroom for a source of assistance and scanning their proximal learning center for indications that others needed help. Many peer assistance sequences began with one child volunteering help to another. A substantial variability in performance and achievement levels apparently compensated for age-graded classrooms, so that the children adapted by turning to a peer they thought likely capable of helping (Jordan 1985).

Another significant home-school difference: emphasis on literacy activities was greater in the peer centers, and the range of activities available more restricted. However, there was some literacy activity at home, often both child and sib initiated. During home visits for interviews, school homework and papers were observed being used as part of sibling group play activities. For example, in one family the target child "played school" with older siblings, using already completed homework to make the play more realistic. Completed pages were erased, and answered again. However, frequency of common activities between home and school was limited, and there was little overlap between tasks assigned by adults at home and the tasks in peer learning centers.

Although the freedom to select, initiate, and modify activities was less available in the KEEP centers than in natal settings, some compelling overlaps emerged. They shared these common elements:

1. Flexible access to other children of equal, greater, or lesser ability and skill
2. Influence over kinds of interactions
3. Opportunities to actively explore range of activities
4. Self-generated creation and redesign of activities
5. Limited direct adult direction and monitoring

Plausibly, we concluded that children experience home-school compatibility in the interactional flexibility and opportunities for child-child assistance within the peer centers while realizing that in many respects KEEP centers did not mirror or replicate natal sibcare settings. A variety of methodological lenses proved helpful in coming to this conclusion. Beginning with the structured interviews in Nanakuli that failed to detect sibcare, to the ethnographic observations that did, to the pragmatic discovery in the lab school that peer centers worked well, to a combination of systematic and qualitative interviews and observations that identified subtle overlaps between children's home and school experiences.

Yet for all the multimethodological lenses used, a basic question remained unanswered: Did children in the Princess's lab school learn to read in part because they had access to particularly culturally compatible peer learning centers? Or perhaps peer learning centers would be an instructional practice good for all—a case that might be made using the effective instruction standards identified by The Center for Research Education, Diversity, and Excellence (CREDE). One of CREDE's five standards holds that learning occurs effectively when experts and novices work together for a common product or goal, and are therefore motivated to assist one another. Experts can be teachers, or more capable peers. "Working together allows conversation, which teaches language, meaning, and values in the context of immediate issues" (CREDE Standards, no date).

Indeed many of the CREDE's recommendations to foster peer teaching and learning were carried out in the KEEP peer centers:

Design activities requiring student collaboration to accomplish a joint product.

Arrange classrooms to accommodate students' individual and group needs to communicate and work jointly.

Organize students in a variety of groupings, such as by friendship, mixed academic ability, language, project, or interests, to promote interaction.

Plan with students how to work in groups and move from one activity to another, such as from large-group introduction to small-group activity, for cleanup, dismissal, and the like.

Manage student and teacher access to materials and technology to facilitate joint productive activity.

Monitor and support student collaboration in positive ways.

The evolved reading program had many elements in addition to peer learning centers. To maintain a vibrant learning environment, KEEP used a positive classroom management approach. Frequent assessments targeted each individual's learning needs, smoothing progress through the stages of beginning reading, and identified those children who needed more intensive instruction. Reading comprehension lessons were taught using a conversational-approach in small groups, permitting elements of a common Hawai'ian narrative style ("talk-story") embedded in carefully planned and conducted instruction.

When a random clinical trial in a public school demonstrated the superiority of the reading program, KEEP researchers were still investigating and debating the role played by cultural accommodations. Ironically, recursively employed multiple methods first led the KEEP team away from a focus on cultural hypotheses in their search for an instructional program that worked, and then back again when we tried to interpret the reasons the reading program worked well. For example, Weisner, Gallimore, and Jordan's (1988) multimethod study of natal sibcare and KEEP learning centers proposed a cultural accommodation that plausibly contributed to the program's success—providing opportunities for Hawai'ian students to flexibly rely on self-regulated and peer group-regulated activities. Would peer learning centers in an affluent suburban school suggest the same? We never did that study, and I don't think anyone has, leaving a critical gap in the evidence.

Final Words

When problems are puzzles for which unique solutions exist, technicians can take over. But when problems are defined through the process of attempting to draft acceptable solutions, then analysts become creators as well as implementers of policy: "This particular problem may not be solvable . . . how about substituting one that can be solved?" (Pressman and Wildavsky 1984, 176).

KEEP treated the search for an effective reading program in ways similar to the evolution of a forest from grasslands to shrubs to tall timber (Tharp and Gallimore, 1979; 1982). At each stage, different methods were relatively more useful and impactful. Personal knowing, ethnography, systematic observation, and quasi-experimental "tinkering" were used through a recursive succession of trials, errors, discoveries, and refinements. Program R&D shaped the questions. Questions dictated the method. We learned, tinkered, and asked new questions.

How much cultural accommodation contributed to the KEEP program's success was another instance of the first law of education R&D. It depends on the lens one chooses to examine the evidence. Cultural accommodations did or did not are not the only options. Pulling back to a wider angle suggests another interpretation based on studies of early literacy development in many cultural communities.

In brief, communities vary greatly in the amount of early literacy experiences a child has before entering kindergarten. In communities where parents use literacy and numeracy as tools to earn a living, children might enter school with storybook reading experiences exceeding a thousand hours. In blue-collar communities where literacy is not used for subsistence or recreation, children might have a few hundred hours. Communities differ also on how much a child is treated as an interlocutor, engaged in conversation about texts, everyday matters, environmental print, e.g., billboards, etc. KEEP's reading program evolved to be flexible enough to accommodate a wide range of home literacy experiences, by providing ample peer learning, extensive opportunities for connected discourse about texts, and access to a reading materials suitable for a wide range of achievement levels. Perhaps the key accommodation was to variable child experience, not to a specific home situation.

There is another confounding factor to consider. More than in most public schools, KEEP focused on professional teacher development (PD) using peer coaches, video feedback, and lesson analysis instead of conventional training vehicles like workshops and courses (Tharp and Gallimore 1988). As a result, KEEP avoided the snare that traps so many attempts at educational reform: failure to implement the intended changes because teachers get too few opportunities to learn how to teach in a way different than they were taught. KEEP tried to make the lab school a place of learning for teachers as well as students. And because the teachers were learning from their experiences teaching the population of the lab school, perhaps the real R&D was the thousands of small improvements they gradually identified and implemented day to day. What to make of the lab school's results depends on what lens you choose.

Finally, I like believing the KEEP proved anthropologists were on the right side of the deficit-difference wars that began in the 1960s. Children from disadvantaged communities like those in Hawai'i bring strengths, not deficits, to school. Like children everywhere, most are active, eager learners, and given good teaching do as well as their counterparts from other communities. The Hawai'ian students of KEEP proved fully capable of adapting to a variety of conventional public school settings, routines, curricula, and instruction. Their successes did not require a radical program shift, classrooms segregated by cultural experience, or reforms with little chance of being implemented in public schools. A highly culturally specific program was not necessary, though a few accommodations helped. Through multiple mixed methods research projects to answer questions that led to trial, error, experiment, implementation, refinement, and evaluation, the Princess's lab school accomplished what mattered most to parents––their children learned to read.

I also like to believe that the same is true for children in any community, depending on the willingness of adults to talk teaching and be open to strange ideas—as strange as ethnography was for a youthful, objective psychologist doing research in education—to improve it.

References

CREDE. n.d. Joint Productive Activity. Retrieved August 15, 2013, from http://crede.berkeley.edu/research/crede/jpa.html.

Gallimore, Ronald, and Alan Howard, eds. 1968. *Studies in a Hawaiian Community: Namakamaka O Nanakuli.* Pacific Anthropological Records no. 1, Department of Anthropology, B. P. Bishop Museum, Honolulu.

Gallimore, Ronald, Joan W. Boggs, and Cathie Jordan. 1974. *Culture, Behavior, and Education: A Study of Hawaiian-Americans.* Beverly Hills, CA: Sage Publications, 1974.

Jordan, Cathie. 1978. Teaching/Learning Interactions and School Adaptation: The Hawaiian Case. Report no. 81. Honolulu: Kamehameha Early Education Project, The Kamehameha Schools/Princess Bernice Pauahi Bishop Estate.

———. 1985. "Translating Culture: From Ethnographic Information to Educational Program." *Anthropology and Education Quarterly* 16 (2):106–23.

Pressman, Jeffery L., and Aaron Wildavsky. 1984. *Implementation*, 3rd ed. Berkeley: University of California Press.

Tharp, Roland G., and Roland Gallimore. 1979. "The Ecology of Program Research and Development: A Model of Evaluation Succession." In *Evaluation Studies Review Annual*, vol. 4, edited by Lee B. Sechrest, 39–60. Beverly Hills, CA: Sage Publications.

———. 1982. "Inquiry Processes in Program Development." *Journal of Community Psychology* 10: 103–18.

———. 1988. *Rousing Minds to Life: Teaching, Learning, and Schooling in Social Context.* Cambridge: Cambridge University Press.

Weisner, Thomas S., and Ronald Gallimore. 1977. "My Brother's Keeper: Child and Sibling Caretaking." *Current Anthropology* 18 (2): 169–90.

Weisner, Thomas S., Ronald Gallimore, and Ronald G. Tharp. 1982. "Concordance between Ethnographer and Folk Perspectives: Observed Performance and Self-Ascription of Sibling Caretaking Roles." *Human Organization* 41 (3): 237–44.

Weisner, Thomas S., Ronald Gallimore, and Cathie Jordan. 1988. "Unpackaging Cultural Effects on Classroom Learning: Native Hawaiian Peer Assistance and Child-Generated Activity." *Anthropology and Education Quarterly* 19 (4): 327–53.

Notes

1. The term "sibcare" is used here, according to the norms of the psychology and human development literature, as a common shorthand for sibling caretaking.

PART THREE

Mixed Methods to Explore Cultural Variability

SIX

The Soft Side of Hard Data in the Study of Cultural Values

RICHARD A. SHWEDER

Introduction: A Blast from the Past

I originally wrote this essay in September 1970 while I was engaged in long-term fieldwork in the Hindu Temple Town of Bhubaneswar in Orissa, India. I prepared the document (and then just filed it away until now) as a finger exercise of sorts concerned with the soft side of hard data and the subjective or discretionary aspects of quantitative data analysis and interpretation. But looking back I can see that this previously unpublished demonstration piece marked the starting point of my disenchantment with abstract value questionnaires as an objective method for studying cultural differences in folk understandings of the social order as a moral order. It thus seems appropriate and even timely to revive and revivify the essay now, because the field of moral anthropology has returned to center stage in cultural anthropology in recent decades (Fassin 2012).

That phrase or banner—moral anthropology—is, of course, semantically ambiguous and points in two directions. On the one hand it points in the direction of a moralizing (or even moralistic) anthropology that is critical, judgmental, and normative and concerned with studies of, e.g., inequality, poverty, violence, social justice, and human rights. On the other hand, the phrase points in the direction of the anthropology of morality dedicated to positive science, comparative studies of values, moral reasoning, moral sentiments, and cultural narratives.

Not surprisingly, the ancestral heroes of contemporary moral anthropologists are themselves ideologically diverse: Emile Durkheim, Max Weber, Bronislaw Malinowski, Kenneth Read, Karl Marx, E. P. Thompson, Michel Foucault. Notably, mixed methods (or perhaps more accurately, mixed-up methods) are the research methods employed by card- carrying moral anthropologists. A list of those methods would include archival analysis of legal cases and dispute resolutions, behavioral documentation of folkways and customary practices, structured interviewing, value questionnaires, conversational analysis, cognitive experiments, media analysis, recording neuronal activity in the human brain, etc.

In any case, back in 1970 when I wrote "The Soft Side of Hard Data," I was investigating concepts of the person in Orissa, India. That research later morphed into a comparative project on folk conceptions of the social order as a moral order, which led to the empirical and theoretical development of a conception of the moral domain known as "the Big Three." This comparative approach to the study of morality argues that on a global scale, within any culturally diverse society, and across institutional domains within any cultural group, moral judgments about the right thing to do under such-and-such circumstances are linked to a variety of diverse terminal goods or ultimate values, which come in three broad kinds: moral judgments ultimately grounded in an ethics of autonomy (with its focus on values or moral goods such as harm, rights, and justice and an emphasis on the self as a preference structure with wants entitled to satisfaction); moral judgments ultimately grounded in an ethics of community (with its focus on values or goods such as duty, loyalty, interdependency, and respect for hierarchical authority and an emphasis on the self as a responsible and self-controlling status bearer with a social role to play within a community); and moral judgments ultimately grounded in an ethics of divinity (with its focus on purity, sanctity, cleanliness, and the connection between the natural order and the sacred order and an emphasis on the self as a potentially elevated or dignified token of some divine, transcendent, or higher order of things).

Given that interest in the study of morality and conceptions of the person, I was busy in 1970 reading about quantitative methods for the study of values, such as the ranking and rating procedures associated with abstract value questionnaires (Hays 1963). Value questionnaires ask informants from different cultural groups, ethnic traditions, or social categories to make ratings or rankings of abstract words or context-free stand-alone value concepts, for example, "Which is more important to you, beauty or wealth, freedom or equality, security or privacy, honesty or cleanliness?" Or, alternatively, how important is "obedience" on a five-point scale? How about "loyalty"? How about "self-control"? How about "justice"?

Looking back now, I wish Roy D'Andrade's little-read and astonishingly underappreciated 2008 volume *A Study of Personal and Cultural Values* had been available to me when I was in graduate school. His brilliant book was written much later, when social psychologists where drawing attention to modes of East Asian thought and contrasting them with Anglo-American modes of thought. In the thick of that widespread contemporary discussion of East versus West differences in cognition, D'Andrade developed a quantitative study of what he called the personal values of informants from three groups: American undergraduates at the University of California, Vietnamese refugees to the USA, and Japanese respondents living in Japan. Writing against the current of a cultural psychology focused on East versus West differences, his main take-home message was that he had a very hard time finding significant cultural or group-based differences in the expressed personal values of his American, Vietnamese, and Japanese informants. Between-group variance in the endorsement of abstract value words and phrases was minimal. For eager readers of the anthropology of morality, there was nothing much to write home about concerning cultural differences.

Fortunately Roy D'Andrade is a brilliant culture theorist as well as a virtuoso quantitative methodologist. So, confronted with his findings he went on to draw a useful theoretical distinction, which I would commend to researchers in cultural psychology and moral anthropology. He distinguished the study of personal values (tell me which is more important to you, cleanliness or honesty, liberty or justice?) from a different unit of analysis focused on values (and inevitably beliefs) with respect to something in particular (such as—to pick a not-so- random example—being the chairman of the Center for Psychosocial Studies at UCLA or the Editor of *Ethos*), which he dubbed institutional values. To get a better sense of this distinction: the study of "institutional values" is not an investigation of an individual's evaluation of the relative importance of abstract goods (such as liberty, justice, loyalty, and personal sanctity). Instead it is the study of all the ideas about what is true, good, and instrumental, revealed and made manifest through speech when an informant is questioned about the obligations and expectations associated with role or status-based participation in the customary practices and local institutions which are familiar to the informant from living in his or her own particular society—for example, all the beliefs and values associated with being a widow in a Hindu temple town in India. (I will have more to say about cultural differences in widowhood in a moment.)

Looking back to 1970, I think the unit of cultural and mental analysis described as institutional values by Roy D'Andrade was probably available (at least in theory) to students of John Whiting through a cognate concept that Whiting and Irvin Child had discussed in their 1953 collaboration *Child Training and Personality*. There Whiting and Child managed to combine the comparative study of routine cultural practices (or folkways) and the comparative study of individual mentalities into a single unit of analysis called the custom complex. Simply put, Whiting and Child state that the custom complex "consists of a customary practice and of the beliefs, values, sanctions, rules, motives, and satisfactions associated with it." In my view the study of institutional values is another way of describing the study of the custom complex.

Although Whiting and Child introduced the idea of the custom complex in 1953, its theoretical implications were not widely or fully appreciated at the time. For the most part the idea was not taken up or carried forward by psychological anthropologists working in the 1950s. Nor did the custom complex become a unit of analysis for social psychologists working on the development of value questionnaires. Indeed, it was not until the 1980s and 1990s, when Weisner and others developed a research agenda for the study of the ecological niche (Weisner 1984, 1996; also 2001, 2002) and a so-called practice approach or activity-setting approach took hold among some child development researchers (Goodnow, Miller, and Kessel 1995), that Whiting and Child's conception gained some limited currency and appeal. The study of the custom complex also bears some resemblance to the founder of American social psychology Kurt Lewin's idea of a personal life space (Lewin 1943) and fully anticipates the French sociologist Bourdieu's now-popular idea of a habitus (Bourdieu 1972, 1990). It is the study of the mental side of social habits, which are always bound to particular institutions and social roles in specific cultural settings. In my view, paying more attention to this broader unit of analysis is a good way to make progress in the study of moral anthropology and cultural psychology.

Mixed-Up Methods: Exploring Cultural Differences in Values

The recognition of the bounded or qualified nature of social science generalizations, including the extent to which one's picture of social and psychological reality is dependent on the particular methods one uses to generate "data" so as to interpret what is real (so-called method variance—Campbell and Fiske 1959), goes hand in hand with the study of the custom complex, the ecological niche, and institutional values. That recognition—that social science generalizations are typically narrow in scope—is not new. The philosopher of science Ernest Nagel made the observation in his 1961 book *The Structure of Science* and he cites a reference from 1934. He writes (459): "The conclusions reached by the controlled study of sample data drawn from one society are not likely to be valid for a sample obtained from another society. Unlike the laws of physics and chemistry, generalizations in the social sciences therefore have at best only a severely limited scope, limited to social phenomena occurring during a relatively brief historical epoch within special institutional settings." He makes the point that human actions are mediated by local "technologies and traditions," and although Nagel himself leaves open the possibility (and hopes) that generalizations of broad scope will be discovered, he avers that "the possibility must certainly be admitted that nontrivial but reliably established laws about social phenomena will always have only a narrowly restricted generality" (460). Starting one's research on values by focusing one's interview questions on bounded units such as a particular custom complex, or a particular ecological niche, or the particular behavior in the context of a particular social institution is one way to acknowledge that organizational feature of human social life.

In his 2008 book Roy D'Andrade milked the study of informant judgments about abstract value words and phrases for all they are worth, and came up with very little by way of cultural differences. His research program is especially instructive for those of us interested in psychological differences across human populations because he went into the research fully aware of the many problems with value questionnaires yet not yet prepared to abandon them as a method for the study of values. Thus he writes:

There are well known problems with questionnaires. The same words mean different things to different people. Translations are imperfect. People, however honest
their report, do not always respond to the words for things the way they respond
to things themselves. Someone may think they value something highly when presented with words—for example, how much do you value peace and quiet?—yet
when presented with lots of peace and quiet may find they do not value it as highly
as they thought. And people may simply not be able to answer some questions—
they just do not know how much they value X and may never know. Or they may
be profoundly ambivalent about something, and both value it and disvalue it, so
that no single rating covers the situation. Despite all these problems, with respect
to efficiency and efficacy, there is much to be said in favor of questionnaires for the
study of values. Observation of the choices someone makes cannot tell us what that
person thinks or what he or she feels is good. The most efficient way to find out
what people think is to ask them. One can observe people smoking cigarettes but
they may or may not think smoking is a good thing. (D'Andrade 2008, 13)

(Parenthetically, one does wonder whether declaring one's general
commitment to an abstract value—such as equality or piety or social
justice—and having one's identity as a person associated with such a
public commitment is really a familiar or basic feature of cultural, political, and psychological life in all societies. The method itself and its
very mode of questioning may presuppose a bit too much about fundamental psychological and linguistic practices.)

D'Andrade's volume is full of such pithy methodological observations about value questionnaires and theoretical insights relevant to
the study of similarities and differences in psychological functioning
across cultural groups of the sort pioneered by generations of psychological anthropologists. Nevertheless, his main take-home message
and empirical finding after years of carefully conducted quantitative
research is that Japanese, Vietnamese, and Anglo-Americans do not differ very much in their values, at least not when they are systematically
asked to judge abstract value words or phrases.

I would describe his finding as a potential point in favor of the principle of "method variance," discussed by Campbell and Fiske (1959).
The data one generates on similarities or differences in values across
cultural groups is not independent of the procedures one used to generate the data. The study of informant ratings or rankings of abstract
and decontextualized value words or phrases may not be the best way
to get at cultural differences in the beliefs and values that give meaning and value to the moral worlds institutionalized in different cultural
traditions.

Implicit in the ideas of a custom complex, an ecological niche or an institutional value is the imperative to begin one's research on other societies with fieldwork that documents the local institutional world and customary or habitual practices of members of a distinct cultural group. It is an invitation to then structure one's interviews in such a way that they provoke a discussion of the values and beliefs associated with local institutions or ecological niches, using the native's language to get at the beliefs and values that are important to being, for example, a mother, a teacher, the conductor of an orchestra, a widow; in other words, focus the interview on the folk custom or institution in which a person in such-and-such status plays a significant part rather than treating the informant as a stand-alone individual with a general motivating ideological commitment to abstract values regardless of context. Many Americans on the liberal left who say they value freedom do so because they have in mind concrete, fact-based institutional contexts, for example, the freedom of the *New York Times* to publish classified government documents such as the Pentagon Papers, which activates some master metaphor such as the free market of ideas. But if you press on and concretize the abstract value in a different way, you may discover they are not so sure they value freedom when it is comes down to a free market of goods and services and the institutional context is the workplace, the freedom of employers and employees to enter into labor contracts and the right of skilled workers to be hired for a job regardless of union membership.

Context matters and it needs to be built into our value interviews. There are many ways to do this. After thinking about my own work on cultural differences in moral judgments in the Temple Town of Bhubaneswar, Orissa, India, and Hyde Park, Illinois, USA, in the light of Weisner's notion of an ecological niche and D'Andrade's notion of institutional values, it seemed fortunate to me that the interviewing we did in the early 1980s was role-based and embedded in local customary practices.

Here is an example drawn from that work (Shweder, Mahapatra, and Miller 1990; also see Shweder et al. 1997). Below are two interviews contrasting institutional values in the Hindu Temple Town of Bhubaneswar, Orissa, India, and in the secular community of Hyde Park, Illinois, USA. The custom complex in this instance is widowhood. The interview examines the respondents' ideas about what is true, good, and instrumental with respect to marriage and widowhood. Those ideas are elicited by structuring a series of interrogatives about a particular pattern of behavior by a hypothetical widow. Consider the following behavior: "A widow in your community eats fish two or three times a week."

First, the interview in the Hindu Temple Town:

Is the widow's behavior wrong? (Yes. Widows should not eat fish, meat, onions, or garlic, or any "hot" foods. They must restrict their diet to cool foods, rice, dhal, ghee, vegetables).

How serious is the violation? (A very serious violation. She will suffer greatly if she eats fish.)

Is it a sin? (Yes. It is a great sin.)

What if no one knew this had been done? It was done in private or secretly. Would it be wrong then? (What difference does it make if it is done while alone? It is wrong. A widow should spend her time seeking salvation—seeking to be reunited with the soul of her husband. Hot foods will distract her. They will stimulate her sexual appetite. She will lose her sanctity. She will want sex and behave like a whore.)

Would it be best if everyone followed the rule that widows should not eat fish? (That would be best. A widow's devotion is toward her deceased husband—who should be treated like a god. She will offend his spirit if she eats fish.)

In the United States widows eat fish all the time. Would the United States be a better place if widows stopped eating fish? (Definitely it would be a better place. Perhaps American widows would stop having sex and marrying other men.)

What if most people in India wanted to change the rule so that it would be considered all right for widows to eat fish? Would it be okay to change the rule? (No, it is wrong for a widow to eat fish. Hindu dharma—truth—forbids it.)

Do you think the widow who eats fish should be stopped from doing that or punished in some way? (She should be stopped. But the sin will live with her and she will suffer for it.)

Next consider the parallel interview conducted in Hyde Park, Illinois, with a secular informant:

Is the widow's behavior wrong? (No, she can eat fish if she wants to.)

How serious is the violation? (It is not a violation.)

Is it a sin? (No!)

What if no one knew this had been done? It was done in private or secretly. Would it be wrong then? (It is not wrong in private or public.)

Would it be best if everyone followed the rule that it is all right for a widow to eat fish if she wants to? (Yes, people should be free to eat fish if they want to. Everyone has that right.)

In India it is considered wrong for a widow to eat fish. Would India be a better place if it was considered all right for a widow to eat fish if she wants to? (Yes, that may be their custom but she should be free to decide if she wants to follow it. Why shouldn't she eat fish if she wants to?)

What if most people in the United States wanted to change the rule so that it would be considered wrong for a widow to eat fish? Would it be okay to change it? (No, you can't order people not to eat fish. They have a right to eat it if they want to.)

Do you think the widow who eats fish should be stopped from doing that or punished in some way? (No!)

I submit that one learns far more about cultural differences in moral understanding and folk conceptions of the social order as a moral order from interviews of this type than by asking devout Hindus in India and devout secularists in the USA whether and to what extent loyalty or freedom of choice is good. I hope I have said enough by way of introducing my flash from the past. Below is that 1970 demonstration study expressing doubts about the objectivity and usefulness of value questionnaires as a method for understanding cultural differences in the moral domain.

The Soft Side of Hard Data (1970)

This is a note about uncertainty in the analysis and interpretation of some social science data. I shall show how "hard data" on values in American society may be statistically analyzed so that for every one of four plausible and mutually exclusive interpretations of the data, three others may be advanced that are also plausible and compatible with the facts.

There are three reasons for considering the analysis and interpretation of data indeterminable.

1. There is indeterminateness between the data and the analysis. Each interpretation is inferred from a statistical analysis that draws or ignores some distinctions that potentially exist in the data. The data do not provide us with objective criteria for deciding which distinctions to heed and which to disclaim in the data when performing the statistical analysis. Thus what appears to be a conclusion drawn from the facts is rather an interpretation only loosely constrained by the data.

2. There is indeterminateness between the results of the statistical analysis and the interpretation. Each interpretation is compatible with the results of a statistical

analysis that may be performed on the data. None of the interpretations necessarily follow from the analysis.

There is indeterminateness in evaluating the best interpretation. Any one of the interpretations may be correct and there is no way to judge from the data per se.

Two Faces of Values Data

It is possible for members of diverse social categories to disagree about the relative importance of every value in their value system, and yet almost perfectly agree on the hierarchical ordering of their value system as a whole.

So for any set of value statements, disagreement over the relative importance of each value considered alone may be statistically significant while, simultaneously, agreement about relative importance may be statistically significant for the system as a whole. In fact as the number of values about whose relative importance people can disagree increases, the extent of agreement about the system as a whole may approach perfection.

This paradox makes it possible to analyze values from two points of view that lead to strikingly different interpretations of the degree of similarity of the value systems of members of various categories in society.

A First Analysis and Interpretation

In a study entitled "Values as Social Indicators of Poverty and Race Relations in America," Rokeach and Parker (1970, 98) asked a large sample of Americans to rank two sets of eighteen value statements in terms of their importance as guiding principles in the informant's daily life. The informants varied considerably in the level of their income and education, and in their race.

The results of the study were presented in eight tables. The first and second tables gave the median and composite rank of each of the values as judged by members of different income categories ranging from under $2,000 a year to $15,000 and over. The third and fourth tables gave the same type of information for values as ranked by members of different educational categories ranging from zero to four years of schooling to a graduate-school level of education. The fifth and sixth tables gave the ranks of the values as judged by blacks and whites randomly sampled. The seventh and eighth tables gave the ranks of the values for blacks and whites matched for income and education.

Rokeach and Parker asked the following question of their data: how many of these eighteen values in each of these tables are significantly different in the relative rank assigned to them by members of different social categories? They answered the question by applying the median test to each value in the tables. In table 6.1, I have reproduced some of their data for income categories. The table shows the median and composite rankings of eighteen values by informants of diverse socioeconomic status from poverty to affluence. The results of applying the median test indicate that eleven of the eighteen values are significantly different among income groups.

The results of the statistical analysis performed by Rokeach and Parker are as follows: (1) twenty of the thirty-six values in the two income tables show significant differences among income categories, (2) twenty-five of the thirty-six values in the two education tables show significant differences among educational groups, (3) fifteen of the thirty-six values in two of the racial tables show significant differences between blacks and whites, but this number is reduced to seven when the informants are matched for income and wealth.

Based on the results of their statistical analysis, Rokeach and Parker make an interpretation about the extent of difference in the patterning of values by informants having various social characteristics in American society. Their interpretation is an evaluation of the number of significant differences out of thirty-six possibilities that appear in each pair of income, educational, and racial tables (106, 108). Rokeach and Parker construct the following interpretation: (1) there are significant and pervasive variations in value systems, associated with differences in socioeconomic status in America (106), and the values of the poor differ significantly from the values of the more affluent segments of our society (110). (2) Most of the differences in values between blacks and whites in America can be attributed to differences in socioeconomic status and not to distinctive racial cultures (108).

Their interpretation indicates a tendency toward a "culture of poverty" in America and suggests that black culture is different from white culture only to the extent that a greater proportion of blacks are poor, and not because of a different cultural heritage and tradition. I would add another interpretation to their statistical analysis, which I think

Table 6.1. Value medians and composite rank-orders for informants varying in income (N=1,325)*

Values	Under $2,000 N=139		$2000-$3,999 N=239		$4,000-$5,999 N=217		$6,000-$7,999 N=249		$8,000-$9,999 N=178		$10,000-$14,999 N=208		$15,000 & Over N=95		Median x^2	Test $p =$
	MD.	RNK.	MD.	RNK.	MD.	RNK.	MD.	RNK.	MD.	RNK.	MD.	RNK.	MD.	RNK.		
Ambitious	8	6	6.9	3	6.1	2	6.8	3	6.6	3	5.8	2	6.4	3	8.33	0.215
Broad-minded	8.6	8	7.2	4	8.1	8	8.1	6	7.1	4	6.4	4	7	4	11.92	0.064
Capable	9.5	10	10.5	14	9.8	11	9.3	11	9.8	11	8.4	7	8.8	8	14.98	0.02
Cheerful	9	9	8.6	9	10.6	14	10.3	12	10.7	12	10.2	11	11.3	14	16.33	0.012
Clean	6.4	2	7.3	5	8	7	8.6	8	9.3	10	10.4	12	14.4	17	72.35	0.001
Courageous	7.5	5	8.1	8	8	5	7.5	5	7.4	6	8	5	7.2	5	2.37	0.825
Forgiving	6.4	3	6.5	2	7.3	4	6.3	4	7.4	5	8.1	6	10.7	12	20.23	0.003
Helpful	7.1	4	7.4	6	8	6	8.2	7	8.9	8	9.3	8	9.1	9	17.69	0.007
Honest	3.3	1	3.7	1	3.4	1	3	1	3	1	3.4	1	3	1	4.71	0.582
Imaginative	15.2	18	15.8	18	15.6	18	15.9	18	15	18	14.6	18	11.4	15	29.32	0.001
Independent	10.5	14	10.3	12	10	12	10.7	14	11.4	13	11	13	8.3	6	5.54	0.476
Intellectual	13.9	16	13.4	16	13.3	16	13.6	16	13.1	15	12.1	15	8.6	7	25	0.001
Logical	15.2	17	14.8	17	14.7	17	14.1	17	14	16	12.8	16	10.9	13	36.56	0.001
Loving	10	11	10.3	13	9.5	10	9.1	10	8.8	7	10.2	10	9.8	10	2.47	0.872
Obedient	12	15	12.4	15	13.3	15	13.2	15	14.2	17	14.3	17	15.3	18	27.06	0.001
Polite	10.4	13	10.2	11	10.2	13	10.4	13	11.4	14	11.2	14	13.2	16	26.11	0.001
Responsible	8.2	7	7.8	7	7.1	3	5.8	2	6	2	6	3	5.9	2	33.51	0.001
Self-controlled	10.2	12	9.9	10	9.2	9	9	9	9	9	9.7	9	9.9	11	3.21	0.782

*These data come from Rokeach and Parker (1970, 102) and is table 2 in their study.

the authors would endorse. Since Rokeach and Parker assume that a person's values have social consequences (98) (I take this to mean effects on behavior), their analysis might suggest that (3) behavioral differences between the rich and poor and educated and uneducated can be related to differences in their value preferences.

A Second Analysis and Interpretation

I have reanalyzed Rokeach and Parker's data utilizing different statistics. I have constructed an interpretation of the data that is completely different. I asked the following question: To what degree do members of these various social categories agree in the way they hierarchically rank all the eighteen values in terms of the variable "important to me as a guiding principle in my daily life"? To answer the question I applied Spearman's Rank Order Correlation Coefficient (r_s) and Kendall's coefficient of concordance (W) to the eight tables.

The results of the analysis are as follows:

1. When Kendall's coefficient of concordance is applied to the composite ranks of values across all income categories in my table 1, W= approximately +.84, and the average correlation is high. Average r_s = approximately +.81. The hypothesis that income groups do not agree on the patterning of values must be rejected ($x2_{17}$ = 99.96, significant beyond .001).
2. When Kendall's coefficient of concordance is applied to the composite ranks of values across all educational categories in Rokeach and Parker's table 4, W = approximately +.73, and the average correlation is high. Average r_s = approximately +.68. The hypothesis that educational categories do not agree on the patterning of values must be rejected ($x2_{17}$= 86.87, significant beyond .001).
3. In Rokeach and Parker's table 1 on income differences, the composite rank of values for the most extremely different income categories, namely under $2,000 and $15,000 and over, are highly correlated, r_s = approximately +.65.
4. In Rokeach and Parker's table 3 on educational differences, the composite ranks of values for informants with extremely different educational backgrounds, namely college graduates and those with only zero–four years of education, are highly correlated, r_s = approximately +.63.
5. The composite ranks of values for blacks and whites are highly correlated in Rokeach and Parker's tables 5, 6, 7, 8. Controlling for income and education *does not* increase the correlation of the system of ranks between blacks and whites. The correlations in the four tables are r_s = approximately +.81, +.88, +.84, +.86, respectively. The highest correlation is for their table 6, before the informants were matched for income and education.

The results of this analysis lead me to construct a very different interpretation. I conclude that: (1) patterning of values by Americans is relatively invariant across differences in wealth, education, and race. (2) Any differences in behavior that may exist among members of different races, the rich and poor, the educated and uneducated, have little to do with the values they profess. (3) The value system remains stable while behavior varies with one's position in the social structure. Therefore much of behavior is controlled by one's situation and not one's beliefs about desirable behavior or future goals. In America the value system does not change very much as you increase your income, attain educational degrees, or change your color, or as you exhibit the behavior appropriate to your new status.

An Interlude in Middle Earth

The same quantitative data lent themselves to two entirely divergent interpretations as a result of the statistics used in the analysis. By applying the median test and Spearman's rank order correlation coefficient to some hypothetical data, it is easy to understand how such opposite results can be produced.

Assume some anthropologist wandering through Middle Earth were to discover a society consisting of two hundred members divided equally between two social groups, the dwarves and the elves. After much painstaking effort the anthropologist was able to formulate all the relevant values of the culture, and these were ten in number. Every member of the society expressed these and only these values. But the dwarves and the elves disagreed on how important each value was, relative to all the others.

The anthropologist then asked every member of the society to rank the ten values and found that all the dwarves gave the same rank to each value, and all the elves gave the same rank to each value, but the two groups never agreed on the precise rank of each value. The composite ranks for the two groups are shown in table 6.2.

If these hypothetical data are analyzed with the median test, such as that applied by Rokeach and Parker, we perform a separate analysis of each of the ten values. For each value we compare the distribution of all the dwarves' ranks and all the elves' ranks with the grand median rank.

With such a procedure we can test the hypothesis that the distribution of ranks around the grand median is significantly different for the two groups with respect to value 1. The grand median for the two

Table 6.2. The ranking of ten values by dwarves and elves: hypothetical data

| | Value statement number | | | | | | | | | |
	1	2	3	4	5	6	7	8	9	10
Dwarves composite rank (n=100)	1	2	3	4	5	6	7	8	9	10
Elves composite rank (n=100)	2	1	4	3	6	5	8	7	10	9

Table 6.3. The median test on any value in Table 6.2

	Dwarves	Elves
Above median	100	0
Below median	0	100

groups is 1.5. If we then sort the informants' ranks in relation to the grand median we get the two-by-two table in table 6.3.

The results are obviously significant. There is a significant difference between dwarves and elves in their precise ranking of value 1. The same results are produced by applying the median test to the other nine values. The results of a median test analysis indicate that dwarves and elves differ significantly on every single value in their Middle Earth culture.

If we apply the Spearman rank order test to the same hypothetical data, we perform one analysis on the whole system of ranks of the two groups. We only wish to know the extent of agreement between the two hierarchies of ranks. We take into account the number of values being ranked and the amount of difference in the rank assigned to each value by the two groups. We assess the degree of agreement, nonagreement, or disagreement in relation to the mathematical possibilities for maximum agreement or disagreement. If we apply the r_s to the data in table 6.2, the value systems of elves and dwarves correlate almost perfectly, r_s= approximately +.94. And as the number of values about which elves and dwarves can disagree on relative importance increases, the correlation of the value systems approaches greater perfection. With eighteen values arranged according to the system in table 6.2, the r_s= approximately + .98. The correlation continues to approach unity as the number of values disagreed on enlarges!

A Third Analysis and Interpretation

With this insight from Middle Earth, let us return to Rokeach and Parker's data on American values. It is mathematically possible for very high correlations between rankings to coexist with significant disagreement on the rank of every single value. This fact allows for the construction of a third interpretation of the data. The same data can be analyzed so that: (1) among members of various income and educational categories, forty-five significant differences over the placement of individual values are found out of a possibility of seventy-two differences, (2) the rankings of values of all informants are highly correlated.

The interpretation that is constructed from these results of combining the median test, and the Spearman r_s and Kendall W analyses is as follows: (1) There is truly an American value system, one that all segments of the population share. (2) There are also a large number of significant points of disagreement over the placement of individual values within the system. (3) The sharing of the value system is considerable and indicates that, in spite of differences in social status, we are all members of one somewhat integrated society. (4) The differences in values are considerable and are related to the variations of social status of members of our society.

This interpretation is appealing because it conforms to our common sense notion that two objects or systems can be both similar and different at the same time (for example, the colors blue and green), and because it seems to account for the results of both statistical analyses. The large number of differences over the placement of values discovered by the median test is combined with the high correlations between the total system of ranks discovered in the concordance analysis. The interpretation is compelling because it encompasses both types of statistical results.

A Fourth Interpretation

The results of a further statistical analysis will provide a basis for a fourth interpretation. The number of significant differences in values (as judged by the median test), and the size of the correlation of any two or more systems of ranks (as judged by r_s), are independent measures. Nearly identical correlations in the overall ranking can exist between rankings where every value is significantly different, or alternatively where none of the values are significantly different. An identical number of significant differences between individual values can exist between rankings that have a perfect negative correlation or, alternatively, a nearly perfect positive correlation.

In table 6.4, assume that each ranking is the ranking of members of different social categories. Assume that agreement within each social

Table 6.4a and Table 6.4b. A comparison of four rankings of values showing the independence of results of the median test from results of Spearman's correlation coefficient

	Values										
Ranking 1	1	2	3	4	5	6	7	8	....	17	18
Ranking 2	1	2	3	4	5	6	7	8	....	17	18
Ranking 3	2	1	4	3	6	5	8	7	....	18	17
Ranking 4	18	17	16	15	14	13	12	11	....	2	1

	Median test number of significant differences in individual rank	rs correlation of two rankings
Rankings 1 & 2	0	+1.00
Rankings 1 & 3	18	+0.98
Rankings 1 & 4	18	−1.00

category about that ranking is complete. Rankings 1 and 2 and rankings 1 and 3 have nearly identical correlations (+1.00 and +.98) and the extreme opposite number of differences in individual ranks (0 and 18). Rankings 1 and 3 and rankings 1 and 4 have the same number of individual differences in rank (18) and completely opposite correlations (+.98 and −1.00).

The same number of differences in individual ranks can exist in systems that are completely unalike as well as in systems that are identical. This means that the median test fails to make an important distinction among those values that are found to be significantly different in their individual rank. It does not distinguish among values in terms of the extent of difference between their ranks. It is precisely the extent of difference that determines the extent of correlation of the two rankings.

The Spearman r_s statistic is defined as $1 - (6(\Sigma_1 D2_1) \div N(N2-1))$. The two variables in the formula are D, the size of the difference in rank of each object in the two rankings, and N, the number of objects ranked. In rankings of the same number of objects, N, of course, is a constant. The only variable is D, the size of the difference in ranks for each object in the rankings.

I have already shown in table 6.4 that the same number of significant differences in the median test can tolerate rankings whose correlations range from −1.00 to +.98. It follows that when analyzing the data on values it is not useful to count the number of significant differences in the median test results. Rather, we should distinguish each individual difference as a contributor to, or a detracter from, the overall correlation of the rankings.

If one divides the values that Rokeach and Parker discovered to be significantly different in rank into those that contribute to high correlations in the two rankings and those that reduce the similarity of the two rankings, one gets the following results.

1. Forty-one out of sixty-seven cases of significantly different values (60 percent of their findings) have an average difference in rank of three ranks or less. Rankings of eighteen values between which no value is more than three ranks different have minimum correlations of +.84 (r_s).
2. At least fifty of sixty-seven cases of significantly different values (nearly 75 percent of the findings) have an average difference in rank of four or less. Rankings of eighteen values between which no value is more than four ranks different have minimum correlation of +.71 (r_s).
3. At best only seventeen cases out of a possible 144 are different enough to reduce the size of the correlations found between the rankings of all informants.

On the basis of this analysis one might construct the following interpretation: (1) there is truly an American value system, one that all segments of the population share. (2) There are also a small number of significant points of disagreement over the placement of individual values within the system. (3) The sharing of the value system is considerable and indicates that in spite of differences in social status, we are all members of one somewhat integrated society. (4) The differences in values are negligible but are related to variations in the social status of members of our society.

The Four Interpretations

The four interpretations and their statistical foundations are summarized in table 6.5. The four interpretations of the data are alternative and mutually exclusive interpretations. Each is confirmed by a different set of statistical results with which it can be viewed as compatible. If we accept the reference and sense of any one of them, we cannot accept the reference and sense of any other, nor can we limit ourselves to the set of statistical results with which they are compatible.

I include the "sense" of the interpretation in this reasoning about their mutual exclusiveness because in each interpretation's reference, interpretations one and three are not mutually exclusive. It is possible to have pervasive differences in the value system (interpretation one) and at the same time have sharing. This is the reference of the third interpretation. But in their sense, the two interpretations are quite in-

Table 6.5. Summary of four statistical analyses of the data and their interpretations

Interpretation	Statistical Results
1. Pervasive differences in values associated with socioeconomic differences. Behavior variations related to differences in value preferences.	The median test indicates out of a possible 72 differences, 45 significant differences in the rank of values by informants varying in socioeconomic status.
2. Value preferences invariant across differences in socioeconomic status. Behavioral differences not related to differences in values.	The Spearman r_s and Kendall W indicate high correlations between rankings of all informants regardless of socioeconomic status.
3. A value system shared by all socioeconomic categories but a large number of differences in the placement of individual values. Sharing considerable. Differences considerable.	The two sets of results listed above.
4. A value system shared by all socioeconomic categories but a small number of differences in the placement of individual values. Sharing considerable. Differences negligible.	The high correlations in the Spearman and Kendall tests—and the fact that only 25% of the differences found by the median test—detract from the high correlation of the informants' rankings.

compatible. Considered alone, the first interpretation lays emphasis on, or implies the fact that the rich and poor and the educated and uneducated have different value systems. This implication is completely lacking in the third interpretation.

From Data to Analysis

There is a degree of uncertainty between the data and the statistical analysis. The data do not provide us with a criterion that might aid us in deciding which statistical analysis is interpretatively relevant. The data can always be analyzed in different ways, and more and more statistical distinctions can be added. We might, for example, decide that the only important differences are between values whose difference in rank is large enough to produce negative correlations between two rankings. This would reduce the significant differences to less than five percent of all the values ranked.

But the truth of the interpretation does not increase as the number of statistical distinctions upon which it is based is increased. Some differences in the data may be interpretively irrelevant, as I assumed in the fourth analysis and interpretation. The data themselves remain silent on this issue.

The four interpretations are mutually exclusive alternatives. They are all compatible with aspects of the data as shown in a statistical analysis. There is no criterion given by the data per se for preferring any one statistical analysis. It follows that the data do not impel us to adopt one interpretation or another. The facts do not speak for themselves. The only criterion that does seem available for selecting one statistical analysis over another is the interpretation that one personally favors, or hopes to discover in the data, or believes deserves to be true.

From Analysis to Interpretation

Uncertainty is not limited to the step from the data to the selection of a statistical technique for its analysis. There is indeterminateness between the results of the statistical analysis and the interpretation. Although each interpretation is compatible with the results of some statistical analysis, not one of the interpretations necessarily follows from those results. I will consider each interpretation in turn.

The first case begins with an analysis that indicates a large number of statistically significant differences in individual rank. It concludes with the interpretation that pervasive differences in the value system are associated with socioeconomic status. I have demonstrated that the number of individual differences in rank that are significantly different can remain fixed while the degree of correlation of the value system can vary from complete disagreement to near complete unanimity. It can be argued that we cannot ignore the extent of correlation of the rankings when we interpret the value rankings of two groups to display pervasive differences. Thus an assessment of the extent of difference cannot be directly inferred from such statistical results.

The second case begins with an analysis that indicates high correlations between the value systems of all informants. It concludes with an interpretation that value systems are invariant across socioeconomic categories. It is the nature of the correlation coefficient that two systems of ranks can be highly correlated and still display statistically significant differences in every value. Who can say from the data themselves whether a statistical difference as small as one or two ranks is conceptually or behaviorally important or not? It is also possible for two rankings to be highly correlated and still have major differences in rank between a small number of values. For example with eighteen values, if rankers agree on the rank of sixteen of the values, the remaining two values can be twelve ranks apart and the r_s = approximately +.71. These two values with large discrepancies in rank may be the key to all the behavioral differences between the social categories. Or they may be completely irrelevant. The data remain silent on the issue. Thus an assessment of the extent of similarity cannot be directly inferred from these statistical results either.

The third and fourth interpretations do not necessarily follow from the statistical analyses with which they are compatible. The third case begins with a statistical analysis that indicates a large number of statistically significant differences in the placement of individual values between members of various socioeconomic categories, and high correlations between the total rankings of these informants. It concludes with an interpretation that there is considerable sharing of values and considerable differences at the same time. Yet from a strictly statistical point of view the interpretation does not directly follow. Since the number of individual differences in value placement varies independently of the correlation coefficient, it can be argued as above that only a small number of differences are statistically significant. In this case statistical significance will be determined by how much the difference in the individual values detracts from the overall correlation of the rankings of all values. The interpretation that there are considerable differences would then be eliminated.

From the cultural point of view, the third interpretation is only one possible conclusion compatible with its statistical results. The question of whether you place "equality" above "personal pleasure," or vice versa, may place you into one of two somewhat hostile political camps in our contemporary society. How much you place it above or below in importance really may not matter. But the question of whether you feel that "a world of beauty'" is more important than "inner harmony" may have no implications conceptually, politically, or socially to members of our culture. That is to say, we cannot assume that all the values ranked are weighted equally in their social implications in daily life: two rankings of eighteen values may have nine statistically significant differences in individual placement. But if the nine values, which are the same in both rankings, are the nine most relevant values, the value systems of those informants are much more alike than if the values in the same position are the nine least relevant.

The fourth case is equally susceptible to cultural blindness. It interprets high correlations to indicate considerable sharing of the value system. It interprets the small number of individual differences that detract from the overall high correlations to indicate negligible differences in the systems. But it is possible that just those few values that are different in rank are the central values of the culture. The magnitude of the difference that may exist between those few values can also not be ignored. Blacks and whites have high correlations between their rankings of values, yet on the issue of equality they differ by ten ranks (Rokeach and Parker 1970, 109). Equality is a key value of our culture, with a high degree of relevance to the history of race relations in the United States. A difference in relative importance as great as ten ranks for a key value may create deep divisions between blacks and whites. The high correlation of their value systems and small number of significant differences might obscure the cleavage.

Three Stages to Understanding: Data Collection, Statistical Analysis, and Interpretation

I have conceptualized three stages on the path from data to findings in the style of research under consideration (see table 6.6). Each stage may be thought of as self-contained, with principles for adequately applying means to reach its goals. These principles and means have all received a good deal of attention and are relatively well understood. The three stages I have called data collection, analysis, and interpretation.

The goal or output of each stage may be an input for a subsequent stage. Thus data are the output of the data collection stage and are usually the input of the analysis stage. Statistical results are the output of the analysis stage and are usually input for the generation of interpretations and conclusions.

I do not wish to imply that the direction along the path is always from data collection to analysis to interpretation. Expected or hoped-for conclusions and the availability of a particular form of statistical analysis sometimes precede the creation of a measuring instrument.

Table 6.6. Three stages to understanding

Stage	Inputs	Means	Principles	Goals or outputs
Data collection	Phenomena	Measuring instruments	Increase reliability/ decrease experimental bias	Data
			SELECTION	
Analysis	Data	Statistics	Applicability of statistical assumptions: normal distribution, interval scale, etc.	Statistical results
			EVALUATION OF SIGNIFICANCE	
Interpretation	Statistical results	Reason	Logic	Interpretations and conclusions

I believe that in contrast to the attention that has been given to each of these separate stages in research on reliability and experimental bias (data collection stage), on statistical assumptions and their applicability (analysis stage), and on logic and reasoning (interpretation stage), little attention has been devoted to the transition from one stage to another. We need to study more closely the rules or procedures for passing from data to their statistical analysis, and from statistical results to their interpretation and final presentation as findings. I have shown in one case the many degrees of freedom and the great scope for doubt that exist in the transition from data to analysis and from statistical results to interpretation.

Between the data and the analysis of that data is the uncertainty of selection of a statistical tool and the parts of the data to which it will be applied. Between statistical results and their interpretation is the evaluation of significance. It is replete with uncertainties.

The Softening and Silent Ghost of Method Variance

Hard data have an intrinsic impressiveness which, when combined with a fruitful statistical analysis, may compel the reader to accept the interpretation of the data favored by a scientist. By demonstrating some of the degrees of freedom that exist between data and their statistical analysis, and between the results of the statistical analysis and their interpretation, I hope to have suggested that data are more a method of persuasion in most scholarship and not strictly a mirror of nature or of the truth.

D'Andrade's nonfindings are provocative in a very special way: that the American, Japanese, and Vietnamese subjects in his values questionnaire study are so similar in their reported values may be most telling precisely because, from an ethnographic/thick description point of view, the findings not only defy expectation but also don't really ring true. D'Andrade himself wondered about alternative units for the analysis of values, and it seems fruitful to raise skeptical questions about the soft side of the quantitative analysis of abstract value words and consider disconnects in the general process of moving from cultural reality to tools for measuring, analyzing, and interpreting that reality.

Despite the popularity of cross-cultural questionnaires about abstract value words, the results may be problematic if they fail to attend to concrete institutional realities and to the particular custom complexes of members of local communities. Even if certain formal standards for questionnaire construction are met, that method for studying cultural values may be somewhat off the mark precisely because the method typically seeks generality of application by removing parochial or culture-specific questions about whether, for example, it is normatively acceptable for widows to eat fish—which are the types of questions that might highlight the cultural differences one is looking for. Whether doing research in Middle Earth or around the corner, collecting, analyzing, and interpreting data are cognitive enterprises involving selection and evaluation. Since the criteria for selection and evaluation are not to be found in the data per se, the data do more to limit the number of credible interpretations of social and cultural reality than to pick out a correct interpretation. Data speak in a very soft voice if they speak at all. They may well say "You have not yet been disproved" but they never boldly assert "You are right!"

References

Bourdieu, Pierre. 1972. *Outline of a Theory of Practice.* Cambridge: Cambridge University Press.

———.1990. *A Logic of Practice.* Stanford, CA: Stanford University Press.

Campbell, Donald T., and Donald W. Fiske. 1959. "Convergent and Discriminant Validation by the Multitrait-Multimethod Matrix." *Psychological Bulletin* 56 (2): 81–105.

D'Andrade, Roy G. 2008. *A Study of Personal and Cultural Values.* New York: Palgrave MacMillan.

Goodnow, Jacqueline J., Peggy J. Miller, and Frank Kessel, eds. 1995. "Cultural Practices as Contexts for Development." In *New Directions for Child Development*, vol. 67. San Francisco: Jossey-Bass.

Fassin, Didier. 2012. *A Companion to Moral Anthropology.* Malden, MA: Wiley-Blackwell.

Hays, William L. 1963. *Statistics for Psychologists.* New York: Holt, Rinehart and Winston. Lewin, Kurt. 1943. "Defining the field at given time." *Psychological Review* 50: 292–310.

Nagel, Ernest. 1961. *The Structure of Science.* London: Routledge and Kegan Paul.

Rokeach, Milton, and Seymour Parker. 1970. "Values as Social Indicators of Poverty and Race Relations in America." In *The Annals of the American Academy of Political and Social Science*, vol. 388, March: 97–111.

Shweder, Richard A., Manamohan Mahapatra, and Joan G. Miller. 1990. "Culture and Moral Development." In *Cultural Psychology: Essays on Comparative Human Development*, edited by J. Stigler, R. A. Shweder, and G. Herdt, 1–82. New York: Cambridge University Press.

Shweder, Richard A., Nancy C. Much, Manamohan Mahapatra, and Lawrence

Park. 1997. "The Big Three of Morality (Autonomy, Community, Divinity) and The Big Three Explanations of Suffering." In *Morality and Health*, edited by A. Brandt and P. Rozin, 119–72. New York: Routledge and Kegan Paul.

Weisner, Thomas S. 1984. "A Cross-Cultural Perspective: Ecological Niches of Middle Childhood." In *The Elementary School Years: Understanding Development during Middle Childhood*, edited by A. Collins, 335–69. Washington, DC: National Academy.

———. 1996. "Why Ethnography Should Be the Most Important Method in the Study of Human Development." In *Ethnography and Human Development*, edited by R. Jesser, A. Colby, and R. A. Shweder, 305–26. Chicago: University of Chicago Press.

———. 2001. "Anthropological Aspects of Childhood." In *International Encyclopedia of the Social and Behavioral Sciences* 3: 1697–1701. Oxford: Elsevier Science Ltd.

———. 2002. "Ecocultural Understanding of Children's Developmental Pathways." *Human Development* 45: 275–81.

Whiting, John W. M., and Irvin Child. 1953. *Child Training and Personality*. New Haven, CT: Yale University Press.

SEVEN

Images of Infancy: The Interplay of Biological Predispositions and Cultural Philosophies as an Arena for Mixed Methods Research

HEIDI KELLER

Consider these three brief interactions between three mothers with their infants:

"Clap your hands," says a mother to her infant, in the midst of conversations with others, while moving the hands of the child.

A mother turns to her infant and says, "I am going to leave you alone so you can play all by yourself" and then leaves the child surrounded by toys.

"Here is aunty. Give aunty a smile. Give aunty a smile, smile please," says a mother to her infant when a visitor comes in.

These brief conversational bouts between mothers and their three-month-old babies represent very different socialization agendas. The first mother is a farmer from rural northwestern Cameroon. For her it is very important that her baby is trained in proper demeanor and behavior in the social group from the very beginning. The second mother lives in the German capital of Berlin. She wants her baby to learn to be alone and not rely on other people too much from the very beginning. The third mother lives in the Indian capital of Delhi. For her the development of the baby's agency is important, but also social references and politeness are crucial from the beginning.

Different views on personhood start from the very beginning of life. These views guide socialization efforts of families and communities and are expressed in parenting ideas and practices. Parenting is therefore a principal reason why individuals in different cultures differ from each other (Keller 2003; LeVine 1977). Parenting, parental care, and caretaking are all activities that render the survival and the physical as well as the psychological development of children, and thus the enculturation of the child. Parenting is guided by images that express the cultural models. Indeed from the very beginning, parents interact with infants based on their images of the kind of person they expect those infants to become. These different images are expressed and embodied in repeated everyday practices within the family or the respective social systems, so that children gradually acquire intersubjective knowledge about themselves, their caregivers, their social environment, and the role they play in this environment (Crossley 2000; Miller and Hoogstra 1992). By coconstructing everyday interactions, caregivers provide the child with a framework for making sense of these experiences; they also provide the child with resources for constructing social meaning, laying the pathway for culture-specific self-ways. Our research with infants and their caregivers in multiple societies has found generalizable patterns, within which the three very different ways that mothers interacted with their infants in the above excerpts make sense. Our research is grounded in evolutionary and neurobiological understandings of infant development and shaped by psychologically informed conceptions of culture, each of which are discussed below in turn.

Neurobiological Dimensions of Infant Development

Infancy constitutes a separate life stage in all primates. In humans, it constitutes the time span between birth and about two years of age and, as such, is a small percentage of the average person's life expectancy (Lamb, Bornstein, and Teti 2002). Humans need this preparatory period to be able to adapt to the complex social environment that constitutes their niche. The extreme helplessness (altriciality) of the human infant has been interpreted as a consequence of a physiological pre-term birth (Prechtl 1984) or the obstetrical dilemma (Washburn 1960) provoked by hominid brain growth. Unlike for other primates' brains, human neonatal brain growth continues in a rapid, fetal-like trajectory for the next year (Martin 1983). Two processes describe the factors typical of the species and the individual in brain development: experience-expectant and experience-dependent processes (Greenough, Black, and Wallace 1987). Experience-expectant processes are common to all members of the species and evolved as neural preparation for incorporating general information from the environment. The overproduction and trimming of synaptic connections between the nerve cells illustrate experience-expectant information storage. Experience-dependent information storage reflects learning and brain development unique to the individual. The neural basis of experience-dependent processes appears to involve the active formation of synaptic connections as a product of experience (Greenough, Black, and Wallace 1987). Connectivity within the brain increases substantially during the first six months of life through augmented dendritic branching; high numbers of synaptic connections are generated. Only those that are activated regularly will survive. Thus, the brain is organized by the electrical and chemical activity of developing neurons and by information received through the senses as much or even more than by the unfolding of a genetic "blueprint." The early experiences influence how subsequent information will be processed, thus affecting future functioning.

Neurophysiological research has therefore indicated that the newborn period can be characterized as the brain imprint period. However, it is not the passive reception of information that constitutes infants' learning but active processes based in an inborn motivation and desire to learn, i.e., to acquire and process information from the environment. Infants' interest in the environment is directed by epigenetic rules (Wilson 1975) or central tendencies (MacDonald 1988) that direct the attention to salient developmental tasks for the respective developmental period. These form sensitive periods during which learning is particularly easy (Boyd and Richerson 1985; see also Keller 2007; Keller and Kärtner 2013). Thus, experience is the product of an ongoing reciprocal interaction between the environment and the brain (Nelson 2005). Accordingly, the neonatal environment has major and lasting consequences for development (Storfer 1999) and is therefore constitutive for cultural development.

Cultural Dimensions of Infant Development

The brief period of infancy has attracted the interest and the attention not only of biologists, neurologists, and physicians, but also of philosophers, psychologists, and anthropologists from Plato's time on (about 350 BC) and perhaps even earlier. Infants are attractive social partners for everybody: they elicit the motivation to care, protect, and stimulate. However, care, protection, and stimulation are dependent on the situational affordances and constraints and therefore expressions of culture.

Thomas Weisner regularly asks his students, "What is the single important thing that one could do to influence the development of [an] infant?" Student answers include physical protection and security, good nourishment, love and attachment, trust, financial security, stimulation. While confirming the importance of all these factors, Weisner argues that the most important one is culture, since culture defines how all the other factors are embodied and expressed (Weisner 2002, 276). Infancy can be said to constitute a lens through which to understand critical cultural decisions and orientations (Gottlieb 2004). Thus, contrary to still-existing views that culture comes more into play as children grow older, culture defines the human condition right from the beginning. Therefore culture can be regarded as the software that gives adaptive direction to the neurophysiological hardware, which is composed by the inherent capacities that all newborns possess (LeVine et al. 1994). In the same vein, Patricia Greenfield (2002) argues that culture selects, emphasizes, and reinforces biological propensities.

Inherent in the previous discussion is the conception of culture as everyday life and experiences, in which children participate from birth on.[1] We therefore understand culture as a socially interactive process with two main components: shared activities (cultural practices) and shared systems of meaning (cultural interpretations) (Greenfield and Keller 2004; Keller 2007). Obviously people differ in their behavioral conventions and norms, beliefs and attitudes. These differences are emergent within environmental conditions and, in particular, sociodemographic differences, such as degree of formal education, which shapes reproductive life strategies such as the onset of parenthood and number of children, as well as the cultural priorities in terms of behaviors and belief systems (Keller 2010; Keller and Kärtner 2013; Weisner 2002; Whiting 1977). Culture can therefore be regarded as the representation of sociodemographic parameters that can be identified in the everyday interactions between adults and infants.

Studying Infants in Context

The starting point of our cross-cultural research program was an interest in identifying universals in parenting. We were lucky to have access to the film archives of the Max Planck Institute in Seewiesen (the former institute of Konrad Lorenz), which its director of that time, Irenäus Eibl-Eibesfeld, and his students had compiled (Keller and Eibl-Eibesfeld 1989). The method of choice was ethological behavioral observation as applied to the filmed episodes. We were especially interested in documenting the universal nature of face-to-face contact, which we could do in social groups as different as Eipo Indians from the Amazon, Trobriand islanders from the Pacific Sea, and German middle-class families. However, the vast quantitative differences in face-to-face exchange between these groups could not be ignored if we accept the assumption that everyday experiences are crucial for children's development. As a consequence, our methodological repertoire needed to be expanded to include methods that allow one to infer meaning from overt behavior. We therefore started interviewing cultural informants about their conceptions of good and bad parenting and related issues. The differences in meaning, sometimes even with respect to the same behavior, were striking and fascinating.

Based in evolutionary thinking as to why particular behaviors have emerged during phylogeny and how they contribute to adaptational processes, as well as in cultural anthropological and psychological conceptions of meaning making, we developed an ecocultural model of development that is bound to a particular methodology (Keller and Kärtner 2013; Keller 2011). We first identify sociodemographic contexts along the milieu of the level of formal education, age at first parenthood, number of children, and family structure or household composition, respectively. These components are not considered as independent variables that need to be statistically controlled in order to measure their impact but as forming contexts that are related to particular norms, values, attitudes, behavioral conventions, and the like. In focus group interviews we try to assess these representations. With local conventions of conduct we recruit participants for our studies. Departing from the initial interest in parenting strategies, we developed a longitudinal research program aimed at uncovering the cultural solution of universal developmental tasks. When children are about three months of age, we assess their learning environment (Whiting 1977), including parenting socialization goals, ethnotheories and behavioral contexts, and interactional regulations, with an array of multiple methods. It is part of cultural/cross-cultural research of this kind that different methods need to be applied in order to generate information that relates to the same constructs. The data are analyzed quantitatively as well as qualitatively (for more information, see Keller and Kärtner 2013 and Keller 2011).

Parenting Varies by Cultural Dimensions of Autonomy and Relatedness

Based on earlier proposals from Markus and Kitayama (1991), Kağit-çibaşi (2007), and others, we have proposed to define culture in terms of models that integrate autonomy and relatedness (Keller 2012; Keller and Otto 2011). Autonomy and relatedness are two human needs and cultural values at the same time. They represent independent dimensions, yet the definition of one influences the definition of the other. We differentiate psychological autonomy as comprising mental processes that are based on self-reflective ways of being, centering on the exploration and reflective awareness of personal desires, wishes, and intentions from action autonomy as the individual's self-regulated capacity to perform (complex) behavioral necessities, including setting goals, planning, and executing actions independently. Both conceptions may concur but need not necessarily, i.e., psychological autonomy may accompany action autonomy, but action autonomy does also work without self-reflective processes.

Relatedness also can appear in two modes. Psychological relatedness means that separate, self-contained individuals establish self-selected relations with others that are defined and negotiated from the point of view of individual autonomy. This conception of relatedness is in the service of psychological autonomy. Hierarchical relatedness is defined as a network of obligatory relationships based on ranked and interdependent roles that are mandatory. In this sense, hierarchical relatedness is the leading principle for action autonomy. However, aspects of all four conceptions can co-occur based on contextual and situational demands (for more details, see Keller and Kärtner 2013).

Indeed, we see different configurations of the conceptions in different sociodemographic contexts. Three cultural models for configuring these conceptions emerge with the three sociodemographic contexts referred to earlier. This certainly does not, however, cover all possibilities in all of humanity. Western middle-class families follow the model of psychological autonomy and psychological relatedness with an emphasis on individuality, unique preferences, influencing the environment, exercising free will, and asserting equality (cf. Markus and Conner 2013). This pocket of the world's population comprises about five percent but dominates human sciences in research and practical applications (Arnett 2008; Henrich, Heine, and Norenzayan 2010). The neglected ninety-five percent (Arnett 2008) are composed of different subgroups, which are not all statistically accessible. An estimated thirty to forty percent of people are subsistence-based farmers in non-Western countries. Their cultural model comprises hierarchical relatedness and action autonomy with an emphasis on rooting oneself in networks and traditions, understanding one's place in the larger whole, respecting and accepting (family) hierarchy, and unconditional commitment to role obligations and responsibilities. A third cultural model consists of possible combinations of all the facets of autonomy and relatedness. It characterizes the educated middle-class families of non-Western countries. It represents a far greater heterogeneity and variability than the other two cultural models.

In the following paragraphs, ideal images of the baby for the different cultural models will be portrayed. These portraits are based on a multitude of different methodological approaches (see Weisner 2005, 2012). First, I drew on the literature of anthropological field observations. Second, I utilized the results of our own cross-cultural research program briefly outlined before. We observe everyday situations in the natural environment, combining spot observations and videotaping social situations. We interview mothers, fathers, grandmothers, and sibling caretakers in order to understand socialization goals and parenting ethnotheories. We also conduct focus group interviews to assess the consensual framework of parenting (for more details, see Keller 2007, 2011; Lamm 2008).

The Western Middle-Class View of the Baby

For a long time, the Western view of infancy has been that of a "blooming, buzzing confusion" (James 1890) or a fog-like state of mind (Stern 1923). Particularly following ethological long-term observations and mapping the infant behavioral repertoire, the notion of the *competent infant* has become prevalent since the early 1970s (Stone, Smith, and Murphy 1973). It is common knowledge today that infants are equipped with particular social and sociocognitive capacities, which enable them to participate in their social environment. Babies are considered as active, separate, and autonomous persons, whose wishes and activities are valid in their own right (Ainsworth et al. 1978; Otto and Keller 2014). This leading principle of child-care philosophy is apparent from the first days of a baby's life. Babies are usually lying on their backs with their interactional partners, mainly the mother or the father bending over them, interacting via face-to-face contact. There is little direct body contact beyond touching, stroking, and patting. The autonomy of the baby is supported with protoconversations, i.e., dyadic verbal/vocal exchanges that are structured like quasi dialogues between adults, with turns and pauses. Prompt and contingent reactions toward infants' signals within a time frame of less than a second allow the baby to experience causality, i.e., their own behavior impacts the environment and leads to predictable outcomes. These interactional experiences support the emergence and stabilization of self-efficacy (Keller 2011). Another characteristic is the emphasis on an autobiographical time line (what happened yesterday, what will happen tomorrow) that initiates the development of a narrative self from early on (Keller 2011).

The interactional structure is child centered so that parents follow the baby's lead. Infants are encouraged to express their preferences and intentions. Good parenting is to prioritize the initiatives of the baby. This behavioral mode is mirrored in voluminous elaborated conversations where the mother and, to a lesser degree, also the father explain the world to the baby, especially his or her inner world. Elaborations are accompanied by an ongoing stream of questions seeking consent and confirmation from the baby for every detail:

> You want to play on your own?
> Do you want to tell me something?
> Do you want Mom to show you the picture book?
> Are you tired?
> Do you want to play with Dad?
> What do you think about this?
> You like that book?

Babies are continuously offered choices as another characteristic of a psychologically autonomous lifestyle with decision competence. (Want to look at Mommy for a second, or are you busy?)

The most subtle signals of the baby are understood as quasi-intentional communicative signals, which are included in the conversational stream. Positive emotionality, which can be regarded as one of the bases of individuality (Shweder and Bourne 1984), is a major topic:

> Hello hello.
> Are you happy?
> Give Mommy a smile, ok?

Related is the unconditional praising of the baby and all of his or her actions. The following is a brief excerpt from a conversation between a Los Angeles (LA) middle-class mother and her three-month-old son:

Okay, you're the tallest boy in the world huh? Look how tall you are. Look at those strong legs. . . . Look how big that big boy is? . . . Super baby, super baby. Look at that, look at that big boy, look at that big boy!

Of course, three-month-old babies do not understand the semantic content of these conversations, yet, the intonation, the segmentation, and other nonverbal elements carry substantial cultural meaning about the self and the image of the child.

The research team around the German biologist Kathleen Wermke has impressively demonstrated how the verbal/vocal environment transmits cultural messages to babies. They analyzed the spectral parameters of newborns' cries and demonstrated that German newborns cry in German intonation in emphasizing the first syllable like Máma, whereas French newborns cry in French intonation in emphasizing the second syllable like mamán (Mampe et al. 2009).

The picture of early independence is complemented with the babies' ability to be alone and spend time on their own. One middle-class mother from LA said to her three-month-old daughter, "I am going to leave you alone so you can play all by yourself." In the interview, she explained:

Mother: "And sometimes they do need time away—uhm—'cause they get overstimulated if there are just too many people around. Or they, you know, sometimes they need just a little quiet time."
Interviewer: "Mhm."
Mother: "Helps them develop a sense of—uhm—independence."
Interviewer: "Oh, mhm, so what's important about independence?"
Mother: "Uhm, that they are able to make decisions for themselves."

Babies, who spend time alone, are usually surrounded by toys. Toys are considered important socialization agents that stimulate babies and train their cognitive competences, which is important for the instantiation of the mental world.

The image of the baby from a Western middle-class perspective can be summarized as follows: The child is in the center. This is apparent in the spatial arrangement, with babies lying on their backs, surrounded by toys, and receiving the exclusive dyadic attention of their caregiver (see figure 7.1). The baby is considered to be self-contained, self-assured, self-conscious, and independent. The baby has rights that the caregiver has to respect and execute: "The sensitive mother gives the baby what his communications suggest he wants. She responds socially to his attempts to initiate social interaction, playfully to his attempts to initiate play. She picks him up when he seems to wish it, and puts him down when he wants to explore." (Ainsworth 1969/2012)

This image of the infant is made possible by (1) economic prosperity that allows exclusive attention and time spent with the baby and (2) high formal education to facilitate verbal elaboration. The few

FIGURE 7.1 A Euro American mother with her three-month-old baby son, being exclusively attentive to his needs and wishes.

children in a nuclear family receive a high material and psychological investment by their parents in order to prepare them for competition with like-raised others.

The Non-Western Subsistence-Based Farmer View of the Baby

Intact subsistence-based village structures have a much slower pace of change than urban contexts, so that lived cultural practices continue more or less over several decades. This is evident, for example, in the fact that the intragroup variability concerning parenting strategies is substantially smaller than in Western middle-class contexts (Lamm and Keller 2007).

Family in this context means a hierarchical system of roles and responsibilities that define the relational pattern of the family. Families represent social systems in which the individual cannot define him- or herself without reference to others. "I am because we are" is a proverb that is popular in many African communities.

The image of the child is that of an apprentice, who needs to be primed for hierarchical relatedness. Nsamenang (1992) reports for sub-Saharan Africa that the major developmental task of infancy is social priming. The baby is seen as more or less passive and simply has to learn to adapt to the requirements of the society. These characteristics of infants are shaped through pragmatic training, apprentice-like in nature (Nsamenang 1992), and responsive control, consisting of bodily closeness while monitoring, instructing, training, directing, and controlling the infant's activities (Yovsi et al. 2009). This training starts early: LeVine and colleagues (1994) observed that Kenyan Gusii mothers are keenly aware to train children for their future roles as soon as they are deemed capable of understanding instructions. These authors labeled this parenting style as pediatric; the goal of the pediatric model is protection through soothing, which the mother meets by following cultural scripts for maternal attention including response to distress, modulating excitement, and commands.

The experience of being a part of a relational network means that babies are never at the center of attention and experience only rare moments of exclusive dyadic attention directed toward them. They are part of all ongoing everyday activities. Caregiving is co-occurring (Saraswathi and Pai 1997) through lived multitasking. The parenting strategy is proximal, i.e., the major parenting systems are body contact and body stimulation. Babies are almost always attached to the bodies of their caregivers: in the lap, on the back, or at the hip. This kind of bodily proximity implies synchronizing of movements and rhythms. Babies experience rhythmical body stimulation also, together with rhythmical vocal/verbal communication, which support the experience of communality and relatedness instead of emphasizing separateness and individuality (Rothbaum et al. 2000; Gratier 2003; Keller et al. 2008). Contingency is expressed bodily also, as Bambi Chapin (2013) has analyzed with Sri Lankan families. Bodily contingency is communicated through behavioral channels rather than distal (visual/vocal).

Another means of blurring the ego boundaries (Rothbaum et al. 2000) is prompt or even anticipatory responses to negative signals, mainly with breast-feeding. In general, the expression of negative emotionality is prevented since it may indicate potentially dangerous health problems (Keller 2007). Moreover the expression of emotionality is generally not esteemed because emotional expressiveness is rather an instantiation of individuality instead of a demonstration of communality. Therefore children learn from early on to control their emotions. Hiltrud Otto (2008) has demonstrated with Northwest Cameroonian Nso farmer families that many one-year-old children do not show distress when a stranger approaches them; a pattern that mothers highly value is "a good child is a calm child" (see also Gottlieb 2004 for a discussion of stranger anxieties from a cultural point of view).

Verbal conversations are instructions, telling the baby what to do and what not to do. Questions are rare, as is praise. A typical conversation may look like the following excerpt from a mother's conversation with her three-month-old baby:

(Mother talks to others, smiles and arranges the child's clothes.)
"Clap your hands." (Mother talks to others. When child vocalizes,
 Mother shakes child's arms and smiles.)
"Ting ting ting ting."
"Ting ting ting ting."
"Ting ting ting ting."
(Mother lifts child from the arms up and down.) "Up ! Down! Up! Down!"
(Child vocalizes; Mother talks to others).
(Mother shakes the hands of the child.) "Clap your hands oh!"
(Mother shaking the hands of the child together.) "Shake your waist oh.
Be dancing faay!" (Mother talks to others.)

It is apparent that the conversational structure and style are quite different from the Western middle-class scenario. The conversation with the child consists of brief instructions and descriptions of actually occurring behavior. The mother is simultaneously engaged in a lot of other social activities while she is interacting with the baby. This caregiving arrangement implies that babies are also never alone (Keller 2013). They are integrated in multiple caregiving arrangements (Weisner 2014), within which the mother may or may not play a special role (Otto and Keller 2014). Other caregivers often include siblings, aunts, and uncles as well as other relatives living in the household and neighbors. Fathers are often not actively involved in caretaking during infancy; their role is rather to grant physical and economic security (Lamm and Keller 2012). However, boys are caregivers until they become initiated into the male societies, with accompanying gender segregation.

Part of the apprenticeship model is practical training of the infant, especially in areas where the acceleration of developmental achievements is highly esteemed. For these infants, mothers do not seek to discover the infant's inner world or augment a sense of a separate self, but instead seek to develop action competencies, especially the training of gross motor skills. These skills—in particular sitting, standing, walking—are trained in interactional situations through motor stimulation of the infant's body but also through specially designed training units, like sitting in holes or containers and walking between poles or with special devices (see figure 7.2).

These modes of motor training also seem to confirm cultural continuity, since anthropologists from the 1950s on have documented very similar practices (Super 1976). Also, migrants seem to preserve this particular mode of parenting, as Cecilia Carra and collaborators (2013) have demonstrated with Northwest African migrants in Northern Italy.

The early motor competences support the acquisition of early action autonomy, which allows even young children to independently contribute to the family functioning with doing chores, running errands, and minding siblings and relatives. Different researchers have observed one-year-old children manipulating machetes with the full consent and even support of the family (e.g., Hiltrud Otto for the Cameroonian Nso, Dan Everett for the Piraha Indians in the Brazilian virgin forest, and Barry Hewlett for the Ngandu farmers in Central Africa).

This image of the child and resulting parenting goals are grounded in the necessities of subsistence-based farming, which needs the unconditional cooperation of the family as a whole. Accompanying low degrees of formal education support an action- oriented attitude, which is based in the here and now of duties and responsibilities. Mul-

FIGURE 7.2 A Cameroonian Nso mother playing with her three-month-old infant daughter, providing her with extensive motor experiences.

tiple caregiving arrangements and co-occurring care socialize children into the network of responsibilities in order to fulfill their place in the family hierarchy.

The Non-Western Middle-Class View of Infants

Non-Western middle-class families form a much more heterogeneous cultural context than the Western middle-class and the subsistence-farming communities. Accordingly, images of the child and children's learning environments are more diverse. Moreover, there is much less research concerning infants and infancy among these families than in the two other cultural environments. Non-Western middle-class families coordinate autonomy and relatedness for the socialization of their children in manifold ways, including the combining of seemingly contradictory dimensions from a Western perspective. The high degree of formal education primes an emphasis on psychological autonomy; however, this can have either an individual or a communal focus and can be combined with psychological relatedness as well as with hierarchical relatedness.

Educated non-Western urban middle-class families raise their children in multigenerational networks that are smaller than the rural joint households but definitely larger than the Western two-generation nuclear families. Larger social networks are associated with lived interpersonal responsibilities (Chaudhary 2004; Miller and Bersoff 1992; Miller, Bersoff, and Harwood 1990; Miller and Luthar 1989; Wang and Chaudhary 2005). Reports from Indian Hindu, Chinese, Japanese and Korean, Costa Rican, and Brazilian middle-class families have shown that interpersonal relations and helping others are understood in moral terms. The sense of objective obligation is based in the perception of maturity and personal fulfillment owing to an intrinsic and obligatory perspective on relationships that is in contrast with the voluntary approach to social relationships that is stressed in Western urban middle-class contexts. At the same time, non-Western middle-class families place much more emphasis on psychological autonomy than do lower-class families or families from subsistence-based backgrounds. This is attributable to their high level of education and the fact that their occupations require flexibility and self-determination (Raman 2003; Sinha and Tripathi 1994; Verma and Saraswathi 2002). Thus children are encouraged to be independent and assertive as well as respectful and sensitive to others.

The parenting strategies concerning babies are a combination of the proximal and distal styles in numerous possible combinations. There may be equal amounts of distal parenting as in Western middle-class families combined with equal amounts of proximal parenting as in rural farmer families. There may be also less body contact and body stimulation than in the rural farmer families and less face-to-face contact and object play than in the Western middle-class families. And there may be differences and similarities in individual parenting systems (Keller 2007). However, the quantitative analyses of things like body contact and object play do not fully recognize the dynamics of parenting strategies. Similar behavioral strategies may be rooted in completely different meaning systems. For example, extended face-to-face contact may be regarded as a scenario for training and health checks rather than a channel for establishing a psychological relationship (Keller 2007).

A particular style of parenting in Southeast Asian middle-class families has recently been the subject of vivid discussion in scientific outlets as well as parents' blogs. Based on Amy Chua's *Battle Hymn of the Tiger Mother* (2011), tiger parenting has sparked very controversial reactions (see also special issue of the *Asian American Journal of Psychology*, Juang, Qin, and Park 2013). Tiger parenting is defined as highly controlling and authoritarian, requiring unquestioning child obedience in order to bring the best achievements out of the child. However, there seems to be substantial interindividual variability, since Kim and colleagues (2013) report that only 20 percent of their study with participants of Asian heritage practiced tiger parenting. In any case, the principles of tiger parenting are rooted in hierarchical relatedness. Chua may have exaggerated the strategy, as do many Western middle-class parents with their autonomy education. The image of the child in non-Western educated families may be manifold. Nevertheless, obedience and respect are crucial components, whereas individuality and its concomitants may vary.

Implications for Application and Policy

Although the evidence for cultural pathways of development is substantial, this knowledge is rarely translated into applied programs in the clinical/counseling or the educational fields. This is particularly pertinent to the situation of migrants in Western societies. The vast majority of migrants in Western societies come from rural non-Western villages with a socialization agenda directed toward hierarchical relatedness. The inevitable confrontation with Western ideology often results in distrust, withdrawal, and rejection. Thus, services that could be potentially beneficial are not at all targeted, since they adhere to an ideology that families consider as harmful and detrimental. Especially the lack of emphasis on respect and the apparent support of individuality and expression of feelings and opinions are regarded as harmful to children's development and well-being (Keller 2011, 2013).

This problem has even wider implications, since transnational programs in the domain of ECCE (Early Childhood Care and Education), as supported by the major funding organizations like WHO, UNICEF, and others, also follow to a large extent the Western philosophy without reflecting the applicability in non-Western contexts. The following example is based in a real need situation and demonstrates the culturally insensitive—and therefore largely ineffective but nevertheless expensive—investments.

Worldwide, breast-feeding is considered the optimal nutritional asset for infants during the first months of life. However, practices of breast-feeding may be differently beneficial, especially in environments of starvation and poverty. In a UNICEF-sponsored study in Liberia, Yovsi et al. (2010) found that strong beliefs persist—especially among ethnic groups predominant in southeastern Liberia—that prelacteal feeds, including water, are necessary for health and social reasons. As a result, beginning breast-feeding is sometimes delayed by several days and therefore puts infants in dangerous situations.

Since adequate breast-feeding support for mothers and families could save many young lives, international organizations like WHO and UNICEF support policy recommendations and intervention programs promoting breast-feeding. Most of those programs are based on Western middle-class standards of parenting and child care that stress exclusiveness between mother and baby and face-to-face positions to create the special bond that is deemed necessary for healthy development. However, Yovsi et al. (2010) found strong contraindications against exclusive breast-feeding in rural Nigerian women, coupled with the view that exclusive breast-feeding represents a Western practice that is considered inappropriate.

In a recent UNESCO paper in the Early Childhood Care and Education Working Papers Series, Serpell and Nsamenang (2014) make a strong plea for ECCE initiatives in rural areas to build on the strengths of indigenous cultures by respecting their meaning systems and adapting their demonstrably beneficial practices. They especially address the situation in Africa, which certainly has some similarities with other indigenous conceptions. They report on indigenous games and songs as a neglected fund of knowledge for the enrichment of ECCE curricula and child-to-child educational strategies. They also note the importance of the use of indigenous languages as reflecting cultural practices and resources, thus promising greater benefit to health and education. Serpell and Nsamenang (2014) in their thoughtful analysis pose questions such as: "Does modern science really show that the current practices of middle-class, cosmopolitan Western families are (a) superior in effectiveness to the traditional practices of rural African communities, and (b) transposable into low-income African communities without disturbing the prevailing sociocultural system, threatening the psychological well-being of parents and undermining their confidence in their own parenting skills?" (20).

These questions were not posed before Western psychology was applied worldwide. However, in the fields of application and policy, readiness for a change is also dawning.

Conclusion

I have portrayed three different cultural milieus that hold rather different images of infancy and infants. It is important to stress that the generalizations described here do not capture all the variability on this planet, particularly that relating to sociodemographic parameters and economic bases. For example, it has been demonstrated that foragers (Aka, Fulani) differ from farmers (Ngandu, Nso) in their caretaking strategies and primary care systems with babies (Hewlett 1991; Yovsi and Keller 2011) and it may be that with further research a fourth ideal type or image of infancy for the forager-family milieu may emerge. Therefore there is evidence that parenting strategies vary with the economic system of the family. Religion, which is often related to family life in public discourses, did not have an influence on parenting and caregiving in our studies. For example, Indian Hindu farmers did not differ in their parenting practices from Nso Christians or Muslim farmers (Keller 2007). Religiosity, i.e., the lived intensity of religious practices, certainly has an influence, so that highly religious people can be considered to differ in their parenting from secular ones, possibly no matter if they are Muslims, Christians, Jews, or belong to any other religion. This is certainly an arena for future research.

It is obvious that different socialization strategies are meaningful in their respective contexts because they are adapted to the moral world of the families and communities (Weisner 1998, 2002). There is an internal consistency between socialization goals, ethnotheories, and parenting practices that inform children about the social world with their specific standards, conventions, and norms in which they live. Even so, cultures are not static entities. Cultures are dynamic systems that change with environmental change. Cultural change in parenting infants has been demonstrated with respect to historical change associated with higher educational achievements (Keller and Lamm 2005; Greenfield 2009), generational change (Lamm et al. 2008), as well as contextual change associated, e.g., with migration (Carra et al. 2013). While the dimensions of autonomy and relatedness are still prevalent in parenting, they also transform and change their meaning with shifting socioeconomic factors.

In order to assess continuity and change in socialization strategies and children's learning environments, longitudinal as well as cross-sectional research strategies need to be further employed as well as ethnographic field observations and interviews. For our studies, using these mixed methods mattered because the different layers of socialization strategies, i.e., socialization goals, parenting ethnotheories, and behavioral contexts and practices cannot be fully understood with the same methodological repertoire. We found it especially fruitful to combine methods that originate from different research paradigms that sometimes are considered incompatible (Reese and Overton 1970). This kind of triangulation is especially important for understanding children's developmental trajectories: the quantitative analysis of interactional experiences as observed in everyday situations is incomplete without the subjective meaning systems attached to the behaviors. Only with a multilevel design and mixed method strategies can all the information necessary be amassed for the understanding of images of infancy and their impact on children's development.

References

Ainsworth, Mary D. Salter, Mary C. Blehar, Everett Waters, and Sally Wall. 1978. *Patterns of Attachment: A Psychological Study of the Strange Situation.* Hillsdale, NJ: Lawrence Erlbaum Associates.

Ainsworth, Mary D. Salter. (1969/2012). "Maternal Sensitivity Scales." Retrieved January 22, 2014, from http://www.psychology.sunysb.edu/attachment/ measures/content/ainsworth_scales.html.

Arnett, Jeffery J. 2008. "The Neglected 95%: Why American Psychology Needs to Become Less American." *American Psychologist* 63: 602–14.

Boyd, Robert, and Peter J. Richerson. 1985. *Culture and Evolutionary Process.* Chicago: University of Chicago Press.

Carra, Cecilia, Manuela Lavelli, Heidi Keller, and Joscha Kärtner. 2013. "Parenting Infants: Socialization Goals and Behaviors of Italian Mothers and Immigrant Mothers from West Africa." *Journal of Cross-Cultural Psychology* 44 (8):1304–20.

Chapin, Bambi L. 2013. "Attachment in Rural Sri Lanka: The Shape of Caregiver Sensitivity, Communication, and Autonomy." In *Attachment Reconsidered: Cultural Perspectives on a Western Theory,"* edited by N. Quinn and J. M. Mageo, 143–65. New York: Palgrave Macmillan.

Chaudhary, Nandita. 2004. *Listening to Culture: Constructing Reality from Everyday Talk.* New Delhi, India: Sage.

Chua, Amy. 2011. *Battle Hymn of the Tiger Mother.* New York: Penguin Press.

Crossley, Michele L. 2000. *Introducing Narrative Psychology: Self, Trauma and the Construction of Meaning.* Buckingham, UK: Open University Press.

Gottlieb, Alma. 2004. *The Afterlife Is Where We Come From.* Chicago: University of Chicago Press.

Gratier, Maya. 2003. "Expressive Timing and Interactional Synchrony between Mothers and Infants: Cultural Similarities, Cultural Differences, and the Immigration Experience." *Cognitive Development* 18: 533–54.

Greenfield, Patricia M. 2002. "The Mutual Definition of Culture and Biology in Development." In *Between Culture and Biology: Perspectives on Ontogenetic Development*, edited by Heidi Keller, Ype H. Poortinga, and Axel Scholmerich, 57–78. Cambridge: Cambridge University Press.

———. 2009. "Linking Social Change and Developmental Change: Shifting Pathways of Human Development." *Developmental Psychology* 45 (2): 401–18.

Greenfield, Patricia M., and Heidi Keller. 2004. "Cultural Psychology." In *Encyclopedia of Applied Psychology*, edited by Charles Spielberger, 545–53. Oxford, UK: Elsevier.

Greenough, William T., James E. Black, and Christopher S. Wallace. 1987. "Experience and Brain Development." *Child Development* 58: 539–59.

Henrich, Joseph, Steven J. Heine, and Ara Norenzayan. 2010. "The Weirdest People in the World?" *Behavioral and Brain Sciences* 33: 61–83.

Hewlett, B. S. (1991). "Demography and Childcare in Preindustrial Societies." *Journal of Anthropological Research* 47: 1–37.

James, William. 1890. *The Principles of Psychology*, vol. 1. New York: Holt.

Juang, Linda P., Desiree Baolin Qin, and Irene J. K. Park. 2013. "Tiger Parenting, Asian-Heritage Families, and Child/Adolescent Well-Being." Special Issue of the *Asian American Journal of Psychology* 4 (1).

Kağitçibaşi, Çigdem. 2007. *Family, Self, and Human Development across Cultures: Theories and Applications*. Mahwah, NJ: Lawrence Erlbaum Associates.

Keller, Heidi. 2003. "Socialization for Competence: Cultural Models of Infancy." *Human Development* 46 (5): 288–311.

———. 2007. *Cultures of Infancy*. Mahwah, NJ: Erlbaum.

———.2010. "Linkages between the Whiting Model and Contemporary Evolutionary Theory." *Journal of Cross-Cultural Psychology* 41 (4): 563–77.

———. 2011. "Biology, Culture and Development: Conceptual and Methodological Considerations." In *Fundamental Questions in Cross-Cultural Psychology*, edited by Fons J. R. van de Vijver, Athanasios Chasiotis, and Seger Breugelmans, 312–40. Cambridge: Cambridge University Press.

———. 2012. "Autonomy and Relatedness Revisited. Cultural Manifestations of Universal Human Needs." *Child Development Perspectives* 6 (1):12–18.

———. 2013. "Attachment and Culture." *Journal of Cross-Cultural Psychology* 44 (2): 175–94.

Keller, Heidi, and Irenäus Eibl-Eibesfeldt. 1989. "Concepts of Parenting: The Role of Eye-Contact in Early Parent-Child Interactions." In *Heterogeneity in Cross-Cultural Psychology*, edited by Daphne M. Keats, Donald Munro, and Leon Mann, 468–76. Amsterdam/Lisse: Swets and Zeitlinger.

Keller, Heidi, and Joscha Kärtner. 2013. "Development—The Cultural Solution of Universal Developmental Tasks." *Advances in Culture and Psychology*, vol. 3, edited by Michele J. Gelfand, Chi-yue Chiu, and Ying-yi Hong, 63–116. Oxford: Oxford University Press.

Keller, Heidi, and Bettina Lamm. 2005. "Parenting as the Expression of Sociohistorical Time: The Case of German Individualism." *International Journal of Behavioral Development* 29: 238–46.

Keller, H., and Hiltrud Otto. 2011. "Different Faces of Autonomy." In *Socioemotional Development in Cultural Context*, edited by Xinyin Chen and Kenneth H. Rubin, 164–85. New York: Guilford Press.

Keller, Heidi, Hiltrud Otto, Bettina Lamm, Relindis D. Yovsi, and Joscha Kärtner. 2008. "The Timing of Verbal/Vocal Communications between Mothers and Their Infants: A Longitudinal Cross-Cultural Comparison." *Infant Behavior and Development* 31: 217–26.

Kim, Su Yeong, Yijie Wang, Diana Orozco-Lapray, Yishan Shen, and Mohammed Murtuza. 2013. "Does 'Tiger Parenting' Exist? Parenting Profiles of Chinese Americans and Adolescent Developmental Outcomes." *Asian American Journal of Psychology* 4 (1): 7–18.

Lamb, Michael E., Marc H. Bornstein, and Douglas M. Teti. 2002. *Development in Infancy* (4th ed.). Mahwah, NJ: Erlbaum.

Lamm, B., H. Keller, Relindis D. Yovsi, and Nandita Chaudhary. 2008. "Grandmaternal and Maternal Ethnotheories about Early Child Care." *Journal of Family Psychology* 22 (1): 80–88.

Lamm, Bettina. 2008. "Children's Ideas about Infant Care: A Comparison of Rural Nso Children from Cameroon and German Middle-Class Children." PhD diss., University of Osnabrück. http://repositorium.uni-osnabrueck .de/handle/urn:nbn:de:gbv:700-2008080129

Lamm, Bettina, and Heidi Keller. 2007. "Understanding Cultural Models of Parenting: The Role of Intracultural Variation and Response Style." *Journal of Cross-Cultural Psychology* 38 (1): 50–57.

———. 2012. "Väter in Verschiedenen Kulturen [Fathers in Different Cultures]." In *Das Väter-Handbuch*, edited by Heinz Walter and Andreas Eickhorst, 77–88. Gießen: Psychosozial-Verlag.

LeVine, Robert A. 1977. "Child Rearing as Cultural Adaptation." In *Culture and Infancy: Variables in the Human Experience*, edited by P. Herbert Leiderman, Steven R. Tulkin, and Anne Rosenfeld, 15–27. New York: Academic Press.

LeVine, Robert A., Suzanne Dixon, Sarah LeVine, Amy Richman, P. Herbert Leiderman, Constance H. Keefer, and T. Berry Brazelton. 1994. *Childcare and Culture: Lessons from Africa*. New York: Cambridge University Press.

MacDonald, Kevin B. 1988. *Social and Personality Development: An Evolutionary Synthesis*. New York: Plenum Press.

Mampe, Birgit, Angela D. Friederici, Anne Christophe, and Kathleen Wermke. 2009. "Newborns' Cry Melody Is Shaped by Their Native Language." *Current Biology* 19 (23): 1994–97.

Markus, Hazel Rose, and Alana Conner. 2013. *Clash! 8 Cultural Conflicts That Make Us Who We Are*. New York: Hudson Street Press.

Markus, Hazel R., and Shinobu Kitayama. 1991. "Culture and the Self: Implications for Cognition, Emotion, and Motivation." *Psychological Review* 98 (2): 224–53.

Martin, Robert D. 1983. *Human Brain Evolution in An Ecological Context: Fifty-Second James Arthur Lecture.* New York: American Museum of Natural History.

Miller, Joan G., and David M. Bersoff. 1992. "Culture and Moral Judgment: How Are Conflicts between Justice and Interpersonal Responsibilities Resolved?" *Journal of Personality and Social Psychology* 62: 541–54.

Miller, Joan G., David M. Bersoff, and Robin Harwood. 1990. "Perceptions of Social Responsibilities in India and in the United States: Moral Imperatives or Personal Decisions?" *Journal of Personality and Social Psychology* 58 (1): 33–47.

Miller, Joan G., and Sundanda Luthar. 1989. "Issues of Interpersonal Responsibility and Accountability: A Comparison of Indians' and Americans' Moral Judgments." *Social Cognition* 7 (3): 237–61.

Miller, Peggy J., and Lisa Hoogstra. 1992. "Language as Tool in the Socialization and Apprehension of Cultural Meanings." In *New Directions in Psychological Anthropology*, edited by Theodore Schwartz, Geoffrey M. White, and Catherine A. Lutz, 83–101. Cambridge: Cambridge University Press.

Nelson, Charles A. 2005. "Neuroscience and Developmental Psychology: An Arranged Marriage or a Marriage of Love?" Paper presented at the 17th Congress of the Developmental Psychology of the German Society for Psychology, Bochum, Germany, September.

Nsamenang, A. Bame. 1992. *Human Development in Cultural Context: A Third World Perspective.* Newbury Park, CA: Sage.

Otto, H. (2008). "Culture-Specific Attachment Strategies in the Cameroonian Nso: Cultural Solutions to a Universal Developmental Task." PhD diss., University of Osnabrueck, Osnabrueck, Germany.

Otto, Hiltrud, and Heidi Keller, eds. 2014. *Different Faces of Attachment.* Cambridge: Cambridge University Press.

Prechtl, Heinz. 1984. *Continuity of Neural Functions from Prenatal to Postnatal Life.* London: Spastics International Medical Publications.

Raman, Vasanthi. 2003. "The Diverse Life-Worlds of Indian Childhood." In *Family and Gender: Changing Values in Germany and India*, edited by Margrit Pernau, Imtiaz Ahmad, and Helmut Reifeld, 84–111. New Delhi, India: Sage.

Reese, Hayne W., and Willis F. Overton. 1970. "Models of Development and Theories of Development." In *Life-Span Developmental Psychology: Research and Theory*, edited by Paul B. Baltes, Ulman Lindenburger, and Ursula M. Staudinger, 115–45. New York: Academic Press.

Rothbaum, Fred, Martha Pott, Hiroshi Azuma, Katzuo Miyake, and John Weisz. 2000. "The Development of Close Relationships in Japan and the United States: Paths of Symbiotic Harmony and Generative Tension." *Child Development* 71 (5): 1121–42.

Saraswathi, T.S., and Shefali Pai. 1997. "Socialization in the Indian Context." In *Asian Perspectives on Psychology*, edited by Henry S. R. Kao and Durganand Sinha, 74–92. New Delhi, India: Sage.

Serpell, Robert, and A. Bame Nsamenang. 2014. "Locally Relevant and Quality ECCE Programmes: Implications of Research on Indigenous African Child Development and Socialization." ECCE Working Papers Series. Paris: UNESCO.

Shweder, Richard A., and Edward J. Bourne.1984. "Does the Concept of a Person Vary Cross-Culturally?" In *Culture Theory: Essays on Mind, Self, and Emotion*, edited by Richard A. Shweder and Robert A. LeVine, 158–99. Cambridge: Cambridge University Press.

Sinha, Durganand, and Rama Charan Tripathi. 1994. "Individualism in a Collectivist Culture: A Case of Coexistence of Opposites." In *Individualism and Collectivism: Theory, Method, and Applications*, edited by Uichol Kim, Harry C. Triandis, Sang-Chin Choi, and Gene Yoon, 123–36. Thousand Oaks, CA: Sage.

Stern, William. 1923. *Psychologie der frühen Kindheit [Psychology of Early Childhood].* Leipzig, Germany: Quelle and Meyer.

Stone, Joseph, Henrietta Smith, and Lois Barclay Murphy. 1973. *The Competent Infant.* New York: Basic Books.

Storfer, Miles. 1999. "Myopia, Intelligence, and the Expanding Human Neocortex: Behavioral Influences and Evolutionary Implications." *International Journal of Neuroscience* 98: 153–276.

Super, Charles M. 1976. "Environmental Effects on Motor Development: A Case of African Infant Precocity." *Developmental Medicine and Child Neurology* 18: 561–67

Verma, Suman, and T. S. Saraswathi. 2002. "Adolescence in India: Street Urchins or Silicon Valley Millionaires." In *The World's Youth: Adolescence in Eight Regions of the Globe*, edited by B. Bradford Brown, Reed W. Larson, and T. S. Saraswathi, 105–40. Cambridge: Cambridge University Press.

Wang, Qi, and Nandita Chaudhary. 2005. "The Self." In *Psychological Concepts: An International Historical Perspective*, edited by Kurt Pawlik and Gery d'Ydewalle, 325–58. Hove, UK: Psychology Press.

Washburn, S. L. 1960. "Tools and Human Evolution." *Scientific American* 203 (Sept): 63–75.

Weisner, T S. 1998. "Human Development, Child Well-Being, and the Cultural Project of Development." *New Directions for Child Development* 81 (January): 69–85.

Weisner, Thomas S. 2002. "Ecocultural Understanding of Children's Developmental Pathways." *Human Development* 45: 275–81.

Weisner, Thomas S., ed. 2005. *Discovering Successful Pathways in Children's Development: Mixed Methods in the Study of Childhood and Family Life.* Chicago: University of Chicago Press.

———. 2010. "John and Beatrice Whiting's Contributions to the Cross-Cultural

Study of Human Development: Their Values, Goals, Norms, and Practices." *Journal of Cross-Cultural Psychology* 41 (4) (April 8): 499–509.

———. 2012. "Mixed Methods Should Be a Valued Practice in Anthropology." *Anthropology News* 53 (5): 3–4.

———. 2014. "The Socialization of Trust: Plural Caregiving and Diverse Pathways in Human Development across Cultures." In *Cultural Variations on a Universal Human Need: Different Faces of Attachment*, edited by Hiltrud Otto and Heidi Keller, 263–78. Cambridge: Cambridge University Press.

Whiting, John W. M. 1977. "A Model for Psychocultural Research." In *Culture and Infancy*, edited by P. Herbert Leiderman, Steven Tulkin, and Anne Rosenfeld, 29–47. New York: Academic Press.

Wilson, Edward O. 1975. *Sociobiology: A New Synthesis*. Cambridge, MA: Harvard University Press.

Yovsi, Relindis D., Joscha Kärtner, Heidi Keller, and Arnold Lohaus. 2009. "Maternal Interactional Quality in Two Cultural Environments: German Middle Class and Cameroonian Rural Mothers." *Journal of Cross-Cultural Psychology* 40: 701–07.

Yovsi, Relindis D., and Heidi Keller. 2011. "Breastfeeding: An Adaptive Process." *Childhood: A Global Journal of Child Research* 31 (2): 147–71.

Yovsi, Relindis D., Kinday Sambo, Benson Barh, and Genevieve Barrow. 2010. *A Qualitative Study of Maternal and Newborn Care Practices in Liberia*. Monrovia, Liberia: MOHSW-UNICEF.

Notes

1. This does not, of course, preclude that culture is already expressed and powerful prenatally in pregnancy customs, food prescriptions, and the like.

EIGHT

Beyond the Randomized Control Trial: Mixed Methods That Matter for Children's Healthy Development in Cultural Context

SARA HARKNESS AND CHARLES M. SUPER

On March 12, 2014, David Greene interviewed Ronald Kessler of Harvard Medical School on National Public Radio about the outcomes of an experimental program to move single mothers and their young children (aged three to eight years) out of public housing in the inner city and into more affluent areas in the suburbs (Greene 2014). The federally funded study—known as Moving to Opportunity—of which Professor Kessler was a principal investigator, was designed as a randomized control trial (RCT), the current gold standard of intervention research. The hope was that these young families would thrive in a more favorable environment where both job prospects and a good education would be easier to access. Unfortunately however, a follow-up study (Kessler et al. 2014) found mixed results: although the move appeared to be beneficial for girl children, it was associated with negative results for boys, who were more depressed, had more conduct problems, and were more likely to suffer from post-traumatic stress syndrome than did boys in the control group who were not relocated.

As interviewer, David Greene wanted to know why. In response to this question, Professor Kessler explained that the answer was not that easy, given the research design and methods. As he put it, "Well, it's important to say at the onset that the experiment's job was to see would there be effects, does neighborhood make a difference? And we showed experimentally that it clearly does. Why the effect exists is not something the experiment was designed to give us definitive evidence for."

Kessler continued, "However, we were fortunate that we had fieldworkers go into the neighborhoods, observe what was going on; and they have some insights into why they think these differences [between results for girls and boys] exist." As he further explained, the fieldworkers noticed that "little girls were embraced by the neighborhoods and seemed to have better interpersonal skills, whereas the boys somehow were thought to be a threat by the community, so they were pushed away and in fact, in some cases, had worse things happen to them." Kessler concluded that "the kinds of qualitative evidence that our research team came up with" suggested that the boys "couldn't make a really good adjustment," but again cautioned, "We just don't know because it wasn't one of the things we had prepared ourselves for at the beginning." He added that in the future, it would be important for public housing funds—currently $37 billion a year—to include programs "that help these new families integrate optimally into better neighborhoods" rather than "just using that money to put a roof over someone's head. . . ."

Many comments about this interview could be made (and in fact were sent in by listeners), including about why boys suffering from post-traumatic stress syndrome should be blamed for not "adjusting well" to their new neighborhoods, and what this says about racism in the United States—assuming, probably correctly, that the families from the inner city were mainly African American, whereas the residents of the suburbs were mainly white. From a research perspective, however, the interview was startling in its apparent disregard of methodological problems in both the original design and the eventual interpretation of results. To plan a project of this size focused simply on *whether* the intervention made a difference on average, without systematically investigating *why* it did (or did not) and *for* whom, seems dramatically short-sighted. To then rely on the personal impressions of fieldworkers as "qualitative evidence" only compounds the problem. The results of the study—beneficial effects for girls, adverse effects for boys—are no more complex than might have been anticipated for an ecological intervention of this magnitude, yet after spending millions of dollars on the study (as well as on the intervention itself), the researchers apparently had nothing more than anecdotal evidence to answer the fundamental questions that should have been addressed at the outset.

Unfortunately the dictates of "rigorous" scientific research typically mandate just this. The result is that conclusions about the meaning of the results are left largely to speculation, with no guidance on how the program in question might be modified to produce better results and, at a minimum, how it might avoid doing harm to the participating families and their children. It also seems likely that a more comprehensive approach, using a mixture of methods, would significantly reduce program costs in the long run.

In this chapter, we consider the usefulness of mixed methods for both basic and applied research about children's development in cultural context in order to address the basic question of what aspects of children's environments matter and how they interact together to support (or detract from) healthy development. Using the theoretical framework of the "developmental niche" as a guide, we examine the ways that methods from several academic traditions can be combined, illustrating with both our own cross-cultural research as it has developed over the course of our careers and mixed methods studies of interventions by ourselves and others. The chapter, part personal narrative and part critique, will include a revisit to the study introduced earlier, where some methodological surprises await. We conclude that the use of mixed methods is essential for applied research that addresses the complexities of what happens when new programs or interventions are introduced to groups of people, going beyond the "whether" question to consider how it works, under what circumstances, in what ways, and for what people. Taking this approach, researchers and their community and implementation partners can produce findings that are actually useful for both program improvement and for increasing our understanding of human behavior and development in context—in short, mixed methods in are indeed "methods that matter" for both science and practice.

Mixed Methods: An Old and New Construct

Our own use of mixed methods has spanned several decades, beginning with our graduate training in the 1970s under John and Beatrice Whiting, Jerome Kagan, and others associated with the Department of Social Relations at Harvard at that time—an historical high point of interdisciplinary cross-fertilization and collaboration (see LeVine, chapter 1). In that environment, it seemed only natural to draw from methods in both psychology and anthropology for the construction of field research designs. Thus, our three years of research (from 1972 to 1975) in a rural Kipsigis village of western Kenya incorporated a wide array of tools, including household surveys, ethnographic and semistructured interviews, systematic behavior observations, recordings of naturalistic child language, and standardized developmental tests. In one example of what is now recognized as mixed methods research, we combined an examination of children's behavior in a cognitive testing situation with what we had learned through our research on the speech environments of young children in that community. Specifically, children's apparent inability to retell a simple story to a local adult tester turned out to be more a matter of how this routine violated sociolinguistic norms than a true measure of the children's ability to remember the story; in one instance, for example, a child who had been unable to respond to the tester recounted the story accurately to his sibling later at home. Other research on child language socialization that we were carrying out at the same time showed that, as we concluded (Harkness and Super 1977/2008), culturally based goals for child language development were directed more toward the acquisition of comprehension than of speech production.

Of course, we were not unique in this eclectic approach. As psychologists Bartholemew and Brown (2012) have recently noted:

Mixing methods is not new. Seminal researchers like Jean Piaget used a combination of observations, quasi-experiments, and interviews to investigate children's thought and development (Müller, Carpendale, and Smith 2009). Researchers have also used both qualitative and quantitative research across their careers. Whiting and Whiting (1975) used extensive observations and interviews to better understand childhood in the Six Cultures study. However, many of these studies were conducted before we thought about mixed methods as a "field of research" worthy of discussion in and of itself and before avenues of publication were available for the mixing of methods in a single study. (179)

In other words, from the perspective of mainstream psychology and related fields, it appears that the use of mixed methods was prehistorical in the sense that, although it existed, it was not recognized as such in the scientific literature on which psychology and other disciplines were being built.

Given our own background in the "prehistoric" use of mixed methods, it came as a surprise to discover more recently that "mixed methods" is now regarded as innovative and in fact controversial, engaging the "paradigm wars" between the positivist or empiricist model on one side, and the constructivist or phenomenological model on the other (Tashakkori and Teddlie 2008, 7), even as it attempts to build bridges between them. In this conflict, quantitative methods ("designed to collect numbers") are often seen as unbiased and objective, whereas qualitative methods ("designed to collect words") tend to be seen as subjective and thus vulnerable to personal biases (Caracelli and Greene 1993, 232). Tashakkori and Teddlie (2008) have traced the historical development of mixed methods approaches in the social and behavioral sciences from the 1950s to the present, showing how various combinations of qualitative and quantitative data have been used together or sequentially during various phases of a study or research program. Relatedly, as described by Bartholemew and Brown (2012), several typologies of mixed methods research designs have been developed. However, these authors do not discuss which particular methods—for example, observations, questionnaires, interviews, tests—have been actually used in these models.

In reality, the distinction between qualitative and quantitative methods can be difficult to maintain, since the collection of numbers usually involves words (whether in a questionnaire or in the context of an observation), and data consisting of words can be represented in the form of numbers. Our working assumption has been that all quantities refer to some quality, and all qualities can be present to some quantifiable degree (Harkness et al. 2006, 8). The use of mixed methods in our collaborative international research has been essential for our efforts to understand local meanings, for incorporating culturally distinctive constructs into frameworks that enable comparison across cultures, and for establishing a higher level of confidence that we "got it right"—with the caveat that there is always more to learn. In this chapter, we illustrate the development and application of mixed methods with reference to a series of cross-cultural studies of parents and children. This process was informed by the theoretical framework of the developmental niche (Super and Harkness 1986), whose structure lends itself readily to the incorporation of a variety of methodological approaches.

The Developmental Niche and Mixed Methods

The developmental niche is a theoretical framework for the integration of concepts and findings from multiple disciplines concerned with the development of children in cultural context (Harkness and Super 1992b; Super and Harkness 1986, 1999). We had originally developed this construct to deal with both the variability and thematicity evident in the multiple studies that we carried out on child development and family life in a Kipsigis village of Kenya in the 1970s (Harkness 1987, 1990; Harkness and Super 1977/2008, 1983, 1985a, 1985b, 1985c, 1987, 1992a, 1992b; Super 1976, 1983, 1991; Super and Harkness 1974, 1982, 1986, 1994a, 2009; Super, Harkness, and Baldwin 1977; Super, Keefer, and Harkness 1994). Two overarching principles reflect the influences of cultural anthropology—especially the seminal work of John and Beatrice Whiting—and developmental psychology (e.g., Bell 1968): First, that a child's environment is organized in a nonarbitrary manner as part of a cultural system; and second, that the child's own disposition, including a particular constellation of attributes, temperament, skills, and potentials, affects the process of development.

At the center of the developmental niche (see figure 8.1) is the individual child. In one sense, the niche can be described only for a single child in one cultural place, with his or her particular set of inherited characteristics (Super and Harkness 1994b). Nevertheless, the framework is equally useful in deriving a generalized description of recurring patterns characteristic of particular cultural communities. Surrounding the child are the three major subsystems of the developmental niche: (1) physical and social settings of the child's daily life; (2) customs and practices of care; and (3) the psychology of the caretakers. The physical and social settings in which the child lives provide a scaffold upon which daily life is constructed, including where, with whom, and in what activities the child is engaged. Culturally regulated customs and practices of child care are particularly meaningful activities that are repeated over time and embedded in the settings of the child's life. Many such customs or habits are so commonly used by members of the community and so thoroughly integrated into the larger culture that individuals need not particularly rationalize them. To members of the culture, they seem obvious and natural solutions to everyday problems, developmental requirements, or social needs; their cultural nature becomes evident only when viewed from an outsider's perspective or when challenged in practice. Often these customs express

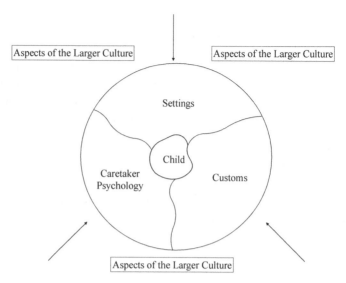

FIGURE 8.1 The Developmental Niche.

deeply held beliefs and related emotions about the nature of the child and about the proper functions of a good parent. Finally, the psychology of the caretakers includes both the emotional experience and the cultural beliefs of parents and others (for example, teachers or health care providers). In much of our more recent research, we have focused in particular on "parental ethnotheories," or cultural models of parenting and child development (Harkness and Super 1996). Like customs of care, parental ethnotheories are often implicit, taken-for-granted ideas, and they have strong motivational properties; ethnotheories are often related to each other both across domains and in hierarchical fashion.

The three subsystems of the developmental niche—settings, customs, and caretaker psychology—share the common function of mediating the child's developmental experience within the larger culture. Three corollaries of this basic framework specify further how it works in children's lives and what researchers should keep in mind.

First, the three components of the developmental niche operate together with powerful though incomplete coordination as a system. Thus, in an internally stable cultural environment, customs of care express or "instantiate" parental ethnotheories about the child, and they are further supported by the physical and social settings of daily life. Of course, the environments of children and their families are rarely completely consistent, but looking across the three subsystems of the niche tends to illuminate cultural themes that are found in multiple domains.

The second corollary of the developmental niche recognizes external sources of change, which may initially affect one subsystem in particular. For example, rapid economic and political change in China, including the one-child policy, quickly led to changes in the settings of children's daily lives, as large families were replaced by very small ones. This change has been associated in turn with changes in customs and practices of care, and probably with parental psychology. Thus change that directly affected one subsystem of the niche can have a cascade of effects on the other subsystems, as the whole system works to reestablish equilibrium.

Last but not least, the third corollary of the developmental niche reiterates the developmental principle that the child at the center of the niche plays an active role in its construction and change over time. Thus for example, parents may adapt customs of care to small children who have difficulty approaching new social situations, and the interactive parent-child relationships may consequently develop along particular paths as the child matures (see, e.g., Bernheimer, Gallimore, and Keogh, chapter 16).

The developmental niche framework lends itself readily to the use of mixed methods in research. The three components of the niche, in and of themselves, necessarily entail different kinds of data collection (Super and Harkness 1999). Measuring the physical and social settings of the child's life requires observation and documentation, which can be accomplished in a variety of ways including participant observation, observations of the child's activities at various times of day, or activity logs created by a family member or outside observer to map the child's activities and settings. Customs, likewise, can be observed; in fact, they are sometimes identified through observations of the child's physical and social settings. Learning about the meaning of customs—whether daily practices such as cosleeping or more formalized customs related to the celebration of holidays—can best be accomplished through a combination of observation and interviews, in which parents or other caretakers can be asked to explain the custom (the naive outsider as interviewer is particularly useful for this situation). Last, parental ethnotheories and other aspects of the psychology of the caretakers are most readily accessed through talk, including interviews, focus group discussions, or other verbal modalities; or questionnaires derived from them; or finally from more formal cognitive methods such as similarity judgments and multidimensional scaling (Harkness and Super 1992c; Weller and Romney 1988).

Thus if we strive to understand children's lives in a way that takes into account the cultural systems in which they are embedded, as well as the particularities and processes of their development, multiple kinds of methods must be utilized. Further, if we want to be able to address *why* questions about human development in real-world contexts—as the Kessler study cited at the beginning of this chapter begs—the scope of inquiry necessitates a mixture of methods.

Mixed Methods in the Study of Parenting Beliefs and Practices: A Personal Journey

In the years that followed our studies in Kenya, we carried out research with US parents back home, focusing increasingly on the culturally shared ideas that helped shape parenting practices and ultimately the course of children's development. The cumulative insights and research methods that came with them, in turn, laid the groundwork for our next research adventure in another culture.

As the calendar year rolled over from 1991 to 1992, we and our four children (aged seven to eighteen years) arrived in the Netherlands for a semester-long stay in a Dutch village that we refer to as "Bloemenheim," in recognition of its location in the bulb-growing district between Leiden and The Hague, with an academic base provided by the Faculty of Social and Behavioral Sciences, Leiden University. The scientific purpose of the visit was to carry out a comparative cross-cultural study of the construction, expression, and developmental implications of parental ethnotheories as key elements in the transmission of cultural knowledge. Through replication and extension of our earlier research on American parents (Harkness, Super, and Keefer 1992), this new study was intended to advance knowledge about how middle-class parents in Western postindustrial societies create cultural understandings of their children, how they communicate these to children, and how characteristics of individual children (especially age, sex, and temperament) affect parents' cultural belief systems.

A more specific rationale for the project concerned the paucity of information on cultural variations in parental thinking and practice among urbanized Western societies—then as now these societies are largely undifferentiated in the developmental literature, especially regarding educated middle-class families. We believed, to the contrary, that there is rich variability among Western cultures, and furthermore that the socioeconomic similarities among them would be helpful for applying lessons learned there to issues in parenting and education in the United States. In addition we hoped that this research would contribute to the development of systematic methods for studying parental ethnotheories in action in a variety of cultural contexts.

Constructing a Study Sample in the Netherlands

Our previous research with American parents had shown that cultural models of parenting are constructed in the process of becoming a parent, and they are elaborated in relation to the challenges of parenting children of various ages (Harkness, Super, and Keefer 1992). Based on this premise and following the structure of that research sample, we recruited a group of sixty families living in Bloemenheim. The town center, accessible by bicycle and by foot (and by car if one were willing to search for one of the few available parking spaces), consisted of tightly clustered, mostly two-story buildings containing specialty shops for breads, cakes, fish, vegetables, cheeses and wine, as well as a couple of small supermarkets. Clothing stores, a few restaurants and cafes, flower shops, a hardware/household shop, a travel agency, and a bicycle shop added to the variety of storefronts, with a church and a children's park located at the epicenter. The town center was completely occupied once a week by a street market that rotated among several towns, where one could buy not only foods and fresh flowers but also clothing, housewares, and even Dutch lace for the customary window dressings.

The local elementary school our seven-year-old son attended—the oldest of the town's schools—sat solidly on the main street that wound its way past the town center. Other, newer schools (all public, but connected to various religious denominations) were located in other neighborhoods close by. Our son's school, and in particular one of the mothers in his class who had extensive international experience as a flight attendant, became the starting point for sample recruitment following the snowball method. We were fortunate that within a short time, we were able to construct the full sample of families, with groups of twelve families (balanced for sex and birth order of the "target" child) at each of five age points to match our US study (six months, eighteen months, thirty-six months, 4.5 years, and seven-eight years of age). All families were broadly middle-class native Dutch, with at least one parent employed outside the home and no major health issues. Despite these shared characteristics, the sample was in some ways quite diverse, including bankers and bakers and bulb farmers among the fathers, and nurses, teachers, housekeepers, and full-time homemakers among the mothers. We made no attempt to control for mothers' employment, but found that in fact the great majority of mothers worked no more than half-time (including teachers, who shared a single classroom).

Variants of this approach to sample construction, as well as other strategies, were later used by our international team of colleagues to construct comparative samples in identifiable populations of five other countries (Italy, Spain, Sweden, Poland, Australia) and a new sample centered in northeast Connecticut for a study focused on parental ethnotheories and children's transition from home to school (the International Study of Parents, Children, and Schools: ISPCS). Each cultural site was specified by its particular location (e.g., a town or city) within the broader cultural context of its home country. For the ISPCS, a corresponding sample of teachers was constructed based on the ages and locations of children in the sample. The question of how generalizable the findings from these community-based samples might be to their home country was not at issue in this research; rather, we sought to study and compare a small number of definable "cultural places" within Europe and the British diaspora that were each located within broader parameters of shared history, social structure, and ways of life. Readers of the findings from these places would thus be able to make their own judgments of how typical they were of the larger nation-state where they were located. In short, our research strategy was cross-*cultural* (taking advantage of cultural boundaries created by the countries in which our study communities were located) rather than cross-*national* (attempting to compare aspects of parenting across nations as a whole).

Developing a Repertoire of Mixed Methods

Our set of methods for both the first Dutch study (and its American predecessor) and the later ISPCS samples was based on the developmental niche framework. Physical and social settings, the first subsystem of the niche, were documented through seven-day "parental diaries," structured as a log of activities, locations, and persons present, as these changed over the course of the day. Parents were instructed to begin a new line each time any of these aspects changed. Thus, the first line of a parental diary kept by the parents of a Dutch three-year-old girl notes the time she gets up (7:00) and her first activity of the day—a shower with her father. The next line of this child's diary notes a new time (7:30) and location (at the dining table in the family living room), and a new cast of characters: Marja's mother, father, seven-year-old sister, and five-year-old brother. The diary takes us, line by line, through the settings and activities of Marja's day, including accompanying her mother while taking her older siblings to school and picking them up, playing by herself at home and outside with neighborhood children, and finally an early evening supper and off to bed (see Harkness and Super 2012 for a fuller narrative).

The parental diaries proved to be useful for a variety of purposes, including analyses of time allocation to different locations, patterns of wake and sleep, and social and cognitive stimulation. They also provided the basic skeleton for an ethnographic portrayal of a particular child's day. Thus, for example, Marja's diary was easily transformed into a narrative that begins as follows:

Marja's day begins with a shower with Daddy at 7:00, followed by family breakfast with her mother, father, her seven-year-old sister, and her five-year-old brother. By 8:15, Marja's sister has left for school. It's just a 5-minute bike ride away and usually their mother rides with both children on their own bikes while Marja sits in her toddler seat on the back, but today Mother will take the car as Marja's brother is staying home with a cold. When they get back home, Marja plays in the living room counting pennies in her piggy bank, then goes out to ride her bike in the child-safe neighborhood streets. At the end of the morning, it's time to go back to school to pick up Marja's sister, along with a younger neighbor child who will spend the afternoon at their home. They all have lunch together, then at 1:00 Mother takes Marja's sister back to school and Marja to the "Children's Playroom," where children her age go for a couple of hours twice a week in order to get used to being in a group outside home, prior to entering school the following year. (Harkness and Super 2012, 498)

The parental diaries were also key to learning about customs and practices of care, the second subsystem of the developmental niche, in conjunction with semistructured parent interviews. The interviews were conducted with both parents together, in their home at a time convenient to them (generally the evening after the children were off to bed—which in the Dutch case usually meant by 7:30 p.m.). At the time of their interview, the parents had already filled out a week of diaries, following an earlier visit when the whole project was explained, informed consent was obtained, and parents received their packet of "homework." Thus in sitting down for the interview, we began with a review of the diaries and asked parents to tell us the story of one of the days they had documented. This provided an opportunity to learn about the practices that not only marked the portions of the child's day but also carried cultural meanings to parents. A brief look at Marja's day as described above suggests several features that were routine to families with young children in Bloemenheim: for example, the morning shower with Daddy, breakfast together as a family, riding a bicycle in the streets without immediate adult supervision, and the customary use of a preschool-like setting, explicitly for social rather than cognitive developmental purposes. As parents described these activities and settings, we asked them (taking a traditional ethnographic approach) to explain their significance or importance to us, the uninitiated visitors. Their answers to these questions helped us to learn not only about customs and practices of care, but also about the ideas and related feelings that shaped them—which, insofar as they turned out to be shared by more parents in our sample, represented parental ethnotheories, part of the third subsystem of the developmental niche.

Since parental ethnotheories were the core of the research, we wanted to know something about the sources of parents' ideas, so we asked about their memories of their parents as parents, in addition to exploring current sources of advice and support—we also explored the latter through a questionnaire that we constructed. We wanted to know about cultural models of the child, and we found, following Kohnstamm and associates' research on the "big five" personality factors (Kohnstamm et al. 1996), that asking parents to describe their child to someone like us who didn't actually know the child provided excellent evidence for what kinds of qualities parents chose to highlight about their child. Especially in the later ISPCS, we wanted to learn about parents' ideas regarding children's education, so we asked them how they thought they could help their child be successful in school, and what kinds of qualities they hoped for in their child's school. As the last question in the interview, we asked parents what they thought was most important for their child's development at that moment, and how they thought they could help. By the time we arrived at this summary question, parents had had a chance to reflect on various aspects of their parenting ideas and practices, and they often produced quite eloquent summary statements.

From a methodological point of view, the parent interviews in these studies were distinctive in several ways. First, it is more typical to interview parents individually rather than together, and in fact this was our initial choice with the American study. We soon found, however, that it was not convenient for these busy parents to find two separate occasions for each to be interviewed at home, and furthermore, they frequently referred to each other's opinions anyway. The interviews with parents together worked much better as a conversational format, and we made sure to get each parent's view on major points, counting on the relatively egalitarian relationships between spouses. Related to the conversational format of the interviews, we worked from a list of about ten questions but allowed the order to vary as it followed the parents' own line of talk. The interviews were tape-recorded and later transcribed in the original language. Coding systems were worked out collaboratively among members of the international team, with English used as the ultimate language of coding and analysis. In the two Dutch studies, the present authors carried out almost all the interviews, with the assistance of Dutch master's students at the University of Leiden, who participated in the project and wrote up parts of the results in fulfillment of degree requirements. Since we were just learning Dutch during the first visit, we adopted a mode of interviewing in which we asked our questions in English (which was mostly understood by these parents) but requested that they respond in Dutch. Having a native Dutch research assistant present made this conversationally feasible, and we in turn generally understood enough of what parents said to continue without frequent breaks for translations.

Other measures in both studies also related to the developmental niche framework. For example, demographic background questionnaires (including the parents' town of origin and international experience as well as education and occupation, and the composition of the household) provided information relevant to parental ethnotheories as well as basic knowledge about the physical and social settings of the child's daily life. Aspects of the parents' experience as parents were accessed through checklists on the backs of the daily diary sheets—for example, of contact with the extended family, with the child's school, and with other parents (in the second study), and of stresses and satisfactions related to parenting. In the ISPCS, parents also filled out a questionnaire rating a list of common descriptors (e.g., happy, persistent, strong-willed) in relation to their importance for children's success in school. The child's contribution to his or her own developmental niche (corollary three of the framework) was tapped through temperament questionnaires (Carey and McDevitt 1978) filled out by both parents. In addition, in the first Dutch study, a fine-grained recording of mother-infant interaction and infant behavior at six months of age was obtained through live coding of naturalistic observations at three different times of day.

Our mixed methods approach over the course of the first US study, followed by the comparative Dutch study and then the seven-culture collaborative International Study of Parents, Children, and Schools, provided a wealth of data that could be used in a variety of combinations to address not only our original questions but also other ones that came up during the course of the research—a process that was possible only with a truly collaborative and open approach to the formulation of research constructs and design (Harkness et al. 2006). Both the answers to original questions and the new questions resulted in the modification of previous methods and the addition of new ones in subsequent studies, a process that has continued to the present, making mixed methods a concept that can be thought of across as well as within individual research projects. In the following section, we describe one particular line of inquiry that started with the first Dutch study and that has been further developed in subsequent research, involving a series of both methodological and theoretical advances.

The Three R's of Dutch Child Rearing

It was not long after our arrival in Bloemenheim in the opening days of 1992 that we started learning from Dutch parents about the concept of the three R's as a guide to healthy child development. First appearing in print more than a century ago (van Hulst 1905) and long promulgated by the Dutch National Health Service's Consultation Bureau for families (Ten Hoopen 2005), the three R's—*rust* (rest), *regelmaat* (regularity), and *reinheid* (cleanliness) form a triad of principles that function together as a coherent cultural model with strong motivational properties. The parents in our study did not talk a lot about cleanliness—although they described the daily bath in some detail—but they were highly attentive to their children's need for a regular and restful daily (and nightly) routine. Sleep was described as important for physical growth, for avoiding fussiness and promoting a calm, positive mood and plenty of energy for enjoying each day. Indeed lack of sleep, a disruption of the normal routine, or too much stimulation were typically offered as explanations of the child's occasional negative behavior. We found these ideas and described practices fascinating, as they were a strong contrast to the concern with providing adequate stimulation for optimal development that we heard so much about from the US parents in both our earlier and subsequent studies (Harkness et al. 2007; Super et al. 1996). Without planning it ahead of time, we had stumbled on the perfect cultural counterpoint to prevailing American ethnotheories and practices—all within the bounds of the supposedly uniform Western world.

Our first published report on the three R's (coincidentally written during our second stay in Bloemenheim four years later) used several different methods to document the ethnotheory, related parenting practices, and aspects of infant behavior that could be interpreted as their developmental outcome (Super et al. 1996). The interviews provided detailed examples of how parents thought about the importance of rest and regularity as two intertwined ideas: as one mother of an eighteen-month-old said, "To bed on time, because they really need rest to grow, and regularity is very important when they are so little. If she gets too little rest, she is very fussy" (Super et al. 1996, 455). Systematic coding of several themes about sleep that parents described in the interviews, compared with our US parent interviews, showed marked differences in what these two groups of parents focused on. The US parents talked about their infants' and young children's sleep development as innately based, but often problematic for themselves as parents—something that might require special strategies to accelerate this natural process. The Dutch parents, in contrast, rarely talked about any of these ideas; instead, they focused their comments on the importance of sleep and even more, the negative sequelae if the child did not get enough.

Two other kinds of data showed how the Dutch three R's contrasted with the less consciously articulated ethnotheories and related practices of the American parents we had previously studied. First, analysis of parental diaries in both groups showed that the Dutch children were indeed getting more sleep than their American counterparts—two hours more at six months of age, gradually diminishing but not disappearing by the time the children were between four and five years of age. The Dutch children were going to bed a great deal earlier than the American children, a difference that again was most dramatic at the earliest age (with an average bedtime difference of almost two hours) but was maintained to the oldest group (still almost an hour). Analyses of the diaries also showed less variability within the Dutch group, as reflected in a measure of variability around the mean (the standard deviation), and even within a single child's bedtimes on the seven days of the parental diary. Second, the timed infant observations of the Dutch mothers and their children at six months of age, compared with other mother-infant observations we had collected in another previous US study, showed a series of statistically significant differences, with the Dutch infants more often in a "quiet alert" state in contrast to the US infants, who were more often in the "active alert" state. Further, the US infants engaged in more gross motor activity (such as moving arms and legs actively), and their mothers were observed to touch and talk to their babies more than in the Dutch case (see figure 8.2).

Our exploration of the Dutch three R's contributed to further theoretical and methodological advances. As a widely shared cultural model, the three R's provided a well-elaborated instance for building a heuristic model (see Figure 8.2) of how parental ethnotheories are formed and how they ultimately are expressed in practices that have consequences for children's development (Harkness and Super 2005). The Dutch parents' beliefs about rest and regularity also resonated well with our growing interest in the development of infants' self-regulation and reactivity in cultural context, which became the focus of our most recent cross-cultural research project, the International Baby Study (IBS).

The IBS adds a new methodological dimension by exploring key aspects of how a child biologically experiences his or her developmental niche and develops a disposition within it. We incorporated measures of infant salivary cortisol (the so-called "stress hormone," but more accurately a measure of preparation for activity) to capture both its diurnal patterning and its change in response to mildly stressful events (e.g., a bath at two weeks of age). This technique allows us to explore how cultural beliefs and practices shape patterns of arousal and rest in human biological systems. In addition, we attached a small "actigraph" (a kind of micropedometer) to the baby's ankle for a forty-eight-hour period, providing an objective measure of the level of physical activity, of the amount and timing of sleep, and even of the internal architecture of sleep phases. Preliminary results suggest a broad range of specific differences between the two cultural groups: compared to the Dutch sample, the US infants are more physically active while awake, they are awake more and for longer bouts (but sleep less and in shorter bouts), they spend more of their sleep in the active (not quiet) phase, and they appear to maintain higher levels of salivary cortisol.

We started this sequence of investigations with an interest in how parental ethnotheories worked, using several kinds of methods. The initial answers led to new questions, new samples, and new methods. We are now arriving at an unexpected picture of cultural differences,

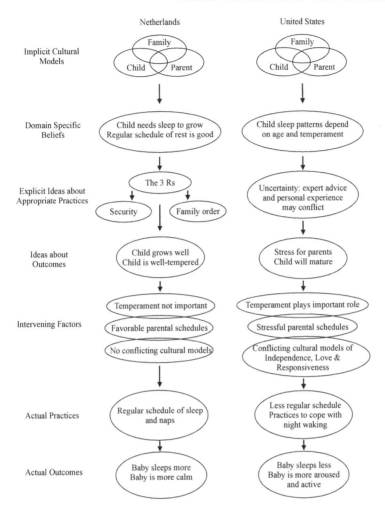

FIGURE 8.2 Parental ethnotheories, practices, and actual outcomes.

differences that may matter for the health and growth, for the skills and risks of infants and children.

Using Mixed Methods to Understand Process in Interventions

Although most of our own work has used mixed methods in the service of basic research on children and families in cultural context, the same kind of approach is equally well suited to the design and evaluation of interventions to promote healthy child development. Several examples can be drawn from the literature on "positive deviance." This concept, advanced especially by Zeitlin and her colleagues (Zeitlin, Ghassemi, and Mansour 1990), starts with this observation: even in the most difficult environments of poverty and deprivation, some families do better than others in raising relatively well-nourished and healthy children. It then asks, "What are these families doing that is different from the less-successful ones?" In one three-month study in the barrios surrounding Managua, Nicaragua, (Engle et al. 1996), the researchers derived several numerical scales based on interviews with mothers about their beliefs about feeding young children (e.g., "When a child doesn't finish his meal, is it better to leave him alone, or help him to finish it?" became part of a "Help" scale). This was followed with naturalistic behavior observations and, ultimately, measures of child nutrition and growth. The results confirmed the core hypothesis that a mother's beliefs about responsibility for ensuring that her child actually eats is related to the child's physical growth, pointing to a window for subsequent intervention.

Another project in this tradition included a quasi-experimental intervention as well as the initial evaluation to identify "positive deviants." Rates of infant diarrhea and malnutrition were a major public health issue in rural Bangladesh in the decades after independence. A research and intervention study was undertaken to identify and evaluate low-cost interventions that might reduce these rates (Zeitlin et al. 1990). In the study villages, the prevalence of infant diarrhea was over sixty percent at one year, and the median weight-for-age was more than two-and-one-half standard deviations below the international norm. Maternal interviews, nonintrusive behavior observations, and the collection of demographic and health information on the infants provided data for quantitative analysis identifying behaviors associated with positive outcomes, mostly having to do with specific routes of contamination through unsanitary practices. A "Clean Life" program of maternal education was developed in collaboration with community members and leaders, which focused on ground sanitation, food sanitation, and personal hygiene, all involving behavior change or affordable materials (Ahmed et al. 1991). Evaluation after only five months indicated substantial health gains: Severe malnutrition, which had been ten percent higher at baseline in the intervention group than in the comparison group, was now thirty percent below (Ahmed et al. 1993). Crucially, the postintervention evaluation identified (through direct observation) which specific family behaviors linked the interventions with positive results, thus allowing subsequent refinement. Ultimately the program was adopted by BRAC, a national (now international), nonprofit NGO, and applied widely across the country.

Although the positive deviance approach highlights questions concerning *who* is helped and through what mediating *processes*, mixed methods more generally draw attention to factors that underlie average results. An interdisciplinary group drew on this strength in studying the implementation and effects of New Hope, a social and economic intervention project undertaken in Wisconsin during the era of dramatic welfare reform (Duncan, Huston, and Weisner 2007). More interesting than the overall results (which were positive: poverty rates declined compared to the comparison group) is the new understanding of why some families benefitted greatly from the program while others did not. Specifically, the families who benefitted most from the new services offered through the New Hope program were those who needed extra help, but who were not too overwhelmed with an overload of personal challenges to take advantage of more resources; in the words of the researchers, families who already had "sustainable daily routines" were more capable of fitting in further activities such as day care for the children or educational opportunities for the parents. This insight was central for not only understanding how the program worked, but also how future efforts in this area might be enhanced.

Discovering Explanations for Surprising Results: The Moving to Opportunity Project Revisited

We opened this chapter with a critique of the research design and methods (as specified in a traditional randomized control trial approach) of a large social experiment, the Moving to Opportunity project. Our comments were based on a description of the project provided in a radio interview by one of the project's principal investigators. As we looked further into the published literature behind the interview, however, we were surprised to find that mixed methods had in fact been used to explain the findings of differential effects on boys compared to girls (Briggs, Popkin, and Goering 2010; Clampet-Lundquist et al. 2011). Notably, these studies, which were separately funded and which were carried out after the project was completed, were barely mentioned in the article in the *Journal of the American Medical Association* (Kessler et al. 2014), which was the immediate basis for the interview. Nevertheless, the later studies, although carried out with much smaller budgets and small samples, did manage to uncover some plausible explanations for why girls who were moved to lower-poverty communities fared better on average than their peers in the control group, whereas the opposite was true for boys. Interestingly from our perspective, the findings of the study fit neatly into the developmental niche framework, as they included differences in the settings that boys and girls chose to inhabit in their daily lives, their customary forms of entertainment, and their gender-specific ideas about self-presentation. In addition, Briggs, Popkin, and Goering (2010) tell a candid story about the many ways in which the pristine design of the project failed to be matched by messy reality on the ground—for example, less than a quarter of the families who were randomly selected for moving to a low-poverty neighborhood actually chose to take advantage of this opportunity; and of those who did, the great majority moved again after the required year in residence to other communities more similar to their former homes in the inner city.

Summary and Conclusions: Why Do Mixed Methods Matter?

In this chapter, we have considered the contributions of mixed methods to both basic scientific research and to interventions for children's healthy development in cultural context. Several principles could be drawn from this review, and they are worth summarizing here:

1. Mixed methods include a variety of different ways of measuring both the qualities of things and their quantity of occurrence. For example, in the back-and-forth of listening to parents, reading and coding their discourse, and deriving numerical counts of themes and related practices, it makes little sense to insist that certain kinds of data are by nature "qualitative" in contrast to other "quantitative" data. The same argument could be made for the analysis of observational and even questionnaire data.
2. The use of a theoretical model such as the developmental niche, and relatedly parental ethnotheories, is helpful for keeping track of the complexities of both environment and development in a way that facilitates their integration.
3. As a construct, mixed methods can be considered both within individual studies and across a series of studies as they contribute to a developing research agenda over time. This idea may be helpful to keep in mind as it reminds us that we do not need to do everything in any given study; rather, a series of studies using different methods can validate and elaborate on previous findings—or identify

previous gaps in our understanding that can be remediated through further research. This triangulation of methods for iterative improvements in research is particularly important in intervention research, to understand process and to prevent unanticipated harm.

4. The technical and intellectual resources for mixed methods research are constantly growing and changing, as new instruments for collecting and analyzing data become available, and as we learn from ongoing experiences, our own and others.' The metaphorical representation of mixed methods might thus look more like a tree than a box of tools.

5. For cross-cultural mixed methods research (or for any research that concerns people in their sociocultural milieu), one essential "method" is to actually "be there," to collect data that include either meaningful direct contact with the research participants or indirect contact through close and continuing collaboration with others who are in the field. This principle underlines the importance of egalitarian collaborative research relationships that are sustained over the course of several studies over time.

6. Thus, mixed methods research must always be a collaborative enterprise because no one individual is likely to have a full command of all the kinds of methods that could be applied to a given research question. Likewise, in the comparative cross-cultural context, many cultural perspectives, and the cultural expertise that goes with them, are essential for making progress toward an increasing understanding of both cultural specifics and more widely shared patterns of ideas and behavior.

In the cross-cultural study of children and families, it follows from these principles that mixed methods provide a stronger basis for discovering new ethnotheories, their representation in action, and their implications for children's development than would any one method alone. As we expand our understanding of the many dimensions of children's development, emerging new methods can parallel—and indeed stimulate—the elaboration of new conceptual models. For the research described here, the use of mixed methods helped us to discover aspects of parenting and child development that matter a great deal to parents, teachers, and human service providers in a variety of cultural settings. It matters, for example, to know that there is more than one strategy for bringing up children to be successful members of their communities, and that some such variation is culturally close at hand—just on the other side of the Atlantic pond. It also is helpful to realize that child development can be thought of as a multistranded process, with different cultures emphasizing different strands—sometimes to the neglect of other equally important ones.

For intervention research such as the Moving to Opportunity project, mixed methods matter for ethical as well as scientific reasons. Moving families from one sociocultural context to another very different one was a bold move, with potential for harm as well as good, as the later research results showed. Using mixed methods to study the experiences of these families as they crossed the divide from urban public housing to suburban communities could have alerted the researchers to the developing threats to the young boys who ended up experiencing post-traumatic stress syndrome and other adverse health effects. Further implications of using a more holistic set of mixed methods, instead of the classic randomized control trial with its tunnel vision of variables to be measured, would include a shift to intervention research designs that allow for change along the way, as new findings point to both new opportunities for learning and new risks that had not been previously considered. Mixed methods for the study of children and families in cultural context do matter—for science, for practitioners, and ultimately for children and families themselves.

Acknowledgments

We are grateful for the generous support our work referenced here received from the Carnegie Corporation of New York, the William T. Grant Foundation, the Spencer Foundation, the National Institutes of Health (USA), the National Science Foundation (USA), and the Fulbright Scholar Program of the Department of State (USA). All statements and views expressed here are the sole responsibility of the authors.

References

Ahmed, N. U., M. F. Zeitlin, A. S. Beiser, C. M. Super, and S. N. Gershoff. 1993. "A Longitudinal Study of the Impact of Behavioral Change Intervention on Cleanliness, Diarrhoeal Morbidity, and Growth of Children in Rural Bangladesh." *Social Science and Medicine* 37 (2): 159–71.

Ahmed, N. U., M. F. Zeitlin, A. S. Beiser, C. M. Super, S. N. Gershoff, and M. A. Ahmed. 1991. "Community-Based Trial and Intervention Techniques for the Development of Hygiene Intervention in Rural Bangladesh." *International Quarterly of Community Health Education* 12 (3):183–202.

Bartholomew, T. T., and J. R. Brown. 2012. "Mixed Methods, Culture, and Psychology: A Review of Mixed Methods in Culture-Specific Psychological

Research." *International Perspectives in Psychology: Research, Practice, Consultation*, no. 1 (3):177–90.

Bell, R. Q. 1968. "A Reinterpetation of the Direction of Effects in Studies of Socialization." *Psychological Review* 75: 81–95.

Briggs, Xavier de Souza, Susan J. Popkin, and John Goering. 2010. *Moving to Opportunity: The Story of an American Experiment to Fight Ghetto Poverty.* New York: Oxford.

Caracelli, V. M., and J. C. Greene. 1993. "Data Analysis Strategies for Mixed-Method Evaluation Designs." In *The Mixed Methods Reader*, edited by Vicki L. Plano Clark and J. W. Cresswell, 230–50. Thousand Oaks, CA: Sage.

Carey, W. B., and S. C. McDevitt. 1978. "Revision of the Infant Temperament Questionnaire." *Pediatrics* 61 (5): 735–39.

Clampet-Lundquist, S., J. R. Kling, K. Edin, and G. J. Duncan. 2011. "Moving Teenagers Out of High-Risk Neighborhoods: How Girls Fare Better Than Boys." *American Journal of Sociology* 116 (4): 1154–89.

Duncan, Greg J., Aletha C. Huston, and Thomas S. Weisner. 2007. *Higher Ground: New Hope for the Working Poor and Their Children*. New York: Russell Sage.

Engle, Patrice, Marian Zeitlin, Yadira Medrano, and Lino Garcia M. 1996. "Growth Consequences of Low-Inclome Nicaraguan Mothers' Theories about Feeding 1-Year-Olds." In *Parents' Cultural Belief Systems: Their Origins, Expressions, and Consequences*, edited by S. Harkness and C. M. Super. New York: Guilford.

Greene, David. 2014. "Study: Boys Report PTSD When Moved out of Poverty." In *Morning Edition*: NPR.

Harkness, Sara. 1987. "The Cultural Mediation of Postpartum Depression." *Medical Anthropology Quarterly* (new series) (2):194–209.

Harkness, Sara. 1990. "A Cultural Model for the Acquisition of Language: Implications for the Innateness Debate." *Developmental Psychobiology* 27 (7): 727–40.

Harkness, Sara, and C. M. Super. 1977/2008. "Why African Children Are So Hard to Test " In *Cross-Cultural Research at Issue*, edited by L. L Adler, 145–52. New York: Academic Press. Reprinted in R. A. Levine & R. S. New (eds.), *Anthropology and Child Development: A Cross-Cultural Reader*, 182–86. Malden, MA: Blackwell.

Harkness, Sara, and C. M. Super. 1983. "The Cultural Construction of Child Development: A Framework for the Socialization of Affect." *Ethos* 11 (4): 221–31.

Harkness, Sara, and C. M. Super. 1985a. "Child-Environment Transactions in the Socialization of Affect." In *The Socialization of Emotions*, edited by M. Lewis and C. Saarni, 21–36. New York: Plenum.

Harkness, Sara, and C. M. Super. 1985b. "The Cultural Context of Gender Segregation in Children's Peer Groups." *Child Development* 56: 219–24.

Harkness, Sara, and C. M. Super. 1985c. "The Cultural Structuring of Children's Play in a Rural African Community." In *The Many Faces of Play*, edited by K. Blanchard, 96–101. Champaign, IL: Human Kinetics Publishers.

Harkness, Sara, and C. M. Super. 1987. "Fertility Change, Child Survival, and Child Development: Observations in a Rural Kenyan Community." In *Child Survival: Anthropological Perspectives on the Treatment and Maltreatment of Children*, edited by N. Scheper-Hughes, 59–70. Boston: D. Reidel.

Harkness, Sara, and C. M. Super. 1992a. "The Cultural Foundations of Fathers' Roles: Evidence from Kenya and the United States." In *Father-Child Relations: Cultural and Biosocial Contexts*, edited by Barry S. Hewlett, 191–211. Hawthorne, NY: Aldine de Gruyter.

Harkness, Sara, and C. M. Super. 1992b. "The Developmental Niche: A Theoretical Framework for Analyzing the Household Production Of Health." *Social Science and Medicine* 38 (2): 217–26.

Harkness, Sara, and C. M. Super. 1992c. "Parental Ethnotheories in Action." In *Parental Belief Systems: The Psychological Consequences for Children*, 2nd ed., edited by I. Sigel, A. V. McGillicuddy-DeLisi, and J. Goodnow, 373–92. Hillsdale, NJ: Erlbaum.

Harkness, Sara, and C. M. Super. 1996. "Introduction." In *Parents' Cultural Belief Systems: Their Origins, Expressions, and Consequences*, edited by Sara Harkness and C. M. Super, 1–23. New York: Guilford.

Harkness, Sara, and C. M. Super. 2005. "Themes and Variations: Parental Ethnotheories in Western Cultures." In *Parental Beliefs, Parenting, and Child Development in Cross-Cultural Perspective*, edited by K. H. Rubin and O.-B. Chung, 61–79. New York: Psychology Press.

Harkness, Sara, and C. M. Super. 2012. "The Cultural Organization of Children's Environments." In *The Environment of Human Development: A Handbook of Theory and Measurement*, edited by L. C. Mayes and M. Lewis 498–516. New York: Cambridge University Press.

Harkness, Sara, C. M. Super, and C. H. Keefer. 1992. "Learning to Be an American Parent: How Cultural Models Gain Directive Force." In *Human Motives and Cultural Models*, edited by R. G. D'Andrade and C. Strauss, 163–78. New York: Cambridge University Press.

Harkness, Sara, C. M. Super, U. Moscardino, J.-H. Rha, M. J. M. Blom, B. Huitrón, C. A. Johnston, M. Sutherland, O.-K. Hyun, G. Axia, and J. Palacios. 2007. "Cultural Models and Developmental Agendas: Implications for Arousal and Self-Regulation in Early Infancy." *Journal of Developmental Processes* 1 (2): 5–39.

Harkness, Sara, U. Moscardino, M. Rios Bermudez, P. O. Zylicz, B. Welles-Nyström, M. J. M. Blom, P. Parmar, G. Axia, J. Palacios, and C. M. Super. 2006. "Mixed Methods in International Collaborative Research: The Experiences of the International Study of Parents, Children, and Schools." *Cross-Cultural Research* 40 (1): 65–82.

Kessler, R. C., G. J. Duncan, L. A. Gennetian, L. F. Katz, J. R. Kling, N. A. Sampson, L. Sanbonmatsu, A. M. Zaslavsky, and J. Ludwig. 2014. "Associations of Housing Mobility Interventions for Children in High-Poverty Neighborhoods with Subsequent Mental Disorders During Adolescence." *Journal of the American Medical Association* 311 (9) :937–48. doi: 10.1001/jama.2014.607.

Kohnstamm, G. A., C. F. Halverson, V. L. Havill, and I. Mervielde. 1996. "Parents' Free Descriptions of Child Characteristics: A Cross-Cultural Search for the Roots of the Big Five." In *Parents' Cultural Belief Systems: Their Origins, Expressions, and Consequences,* edited by Sara Harkness and C. M. Super, 27–55. New York: Guilford.

Super, Charles M. 1976. "Environmental Effects on Motor Development: The Case of African Infant Precocity." *Developmental Medicine and Child Neurology* 18: 561–67.

Super, Charles M. 1983. "Cultural Variation in the Meaning and Uses of Children's Intelligence." In *Expiscations in Cross-Cultural Psychology,* edited by J. G. Deregowski, S. Dziurawiec, and R. C. Annis. Lisse, Netherlands: Swets & Zeitlinger.

Super, Charles M. 1991. "Developmental Transitions of Cognitive Functioning in Rural Kenya and Metropolitan America." In *The Brain and Behavioral Development: Biosocial Dimensions,* edited by K. Gibson, M. Konner, and J. Lancaster, 225–57. Hawthorne, NY: Aldine.

Super, Charles M., and Sara Harkness. 1974. "Patterns of Personality in Africa: A Note from the Field." *Ethos* 2 (4): 377–86.

Super, Charles M., and Sara Harkness. 1982. "The Infant's Niche in Rural Kenya and Metropolitan America." In *Cross-Cultural Research at Issue,* edited by L. L Adler, 47–56. New York: Academic Press.

Super, Charles M., and Sara Harkness. 1986. "The Developmental Niche: A Conceptualization at the Interface of Child and Culture." *International Journal of Behavioral Development* 9: 545–69.

Super, Charles M., and Sara Harkness. 1994a. "The Cultural Regulation of Temperament-Environment Interactions." *Researching Early Childhood* 2 (1): 59–84.

Super, Charles M., and Sara Harkness. 1994b. "Temperament and the Developmental Niche." In *Prevention and Early Intervention: Individual Differences as Risk Factors for the Mental Health Of Children—A Festschrift for Stella Chess and Alexander Thomas,* edited by W. B. Carey and S. A. McDevitt, 15–25. New York: Brunner/Mazel.

Super, Charles M., and Sara Harkness. 1999. "The Environment as Culture in Developmental Research." In *Measurement of the Environment in Developmental Research,* edited by T. Wachs and S. Friedman, 279–323. Washington, DC: American Psychological Association.

Super, Charles M., and Sara Harkness. 2009. "The Developmental Niche of the Newborn in Rural Kenya." In *The Newborn as A Person: Enabling Healthy Infant Development Worldwide,* edited by J. K. Nugent, B. Petrauskas, and T. B. Brazelton, 85–97. New York: Wiley.

Super, Charles M., Sara Harkness, and L. Baldwin. 1977. "Category Behavior in Natural Ecologies and in Cognitive Tests." *The Quarterly Newsletter of the Institute for Comparative Human Development* 1: 4–7.

Super, Charles M., Sara Harkness, N. van Tijen, E. van der Vlugt, J. Dykstra, and M. Fintelman. 1996. "The Three R's of Dutch Child Rearing and the Socialization of Infant Arousal." In *Parents' Cultural Belief Systems: Their Origins, Expressions, and Consequences*, edited by Sara Harkness and C. M. Super, 447–66. New York: Guilford Press.

Super, Charles M., C. H. Keefer, and Sara Harkness. 1994. "Child Care and Infectious Respiratory Disease during the First Two Years of Life in a Rural Kenyan Community." *Social Science and Medicine* 38 (2): 227–29.

Tashakkori, Abbas, and Charles Teddlie. 2008. "Introduction to Mixed Method and Mixed Model Studies in the Social and Behavioral Sciences." In *The Mixed Methods Reader*, edited by Vicki L. Plano Clark and John W. Creswell, 7–26. Thousand Oaks, CA: Sage.

Ten Hoopen, Els. 2005. *Groeiboek*. Den Hague: Gemeente Den Haag.

Van Hulst, Anna G. 1905. *Reinheid, rust en regelmaat: Een beknopte uiteenzetting, hoe moeders hare zuigelingen op de minst omslachtige wijzie goed kunnen verzorgen. [Cleanliness, Rest, and Regularity: A Brief Statement Concerning How Mothers May Provide Good Care for Their Infants in the Most Straightforward Manner.]* Harlingen: Provinciale Friesche Groene-Kruis Fonds.

Weller, S. C., and A. K. Romney. 1988. *Systematic Data Collection*. Newbury Park, CA: Sage.

Zeitlin, M. F., H. Ghassemi, and M. Mansour. 1990. *Positive Deviance in Child Nutrition*. Tokyo: United Nations University.

Zeitlin, M. F., C. M. Super, M. Beiser, G. Gulden, N. Ahmed, M. Ahmed, and S. Sockalingam. 1990. *A Behavioral Study of Positive Deviance in Young Child Nutrition and Health in Bangladesh*. Report to the Office of International Health, USAID.

NINE

Methods to Inform Public Problems: Toward an Ecocultural Framing of Poverty

EDWARD D. LOWE

What can we learn about an important public problem like poverty when we work between statistical and qualitative information as we are invited to do in the illustration below (figure 9.1)? Why does mixing social research methods in this way matter? A narrow answer is that it matters for producing more reliable, more valid, or at least more convincing research findings. Here I take a broader view by showing that in modern technocratic societies, mixed research approaches are not just useful for conducting research, they also are critically important for focusing public attention on key social problems, shaping public debate about how to solve them, and assessing how well we are realizing those solutions.

Why should everyone worry about the role of research methods in shaping how we address important social problems? Why not just leave it up to the experts? John Dewey ([1927] 2012) gives us a clear answer in *The Public and Its Problems: An Essay in Political Inquiry*. In that essay, Dewey was responding to critics of the promise of modern democracy who claimed that the people of large modern states are just too ignorant and prejudiced, too

What Does it Mean to be "Poor" in the U.S.?

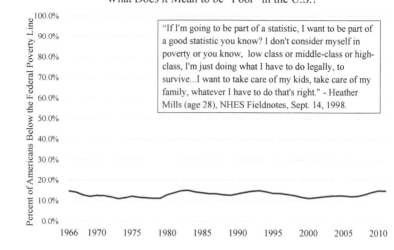

"If I'm going to be part of a statistic, I want to be part of a good statistic you know? I don't consider myself in poverty or you know, low class or middle-class or high-class, I'm just doing what I have to do legally, to survive...I want to take care of my kids, take care of my family, whatever I have to do that's right." - Heather Mills (age 28), NHES Fieldnotes, Sept. 14, 1998.

Source: US Census Bureau

self-interested, too socially heterogeneous and isolated, and too easily misled to be trusted with having a decisive voice is defining a nation's collective interests and in directing public policies toward the common good. Therefore, the critics charged, modern government and the administration of public policy was best left to a class of highly trained, specialized technical experts who would use the findings of the modern social sciences to advise the leaders in government. But, the old professor of philosophy knew well that power tempted the apparently wise and expert to believe that they were actually wise and expert. As a result, the governing elite and their technocratic advisers tended to lose sight of the lives and needs of the people they serve (Rogers 2012). Only through democratic processes where the people have a voice could government effectively meet the diverse and dynamic needs of the people.

That said, Dewey agreed that effective direct democracy in any large, complex polity is impossible. The problems of a modern technologically sophisticated society were too numerous and too complex for the people and their elected representatives to have mastery over all or any of them: modern democratic institutions need experts to inform policy-making. The challenge, Dewey argued, is to develop a cooperative process of social inquiry among the general public, elected representatives, and the experts charged with informing both (Rogers 2012).

So, when we study how methods matter for addressing our public problems, a critical question we must ask is how well those methods invite the participation of the relevant publics or, on the other hand, how well they reflect the uninformed assumptions of a highly trained, but out of touch, technocratic class.

In this chapter, I show how methods matter for the way we understand, measure, and address poverty, one of the most important public problems for societies around the world. I begin with a consideration of how national poverty statistics like those in the illustration above are operationalized as quantitative measures. I argue that these approaches are often informed by expert assumptions about the lives of the poor and the nature of poverty with very little direct study of the lived experiences of people who struggle with chronically inadequate levels of income in those societies. So, the understanding of poverty that informs official statistics and the policies that are then put in place to alleviate poverty do not adequately reflect the on-the-ground nature of poverty very well. What is needed is some means of better understanding these lived experiences. Ethnographic studies can help but often fail to contribute to robust theoretical models that bridge ethnographic insight on the microlevel with more effective quantitative measures of poverty that are needed for assessment at a macro level. I argue that placing ethnographic insights into an ecocultural framework is one solution to better bring these two levels of analysis together; I finish with an ethnographic case to demonstrate my point.

What Is "Poverty"?

If we look at Heather Mills's quote juxtaposed against the official poverty rates for the United States between 1966 and 2011 in figure 9.1, we can ask what understandings of poverty are implicit in these two sources, one a quantitative measurement, the other an ethnographic vignette. In September 1998, Heather Mills, a pseudonym, was among forty-four families who took part in the New Hope ethnographic study (see Lowe and Weisner 2004; Bos et al. 1999 for more details) that was designed to understand how an antipoverty intervention called New Hope fit into the broader concerns of these families struggling against economic adversity in two low-income neighborhoods of Milwaukee, Wisconsin.

Heather's quote resonates well with the public conversations surrounding poverty in the United States. First, that what it means to be "in poverty" is generally contested and understood in moral (i.e., how things ought to be) as opposed to objective terms. So people rarely view themselves as "poor" even if their income is too low to meet their needs for a period of time. The second insight we can take away is that social statistics have become everyday symbolic devices for talking about poverty and one's social well-being more generally.

Heather did not believe that she was poor, and if we examine her reported income for the year 1997, we find that the household she headed was not poor in terms of the United States official definition of poverty. Heather earned $22,000 in 1997, about $9,000 more than the official poverty threshold for a family of three ($12,931 in 1997). But, this comparison assumes that Heather's understanding of poverty and the official definition are the same. Are they? This is not just a question of the symbolic elaboration of a particular term —poverty—but, as far as government measurements are concerned, also a methodological question about the operationalization of a key construct used to construct one of the most important statistics in modern social policy, the official poverty rate. So, when the United States Census Bureau (DeNavas-Walt, Proctor, and Smith, 2013, 14) reports that 15 percent, or 46.2 million Americans, are poor, what do they mean? What are the methods used to measure poverty from one year to the next? How well does the official definition and measurement of this key indicator of societal well-being capture the degree to which Americans like Heather are struggling economically?

Absolute Definitions of Poverty

Many think that poverty has something to do with an inability to afford certain basic material necessities for survival. This view reflects the way many, but not all, important economic organizations and national statistical offices define poverty. For example, the World Bank (2011) defines poverty thus: "A person is considered poor if his or her consumption or income level falls below some minimum level necessary to meet basic needs. This minimum level is usually called the 'poverty line.'" But, what are "basic" needs? Many people probably would agree that basic needs as those necessary for survival like food, housing, and clothing. Once these necessities are taken care of, one is no longer poor.

This is the understanding of poverty that the United States Census Bureau uses in its "poverty thresholds" each year to measure and report the poverty rate. How the United States Census Bureau created these poverty thresholds shows how important official statistics that are used to measure levels of societal well-being are often developed from within closed circles of policy experts and only vaguely informed by the public they seek to represent. Once adopted, these operationalized measures become essentially frozen over time, potentially leaving us with measures that are increasingly at odds with on-the-ground realities.

All official statistics have a history, and these measurement histories are revealing about the how well these statistics might reflect the needs and capabilities of a nation's people (Himmelfarb 1991). The official poverty thresholds used by the US Census Bureau were operationalized by Mollie Orshansky of the US Social Security Administration in 1963–1964 and have since been adjusted each year for inflation without revision (Fisher 1997). Orshansky started by selecting a "minimum food budget," the amount of income necessary, given the size of the family and its farm or nonfarm status, to afford what US Department of Agriculture nutritionists defined in 1955 as a minimally adequate economy food plan—apparently with little study of actual food use for families in the United States at the time (Fisher 1997, 6). Using the few survey studies available at the time as a guide, Orshansky reasoned that a minimum income threshold for poverty would be three times the amount needed to afford the USDA economy food plan, with a multiplier added in to adjust for the size of the household. The assumption is that below this level of income, the family or individuals concerned could become malnourished. These thresholds have remained in place since that time and are adjusted for inflation each year by the US Census Bureau (Fisher 1997).

If poverty is defined as an inability to afford basic needs for survival, then policies and programs can target either overall income levels that should be adequate to provide these specific needs, or voucher programs that can be used to purchase specific survival needs like food, housing, and utilities services. A tight linkage exists between the theoretical definition of poverty, the method of its measurement, and the design of welfare programs that can reduce the overall poverty rate. It also limits who is eligible for assistance: if you are officially poor or nearly so you can apply for certain forms of assistance. If you are not poor or nearly so by official standards, you cannot apply for assistance even if the particular circumstances of a person or family present extreme financial difficulties like needing an expensive treatment for a chronic health condition, for example (Sen 1992).

This method for operationalizing the official absolute poverty thresholds in the United States, as in many other countries, was a prod-

uct of expert technocratic assumptions about how people ought to behave in conditions of economic adversity, rather than how people like
Heather actually experience periods of income inadequacy and act to
cope with it. The process was not democratic in Dewey's sense, as no
studies of local experiences with financial inadequacy were conducted
to inform the definition of the official poverty measure. The "poverty
thresholds," therefore, cannot adequately capture the diverse experiences of struggling within contexts of income inadequacy for individuals and likely do not inform adequate policy responses to these problems (Sen 1992). The emphasis on a limited set of basic material needs
also fuels conservative criticism of official definitions of poverty as being too generous in spite of the very low thresholds set! This is because
studies find that most poor households have apparent luxuries like re-
frigerators, microwaves, and televisions and therefore cannot be on the
brink of being undernourished or suffering from other forms of serious
deprivation (e.g., Rector 2011).

Relative Poverty

Another way to define poverty is in relative rather than absolute terms.
An excellent argument for why we need a relative definition, particularly in affluent societies, how to define it, and how to address it can be
found in the work of the famous liberal economist John Kenneth Galbraith. Writing from the vantage point of the unprecedented affluence
in the two decades following World War II, Galbraith ([1958] 1998)
takes up the troubling question of how to reinvigorate public concern
for the "position of poverty," given the secular pattern of improving
living standards in the United States and Europe at that time. Galbraith
defined relative poverty as follows: "People are poverty-stricken when
their income, even if adequate for survival, falls radically behind that of
the community. They cannot have what the larger community regards
as the minimum necessary for decency; and they cannot wholly escape, therefore, the judgment of the larger community that they are indecent. They are degraded for, in the literal sense, they live outside the
grades or categories which the community regards as acceptable (235)."
This definition shifts the emphasis from the ability to afford material
necessities to the ability to afford a minimum level of socially defined
needs and how the acquisition of these social needs reflects one's inclusion into to the rest of society. Galbraith's claim is that a "decent" consumer lifestyle would minimize the stigma of being judged as indecent
and possibly also resentment toward wealthier classes that could fuel

social instability, a long-standing worry among liberal social reformers dating back to at least the late nineteenth century (Himmelfarb 1991).

Many countries have adopted this relative definition of poverty in their official measurements. However, operationalizing these measures is difficult because each country and even regions within countries have different shared ideals of what lifestyle might indicate a minimum level of decency. So operationalizing a single measure based on some particular set of acquired items that would represent a minimum level of decency is not likely to be valid across these contexts. In order to work around this problem, many countries operationalize relative poverty as some set percentage below the national median income. For example, the European Union, which defines general poverty in terms of social exclusion rather than material hardship, has adopted a threshold of 60 percent of national median income to indicate being "at-risk" for poverty (European Anti-Poverty Network 2014). To place this operationalization of poverty in the context of Heather Mills's economic experiences discussed earlier, her income in 1997 would have placed very near, and possibly below, this relative threshold. At that time, the national median income in the United States in 1997 dollars was $36,210 (DeNavas-Walt, Proctor, and Smith 2013), and 60 percent of this—$21,726—was just a few hundred dollars less than Heather's reported income of $22,000 that year. So, while far from poor by the official standards of the United States, she was on the threshold of poverty by the European Union standard.

If the concern in cases of relative poverty is social exclusion, then it is important to understand what the source of this exclusion might be in order to make changes that could improve the situation. Galbraith ([1958] 1998) argued that the causes of being unable to earn minimally adequate levels of income were either from being relegated to some "island of poverty" where everyone was poor, such as in a resource-poor rural region, or an urban slum—which he called insular poverty—or because of personal deficiencies and other personal barriers to fuller social participation, such as mental illness, poor health, low levels of educational achievement, or generally being unable to adapt to the demand of industrial life, which he labeled case poverty.

What policy solutions exist for addressing relative poverty in modern affluent societies? Galbraith's answer depended on whether or not the risk for impoverishment is the result of case poverty or insular poverty. For case poverty, any suffering that results from impoverishment is either (a) deserved, due to the person's moral defects or (b) undeserved, due to something like a chronic health problem—but mainly the concern of the charitable inclinations of the compassionate. In any case, since these varied on a case-by-case basis, they are not a major concern for society at large (Galbraith [1958] 1998, 238). For insular poverty, it is the moral obligation of society and its public to devote time and treasure to identify and collectively remove those environmental, geographical, or social-structural barriers to full economic participation. This would entail the creation of the modern welfare state, dedicated to ensuring the "public welfare," that is not just survival, but survival at a minimum level of socially defined "decency" (Bauman 2005). This means heavily investing in the public infrastructure of highly impoverished and economically isolated communities, particularly in those services that can benefit children. For Galbraith ([1958] 1998), these include "high-quality schools, strong health services, special provision for nutrition and recreation . . . to compensate for the very low investment which families are able to make in their own offspring" (241). In addition to these programs, programs that would address the environmental and geographical barriers, such as high-quality housing programs, mass transportation to and from all neighborhoods in the city and surrounding regions, clean air, and clean water in the local environment would be added. Finally, he recommended programs to alleviate educational deficiencies and improve treatment of mental and physical disorders in order to encourage as many as possible to move out of the pitiable status of case poverty and into the ranks of the productively employed.

One of the concerns with this discourse of case and insular poverty as social exclusion is that it too easily reproduces Oscar Lewis's (2002) distinction between those mired in a "culture of poverty," whose deeply ingrained patterns of social organization, shared habits and worldviews, and mental health would render them unable to participate in a society during times of growing economic prosperity, and those mainstream poor who, while economically struggling, still shared the habits and worldviews of the majority that would enable them to take advantage of brightening economic circumstances or fight for them through popular social movements. For those retrograde poor mired in the culture of poverty, the only solution was to retrain or reprogram them so that they may rejoin society's mainstream. Galbraith's argument is also reflective of William Julius Wilson's (1990) early work on the "underclass," where sociospatial segregation prevented those who live in neighborhoods of concentrated poverty left people unable to learn about and adopt middle-class values and work habits that could inoculate them against cultural pathologies of poverty like teenage single-motherhood, the underground economy, drugs, crime, and violence (Goode 2002, 287). Regardless of the term used, if a person was in case poverty, a culture of poverty, or the underclass, that person was essentially and identifiably "'Other': people who are socially different, isolated from normal citizens and threatening to society through crime, violence, and other moral lapses" (Goode 2002, 280).

I am not sure that the view of life for people relegated to Galbraith's islands of poverty is better. For example, Heather Mills's concerns were not clearly about being in a state of social exclusion, of already being "Other," or judged as indecently isolated from society's mainstream. Her complaint was not one of having failed to *achieve* some minimal level of acceptable social decency but one of feeling challenged by her *capability* to sustain the level of social decency that she had already achieved and possibly doing a bit better (see Sen 1992 for a discussion of the importance of capability versus achievement in poverty research). In other words, to assume that relative poverty marks the line between social inclusion and exclusion quite possibly misses the many ways that people struggle to sustain various forms of social inclusion, even if these efforts are not quite fully realized. This may reflect a problem with definitions of relative poverty in general, as it is built on the assumption that the relative poverty threshold marks off the line between social decency and social indecency. But this assumption seems to come more from the way elites and the educated middle-classes have talked about poverty in the context of growing affluence since the nineteenth century (Himmelfarb 1991), rather than from seeking the input of people like Heather and Samantha Wood (see below), who are actually struggling with inadequate income in these societies.

Toward an Ecocultural Perspective on Poverty

As modern states and their publics attempt to understand, measure, and address levels of poverty in the society, there is often a lack of democratic input from the poor themselves. The problem is at least partly methodological, as I have described above, where the methodological limitations associated with the formal operationalization of statistical measures used to inform social policy often produce a significant gap between the assumptions of expert researchers and policy advocates about the lives of the poor and what those lives are actually like. Since the 1960s, ethnographic studies of everyday life in low-income neighborhoods have sought to fill this void (see Goode 2002; Morgan and

Maskovsky 2003 for reviews). Among most urban ethnographers, there has been a pronounced movement away from characterizations of the poor as Other, or living on the other side of social decency. Rather, "poor people are rehumanized as competent and moral *social* actors" (Goode 2002, 280, emphasis added) whose everyday struggles are related to political and economic constraints and whose seemingly irrational behaviors can be shown to make sense as ingenious strategies for survival, given these constraints.

Ethnographic studies are important for informing public debates and public policy about poverty. They are particularly valuable for documenting the many diverse strategies poor people use in the constant struggle to realize meaningful forms of social participation in spite of powerful financial and institutional constraints. But ethnographic findings are often difficult to connect to larger aggregate constructs like the poverty rate that are needed when defining and describing progress on important public problems. What is needed is a theoretical framework for understanding and framing ethnographic findings that can provide a conceptual bridge between the micro- and the macrolevels of analysis to better understand the way we define, study, and attempt to alleviate poverty.

This is precisely the ambition of an ecocultural framing of human development and well-being (e.g., Weisner 1997, 2002). The ecocultural framework (there are others) that Thomas Weisner and I have written about (Lowe 2003; Lowe and Weisner 2004; Weisner and Lowe 2005), begins from the microlevel of analysis, viewing individuals as always embedded in a number of networked activity settings, often organized around the production and reproduction of particular socially directed routines. These socially, geographically, and temporally distributed sites of activity are associated with the production of the kinds of activities that collectively make meaningful social participation possible and also give it its local quality and characteristics. These activity settings are distributed among the various sites of meaningful and necessary social action like the household and neighborhood, the office, factory, workshop, or field, religious sites, and shops or markets. These are the primary sites for practical work aimed at the (re)production and distribution of material culture and its practical symbolic correlates, and sites of action aimed at the production of political society, which might include the kin-based lineage group, neighborhood association, town council, school, religious temples, and various political associations, leisure societies, etc.

In ecocultural terms, the potential for sustained health and social well-being is promoted through the creation of a reasonably sustainable routine of everyday life. The challenge of crafting a sustainable routine is grounded in a particular sociohistorical period, neighborhood, and institutional contexts, with varying kinds of public and private supports. The well-being of individuals is ultimately a reflection of their abilities to sustain and adaptively adjust these daily routines to the demands of their memberships across multiple associations (Weisner 2002).

These daily routines are the familiar chains of activities and events that make up people's daily lives and are often concentrated within particular settings (Weisner 2002). For example, from within the setting of a middle-class household in many American suburbs, one can find a series of routine tasks that support the reproduction of the family and its members, including "getting up" routines, having breakfast together, driving children to school, doing homework, watching TV, doing household chores, eating dinner, sharing bedtime stories, and then nighttime "off to bed" routines to finish the day. In crafting a sustainable daily routine, these household activities must be negotiated against the demands of the other settings (e.g., the job, the extended family, church, school, shopping markets, card club, etc.). How much flexibility the members of a household have in selecting among the activity-based demands of competing settings is a reflection of the relative power of these others, particularly those that are dominant institutions in society (e.g., employers and government agencies) and therefore can enforce sanctions for failing to prioritize their activities (such as spending eight hours at the office or submitting income tax forms by April 15th) over the household's activities.

Second, sustaining daily routines is also a reflection of the availability and quality of the necessary components of the activities that make up the routine itself. Altogether, these components fall into four main groups (adapted from Weisner 1984):

1. The practical behavioral tasks associated with the activity (e.g., the activity "family dinner" often consists of preparing and cooking food, setting the table, sitting and eating together, discussing the day's events, managing conflicts and disagreements that erupt from time to time, cleaning the dirty dishes, etc.).
2. The socially distributed embodied conventional understandings, goals, and values as cultural scripts and cultural models associated with the activity. These include knowing how and when to do the tasks that make up the activity (e.g., its cognitive script); knowing why the tasks matter for the larger activity and what larger values, interests, and aesthetics its proper realization signifies (e.g.,

167

"families that eat together, stay together"); and what appetites, emotions, and motives are cultivated, satisfied, or suppressed through the activity.

3. The material, spatial, and temporal resources needed for the activity (e.g., food, plates, kitchen, electricity, an available hour for all participants in the evening, etc.).

4. The social supports as they are distributed among the people who are expected to contribute to the various other elements of the activity.

Activities are unlikely to be sustained if: (1) no one is reliably available to support the activity's various tasks; (2) material, temporal, or spatial resources that are essential for the activity are either unavailable, inadequate, or unreliable; (3) those available to participate in the activity are not committed to doing so—they might not know how to complete associated tasks, not understand why the activity is valuable, would rather be doing something else, lack the emotional energy or desire to participate, or are outright hostile to the activity and/or its other available participants; and, (4) those available for the activity are physically unable to complete the behavioral tasks associated with the activity (see Weisner 2002 for an alternative phrasing of this list).

Finally, it matters how one's multiple involvements across multiple activity settings support or constrain the activities of the daily routine. For example, if one must work eight to ten hours, five or more days a week at one or more jobs to earn enough money to pay for basic needs like rent, utilities, and food, then one's time for household activities is severely constrained. Children who are assigned six to eight hours of mindless, repetitive homework a night to satisfy the demands of an assessment-mad school administration and federal funding apparatus are not going to have much time for family activities, no matter how many family games and outings parents might plan. Even when overworked parents and children do have the time for some healthful labor and enjoyable shared action, they may be too physically and mentally drained to actually participate.

This all leads to a consideration of an ecocultural definition of poverty: people, families, and households are impoverished when the level of material resources, social supports, embodied conventional understandings and capacities for action, and the levels of coherence among multiple domains of daily activity do not enable them to realize minimally sustainable routines necessary for the realization of healthful levels of personal well-being, supportive and cooperative connections to others, and a sense of meaningful societal participation and inclusion. This definition moves us closer to an understanding of poverty that emphasizes the ongoing *capability* to sustain these pursuits (i.e., healthful and meaningful "beings and doings" or *functionings*) on an everyday basis rather than merely the past *achievement* of some minimum level of material adequacy or social decency (Sen 1992, 39).

A Year in the Financial Life of Samantha Wood

As a demonstration of my argument, I now present an ethnographic case summary for another participant in the New Hope ethnographic study, Samantha Wood. Samantha was selected as a critical case (Kuzel 1999) for this section of the paper because she had a difficult time constructing a viable and sustainable daily routine, particularly as a result of tradeoffs she felt she had to make among the many competing activities, resources, and constraints within her family's ecocultural circumstances. When she entered the study in the spring of 1998, Samantha, a young African American single mother of four (two boys and two girls), was living in one of Milwaukee's racially segregated "Northside" neighborhoods. Samantha's income was well below the official poverty threshold of $19,380 for a family of five in 1997 for the entire three-year period of the ethnographic study. Her reported earnings from employment were just $7,090 in 1998, about $5,200 in 1999, and about $6,550 in 2000. But even with additional financial supports from food stamps, WIC, and the Earned Income Tax credit, Samantha's household remained below the federal poverty line. In spite of this very low level of income, Samantha's story is not one of material deprivation, social isolation, or social exclusion and social indecency. Her story reflects a fierce, if uneven, struggle to weave together those material, social, and symbolic resources that were available in an attempt forge a daily routine that provided both a sense of material sufficiency and meaningful social inclusion for her children and for herself. How Samantha managed her income flows to meet the diverse expenditure demands across the activities that she struggled to assemble into workable daily routines is the focus of the following summary of one year in her life, based on multiple ethnographic visits by members of the New Hope ethnographic team and a thematic analysis of the field notes from those visits.

Managing Income

Activities that bring money into the household and facilitate the management of money (e.g., savings) are among the most important in any daily routine. While wealthier households often rely primarily on a main source of income (e.g., earnings from employment), many lower-income households must carefully manage multiple income streams (Edin and Lein 1997; Mistry and Lowe 2006). Over the course of the first year of the Ethnographic Study, Samantha cobbled together income from employment at two low-wage service jobs, food stamps, WIC payments and housing subsidies, the Earned Income Tax Credit, child support payments from the father of her youngest child, and support from her immediate family.

It was difficult for Samantha to manage many of these income sources. Often gains in one area would lead to reductions in another, particularly in the dynamic relation between her earnings from employment and the food stamps and housing subsidy. In July of 1998, Samantha was working about fifty hours a week at a local dry cleaner. But the extra work came with a financial penalty from the welfare programs. This situation seemed unfair to Samantha. She reported that when her earnings from work increased, these agencies would cut her benefits. She felt she could never get ahead financially as a result.

That summer, Samantha was proud of working long hours to support her household; but working so much also meant that she went home too exhausted to tend to the many tasks and activities that needed to be done at home. Also, her job at a dry cleaning service gave her little flexibility: when her youngest son was sick and not allowed to go to the day-care center, Samantha had to bring the child with her to work so that she could earn the desperately needed money. During this time, Samantha also looked forward to receiving some mandated child support from her youngest son's father; however, she reported that she never knew when it would come. The amount she received was negligible in any case, about $13.00 per payment.

The pressures of striking a balance in her daily routine between work and the household proved too much. By November, Samantha was working fewer than ten hours a week at a national video store, making $5.35 an hour. In August, she had been fired from her better-paying job at the dry cleaner after missing work when she took her son to see a doctor. She did not get a doctor's note that would allow her to excuse her absence, so her supervisor fired her on the spot.

After that, Samantha reported that she liked being home even though she was stressed out over her financial situation. Her financial stress of being behind on her bills was not as bad as the stress she experienced while working full-time—which included missing her children, keeping the house clean, scheduling the family's activities, and still not earning enough to stay ahead of her bills.

Like other women in poor, predominantly African American neighborhoods (Stack 1974), during that fall of 1998, Samantha relied often on her family and friends for additional financial help. Her mother provided help paying her bills and bought Samantha's daughters new winter coats. Samantha borrowed $20 from one friend or another as needed. Her family bought Christmas presents for her children that year. But according to Samantha, "everybody [was] struggling"; so giving Samantha help meant that her mother or friend might have to forgo paying one of their own bills. Samantha was careful to repay the people to whom she owned money in a timely way; she was keen to keep family and friends as future supports during difficult times. Finally, while family members were often willing to help, the timing of their support was often uncertain. Samantha discussed her brother as an example; while willing to help, the help would only arrive on "him time." Samantha summed up her brother's support: "He's a man and a hustler. He doesn't have any bills to worry about, so he doesn't understand how they work. He doesn't get when things are due, things are due!" (NHES Field Notes, 11/5/1998).

Throughout that year, Samantha took some comfort from the federal food stamps and housing subsidy programs, even if meeting the programs' income and employment reporting requirements was a hassle. These supports meant that no matter how desperate her financial situation, she could still keep a roof over her head because she lived in subsidized housing. Food stamps allowed her to make sure her children had something to eat. Samantha also took advantage of the Earned Income Tax Credit, which provided her with a large lump sum to catch up on some bills, pay back personal debts, and purchase things that her children needed or wanted but that she was unable to purchase with her regular income.

Expenditures for Survival and Social Inclusion

Income and expenditures were networked together into larger chains of activity that are part of the daily routine. But, given chronic income inadequacy, Samantha struggled with the tensions that made it difficult to sustain a routine without experiencing considerable stress. We already have seen how Samantha's work schedule took time and energy away from a cluster of household activities such as seeing the children, keeping the house clean, scheduling time to meet competing demands, and paying the bills. She also experienced considerable stress associated with the constant juggling of the different expenditures for the household and her family. These expenditures included essential monthly bills that kept food on the table, a roof over their heads, and some clothes for the children. But expenditures that produced a sense of meaningful social inclusion, particularly for her children, mattered just as much.

Staying on top of monthly bills was a constant challenge. Throughout the first year of the study, Samantha would discuss her challenges in paying household bills and essential weekly expenditures, which included her rent, gas and electricity, food, the phone bill, and the cable bill. It also included her bill at the child-care center, payments for furniture that she had purchased on credit, and car payments and the associated insurance payments. Of course, as many readers will appreciate, paying the bills is a fundamental monthly activity for managing a household in the United States. But for Samantha, paying the bills each month was not just a matter of survival. It was also a means of working toward larger social goals. One bill that she struggled the hardest to pay was her car payment because Samantha felt having a good credit report from paying for her car would enable her to purchase a house one day, saying, "This car is my credit for life."

Samantha also regularly discussed her struggles to purchase things that she or the children needed or wanted. For example, in the summer of 1998, the main topic of discussion was buying a few new clothes, shoes, and accessories for herself and her children. Given that she often had about $15 left over from her paycheck after covering the monthly bills, these items were often out of reach. But quite often during the year that followed, Samantha would put off paying some bills in order to purchase something that she or her children needed, particularly new clothing. She felt it was important that her children have some new clothes, not only as a matter of necessity but also of decency. She regularly mentioned that it was important to her that her children have decent clothes so others would see that her children were a priority.

Finally, Samantha also discussed her frustrations trying to do enjoyable activities in the community with her children, with her extended family, and with friends. These included being able to attend a major summer festival in Milwaukee, being able to celebrate her and her children's birthdays, having a "good Christmas," and eating dinner out with her children, her mother, and her brothers. Samantha felt that these activities in particular were important ways to feel a sense of so-cial inclusion and, again, to show others that she was a good mother who was able to spend money on her children.

For example, in July 1998, Samantha had hoped she would be able to have her hair and nails done before going out with a friend who had invited her out to celebrate her birthday at a local barbecue chicken restaurant. But she did not have the money. It was in the context of wishing she could do something to look nice for her birthday that she reported that no one would be able to say that she did not put her children's needs ahead of her own. At the same time, Milwaukee was putting on its annual "Summer Feast" fair and Samantha was trying to figure out a way to go to the fair with her children, but the anticipated cost was a problem. It was in the context of these experiences that Sa-mantha would describe her situation as impoverished: "You can't take the kids [to] no kind of enjoyment. You used to be able to take the kids to the zoo—now that isn't even free anymore. School trips at school cost six or seven dollars now, so if I am on welfare my child don't get to go, which is not fair to my child . . . we just can't do it 'cause we are poor" (NHES Field Notes 7/2/1998).

Samantha did find a way to take her children to the fair and put off paying the phone bill for the month. She also planned to take her chil-dren to McDonald's as a treat, hoping they would fill up there and not ask for the much more expensive foods at the fair. She worried, though: her children would see other children enjoying the foods and the rides at the fair and ask for these things too. She wouldn't have the money to pay for much. Her oldest daughter understood Samantha's situation and would not ask, but the younger children were less understanding and would cry if they were not able to enjoy what other children at the fair were enjoying.

One should keep in mind that arranging these enjoyable activities and purchases occurred during a high-tide season in terms of Saman-tha's income. She had been working overtime at the dry cleaner's for several weeks and she felt that she could catch up with the delayed bills in the coming months. She also anticipated a large lump sum from her tax returns and this would also help her get back on track. Samantha clearly had a long-term view for managing the different activities and their costs during that summer. When circumstances changed in Sep-tember of that year, after she was fired from the dry cleaning job, Sa-mantha would cut back sharply. In November and December, as the Christmas holidays were approaching, Samantha told her children that they were not likely to get anything from her, and they did not. Her mother and her brothers would end up filling the gap, making sure that there were plenty of gifts on Christmas day.

Finally, reflecting the importance of supporting her reciprocal support network among family and friends, Samantha used money to help them out when she could and even treat them to a few nice things. She relied heavily on the financial support of family and friends during the year. So, when she received a large lump sum from her tax refund in the winter of 1999, Samantha reciprocated the support of her mother and brothers. In addition to buying them a number of practical items and helping them pay some bills, she treated them and her children to a number of dinners out at places she could "never normally afford" (e.g., Chuck E. Cheese's). This was important to Samantha; her family had really helped out during the past year when finances were tight, so it was important that she treat them to something nice in return.

The Ups and Downs of Poverty

What was the nature of Samantha's poverty? Samantha often reported feeling "stressed," "sad," or "depressed" when she fell behind on everything she needed to purchase or pay. She also reported that it "felt good" when she finally realized moments of "catching up," only to report feeling stressed and depressed again a few months later. Although Samantha was proud to make sure that there would always be food on the table and a roof over her head, she did struggle regularly and thus did suffer some material hardship. She also reported her belief that the household bills should be paid before purchasing the things she and her children wanted and needed or before providing her children with some kinds of enjoyment. But in practice she would make hard choices throughout the year between staying current on the household bills and purchasing things or activities for the family. Sometimes she would prioritize the household bills, sometimes the car payment or small purchases for the children and herself, and sometimes she would prioritize some enjoyable activities, particularly for important community and family ritual events. Samantha's stressful life was not a product of her inability to afford basic needs for survival. She was not poor in that sense.

Nor had Samantha fallen into some "underclass," where she was unable to afford a consumer lifestyle, placing her below a minimum grade of decency in the eyes of the public. She did worry about how others viewed her. For this reason, she bought her children things from time to time and provided them some enjoyable activities out in public, particularly those associated with community fairs and family celebratory rituals. Samantha was not poor because of a lack of decency.

If anything, Samantha's struggle reflected her attempts to both keep the family fed, housed, and clothed while also providing things that afforded some sense of social inclusion and cooperative social connections, even if these were at best only marginally realized. This triple struggle to realize important "beings and doings" (Sen 1992, 39) like staying alive, staying connected and supported, and realizing at least a marginal experience of social decency defined Samantha's impoverishment over the course of that year.

What contributed to Samantha's uneven, diminishing realization of these beings and doings? One of the values of having longitudinal case data is that we can more clearly see some of the causal processes at work (Maxwell 1992). Obviously, Samantha's major challenge was that her income simply did not meet her needs. But why is that? Samantha was mentally and physically healthy and able to do wage-work during this time. Samantha valued work and being able to independently support her children. She also valued keeping her household in order and being able to care directly for her own children. At the same time, she struggled to realize a routine that would convey a sense of social inclusion in the wider community.

Samantha's working conditions were a lot like those of others working in the low-wage American postindustrial service economy (Newman 2000): her hours fluctuated wildly and her jobs did not always provide the flexibility she needed to take care of her children at home. Samantha enjoyed and valued earning income to provide for her children, but her jobs were difficult, low-status service positions. As a result, she did not keep the jobs very long. Moreover she lived in a sociospatially segregated city. The African American neighborhood in which she lived did not have the better-paying, more flexible jobs that, at the time, were more abundant in the suburbs and downtown areas, a pattern typical of many cities in the postindustrial United States (Harvey 2012; Soja 2010).

Another challenge for Samantha reflects the nature of the social supports available to her. She did receive regular help from her brothers and mother and also from her friends and some other women that she knew from church. But living in an economically and racially marginalized part of town meant that "everyone was struggling," as Samantha described it. Her social network was supportive, but both the level and timing of the support were unreliable.

Not having an able adult partner in the home to help with the household demands and income needs certainly did not help. Samantha was receiving a modest amount of money from one child's father, but this did not offset the demands of managing household tasks, activities, or significant expenses. Here again, one suspects the effect of sociospatial segregation and the associated condition of American apartheid (Massey and Denton 1993) on Samantha's likelihood of forming a stable adult partnership (Mullings 1995).

Institutional social supports helped. The food stamps and subsidized housing Samantha received gave her confidence that she could keep her children housed and fed. The Earned Income Tax Credit was also a great help, so long as Samantha could work enough hours to remain eligible for the credit. However, the reporting requirements made these a logistical hassle and, in the case of means-tested supports like food stamps and housing subsidies, tended to work against her efforts to earn income through employment, where the amount she received from food stamps and rent subsidy would be lowered in tandem with increased income from working longer hours. Having affordable and desirable child-care options also helped. But the costs often meant Samantha's children were in and out of child care as her income fluctuated.

Finally, transportation loomed large in Samantha's story. She needed a reliable car to get around efficiently and worked hard to stay current on her car payments in an effort to protect her credit rating for the future. Having access to a car had a significant positive impact on the likelihood of being able to find stable, full-time work with regular pay (Yoshikawa et al. 2006). If Samantha lived in a city with a well-designed, efficient, and accessible mass-transit system, how else might she have used the money designated to the car payment, gasoline, insurance, and car repairs?

In the end, one senses that Samantha's particular ecocultural circumstances that make the project of constructing a minimally sustainable routine so challenging emerge out of how they are embedded in larger regional, national, and global processes that reflect the distribution of institutional power and enduring racial dynamics that so powerfully mark uneven urban development processes in the United States and elsewhere (Soja 2010; Harvey 2012). In Samantha's story, we can appreciate the power of business interests to dictate the terms of employment in ways that make sustaining a home life increasingly difficult. There are also real-estate interests and institutional class-bias and racism that combine to segregate many urban residents from the sites of economic and social opportunity in nearby city neighborhoods (e.g., Small 2004). The finance, real-estate, and insurance sectors have also been significant players in limiting the development of efficient, city-wide public transportation networks in many cities (Soja 2010). The exclusion of many of the city's poorest residents from how state and municipal resources are deployed in the city can also have a significant impact on creating the conditions that create Samantha's poverty.

Public supports like food stamps do help families like Samantha's, but they only perpetuate a public dissatisfaction with the problems of the "dependent poor." These public supports ignore Dewey's (2012) reminder that society and its members are impoverished "by the domination of one form of association, the family, church, economic institutions over other actual possible forms" (Kindle ed., loc. 2784). For much of the modern industrial era, capitalist institutions dominate all other forms of association. Solutions must go beyond providing limited means-tested public welfare programs that address "basic needs" or needs for "decency." It means a public struggle for what Henri Lefebvre (1996) called "The Right to the City" (see also Harvey 2012), a struggle that ensures a chance for individuals, families, and households to forge and sustain meaningful, productive, and healthful daily routines of everyday life.

Conclusion: Why Multiple Methods Matter for the Public and Its Problems

How poverty is defined and measured has significant consequences for how we address it in our society. Too often, our understanding of poverty is highly selective, emphasizing either a lack of basic necessities or highly stigmatizing social exclusion that may not adequately reflect the actual experiences of the poor. Yet these assumptions inform most official poverty measurements and the public policies and programs aimed at making things better, raising concerns about the adequacy of both in addressing this pressing public problem. In large, complex societies like our own, ethnographic studies have been invaluable for giving voice to the poor for more than a century (Himmelfarb 1991; Goode 2002); but too often it is difficult to translate ethnographic insight into larger-scale public policy solutions. Using an ecocultural framework to analyze and present ethnographic material can help by showing how personal and environmental opportunities and constraints powerfully shape our everyday projects to construct and sustain daily routines that adequately satisfy our basic material needs, our supportive social ties, and a meaningful sense of societal inclusion, which are the keys to a flourishing human life. These ecoculturally framed and ethnographically grounded insights suggest that national measures of poverty could and should go beyond the simple definition of low-income thresholds and be expanded to consider measuring both levels of social connection and societal inclusion as indexed by social participation—a suggestion that has recently been championed by three of the world's most prominent voices in the field of sustainable human development (Stiglitz, Sen, and Fitoussi 2009).

Acknowledgments

This chapter was originally prepared for the "Methods that Matter" conference held at the University of Miami, Ohio, Sept. 19–21, 2013, which was generously funded by the Society for Psychological Anthropology and the Robert Lemelson Foundation. I am thankful to Carol Worthman, Carolyn Pope Edwards, Michael Schnegg, and M. Cameron Hay for their patient reading and very helpful recommendations for improving this chapter.

References

Bauman, Zygmunt. 2005. *Work, Consumerism, and the New Poor*, 2nd ed. New York: Open University Press.

Bos, Hans, Aletha Huston, Robert Granger, Greg Duncan, Tom Brock, Vonnie McLoyd. 1999. *New Hope for People with Low Incomes: Two-Year Results of a Program to Reduce Poverty and Welfare Reform*. New York: Manpower Demonstration Research Corporation Press.

DeNavas-Walt, Carmen, Bernadette D. Proctor, and Jessica C. Smith. 2013. *Income, Poverty, and Health Insurance Coverage in the United States: 2012*. United States Census Bureau, P60-245. U.S. Government Printing Office, Washington, DC.

Dewey, John. 2012. *The Public and Its Problems: An Essay in Political Inquiry*, edited by M. Rogers. Kindle Edition. University Park, PA: The Pennsylvania State University Press.

Edin, Kathy, and Laura Lein. 1997. *Making Ends Meet: How Single Mothers Survive Welfare and Low Wage Work*. New York: Russell Sage Foundation.

European Anti-Poverty Network. 2014. "How Is Poverty Measured?" http://

www.eapn.eu/en/what-is-poverty/how-is-poverty-measured. Accessed July 30, 2014.

Fisher, Gordon M. 1997. "The Development and History of the U.S. Poverty Thresholds—A Brief Overview." *Newsletter of the Government Statistics Section and the Social Statistics Section of the American Statistical Association.* Winter: 6–7.

Galbraith, John Kenneth. 1998. *The Affluent Society.* Fortieth Anniversary Edition. Boston: Houghton Mifflin Co.

Goode, Judith. 2002. "How Urban Ethnography Counters Myths about the Poor." In *Urban Life: Readings in the Anthropology of the City,* edited by G. Gmelch and W. P. Zenner, 279–95. Longrove, IL: Waveland Press.

Harvey, David. 2012. *Rebel Cities: From the Right to the City to the Urban Revolution.* London: Verso.

Himmelfarb, Gertrude. 1991. *Poverty and Compassion: The Moral Imagination of the Late Victorians.* New York: Knopf.

Kuzel, Anton. J. 1999. "Sampling in Qualitative Inquiry." In *Doing Qualitative Research,* edited by Benjamin F. Crabtree and William L. Miller, 33–45. Thousand Oaks, CA: Sage.

Lefebvre, Henri. 1996. "The Right to the City." In *Writings on Cities,* edited and translated by Eleonore Kofman and Elizabeth Lebas, 147–59. Malden, MA: Blackwell Publishing.

Lewis, Oscar. 2002. *The Culture of Poverty.* In *Urban Life: Readings in the Anthropology of the City,* edited by George Gmelch, Robert Kemper, and Walter P. Zenner, 269–78. Longrove, IL: Waveland Press.

Levine, Marc. 2002. *The Economic State of Milwaukee's Inner City, 1970–2000.* Milwaukee: University of Wisconsin, Center for Economic Development.

Lowe, Edward D. 2003. "Identity, Activity, and the Well-Being of Adolescents and Youth: Lessons from Young People in a Micronesian Society." *Culture, Medicine, and Psychiatry* 27: 187–219.

Lowe, Edward D., and Thomas S. Weisner. 2004. "'You Have to Push It—Who's Gonna Raise Your Kids?' Situating Child Care and Child Care Subsidy Use in the Daily Routines of Lower Income Families." *Children and Youth Services Review* 26 (2): 143–71.

Massey, Douglas, and Nancy A. Denton. 1993. *American Apartheid: Segregation and the Making of the Underclass.* Cambridge, MA: Harvard University Press.

Maxwell, Joseph. 1992. "Understanding Validity in Qualitative Research." *Harvard Educational Review* 62 (3): 279–300.

Mistry, Rashmita S., and Edward D. Lowe. 2006. "What Earnings and Income Buy—'The Basics' Plus 'a Little Extra': Implications for Family and Child Well-Being." In *Making It Work: Low-Wage Employment, Family Life, and Child Development,* edited by Hirokazu Yoshikawa, Thomas S. Weisner, and Edward D. Lowe, 173–205. New York: Russell Sage Foundation.

Morgan, Sandra, and Jeff Maskovsky. 2003. "The Anthropology of Welfare

'Reform': New Perspectives on US Urban Poverty in the Post-Welfare Era." *Annual Reviews of Anthropology* 32: 315–38.

Mullings, Leith. 1995. "Households Headed by Women: The Politics of Race, Class, and Gender." In *Conceiving the New World Order: The Global Politics of Reproduction*, edited by Faye Ginsburg and Rayna Rapp, 122–39. Berkeley: University of California Press.

Newman, Katherine. 2000. *No Shame in My Game: The Working Poor in the Inner City*. New York: Vintage Books.

Rector, Robert. 2011. "A Poor Definition of Poverty." *The Oregonian*, July 25, 2011. http://www.oregonlive.com/opinion/index.ssf/2011/07/a_poor _definition_of_pov-erty.html.

Rogers, Melvin. 2012. "Introduction: Revisiting the Public and Its Problems." In *The Public and Its Problems: An Essay in Political Inquiry*, by J. Dewey, edited by M. Rogers. Kindle Edition. University Park, PA: The Pennsylvania State University.

Sen, Amartya. 1992. *Inequality Reexamined*. New York: Russell Sage Foundation.

Small, Mario Luis. 2004. *Villa Victoria: The Transformation of Social Capital in a Boston Barrio*. Chicago: The University of Chicago Press.

Soja, Edward. 2010. *Seeking Spatial Justice*. Minneapolis: University of Minnesota Press.

Stack, Carol. 1974. *All Our Kin*. New York: Basic Books.

Stiglitz, Joseph, Amartya Sen, and Jean Paul Fitoussi. 2009. *Report by the Commission on the Measurement of Economic Performance and Social Progress*. The Commission on the Measurement of Economic Performance and Social Progress. http://www.stiglitz-sen-fitoussi.fr/en/index.htm.

Weisner, Thomas S. 1984. "Ecocultural Niches of Middle Childhood: A Cross-Cultural Perspective." In *Development During Middle Childhood: The Years from Six to Twelve*, edited by W. A. Collins, 335–69. Washington, DC: National Academy of Sciences Press.

———. 1997. "The Ecocultural Project of Human Development: Why Ethnography and Its Findings Matter." *Ethos* 25 (2): 177–90.

———. 2002. "Ecocultural Understanding of Children's Developmental Pathways." *Human Development* 174: 275–81.

Weisner, Thomas S., and Edward D. Lowe. 2005. "Globalization and the Psychological Anthropology of Childhood and Adolescence." In *A Companion to Psychological Anthropology: Modernity and Psychocultural Change*, edited by Connerly Casey and Robert Edgerton, 315–36. Oxford, UK: Blackwell Publishers.

Wilson, William Julius. 1990. *The Truly Disadvantaged: The Inner City, the Underclass, and Public Policy*. Chicago: University of Chicago Press.

World Bank. 2011. "Poverty Analysis: Overview." http://web.worldbank.org/ WBSITE/EXTERNAL/TOPICS/EXTPOVERTY/EXTPA/0,,contentMDK: 22397595~pagePK:210058~piPK:210062~theSitePK:430367,00.html, accessed August 8, 2013.

Yoshikawa, Hirokazu, Edward D. Lowe, Thomas S. Weisner, JoAnn Hsueh, Noemí Enchautegui-de-Jesús, Anna Gassman-Pines, Erin B. Godfrey, Eboni C. Howard, Rashmita S. Mistry, and Amanda L. Roy. 2006. "Pathways through Low-Wage Work." In *Making It Work: Low-Wage Employment, Family Life, and Child Development,* edited by Hirokazu Yoshikawa, Thomas S. Weisner, and Edward D. Lowe, 27–53. New York: Russell Sage Foundation.

PART FOUR

Mixed Methods and Collaborative Research

Collaborative Research on Emergent Literacy: Capturing Complex Mixed Methods Data and Tools for Their Integration and Analysis

ELI LIEBER

Why Mixed Methods?

Simply because life is more complicated than can be adequately represented by the numbers and categories common to more quantitative methods, and life has important patterns that can be impossible to represent without the rich stories, observations, and videos common to more qualitative methods. To understand the complexities and patterns of life that surface as public problems, research teams today are crossing disciplinary (and methodological) boundaries in numbers like they haven't for a generation (see LeVine, chapter 1). I focus here on the ability to read, a quintessential component of education and citizenship in a democratic society. Literacy thus is considered crucial and the linchpin of national education policies and programs. Yet in public schools in the United

States, some children were slipping through the cracks—they couldn't read or couldn't read fluently. Why?

This is the type of question that mixed methods research can answer. For decades there have been pockets of teams working to conduct mixed methods research in the absence of more formal disciplinary guidelines and standards. The richness of these data led to unique challenges for their management and analysis, because of an absence of tools designed to meet the specific demands of collaborative mixed methods research.

With the recent rapid expansion of mixed methods research, the models, strategies, and tools to do this kind of work have expanded and evolved (Bryman 2006; Creswell and Plano Clark 2007; Greene 2007; Lieber 2009; Lieber and Weisner 2010; Plowright 2011; Repko 2012; Tashakkori and Teddlie 1998; Teddlie and Tashakkori 2009). Key to this work is the idea of problem-driven method and sampling decisions (Collins, Onwuegbuzie, and Jiao 2007; Kemper, Stringfield, and Teddlie 2003; Gorad 2010; Teddlie and Yu 2007) and the notion that pragmatism should be considered in methodological and associated decisions (Biesta 2010; Greene and Hall 2010). In mixed methods studies we gather varieties of data that may include stories, field notes, video/audio recordings, demographics, ratings, and test scores.

Once the qualitative data are collected, we develop coding schemes and code weighting/rating systems (and all associated application criteria), as described below. After the codes and code weights have been applied to the qualitative data, we draw on all of the above to extract the evidence needed to weave our stories, communicate our findings, and address our research questions. This brief description of mixed methods research and analysis, however, belies how difficult it actually is, particularly if one is looking at a complex problem like why some children can't read as well as others. The key question for mixed methods research is how to gather relevant and rich data systematically and analyze them efficiently, so that findings can be quickly generated to show both the rich patterns and the complexities at the heart of the problem under investigation.

Using data from a study on the Home Literacy Environments (HLE) of families, this chapter briefly introduces two tools that enable the systematic gathering and efficient analysis of rich data: the Ecocultural Family Interview (EFI), a flexible model for the systematic collection of rich contextualized information about daily routines and activities (Weisner et al. 1996), and Dedoose, a web application for the management, analysis, and presentation of qualitative and mixed method research data. Dedoose was specifically designed for the needs of collaborative qualitative and mixed methods researchers that were not being met by existing qualitative data analysis or other software. Together, the EFI and Dedoose illustrate how efficiently and effectively today's investigators can carry out complex and valuable mixed methods research, even to address so complex a problem as that of literacy.

The Home Literacy Environment Study (HLE) Background

The Federal 2002 No Child Left Behind Act has created significant financial and logistical challenges for school districts, and there is serious question as to whether student outcomes have benefited from its implementation (Lee 2006). A significant advantage of the No Child Left Behind Act over previous policies is its inclusion of English language learners in assessment and accountability. No Child Left Behind mandates academic assessment of all English language learners within one year of entry into the US school system. It has forced districts to monitor the progress of all non-English speaking students. This puts a heavy burden on already strained school systems. Dillon (2008) reported that nearly fifty percent of schools in California face federal sanctions for failing to reach the required gains in student proficiency increase. This burden is exacerbated further because, although students may make progress in their language development, it becomes increasingly difficult to mainstream English language learners (ELL) or "redesignate" them as non-English language learners after three to four years in the system (Orfield 2006; Rumberger 2006). This is particularly a problem in states like California, where twenty-five percent of students are English language learners (Rumberger 2006); therefore there is new and ongoing attention being paid to old questions regarding what works best for English language learners.

Tabors and Snow (2001) argue that not all English language learner students become English literate in the same way. Rather, they argue that pathways to becoming English literate vary by developmental stage and by English language exposure. First, they found that English literacy skills are learned as a function of age—not all age groups benefit from the same teaching models (Tabors and Snow 2001). Second, they emphasized the need to extend the scope of our knowledge by examining literacy skills and English language learning in preschool age children. Children entering the school system at preschool have a potential advantage to improve their English proficiency before entering elementary school and thus not struggle with or miss the schooling that is not accessible to those with lower English proficiency. Indeed limited English proficiency has been associated with a range of academic achievement deficits (Gallimore and Goldenberg 2001; Goldenberg, Reese, and Gallimore 1992; Reese et al. 2000; Goldenberg and Coleman 2010).

The concern for educators is how to best provide ELL students with the appropriate preschool preparation for kindergarten and subsequent years of schooling. Education researchers have narrowed the relevant skills required to learn to read and write to three umbrella topics (Neuman and Dickinson 2001; Whitehurst and Lonigan 1998): oral language skills (Hart and Risley 1995), phonological awareness, and print knowledge (e.g., Wagner, Torgesen, and Rashotte 1994; Whitehurst and Lonigan 1998). The sensitive period for introduction of these skills appears to be between the ages of three and five—a time when children are mostly cared for at home and in preschools (Dickinson, McCabe, and Essex 2006). Poverty, lower adult education, and ethnic minority status coincide with fewer emergent literacy supports at home and limited access to quality preschools. Given the importance of the HLE on supporting emergent literacy skills, the value of research on the everyday routines and activities associated with emergent literacy skills cannot be overstated (Burgess, Hecht, and Lonigan 2002). Despite the markedly greater role of home experience in literacy development, school settings are easier contexts for research, and thus there is relatively little empirical research on home literacy environments for young English language learners (Farver, Xu, Eppe, and Lonigan 2006; Lonigan 1994; Lonigan, Dyer, and Anthony 1996).

The early development and combination of emergent literacy components may have substantial impact on later literacy compared to the development of isolated literacy skills (Senechal and LeFevre, 2002; Whitehurst and Lonigan, 1998). Prewriting activities such as scribbling, drawing, coloring, painting, and attempting to write letters contribute to a child's developing understanding of symbolic representation and to developing the fine-motor skills needed for writing by hand. Prewriting activities can be supported at home by providing materials (e.g., paper, crayons, books) and supporting the activity, for example through valuing the child's products. Letter-recognition skills include learning the alphabet, often through song, naming letters, and matching letters and sounds. Parents can support early letter-recognition skills through direct teaching such as singing the alphabet song and showing the child his or her name on paper. Prewriting and letter- recognition activities at home have not been well documented in families whose children may be at risk for school success. At young ages, children's vocabulary develops through hearing others use words and practicing using the words themselves. Vocabulary development has been studied in homes, and low-income families tend to expose their young children to fewer words. While some decreased exposure may be attributed to parent education level, there may also be cultural practices that influence involving children in talk. Finally, there is some indication that many of these emergent literacy skills can be fostered by early and frequent experience with books, including being read to by others and physical interaction with board- and cloth-book toys. Reading aloud to the young child has been very well documented as an effective strategy for developing many of these emergent literacy skills. Dialogic reading, a reading aloud experience in which the child is an active participant in discussion about the pictures and story, can encourage a developing vocabulary, increasing comfort and familiarity with books and understanding of symbolic representation (Whitehurst et al. 1988, Whitehurst and Lonigan 1998). While we know that dialogic reading supports emergent literacy, we know little about the reading practices specifically of low-income and immigrant families whose children are seen as having multiple risk factors associated with school success.

The study described here focuses on the co-occurrence of emergent literacy skill development activities in home contexts and the factors that facilitate or obstruct the quality and/or frequency of these activities. The better we can understand the complex within-group variations in how demographics and other factors impact the HLE, the better prepared we will be to encourage and support increases in valuable emergent literacy activities. Existing research commonly focuses on understanding between-group differences of successful home literacy practices (Burgess 2011; Burgess, Hecht, and Lonigan 2002; Whitehurst and Lonigan 1998). In contrast, we focus here on within-group variation to better understand the variations of how working poor, immigrant, minority populations find success in supporting their children's emergent literacy development. The study goals are to describe and evaluate the home literacy practices of families with children starting the prekindergarten year at a Head Start in Los Angeles. Primary attention is paid to the four global areas of activity relevant to literacy development discussed in the literature, together referred to as HLE: prewriting experiences, letter-recognition skills, vocabulary development, and experiences with books (Dickinson, McCabe, and Essex 2006; Tabors and Snow 2001; Hart and Risley 1995; Wagner, Torgesen, and Rashotte 1994; Whitehurst and Lonigan 1998).

Using data from semistructured open-ended interviews and surveys, this study describes the nature and range of participant families' daily routines and activities around key elements of emergent literacy. Distinguishing families based on primary home language, I explore variations in how and how well families support the emergent literacy development of their young children. Further, we used a mixed methods approach to look further into how families were providing these supports in combination with each other as they worked to encourage their children's emergent literacy development.

Methods

The present study is focused exclusively on the qualitative subsample nested within a larger study designed to test the effectiveness of an experimental preschool curriculum with Head Start students in Los Angeles. The overall study included approximately 600 students and their parents, who provided a wide range of survey, demographic, and test data. A subsample of families was randomly selected to participate in more in-depth qualitative investigation. Primary caretakers, usually mothers, participated in face-to-face interviews about the activities surrounding their preschool-aged child at home that are understood to contribute to the child's emergent literacy skill development.

The subsample was drawn from a group of 84 Head Start students and their parents in Los Angeles, with a final sample of 76 families with usable data on the majority of variables analyzed in this study. Of these 76 low-income families, 53 percent of children are male, and 82 percent are of Hispanic origin, with the remaining reporting African American or African American/Hispanic origin; 94.7 percent of the children are US born; the approximate average age of mother and father at the time of the study was 31 and 33 years, respectively; both parents in 63 percent of families were US born; non-US-born parents arrived on average in the United States at 18.5 and 19.2 years of age for mothers and fathers, respectively; and there were an average of 2.98 children and 2.4 adults per household. Sixty-six percent of the families report being married or living with a partner, with the remaining being single (22 percent), divorced/separated (7 percent), or widowed (5 percent). Finally, 24 percent of families reported annual income of less than $5,000; 27 percent earned $5,001–$15,000; 22 percent earned $15,001–

$30,000; 5 percent earned more than $30,000; and 22 percent did not respond.

The Emergent Literacy Ecocultural Family Interview (EFI), developed for this study, was the basis for all face-to-face interviews. This interview is an adaptation of the Ecocultural Family Interview protocol (Weisner et al. 1996). The EFI is a semistructured open-ended interview that focuses on family daily routines as an important indicator of family well-being and child outcomes. The Emergent Literacy EFI was designed specifically to assess the HLE through an exploration of how and why a family goes about organizing the child's daily routine with respect to literacy development. Questions focused on aspects of family activities, routines, beliefs, and values related to the child's literacy development and were designed to encourage interviewees to talk freely about these aspects of their lives. Interviewers sought to learn about family resources and any constraints the family had to live within as they addressed their child's literacy development. Each main topic was first presented in general terms, and the interviewer was provided with sets of probes to help elicit details of the daily life related to the topic. For example, one topic focuses on the primary caretaker's reading to the child. Additional probes were used if parents did not spontaneously provide information on reading times during the day, reading duration, frequency and regularity in a routine, and aspects of the experience itself from both the parent and child perspective—aspects that included reading settings, warmth, and indications of enjoyment and desire for these reading episodes.

Recruitment of families involved coordination with Head Start program leaders and standard informed consent procedures with candidate families. Pairs of trained interviewers visited participant homes and conducted the interviews, each lasting approximately seventy-five minutes. In most cases, consent was obtained to audio record the interview. The audio-recorded data were processed by project staff to generate fieldnote summaries capturing the key content communicated by the parent. Summarized interview data were organized into the eighteen predetermined key topics represented by the interview questions. These data were entered and managed in Dedoose (2014)—a web application for the management, processing, coding, and analysis of qualitative and mixed methods data. Finally, each key topic in a fieldnote summary was assigned a numerical score along a five-point scale based on a coding system representing the range of families in this sample. For the four topics presented here, the average Cohen's Kappa coefficient for inter-rater reliability was .78. Coefficients for data coded with

Prewriting activities, Talking with Child, Letter Recognition, and Reading by Primary Caretaker were .71, .78, .88, and .74, respectively.

A summary of how data in the HLE study were collected, managed, integrated, and analyzed is illustrated in figure 10.1. The A1 and A2 ovals represent the collection of both qualitative and quantitative (mixed method) data. Column A1 details the management of the qualitative data, including audio-tape transcription, identifying themes in preliminary data, and code system development. For example, we developed a code called "Reading by Mother" to code all data in which the mother described when she read to her child. The application of the code entailed identifying, excerpting, and tagging all content in the transcripts related to mother-reading episodes with the Reading by Mother code. Then we analyzed the data by extracting and interpreting all excerpts with the same codes (e.g., extracting all Reading by Mother content; filtering by different groups; and exploring, interpreting, and reporting the findings). Double-headed arrow B represents the iterative development and application of a code rating system. For example, in exploring all reading by mother excerpts, we developed a five-point rating system to index "quality" of reading seen in each excerpt, based on rating criteria. This process allows for a quantitative representation of the qualitative data. When this can be accomplished in reliable ways, these numeral dimensions can be easily integrated with other quantitative data and serve as a mechanism through which qualitative and quantitative data can be connected to one another.

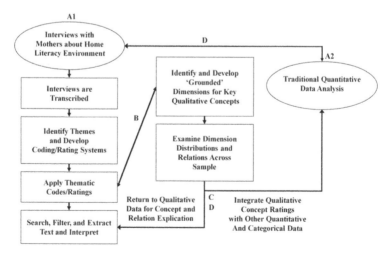

FIGURE 10.1 Home Literacy Environment Study data development and integration.

Intersection C represents a connection point where the rating systems served as a link between quantitative analyses (univariate, bivariate, or multivariate, using the rating scales or the other quantitative data collected in the study) and the qualitative data, enabling exploration to return to the qualitative data to enrich the understanding of purely quantitative findings. For example, when wondering why two variables may be related in different ways for different subgroups, we can return to the qualitative data to explore potential qualifiers unique to these groups. Path D represents how questions and answers gained through more purely qualitative or quantitative analyses can inform how one might then develop questions or approach other aspects of the database—quantitative analysis findings can inform further qualitative investigation and vice versa.

Analyses were carried out from three perspectives. Quantitative Analysis of Variance (ANOVA) is where group differences were discovered (albeit of differing strength) on all four emergent literacy outcome variables: prewriting activities, talking with child, letter recognition, and reading aloud with child. Mixed methods analyses focused on the "how and why" questions that drive decisions about whether or not to engage in such activities and the rationale for doing so. These questions were addressed through the integration of code-application ratings associated with the qualitative data and developed within Dedoose. Finally, qualitative analysis enriched our overall understandings of the more decontextualized quantitative findings.

A main focus of this chapter is to use the HLE study to illustrate how we moved from these rich and diverse raw data, collected via the EFI and complementary survey and test data, to a concise set of findings resulting from both traditional quantitative and qualitative analyses, and then from the interplay between numerical representations of the world and the rich interviews that allowed for more mixed methods perspectives.

Demographic Variation by Language Group: The Quant Side of the Story

Mothers were overwhelmingly reported as responsible for their young children's daily activities and were our main focus here. From a purely quantitative perspective based on self-reported data, table 10.1 presents the variation in mothers' reading characteristics across the three language groups (English, Spanish, and Bilingual). ANOVA results show significant differences in mother-reported language reading skills and satisfaction with these reading skills. Compared to mothers in Spanish and bilingual homes, mothers in English homes were significantly more likely to report greater levels of and satisfaction with their English reading skills and significantly lower and less satisfaction with their Spanish reading skills. Moreover, though not statistically significant, observed differences between Spanish and bilingual mothers' reports were all in expected directions (see table 10.1).

Considering that reading to young children is understood as critical to the development of the child's emergent literacy skills, it is important to recognize that despite significant differences in reported reading skill and satisfaction, we find no differences in the frequency of this activity from a self-reported data perspective. In short, the numbers didn't explain the variation in emergent literacy skill level observed between the children.

Integrating Qualitative Data into the Analysis: Tools and Findings

Integrating quantitative data like those discussed above with the kinds of qualitative narratives and stories we gathered with the Emergent Literacy EFI is essential to gain a holistic understanding of the situation, especially as the quantitative data failed to explain differences in emergent literacy. This kind of integration, or triangulation of data from a mixed methods perspective, requires an analytical structure

Table 10.1. Mother reading characteristics by primary home language

	Primary home language group			
Characteristic	English (n=26)	Spanish (n=27)	Bilingual (n=23)	ANOVA Result
Mother's average English reading skills	$4.31(.79)_{ab}$	$1.48(.77)_a$	$2.18(1.5)_b$	$F_{(2,70)} = 50.11$ $p < .001$
Mother's average Spanish reading skills	$1.94(1.24)_{ab}$	$4.18(.96)_a$	$3.91(1.27)_b$	$F_{(2,62)} = 21.22$ $p < .001$
Mother's satisfaction with English reading skills	$4.16(.89)_{ab}$	$1.65(1.06)_a$	$2.24(1.76)_b$	$F_{(2,69)} = 27.28$ $p < .001$
Mother's satisfaction with Spanish reading skills	$2.12(.49)_{ab}$	$4.48(.64)_a$	$3.82(1.22)_b$	$F_{(2,63)} = 23.98$ $p < .001$

Note: Mother's reading skill/satisfaction with reading skill variables utilized a 5-point scale and was subjected to ANOVA. All comparable mean values with common subscripts differ significantly ($p < .001$).

that simultaneously considers all the different types of data: surveys, interview transcriptions, and field notes. This is key to mixed methods analysis and deserves a parenthetical discussion on how it is possible—which I do here, using the HLE study to exemplify the process before returning below to our mixed methods findings.

The origins of qualitative/mixed methods data management initially focused on the corpora of texts and other associated data collected in the course of anthropological and other qualitative methods. Researchers still tell stories about the organization of these physical documents on tables that they marked up with margin notes, colored notations, and other notation, to "code" content in efforts to discover patterns in the data that spoke to research questions. Others used sticky notes and index cards to look for patterns in their data. The 1980s saw the emergence of efforts to digitize this process in the form of software like NUD*IST and Atlas.ti. These tools greatly improved the efficiency with which investigators could look for meaning in and analyze unstructured data.

Quantitative data analysis can often be easily managed by a member of a research team tasked with running whatever analysis might be required at a particular time. In contrast, qualitative data analysis is an iterative process that is greatly enhanced when multiple perspectives can be considered. As such, the evolution of qualitative investigation, as exemplified in contemporary research, increasingly involves collaboration. Moreover, when mixed methods are employed, it is of great value to have team members who can bring expertise from traditional qualitative and quantitative backgrounds. Thus we increasingly see mixed methods work being carried out by teams with members from varying methodological and disciplinary backgrounds.

Dedoose, previously "EthnoNotes," was developed after recognizing that we faced challenges in our work at UCLA that were not effectively addressed by existing tools or services. Prior to the development of Dedoose, there were no tools for the effective, efficient, and collaborative management, analysis, and interpretation of qualitative and mixed methods data. We had a need and, in 2001, began building a solution. We sought to create a platform-independent "environment" that would support the intuitive, collaborative, and effective management, manipulation, analysis, and interpretation of qualitative and mixed methods research data. Most features needed to be intuitive because many team members were not expert researchers nor analysts—yet we needed them to carry out their tasks accurately and consistently without high training costs. Collaboration was critical, and web applications are natively collaborative. Beyond those basics, the features needed to accommodate all of the typical qualitative data analysis activities while seamlessly integrating demographic and other more quantitative data. Finally, the analytic features needed to accommodate all the approaches qualitative and mixed method researchers may wish to employ. EthnoNotes was released as a commercial service in 2006, and Dedoose, EthnoNotes's reincarnation, was released in late 2010 to meet all of these needs.

The Dedoose architecture was specifically designed to support the efficient and effective management and analysis of data from qualitative and mixed methods perspectives. Figure 10.2 illustrates the relational database nature of Dedoose and the underlying architecture. Useful to understand here is how the different parts of the database are stored separately to allow for efficient management (e.g., documents are well managed in word processors and descriptor data in spreadsheet software). All the pieces are connected through relationships that allow Dedoose's connective features to operate in flexible and nimble ways. Simply, all the data are available for sorting, filtering, and graphing, and Dedoose analytic features are designed to make this process, and the exporting of results in useful forms, as intuitive and efficient as possible. Figure 10.3 offers a snapshot of the HLE Study Dedoose home dashboard.

So in our study, to translate the qualitative data into something that could be analyzed quantitatively to show rich patterns, we used the

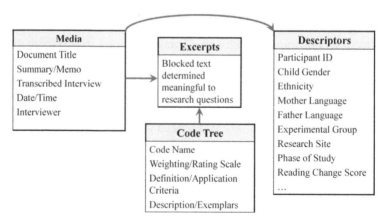

FIGURE 10.2 Dedoose architecture.

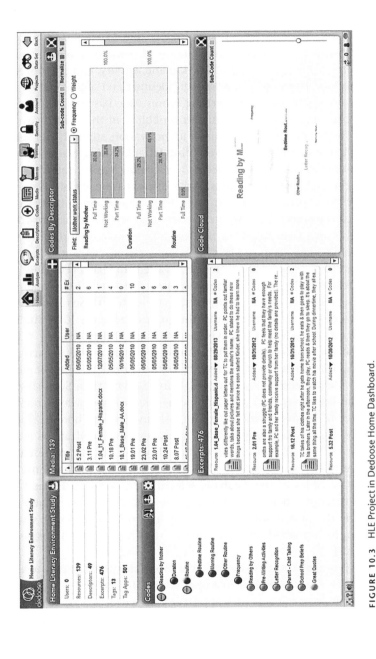

FIGURE 10.3   HLE Project in Dedoose Home Dashboard.

Dedoose code rating system. Note that these rating systems were developed within the context of this study's qualitative data and the application criteria that were developed and assessed across team members to help assure the validity of the ranking system. We found significant differences in the frequency and quality of prewriting skills and activity, prewriting letter-recognition skill and activity, and parent-child conversation. These topic ratings were defined and applied based on the following criteria: (a) prewriting scores were based on the target child's painting, writing, coloring, or scribbling in the home, with issues of frequency, level of pleasure and motivation, support, and spontaneity being considered; (b) prewriting letter-knowledge and activity scores were based on a child's ability to recite, recognize, and write letters of the alphabet, read words, write name, frequency of play with alphabet toys, parent efforts to teach the alphabet, and child's demonstrated curiosity about printed letters and words; (c) parent-child talking ratings were based on the frequency, content, and nature of parent-child conversation. Higher talking ratings were assigned to those families reporting more frequent, varied, and balanced conversation (more equally shared dialogue as opposed to more unidirectional directive talk). Significant ANOVA results for each of these topics reveal a pattern of HLE differences across the groups (see figure 10.4). Statistically significant post-hoc pair-wise comparisons (Tukey's HSD, $p < .05$) show: (a) Spanish homes had higher mean scores on prewriting activity than English and bilingual homes; (b) English homes had higher mean scores in letter-recognition knowledge and activity than Spanish and bilingual homes; and (c) bilingual homes had higher mean scores in parent-child communication than English and Spanish homes. This is a simple example of the many customizable data visualizations available in the Dedoose Analysis Workspace. The visualization represented in figure 10.4 was generated by the creation of a filter to focus only on a subset of codes in the database, selecting the "General Home Language" descriptor field, and choosing the "Weight" display. These visuals and the underlying data are easily exported to MS Excel, where they can be formatted for use in manuscripts and presentations, as in figure 10.4.

This initial quantitative approach to mixed methods analysis reveals substantive differences in three of the four HLE activities across the three language groups, as each appears to place relatively more emphasis on different activities believed to encourage children's emergent literacy development. Variation in these important HLE activities both

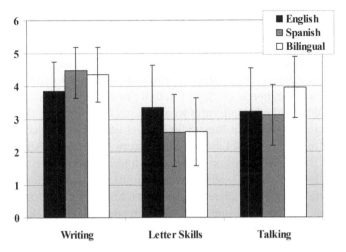

FIGURE 10.4 Significant emergent literacy EFI topics by language group. Note: Emergent literacy EFI topics are scaled (1–5, 5 being higher quality)—ANOVA results for each shown significant at ($p < .05$). "Writing" indicates prewriting activities, "Letter Skills" indicates letter recognition knowledge and activities, and "Talking" indicates parent-child verbal communication.

between language groups and within each group exposes considerable heterogeneity within a population of families commonly categorized as a single group in research and intervention efforts. These findings offer important guidance to specific areas of apparent lower-quality HLE activities by language group. However, we expected similarly unidentified variation in how effectively families within this population set routines and engaged in activities that support their children's emergent literacy development. Thus, we must turn to a more comprehensive mixed method analysis that includes both qualitative and quantitative perspectives to more fully understand variation in the form and levels of these activities and the factors that drive the decisions around them.

How Do Some Families Achieve High Levels of HLE Activity?

Optimal emergent literacy development is believed to occur where experiences related to each of three emergent literacy skill areas (oral language skills, phonological awareness, and print knowledge) take place.

While it is promising to find that many families engage at high levels in one activity or another that support the development of these skills, an evaluation of overall HLE quality required attention to the combinations of routines and activities that are present in support of emergent literacy development. Here we turn our attention to families who demonstrated higher levels of HLE activity in multiple areas.

To understand what activities were making the high HLE so successful in fostering emergent literacy in their children, we needed to limit our data to just those HLE households. Figure 10.5 is a snapshot of the Dedoose Data Selector, where one can set filtering parameters based on any number of Boolean operations and can include parameters for any part of the Dedoose database (i.e., Excerpts, Media, Users, Descriptors). To answer our research question, we narrowed the active data set to only those families whose "Reading by Mother" and "Prewriting Activities" excerpts were rated four or five in terms of quality. This allowed us to identify families meeting certain criteria and then to export the data to represent the patterns shown in figure 10.6.

Figure 10.6 illustrates the percentage of families in each language group who reported high levels across the three critical areas of emergent literacy support activity. High levels of HLE activity is defined for the purposes of this sample as: (a) "Reading by Primary Caretaker (PC)" and "Reading by Others," in which reading was reported to be integral in routines, parents expressed understanding of reading importance, and reading occurred with high frequency and duration; (b) "Prewriting Activities" and "Letter Recognition," in which regular and supported scribbling, drawing, and painting and evidence of child exposure to and practice with letters as symbols (sounding out, alphabet songs, practice letter writing, play with puzzles, games, alphabet books) encouraged skills like writing name/letters, reciting/recognizing letters, and reading simple words; and (c) "Talking with Child" showed evidence of open parent-child communication, regular verbal engagement in conversation beyond daily activities (e.g., past/future events, parent stories of own history, anticipation of kindergarten). Despite the variation observed in each group across support activities, it is promising to find meaningful proportions of each group reporting relatively high levels of emergent literacy support activities in one or more areas deemed critical to children's emergent literacy skill development. Group means show that each group distinguishes itself in specific areas. Specifically: (a) English parents report significantly higher levels of reading by the primary caretaker than Spanish families ($p < .05$); (b) Spanish parents report significantly higher levels of prewriting

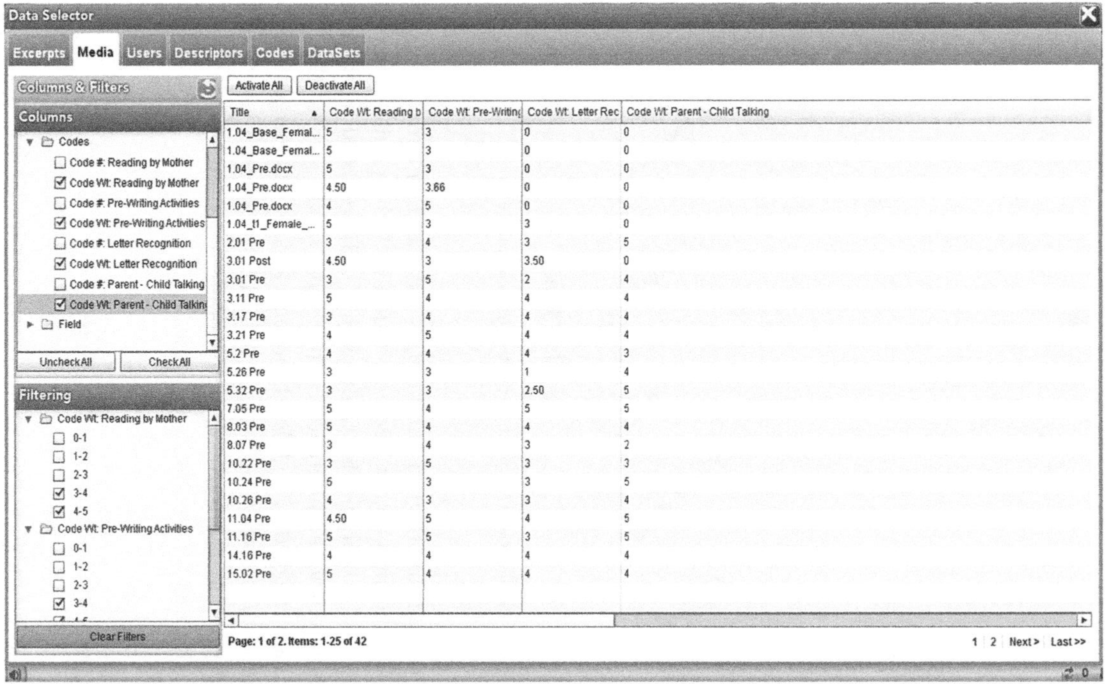

FIGURE 10.5 Finding families rated "High" in HLE activities by language group in Dedoose.

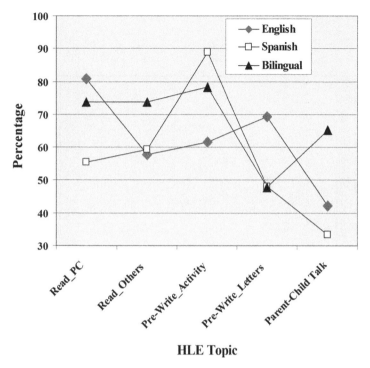

HLE Topic

FIGURE 10.6 Families rated "High" in HLE activities by language group.

activities than the English families ($p < .05$); and (c) bilingual parents report significantly higher levels of talking with their child than either English ($p < .10$) or Spanish families ($p < .05$), as tested by the Z-test for two proportional differences. While these results suggest that most families are engaged in high levels of some aspects of emergent literacy support, it turns out what is more critical for children's emergent literacy development are HLE activities being practiced in combination with each other for all language groups.

High Levels of Combined HLE Activity

While it is desirable to engage in any supportive HLE activities, optimal emergent literacy development will take place when a full range of these activities is present. Figure 10.7 illustrates the percentages of families in each language group that report high levels of activity in multiple areas: reading by PC and others, prewriting and letter recognition, and talking with child in various combinations. The patterns are consistent with those in figure 10.6, as each language group's areas of strengths and weaknesses are apparent. It is particularly intriguing that between ten and twenty percent of families in each language group combine high levels of emergent literacy support activity in all areas, and these families also report regular communication with their children's school. This finding prompts two key questions. How well do these families appreciate the value of combining a full range of HLE activities? Can education and intervention programs find ways to encourage more combined emergent literacy support activity?

Parents of English-speaking families that combined high levels of HLE activities reported having achieved at least a high school education and describe a relatively comprehensive model of understanding the variety of requirements for school success. These parents appreciated their responsibility for providing supportive experiences and monitoring children's progress through communication with the school. For example, one mother recalled that as a child her own mother was not able to help support her learning. This history motivated her to become very involved with her own children's school so they won't be "left behind." Another mother shared how her child showed she is "eager to learn," and expressed a consistent understanding of the skills

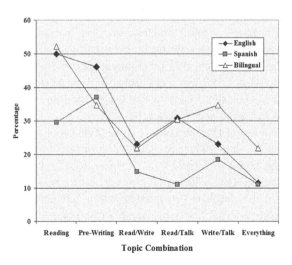

FIGURE 10.7 Percentage of families combining emergent literacy support activities by language group.

her child had and those she needed to acquire to be successful in later academic pursuits.

Spanish-speaking families that combined HLE activities also reported at least a high school education, and expressed appreciation of the demands of school success as well as the importance of preparing their children. Despite possible language obstacles for these primarily Spanish speakers, families reported regular communication with their children's school. For example, in one family the mother and other family members prepared the child for kindergarten by helping her to learn numbers and the alphabet. The mother explained that this help is a "good gateway for other learning because these are the basics," and she believed these would enable her daughter to have confidence once older. This determination and commitment to supporting emergent literacy development is illustrated by another family in which both parents had sought suggestions from the Head Start teacher on how they could help prepare their child for school. The teacher suggested teaching the alphabet and shapes and, in response, the parents devoted time daily to practice these skills with their child.

Bilingual families that combined HLE activities reported relatively less formal education, using both English and Spanish to guide their children's home activities, and taking a practical, school-skills-oriented perspective on activities supporting literacy at home. For example, in one family both parents spent time at home teaching their child things he will be learning in school (e.g., numbers, alphabet, how to behave). They did this so he would "understand what is expected from him once in school." When describing home writing activities, the mother said, "It gives joy to know that by coloring [her child] is also learning things like getting to know colors" in an enjoyable manner. Another mother shared that she "reads to her child like [her] father did with [her] so that her son can develop well."

Overall, we found that families with high levels of activity supporting the development of all three areas of emergent literacy skills have similar beliefs about preparing their children for regular school. These parents described their beliefs and appreciation for how these activities would benefit their children in relatively complete and cohesive ways. Further, despite a variety of differences across home language groups, all recognize the importance of providing all core emergent literacy experiences and finding ways to ensure they are consistently present in the daily routines of their homes. Finally, these parents all report actively communicating with their children's teachers and steadily monitoring their children's progress in the Head Start program.

Conclusions: What Difference Did Mixed Methods Make in the Findings?

The mixed methods employed in this study were critical to the identification and understanding of the deep and contextualized findings. Emergent literacy skill development is just one phenomenon presenting a level of complexity demanding attention from multiple perspectives in order to acquire a level of understanding that can inform effective and sustainable program and intervention development. In this study, ANOVA analyses of group differences by home language revealed that while there was no difference in the reported time mothers read to children, each language group had a particular area of strength in preparing young children for school that was significantly different from the other groups. Specifically, Spanish speakers were more likely to support prewriting activities, like drawing, coloring, and writing letters, through parent involvement and directed scaffolding. These activities were seen as enhancing school readiness. Interestingly, English speakers saw these activities more as children's independent play and expressiveness, not as early literacy skills. Bilingual parents reported providing higher levels for conversational opportunities for their children and were more likely to encourage oral and vocabulary support. Finally, English speakers actively supported letter-recognition activities more than other groups. While it is believed that emergent literacy components are more effective when combined, results in figure 10.7 suggest that Spanish-speaking families showed less comprehensive patterns of HLE activities.

The application of the code-weighting approach and subsequent analysis in Dedoose represents just one mixed method approach used here to understand the diversity of families and settings in the low-income population under examination. The use of these numeric representations of qualitative data allowed for unique profiling and indexing analyses and provided a direct link to the qualitative data for a more contextualized understanding of results. The results from these analyses demonstrate that the habitual practice of categorizing English-language learner students and families as a homogenous group presents an obstacle to properly serving the educational needs of children. In short, while our ANOVA results show patterns of different emphases on HLE activities by language group, our mixed method analyses reveal that more significant for appreciating the nuances related to impacts on child literacy skill development was in-group variation.

Overall, despite the perspective encouraged by deficit models, we find that these low-income immigrant families showed a wealth of emergent literacy development supports in their daily activities and routines. At the same time, it is important to recognize the variation across these home-language groups in terms of education experience, language skills, and immigration background, as these represent the context in which any intervention must be integrated. Further, we find that the HLE activities are not understood in the same ways by each language group. Recognizing and adapting to these variations will enhance the successful adoption and sustainability of education and intervention efforts. Particular group strengths should be identified, encouraged, and capitalized on as culturally consistent and familiar practices that support emergent literacy development within a particular group. This study offers some insight into these "natural" practices that can be used to develop models of other home environments understood to share sociocultural characteristics. Finally, the acquisition of these insights could only have come from a systematic application of mixed methods research strategies and the efficiencies afforded by modern and flexible research models and technologies.

Educators using just the quantitative findings presented here would have been led to an oversimplification of group categories by home language. As demonstrated by this study, the efficiency and effectiveness of education and intervention efforts are limited if they fail to pay closer attention to individual student and family strengths, weaknesses, and background characteristics (see also Tabors and Snow 2001). The costs of this failure to fit support resources to the range of specific needs in target populations are costly to both the students and the provider system. Findings from ecocultural investigations, like that carried out here, can guide the delivery of education and intervention practices and enhance the efficiency and effectiveness of their desired outcomes (Burgess, Hecht, and Lonigan 2002). Particularly if implemented with preschool-aged English-language learner students and families, enhanced fit and effectiveness of services can help ensure these students will enter the school system prepared to succeed (Farver, Xu, Eppe, and Lonigan 2006). That said, this work is more easily encouraged than put into practice. Yet strategies like those of the EFI and tools like Dedoose can help put a structure around the collection of necessary data and a platform for the efficient management, analysis, and presentation of these data.

References

Biesta, Gert. 2010. "Pragmatism and the Philosophical Foundations of Mixed Methods Research." In *Sage Handbook of Mixed Methods in Social and Behavioral Research*, 2nd ed., edited by A. Tashakkori and C. Teddlie, 95–117. Thousand Oaks, CA: Sage Publications.

Bryman, Alan. 2006. "Integrating Quantitative and Qualitative Research: How Is It Done?" *Qualitative Research* 6 (1): 97–113.

Burgess, Steven R. 2011. "Home Literacy Environments (HLEs) Provided to Very Young Children." *Early Child Development and Care* 181 (4): 445–62.

Burgess, Stephen R., Steven A. Hecht, and Christopher J. Lonigan. 2002. "Relations of the Home Literacy Environment (HLE) to the Development of Reading-Related Abilities: A One-Year Longitudinal Study." *Reading Research Quarterly* 37 (4): 408–26.

Collins, Kathleen M. T., Anthony J. Onwuegbuzie, and Qun G. Jiao. 2007. "A Mixed Methods Investigation of Mixed Methods Sampling Designs in Social and Health Science Research." *Journal of Mixed Methods Research* 1 (3): 267–94.

Creswell, John W., and Vicki L. Plano Clark. 2007. *Designing and Conducting Mixed Methods Research*. Thousand Oaks, CA: Sage Publications.

Dedoose, Version 4.5 (2014). A web application for managing, analyzing, and presenting qualitative and mixed method research data. Los Angeles: SocioCultural Research Consultants LLC (www.dedoose.com).

Dickinson, David K., Allyssa McCabe, and Marilyn J. Essex. 2006. "A Window of Opportunity We Must Open to All: The Case for Preschool With High-Quality Support for Language and Literacy." In *Handbook of Early Literacy Research*, vol. 2, edited by Susan B. Neuman and David K. Dickinson, 11–28. New York: The Guilford Press.

Dillon, S. 2008. "Under 'No Child' Law, Even Solid Schools Falter." www.nytimes.com/2008/10/13/education/13child.html, Accessed October, 13, 2008.

Farver, Jo Ann, M., Yiyuan Xu, Stefanie Eppe, and Christopher J. Lonigan. 2006. "Home Environments and Young Latino Children's School Readiness." *Early Childhood Research Quarterly* 21: 196–212.

Gallimore, Ronald, and Claude Goldenberg. 2001. "Analyzing Cultural Models and Settings to Connect Minority Achievement and School Improvement Research." *Educational Psychologist* 36 (1): 45–56.

Goldenberg, Claude, and Rhonda Coleman. 2010. *Promoting Academic Achievement Among English Language Learners: A Guide to the Research*. Thousand Oaks, CA: Corwin.

Goldenberg, Claude, and Ronald Gallimore. "Local Knowledge, Research Knowledge, and Educational Change: A Case Study of Early Spanish Reading Improvement." *Educational Researcher* 20 (8): 2–14.

Goldenberg, Claude, Leslie Reese, and Ronald Gallimore. 1992. "Effects of Literacy Materials from School on Latino Children's Home Experiences and Early Reading Achievement." *American Journal of Education* 100 (4): 497.

Gorad, Stephan. 2010. "Research Design as Independent of Methods." In *Sage Handbook of Mixed Methods in Social and Behavioral Research*, 2nd ed., edited by Abbas Tashakkori and Charles Teddlie, 237–51. Thousand Oaks, CA: Sage Publications.

Greene, Jennifer C. 2007. *Mixed Methods in Social Inquiry.* San Francisco: Jossey-Bass.

Greene, Jennifer C., and Jori N. Hall. 2010. "Dialectics and Pragmatism: Being of Consequence." In *Sage Handbook of Mixed Methods in Social and Behavioral Research*, 2nd ed., edited by Abbas Tashakkori and Charles Teddlie, 119–43. Thousand Oaks, CA: Sage Publications.

Hart, Betty, and Todd R. Risley. 1995. *Meaningful Differences in the Everyday Experiences of Young American Children.* Baltimore, MD: Paul H. Brookes Publishing.

Kemper, Elizabeth A., Sam Stringfield, and Charles Teddlie. 2003. "Mixed Methods Sampling Strategies in Social Science Research." In *Sage Handbook of Mixed Methods in Social and Behavioral Research*, edited by Abbas Tashakkori and Charles Teddlie, 273–96. Thousand Oaks, CA: Sage Publications.

Lee, Jaekyung. 2006. "Tracking Achievement Gaps and Assessing the Impact of NCLB on the Gaps: An In-Depth Look into National and State Reading and Math Outcome Trends." *The Civil Rights Project at Harvard University* (June): 82.

Lieber, Eli. 2009. "Mixing Qualitative and Quantitative Methods : Insights into Design and Analysis Issues." *Journal of Ethnographic and Qualitative Research* 3: 218–27.

Lieber, Eli, and Thomas S. Weisner. 2010. "Meeting the Practical Challenges of Mixed Methods Research." In *Sage Handbook of Mixed Methods in Social and Behavioral Research*, 2nd ed., edited by Abbas Tashakkori and Charles Teddlie, 559–79. Thousand Oaks, CA: Sage Publications.

Lonigan, Christopher. 1994. "Reading to Preschoolers Exposed: Is the Emperor Really Naked?" *Developmental Review* 14 (3): 303–23.

Lonigan, Christopher J., Sarah M. Dyer, and Jason L. Anthony. 1996. "The Influence of the Home Literacy Environment on the Development of Literacy Skills in Children from Diverse Racial and Economic Backgrounds." Paper presented at the annual meeting of the American Educational Research Association. New York, April.

Neuman, Susan B., and David K. Dickinson, eds. 2001. *Handbook of Early Literacy Research.* New York: The Guilford Press.

Orfield, Gary. 2006. "State Capacity to Implement No Child Left Behind: What Have We Achieved?" Paper presented at the annual meeting of the American Educational Research Association. San Francisco, April 7–11.

Plowright, David. 2011. *Using Mixed Methods: Frameworks for an Integrated Methodology*. Los Angeles: Sage Publications.

Reese, Leslie, Helen Garnier, Ronald Gallimore, and Claude Goldenberg. 2000. "A Longitudinal Analysis of the Antecedents of Emergent Spanish Literacy and Middle-School English Reading Achievement of Spanish-Speaking Students." *American Educational Research Association Journal* 37: 633–62.

Repko, Allen F. 2012. *Interdisciplinary Research: Process and Theory*. Los Angeles: Sage Publications.

Rumberger, Russell. 2006. "How Are English Learners Faring Under California's Prop. 227? Findings from a 5-Year Statewide Evaluation." Paper presented at the annual meeting of the American Educational Research Association, San Francisco, April 7–11.

Senechal, Monique, and Jo-Anne LeFevre. 2002. "Parental Involvement in the Development of Children's Reading Skill: A Five-Year Longitudinal Study." *Child Development* 73 (2): 445–60.

SRI International. 2006. "First 5 School Readiness Program Evaluation: Kindergarten Entry Profiles." Accessed March 11, 2008: http://www.ccfc.ca.gov/.

Tabors, Patton, and Catherine Snow. 2001. "Young Bilingual Children and Early Literacy Development." In *Handbook of Early Literacy Research*, vol. 1, edited by Susan Neuman and David Dickinson, 159–78. New York: Guilford Press.

Tashakkori, Abbas, and Charles Teddlie. 1998. *Mixed Methodology: Combining Qualitative and Quantitative Approaches*. Thousand Oaks, CA: Sage Publications.

Teddlie, Charles, and Abbas Tashakkori. 2009. *Foundations of Mixed Methods Research: Integrating Quantitative and Qualitative Techniques in the Social and Behavioral Sciences*. Thousand Oaks, CA: Sage Publications.

Teddlie, Charles, and Fen Yu. 2007. "Mixed Methods Sampling: A Typology with Examples." *Journal of Mixed Methods Research* 1 (1): 77–100.

Wagner, Richard K., Joseph K. Torgesen, and Carol Rashotte. 1994. "Development of Reading-Related Phonological Processing Abilities: New Evidence of Bidirectional Causality from a Latent Variable Longitudinal Study." *Developmental Psychology* 30 (1): 73–87.

Weisner, Thomas S., Jennifer Coots, and Lucinda P. Bernheimer. 1996. "Eco-Cultural Family Interview Field Manual." Unpublished manuscript, UCLA Center for Culture and Health, Los Angeles.

Whitehurst, Grover J., Francine Falco, Christopher Lonigan, Janet Fischel, Barbara DeBaryshe, Marta C. Valdez-Menchaca, and Marie Caulfield. 1988. "Accelerating Language Development through Picture Book Reading." *Developmental Psychology* 24 (4): 552–59.

Whitehurst, Grover, and Christopher Lonigan. 1998. "Child Development and Emergent Literacy." *Child Development* 68: 848–72.

ELEVEN

Lessons Learned from Parents of Adults with Autism in India

TAMARA C. DALEY

In figure 11.1, three young men sit around a table with plates of samosas, cakes, and other treats. It is a birthday party, both for me and for the birthday boy at the head of the feast, his fingers askew in front of his eyes. At the moment the photo was shot, one guest glances away from the camera, while the other gives a penetrating look straight into the lens, a cheek stuffed with a samosa. It is 1996, and the birthday boy and his friends are all teens with autism, each on the verge of adulthood.

The day of this photograph, I had been in India for eleven months, immersed not in Indian culture, but in Indian *autism* culture. I had started with a simple question: If autism exists in India, but they don't call it that, then what DO they call it? This question expanded into many more: Does autism in India "look" like autism in the United States—are the characteristics the same? How do people explain these characteristics? Who is getting diagnosed? What happens to people who don't? Are there differences in the kinds of intervention a child will get? These questions led me through five major cities, more than forty schools, numerous doctors' offices and clinics, and most importantly, into the homes of more than

FIGURE 11.1   Photo of birthday party by Tamara Daley.

one hundred families—all of whom had been given a diagnosis of autism. Toward the end of the year, these questions took me to the capital city of New Delhi and into the home of the birthday boy, where, after eleven months, we celebrated our shared birthday with samosas and pizza.

Different disciplines would approach the questions above using a range of methods. Historically, researchers who study autism have often come from the fields of clinical and developmental psychology, medicine, and psychiatry, where research designs involve control groups and assessments, and in which tasks are commonly completed in a research setting (Burack et al. 2002). When I visited families of autistic children in 1995 and 1996, only very few researchers had published ethnographic research on autism or used more qualitative methods (see Gray 1994; Toomey and Adams, 1995; Connors and Donnellan 1993). Given how little information was available about autism in India, qualitative methods seemed best suited to answer my list of questions. They also happened to be all I knew how to do.

A Limited but Effective Tool Box

I went India armed with only a few research methods in my toolbox, gleaned through part-time positions and whatever I had read about doing fieldwork. I felt unqualified to administer standardized questionnaires or tests, so to understand autism in India, I replicated the methods I had used before: asking questions, observing, and pulling out information from medical reports, which families in India keep with them rather than in clinics ("abstracting," in more technical terms). I did this in home after home, all across the country. Not surprisingly, what I found turned out to be quite interesting. Families told me of their children who didn't speak, or who had seizures, or who seemed overly active. They told of how they had taken their child from doctor to doctor (from "pillar to post!" was a phrase I heard over and over), only to be given one misdiagnosis after another. By copying information from the doctors' reports, I could see why parents were confused: diagnoses were often written as questions, and sometimes no diagnosis was provided at all. Families sometimes waited for years before visiting a doctor, only to spend an average of two more years before receiving a diagnosis of autism (Daley 2004).

I also heard stories of interventions with devastating consequences, such as a young adult whose medications were so high that he lay in a catatonic state almost twenty-four hours a day, and eventually was taken by his mother to a drug rehab facility to wean him off his psychotropic medications. I listened to parents describe the welts their children received from being beaten at their special schools, as they sadly confessed that they had said nothing to the school official. "Why?" I asked, not understanding. "For fear we would be told to leave. And then we would have nowhere to go," was the response. It wasn't long until I saw for myself, in schools I visited, the full range of ways that children with autism were treated in 1996, from children tied to desks and hit with sticks to gentle, innovative, and creative ways of engaging and bringing out the best in a child. This was a period in India where understanding of autism was still limited, and the explosion of global awareness that came in the post-Internet age (Grinker 2007) had not yet occurred.

The methods I used in the mid 1990s mostly answered my research questions. I got incredibly rich information, some of which I quantified (Daley 2004) and other parts I used to develop theoretical arguments (Daley 2002). However these methods had their limitations. It was difficult to make comparisons across families on all but a few variables, and comparisons to families outside India were definitely out of the question. Most of all, it was sometimes hard to know how different aspects of the families' lives fit together, since so much relied on my own ability to make sense of what I had learned.

Expanding Questions to Seek Findings That Would Matter to Families

When I first began working in India in the 1990s, I did not know anyone in India who might be called an autism expert, and I started my fieldwork by following questions that were interesting to *me*. Following questions of interest, in fact, was what I had been taught to do. I was several months into my project when people started to express interest in what I was finding, and they wanted to know how it would help them. It was also about that time that I met some key professionals and advocates in the small but growing autism field, and these individuals further shaped my research approach. I realized that any kind of systematic data would be among the only data of its kind at the time, and it felt incredibly important to ask the right questions—questions that would benefit families in India. One of the key questions I began asking, as a result, was *what would help families most right now?* Fifteen years after my first study, this new question led me to become part of a new project, called Research on Autism and Families in India (RAFIN).

In RAFIN, we committed ourselves from the conception of the project to conduct studies that had high local relevance and potential for impacting disability policy within India. We wanted our findings to not just be "interesting" as a research study contributing to theory and empirical findings for social science, but to provide data that would be helpful to our participants, to other families in India, and to the professionals who work with them.

To meet these two goals, we established a formal collaborative partnership with an Indian nongovernmental organization, Action For Autism (AFA). Beyond being merely a collaboration, this relationship has the elements of community-based participatory research (CBPR), that is, an approach to empirical questions that involves stakeholder participation, research, and action (Hall 1992). We asked our colleagues at AFA to identify the unanswered questions, what they felt needed to be known—we viewed them as the experts, not us. Following their lead, we designed and conducted two studies as part of RAFIN.

One key aspect of both studies was to bring family and community contexts of autism to life through the use of mixed methods. Similar to the 1996 study, the RAFIN projects had semi-structured interviews at the core of data collection, but our mixed methods approach added standardized assessments and questionnaires to the interviews and observations. In this chapter, I describe one of the RAFIN projects, a study of fifty-two families of adults with autism in New Delhi, to highlight the benefits of multiple methods, as well as to emphasize the importance of collaborative partnerships. Through this study, I had the opportunity to revisit fifteen of the families I had met in 1996, including the young men who had attended my birthday so many years earlier. While the RAFIN Adult Study asked many questions, I use the data from just a single question in this chapter. After presenting the findings to this question, I discuss how the information collected can be made *useful*, with community-based participatory research as a key to both doing better research and making findings more locally meaningful.

The RAFIN Adult Study

The RAFIN Adult study included fifty-two families, with a total of fifty-four adults with Autism Spectrum Disorder (ASD; two families had two adults each). All the families came from the greater urban area of New Delhi, which consists of approximately 22.1 million people.

Data collection for the RAFIN Adult Study took place between February and July 2013. Families were interviewed for between two and five hours in their homes, with either two or three members from the research team participating in each visit. Interviews were conducted in the language of choice of the parent, which resulted in sixteen interviews predominantly in Hindi and thirty-six interviews predominantly in English. All interviews were audio recorded and professionally transcribed and translated. A member of the research team separately reviewed the translated files to ensure accuracy. At the time of the interviews, adults ranged in age from eighteen to forty-four years old and parents ranged in age from forty to seventy years old. Selected characteristics of families and adults appear in table 11.1.

Parents completed questionnaires, some of which were developed in the West and some of which we developed. In the RAFIN projects, two constructs in particular figure prominently: empowerment and acceptance. These were first introduced to RAFIN by Indian team members as key outcomes of a parent training program. The RAFIN team spent

Table 11.1. Participant characteristics

	N	%
Sex of adult is male	44	81.5
Age		
18–20	19	35.2
21–25	16	29.6
26–30	9	16.7
31+	10	18.5
Birth order		
Only child	15	27.8
Eldest with younger siblings	21	38.9
Younger with elder siblings	18	33.3
Daytime setting		
Stays at home	22	40.7
Attends educational, vocational, or other setting outside of home	32	59.3
Religion		
Hindu	40	76.9
Muslim	2	3.8
Christian	4	7.7
Sikh	3	5.8
Jain	1	1.9
Two different religions followed	2	3.8
Household type		
Nuclear	35	67.3
Extended or joint	19	36.5
Reported monthly household income (in Rupees)		
Less than 25k	6	11.5
25k to 50k	10	19.2
50k to 75k	7	13.5
75k and above	29	55.8
Mother employed outside the home	26	50.0
Father employed outside the home	39	75.0

considerable time discussing what "empowerment" and "acceptance" meant in an Indian context, and how empowerment in particular may differ from the way it is conceived in the United States, where it is typically focused on increasing both understanding of the disability with capacity to navigate the service delivery system and capacity to advocate on behalf of the child (e.g., Brookman-Frazee and Koegel 2004). Ultimately we developed two short questionnaires and administered these as part of the first RAFIN project, the parent training program evaluation. By the time we initiated the RAFIN Adult study, we had these same measures developed and ready to use. In addition, we included a well-established questionnaire to assess stress, the Parent Stress Index-Short Form (PSI-SF; Abidin 1995). The PSI-SF has been used with parents to examine a wide range of topics, and it has also been previously used in Indian populations, including parents of children with disabilities (John 2012; Gupta, Mehrotra and Mehrotra 2012; Prakash et al. 2013).

A third method used in this study was direct assessment, based on observational tools, semistructured interviews, and self-reported measures. A list of all measures with the method type appears in table 11.2. In contrast to 1996, my tool kit had more than doubled in size.

We conducted the interviews in each family's home, and families completed questionnaires after we left. All visits included either two or three members from the research team. Interviews were conducted in the language of choice of the parent (either Hindi or English), and lasted between two and five hours, often including a meal. We used a

Table 11.2. Overview of measures for the RAFIN Adult Study

Construct	Measure name	Method type	Origin of measure
Daily routines, educational and work history, interventions and medication, sexuality and marriage, social activities, future plans, advice for others	Semistructured interview	Semistructured interview	Developed with AFA
Stress	Parenting Stress Index Short Form (PSI-36)	Questionnaire	Western
Acceptance	RAFIN Acceptance Scale	Questionnaire	Developed with AFA
Empowerment	RAFIN Empowerment Scale	Questionnaire	Developed with AFA
	Parent Advocacy Activity	Questionnaire	Developed with AFA
	Parenting Sense of Competence (PSOC)	Questionnaire	Western
Adult functioning	Vineland Adaptive Behavior Scales (VABS)	Semistructured interview	Adapted
	Social Responsiveness Scale	Questionnaire	Western
	Autism Diagnostic Observation Schedule (ADOS)	Observational assessment	Western
	Glasgow Anxiety Scale (GAS)	Questionnaire (interview)	Western
	Beck's Depression Inventory (BDI)	Questionnaire (interview)	Western

semi-structured interview, but the order of questions was not always the same. We asked about adults' daily routines, educational and work experiences, diagnosis, interventions and medications, social activities, marriage and sexuality, and plans for the future. Regardless of the order of questions, we ended each interview by asking parents to reflect on what would have made their experience easier and concluded with one final question: "*What advice would you share with families of younger children diagnosed with autism?*" This question is the focus of my analysis here.

Advice from Parents of Adults with ASD in India

We asked parents what advice they would offer to families without any a priori hypotheses about what they might say. Even "knowing" a group of these families in the past, I could not begin to guess the direction their lives had taken and therefore what reflections they might share. One thing I knew with certainty was that many of these families had been told to "wait and see" about their child's development, or that their son would "become all right when he turns eighteen." With eighteen as their son or daughter's minimum age to participate in the project, I was extremely interested to see how parents would now make meaning of their current situation, and what could be gleaned from their comments. For the most part, answering this question was not difficult, and parents did not struggle to articulate their response.

All the responses to this question were extracted from transcripts of the interviews, and using Dedoose, a tool for analysis of mixed method data (see Lieber, chapter 10), the responses fell broadly into four categories: (1) advice to the parent about direct actions they could take for themselves, such as becoming trained or learning about autism, seeking professional support, and developing an informal support system; (2) advice to take particular philosophical approaches to life and understanding the child, such as accepting the child or the situation, or not being bothered by small things; (3) advice related to intervention for the child, such as the type of interventions to use, effective strategies, and areas of behavior and development to focus on with the child; and (4) advice about different parenting approaches to the child, such as whether or not to indulge the child and whether or not to use punishment. Figure 11.2 shows the percentage of parents who offered advice in each category; note that many parents offered advice for more than one category. Below I provide some examples of the two greatest areas of advice mentioned by parents (parents taking action

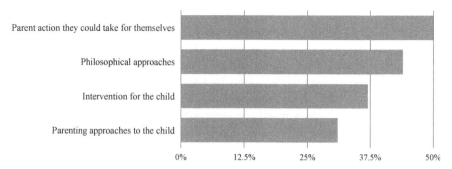

Parent action they could take for themselves

Philosophical approaches

Intervention for the child

Parenting approaches to the child

0%   12.5%   25%   37.5%   50%

FIGURE 11.2   Percentage of parents offering advice in each category (N=52).

for themselves and advice about philosophical approaches) and discuss how these data relate to some of the questionnaires used in this study.

Parent Actions for Themselves: "No Angel Is Going to Come . . ."

Many of the parents in this study received a diagnosis for their children at a time when very few professionals in India knew about autism, and therefore parents were typically on their own to navigate their child's education and development. In the early 1990s, there were few educational options: the first school specifically for children with autism did not open until 1994. Thus parents often learned by trial and error, and as Veena's[1] mother advised, "The best thing is to empower yourself, to enlighten yourself, don't be dependent on professional things." Educating and empowering oneself was a theme that echoed through approximately forty percent of the parent narratives. Some parents put emphasis on the importance of understanding autism, while others explicitly addressed the need for parents to be the ones to work with their child.

Some parents expressed impatience with other parents who might turn over the task of education to schools and others. Maanav's mother, for example, has worked throughout his life. Even while working, she estimated that she spent up to five hours a day working with Manaav, and eventually found success in teaching him to communicate through writing. Her score on the RAFIN Empowerment Scale (RAFIN ES) was in the top half for parents in the sample. In rapid fire, she advised parents: "Get enough knowledge about autism, about yourself. Don't expect anybody to do anything for you. If they do, good, acknowledge it. No angel is going to come. Learn, read, don't limit yourself, be positive, don't cry, increase your network, go visit people, don't confine yourself at your home. Take your child out, let him do what he wants to do. Don't blame yourself. Get full knowledge. NO angel is going to come. If somebody helps, be grateful. Be knowledgeable, read, learn. Don't lament, don't cry." Manaav's mother's strong sense of empowerment comes through clearly as she lists these multiple strategies of positive emotional and behavioral activity, and the success of these strategies seem borne out in Manaav's ability to communicate through writing and basic self-care skills. Yet other data suggest that parent empowerment might vary independently from child outcome.

Jatin's level of functioning is considerably lower than that of Manaav; he is nonverbal and lacks many self-care skills, such as being able to use the toilet by himself. Jatin's mother has stoically tolerated an abusive and uninvolved husband, one who blamed her for Jatin's autism. She is now focused on addressing Jatin's aggression; the force of his blows to her stomach can sometimes knock her over. She has developed strategies to handle both these challenges and her empowerment is clear in the advice she offered:

Firstly, the problem is people blame their destinies that this happened to us. Nobody can say why this happened to you, any child could be born disabled to any parents. Now the problem is there, and you have to face it . . . the blame game is very bad either in the family or in the society. People say that because of you, this happened. This is no reason. You may start finding the reason why the child has born like this, but you should look for solutions, what's the treatment? Don't waste time on reasons, go for treatment.

Jatin's mother continued:

So the main thing is to have knowledge. Knowledge whatever you get, wherever you get . . . I would tell them firstly that it's very important for parents to work with the children. You're expecting things from the school, and what time are you devoting to him at house? The mentality that a miracle would take place, I don't believe in such things. Hard work with the child is very important. If you do 200 percent hard work then maybe the result is five percent; these children require a lot of hard work.

Jatin's mother is willing to put in 200 percent for a five percent return. Her score on the RAFIN ES placed her in the top ten percent of parents in the study, meaning she reports one of the highest empowerment scores of all parents, even though Jatin was in the lowest fifteen percent in terms of his score on community adaptation and self-care functioning.

Some families recommended that parents educate themselves, learn as much as they can, and dig in to work directly with their child, based on their experience of stepping in once the professionals failed them. Tushar's mother was one who was giving "200 percent hard work" from the time I met her, when Tushar was only six. While he attended many schools over the years, she took on his education with single-minded, life-consuming drive. She recalled how she could have bought him shoes with Velcro "like so many parents" when he struggled so much to learn to tie them, but instead, she recalled, "I said, 'he *has* to, he *has* to. Let him take as much as time as he needs.' So, every morning, every evening, 'make this knot, make rabbit ears, make this. . . .' It kept on happening. If he has fingers, he has hands, he can do it, and that is true in so many other areas (italics indicate verbal emphasis)." This level of effort does not come without a cost. Simply stating her life as she sees it, Tushar's mother said that she and Tushar have reached a point where what he needs most is to separate from her, that her deep understanding of him is precisely what is holding him back. Perhaps this transition period may be reflected in her RAFIN ES score, which was just above the mean for parents. Her advice was simple: "Don't do everything alone. It's best to have different professionals working with your kid even in a single day, because it's important for the kid, and it's important to trust professionals." She added, without mincing words: "Because otherwise you will burn out."

Other parents similarly suggested the importance of seeking help from institutes and organizations. But Sakshi's mother warned that the challenge faced by young parents is not that there are too few options, but that there are too *many*. In the past decade, India has become the Wild West for autism "cures," which include a long and dramatic list of approaches that are not typically found elsewhere, some of which have been discredited or have fallen out of fashion elsewhere, and none of which are regulated in India. Shortly after I met Sakshi and her parents, her mother began taking courses to work with children with special needs and continues to work with parents today. Sakshi's mother, therefore, has the perspective both as a parent and a professional, and explained, "I would always tell them to read up because they are very vulnerable around like people even talk about recovery and all these things. So just they need to educate themselves and get empowered. So that then they know who is trying to fool them, or they know which is the best service." Several parents commented that other parents and families were an invaluable source of knowledge as well as support. Pooja was one of the younger participants in the study, having just turned eighteen. She received a diagnosis of autism only one year earlier, though she had been seeing doctors for seizures since she was six years old, and her mother had felt something was different about her since she was two years old. According to Pooja's mother, "It's very important to form a network of parents with similar concerns, that's really important because if I have a problem and the other parent also tells me that she's going through the same thing then at least you realize that this is a problem which the child is facing. Otherwise, many times in our struggle, we would scold her because it was so odd, you just fail to understand. But when there's a network of parents you really understand that this is a problem which is genuine to children with such kind of difficulties, a development disorder, and then you can share the strategies. So one thing foremost important is to have network of parents." Pooja's mother scored in the thirtieth percentile of the RAFIN ES, which may reflect the delayed diagnosis and her sense of needing to "catch up" to be able to help her daughter. Likewise, the advice she offered may be precisely what she lacked during those many years of ambiguity about Pooja and her behavior.

To summarize, the parents that talked about empowerment in their advice emphasized multiple things parents should do to facilitate their and their children's well-being. Educating yourself about autism and the way it affects your own particular child was repeated over and over; digging in and being willing to commit time and energy to achieve goals, however small, was likewise frequently mentioned. One way advice was framed that seemed to reflect parents' individual experiences was that some parents cautioned against relying too heavily on professionals, either because it was important to do the work yourself or because professionals could not be trusted, while other parents advocated more strongly to seek advice and accept support.

Philosophical Approaches: "Acceptance Is the First Thing"

Unlike the advice regarding self-efficacy, which had many elements, parents had one clear message when it came to what philosophical stance should be taken: *accept*. In some cases, parents spoke explicitly of accepting the child, while in others, they spoke of accepting "it"— the situation, the child's autism, life. All together, thirty-seven percent of the study families spoke about acceptance in their response, and twenty-five percent of families specifically used the word "acceptance." In many cases, parents suggested acceptance as the primary or first step that should be taken upon diagnosis. All of these parents from the 1996 sample, who scored in the eightieth percentile or higher on the RAFIN Acceptance Scale (RAFIN AS), are examples of parents who saw acceptance as central for a new parent:

I just tell them that you need to follow the correct path without feeling the social pressures. That's one advice I do give, I tell them that acceptance is the first thing and the moment you start accepting things will become easier for you and for your child. (Nandita's mother)

The most important thing: start feeling proud about your child. Don't think them as a burden. Start enjoying your kid whichever way they are, doesn't matter if he's smart, he's a vegetable, he's good for nothing, start feeling proud. If you're not doing that as parents, forget about the whole world. Why would they care about your child? It's very important thing, first thing. Learn to accept your child as an autistic child or as a disabled child, whatever. Then the next step starts. If you start feeling shy and embarrassed and sad and feel burdened, then nothing can change. Your child will never grow. (Sagar's mother)

Our first advice to all these parents has been, please accept that child, acceptance is the first part, because what happens is we have found that the life of the child is miserable and the life of the parents is also miserable, and the other siblings' life is also miserable only because they just are not willing to accept him, that he is somewhat different from them. Accept him for what he is. (Nikhil's father)

Acceptance is a fundamental part of the philosophy of Action For Autism, so it would follow that some families associated with the organization might have adopted this stance, and for this reason, we included a measure of contact that parents had with AFA. We found that families who included acceptance in their advice reported having significantly greater contact with AFA, $t(50) = -2.23$, $p = .027$. We did *not*, however, observe a significant relationship between scores on the RAFIN AS and contact with AFA. And, there were families who scored high on the RAFIN AS, mentioned acceptance as part of their advice, and had virtually no contact with AFA. Sushant's mother, for example, had visited AFA just once, many years ago, but was one who had much to say about acceptance. She added an additional dynamic to this advice: "I have just one thought. If your husband accepts that the issue is with your child, then your family will be fine. If he doesn't accept it, if the in-laws don't accept it, then your family is wrecked. This is what I feel. That if we'd have accepted Sushant's situation and done something about it then things might have been different . . . Accept, and start making the child do everything. Make him self-sufficient. And everybody in the family should accept that yes, my child has this and should accept it quickly because we accepted it only after he was thirteen years." The comments by Sushant's mother raise the important role of extended family members and the challenges often associated with parenting within a multigenerational household. While not the focus of the current chapter, this was an issue many families had faced. As the advice from Sushant's mother and others suggests, it appears that acceptance is a construct that is not simply something learned from AFA, but a philosophy that families also come to on their own.

Integrating Quantitative Measures of Empowerment and Acceptance

As detailed above, the two most frequent characteristics of parental advice in the interviews were related to empowerment and acceptance, which are two constructs for which we also obtained quantitative data through the questionnaires. On measures of acceptance, empowerment, and stress, an inverse relationship for both mothers and fathers was observed, namely, that parents who reported higher acceptance had lower levels of stress ($r = -.65$, $p < .0001$ for mothers; $r = -.65$, $p < .0001$ for fathers). Similarly, the higher the reported empowerment, the lower levels of stress ($r = -.51$, $p = .001$ for mothers; $r = -.54$, $p = .001$ for fathers). These findings echo work that has been done elsewhere. For example, a similar inverse association has been observed between acceptance and distress in mothers of children with intellectual disability (Lloyd and Hastings 2008). In a group intervention study, Blackledge and Hayes (2006) used Acceptance and Commitment Therapy (ACT) and observed a significant reduction in depression and stress in mothers of children with ASD. More recently the constructs of empowerment and acceptance have been examined together and in conjunction with parent mental health in parents of children with ASD. Both greater acceptance and empowerment were associated with fewer parent mental health problems, but a model that included both processes found that only acceptance was a significant mediator between child problem behavior and parent mental health (Weiss et al. 2012).

I did not have measures like the RAFIN ES and RAFIN AS in 1996. But what if I had? Would young parents be more or less empowered and accepting than older parents? One way to answer this question is through our data from younger families participating in our other RAFIN project, also conducted in New Delhi. Of course, there are many ways in which the mothers who came for the parent training program were unlike my 1996 families. Most obviously, these new mothers were likely to be more empowered than average, since they not only were aware of the importance of training but had committed to a three-month, intensive program, sometimes far from their homes. Compared to twenty years ago, parents of children newly diagnosed with autism have a nearly inexhaustible source of information at their disposal today through the Internet. These young mothers all had received a diagnosis of autism for their children at a relatively young age (unlike Pooja's mother, and others in the adult study), and many came to the training with background information on autism. On the measure of empowerment, therefore, it is not surprising that there were no significant differences between mothers in these two groups. Advice from parents of adults encouraging young parents to learn about autism and send their children to school instead of keeping them home may be unnecessary for these younger families, who, according to our sample, are already doing just that.

Yet the whole premise of asking parents of adults to offer advice to parents of younger children was based on the recognition that these parents may have something important to offer, something that a family may not be able to read on the Internet. Parents of children with autism in India, no matter what age, are tied together by having a child with an especially complex disability in a country where general awareness is still low, stigma is still high, and the extended family is both a powerful and prevalent dynamic that shapes decision making in every facet of life. The piece of advice that came through clearest from parents of adults and was echoed by families of all backgrounds—wealthy or not, large and small: *You have to accept it. The sooner you accept, the better, because once accepted then you start working on it.* In acceptance, parents of younger children still have far to go. Parents of adults with autism reported significantly higher levels of acceptance than parents of young children with autism, $t(81) = -2.52, p = .013$.

The Advantage of Mixed Methods

The findings described above come from a qualitative process of interviewing families that produced rich descriptions, and from the use of standardized questionnaires that produced quantitative data. An option for us would have been to rely on just the interviews and other observations from the visit, since they provide so much information about the families. Plenty of excellent recent work has primarily relied on qualitative methods (for example, see the 2010 issue of *Ethos* "Rethinking Autism, Rethinking Anthropology," N. Bagatell and O. Solomon 2010). Or we could have also relied only on questionnaires, as is common in many psychological and medical studies of autism. Mixed methods gave us the ability to learn much more than either method alone. Consistent with a "multiculture, multiage, multimethod science" (Bornstein 2002), using quantitative measures allowed us to make comparisons and ask questions such as: How do empowerment and acceptance differ between parents of young children and those of adult children with autism? How does acceptance relate to parent well-being? These questions, and more importantly, their answers, are ones that matter to parents and families with autism. Without the explanation of what acceptance means and why it matters, our findings would be far less compelling.

The Significance of Community-Based Research Partnerships

Like all relationships, research partnerships take time and patience, and the relationships that lie at the heart of this project were rewarding both scientifically and personally. Our Indian collaborators helped interpret observations and made sure that we were not jumping to conclusions that were based on our own assumptions. For example, I commented after one interview on how many adults with autism ate their meals alone, and might this be telling in some way about the extent to which adults are isolated from family routines. This was not something that had stood out to anyone else involved in the interviews, however. Through sitting as a team to talk about this, we ultimately concluded that grabbing food or eating in shifts was *not* unusual behavior for an unmarried twenty-something in busy Delhi, particularly in multigenerational and joint-family homes. I should not rush to interpret this practice of eating alone as something specific to families of adults with autism, since it essentially reflected a common pattern of behavior for many families without any members with a disability.

In our partnership, the learning went in both directions. All the research assistants involved in the project had a Master's degree in psychology or a related field, and all of them had taken a research methods course, yet they had virtually no experience conducting open-ended interviews. By the end of the project, the hands-on experience of conducting so many visits had given these researchers the opportunity to hone their interviewing skills and to handle strong emotions and delicate topics. They learned how to use their observations and the experience of the interview to go "off script" to inform their questions; for example, seeing a living room that felt as though no one had entered it in years invariably prompted more probing about whether the family often has guests or neighbors come to the home.

No matter how familiar a researcher may be with a particular construct, engaging local stakeholders in conversations can result in important adjustments to instruments and approaches (Minkler 2005). For each section of our semistructured protocol, we went through multiple iterations of how to ask questions. For example, in asking about daily routines (described in Daley, Weisner, and Singhal 2014), we changed the time frame, the order of questions, where we put our focus, whether we asked about a weekday or weekend, and incorporated other tweaks suggested by our colleagues at AFA before we settled on a method that would be simultaneously feasible and produce the kind of data we wanted *and* the kind of data they needed to convey the essence of the daily experience. "Collaboration" in many cross-cultural settings is focused only on obtaining the cooperation of participants, rather than ensuring meaningfulness of the measures used and correctly interpreting data.

Making It Matter: Local Application

A longstanding tension in psychological anthropology, and one identified as a key ethical consideration in other fields (Marshall 2007), is making research findings translate into meaningful action for the study participants. Mackenzie and colleagues wrote eloquently on this issue, stemming from their work with refugee populations, in which participants complained that researchers "get their PhDs and funding from our stories and they cannot even be bothered to send us a report and a thank you letter . . . We give up our time and share our pain and they cannot give the time to write us a letter" (Mackenzie, McDowell and Pittaway 2007, 305). More than thirty years ago, Mick Bennett put it another way: "Is any person or group I've studied going to benefit anywhere near as much as I?" He argued that cross-cultural psychology should be "as much an applied enterprise as it is a way to have fun, test favorite theories, and get promoted in the process" (Lonner 1979, 34). In 1996, I had the privilege to work with individuals in India who were very aware of how to use data to influence change in the field of autism, and it set me on a course to design studies with Bennett's question at the forefront. Since 2010, I have once again had the privilege to partner with a team committed to conducting research that is not just scientifically useful but also personally relevant to the participants. Improving the experience of parenting a person with autism will take our research, and the participation of our partners at AFA, into the topic of regional and national institutional policies in New Delhi and India.

Acknowledgements

This project is funded through a grant from the Foundation for Psychocultural Research's (FPR) Culture, Brain, Development, and Mental Health (CBDMH), Robert Lemelson, president; Tom Weisner, PI; Tamara Daley, co-PI, and in partnership with Action For Autism, New Delhi (Nidhi Singhal and Merry Barua). FPR-UCLA CBDMH is one of the interdisciplinary programs initiated and funded by the FPR. The RAFIN Adult Study was managed by Deepali Taneja, with key assistance from Sachita Suryanarayan. Additional team members in India were Tanvi Behl, Rubina Pradhan, and Simi Sunny. Rachel Brezis also participated in the project while completing a postdoctorate at UCLA through support from the FPR. This chapter draft benefited greatly from comments and suggestions from Tom Weisner, Nidhi Singhal, Deepali Taneja, and Sachita Suryanarayan.

References

Abidin, Richard R. 1995. *Parenting Stress Index* (3rd ed.). Odessa, FL: Psychological Assessment Resources.

Bagatell, Nancy, and Olga Solomon. 2010. "Special Issue: Rethinking Autism, Rethinking Anthropology." *Ethos* 38 (1): 1–7.

Blackledge, John T., and Steven C. Hayes. 2006. "Using Acceptance and Commitment Training in the Support of Parents of Children Diagnosed with Autism." *Child & Family Behavior Therapy* 28 (1): 1–18.

Bornstein, Marc H. 2002. "Toward a Multiculture, Multiage, Multimethod Science." *Human Development* 45: 257–63.

Brookman-Frazee, Lauren, and Robert L. Koegel. 2004. "Using Parent/Clinician

Partnerships in Parent Education Programs for Children with Autism." *Journal of Positive Behavior Interventions* 6 (4): 195–213.

Burack, Jacob A., Grace Iarocci, Dermot Bowler, and Laurent Mottron. 2002. "Benefits and Pitfalls in the Merging of Disciplines: The Example of Developmental Psychopathology and the Study of Persons with Autism." *Development and Psychopathology* 14 (02): 225–37.

Connors, Jeanne L., and Anne M. Donnellan. 1993. "Citizenship and Culture: The Role of Disabled People in Navajo Society." *Disability, Handicap & Society* 8 (3): 265–80.

Daley, Tamara C. 2002. "The Need for Cross-Cultural Research on the Pervasive Developmental Disorders." *Transcultural Psychiatry* 39 (4): 531–50.

———. 2004. "From Symptom Recognition to Diagnosis: Children with Autism in India." *Social Science and Medicine* 58 (7): 1323–35.

Daley, Tamara C., Thomas Weisner, and Nidhi Singhal. 2014. "Adults with Autism in India: A Mixed-Method Approach to Make Meaning of Daily Routines." *Social Science and Medicine* 116: 142–49.

Gupta, Vidya B., Priyanka Mehrotra, and Naveen Mehrotra. 2012. "Parental Stress in Raising a Child with Disabilities in India." *Disability, CBR and Inclusive Development* 23: 41–52.

Gray, David E. 1994. "Lay Conceptions of Autism: Parents' Explanatory Models." *Medical Anthropology: Cross-Cultural Studies in Health and Illness* 16: 99–118.

Grinker, Roy R. 2007. *Unstrange Minds: Remapping the World of Autism.* New York: Basic Books.

Hall, Budd L. 1992. "From Margins to Center: The Development and Purpose of Participatory Action Research." *American Sociologist* 23: 15–28.

John, Aesha. 2012. "Stress among Mothers of Children with Intellectual Disabilities in Urban India: Role of Gender and Maternal Coping." *Journal of Applied Research in Intellectual Disabilities* 25 (4): 372–82.

Lloyd, Tracey, and Richard Hastings. 2008. "Psychological Variables as Correlates of Adjustment in Mothers of Children with Intellectual Disabilities: Cross-Sectional and Longitudinal Relationships." *Journal of Intellectual Disability Research* (52): 37–48.

Lonner, Walter J. 1979. "Issues in Cross-Cultural Psychology." In *Perspectives on Cross-Cultural Psychology*, edited by Anthony J. Marsella, Ronald G. Tharp, and Thomas J. Ciboroski, 17–45. New York: Academic Press.

Mackenzie, Catriona, Christopher McDowell, and Eileen Pittaway. 2007. "Beyond 'Do No Harm': The Challenge of Constructing Ethical Relationships in Refugee Research." *Journal of Refugee Studies* 20 (2): 299–319.

Marshall, Patricia A. 2007. *Ethical Challenges in Study Design and Informed Consent for Health Research in Resource-Poor Settings.* Geneva: World Health Organization.

Minkler, Meredith. 2005. "Community-Based Research Partnerships: Challenges and Opportunities." *Journal of Urban Health* 82 (2 suppl. 2): ii3–ii12.

Prakash, Ankit, Sheema Aleem, Samina Bano, and Naved Iqbal. 2013. "Stress and Psychological Hardiness of Parents of Physically Challenged Children." *Journal of Indian Health Psychology* 8 (1): 103–13.

Toomey, Janice, and Lawrence A. Adams. 1995. "Naturalistic Observation of Children with Autism: Evidence for Intersubjectivity." *New Directions for Child and Adolescent Development* (69): 75–89.

Weiss, Jonathan A., Mary C. Cappadocia, Jennifer A. MacMullin, Michelle Viecili, and Yona Lunsky. 2012. "The Impact of Child Problem Behaviors of Children with ASD on Parent Mental Health: The Mediating Role of Acceptance and Empowerment." *Autism* 16 (3): 261–74.

Notes

1. All names in this chapter are pseudonyms.

TWELVE

What Makes for the Best Clinical Care? Using Trigger Films to Explore Better Integration of Guidelines and Experience

M. CAMERON HAY, THOMAS S. WEISNER, AND SASKIA K. SUBRAMANIAN

All of us are patients at some time or another. When we go to see our health care providers, we all want to receive the best possible care. So what constitutes the best possible care? Surely, we want our care providers to be up-to-date on the scientific evidence. But is that enough? Don't we also feel more comfortable if they are experienced, particularly if they have experience successfully treating whatever it is we have? And, according to research Hay and colleagues did in the United States on patient access to on-line medical knowledge and its effects on doctor-patient interactions (Hay, Cadigan et al. 2008), we also want the physician to treat us as individuals. In that research, Hay found that patients were hesitant to bring up information they had found online because "I want the doctor to look at me"—in short, patients want to be treated personally and as a person, not as a number or a case (see also Sered and Tabory 1999). Patients, at least the actively coparticipating, informed patients that are common in the twenty-first century in the United States, want experienced, scientific experts who will personalize medicine for them.

Other patients in other contexts will have different expectations and so different scripts; likewise, physicians and their practices vary not only in the United States but certainly around the world—and that does not include the even greater variety of complementary medical practitioners and healers of all kinds. In this chapter, we limit our scope to contemporary biomedicine in the United States. Given the tendency for American patients to want medicine personalized for them by informed experts, we sought to understand what makes for the best possible clinical care from the physician's point of view.

What do physicians think of as the best possible clinical care? Physicians listen to patient narratives or histories, examine symptoms, narrow down the array of possible diagnoses, discuss treatment plans, and order any tests and write any prescriptions, all in increasingly short patient appointment time slots. They do this day in and day out, with a variety of patients walking through the door. Where do they go to get the medical information they need to make a decision about a particular case? How do they weigh scientific or published evidence against the years of practical experience they have treating patients? Do physicians with years of experience weigh their experience and the scientific evidence in the same way that newly minted medical students do? And to what extent are they interested in personalizing their treatment recommendations for the patient at hand?

In contemporary biomedicine in the United States, these are salient questions for patients, providers, and policymakers. Indeed, medicine is in the midst of a crisis in the United States. Escalating medical costs and increasingly poor population health statistics have intensified scrutiny of health care quality, which is increasingly measured by the practice of what is called evidence-based medicine (EBM). The premise of evidence-based medicine is that findings from random control clinical trials, which measure the impact of a treatment protocol on a carefully selected, single-disease patient population, provide the strongest, unbiased scientific data and thus should apply universally. Once published in the medical literature, the findings of the random control clinical trials become the gold standard of medical evidence. And it is this evidence that is synthesized into guidelines for clinical care that also can be used to guide clinical practice and evaluate the quality of that practice. Thus guidelines—for everything from the screening of breast cancer to the timing of childhood vaccines to the prescription of statins in people with heart disease—become the norm for good practice and should be applied to any patient who fits within a diagnostic or demographic category. Not applying the guidelines is considered a deviation from evidence-based medicine, and since the early 1990s there has been considerable pressure, sometimes with moral connotations, for physicians to conform clinical practice to the guidelines, thereby reducing variation between practitioners and improving overall health care outcomes. Or so it was thought. With relatively few exceptions, the push for EBM has had less effect on physician practice than expected (Bassand, Priori and Tendera 2005; Aberegg, Arkes, and Terry 2006; Cabana et al. 1999).

There may be multiple reasons for this, but among them is the importance of clinical experience. In their training, in medical school and during internship, residency, and fellowships, physicians are expected to develop experience in the application of scientific knowledge to patients through an apprenticeship model, in which they "see one" before they are expected to "do one." Medicine has never been just about knowing science. The "art of medicine" is knowing when and how to apply the science. And the importance of clinical experience has been verified with scientific studies: physicians with accurate recall of scientific facts tend to be five to ten times less accurate diagnosticians than experienced physicians who may not recall all of the facts but who can spontaneously recognize the pattern of the case in front of them (Lloyd and Reyna 2009; Coderre et al. 2003). Experience matters when it comes to offering good clinical care, but because it is difficult to assess with administrative or survey scales, it remains an understudied and underappreciated part of the national conversation about how to improve health care quality in the United States. Indeed the push for EBM, while offering a means to systematize care across clinics and use the best scientific evidence available to improve health outcomes, obscures the ontological reality that every medical student, physician, and patient knows: local context, personal experience, and individual biology make a difference.

Naihua Duan (2007) coined the term "Evidence Farming" (EF) to describe the notion of systematically utilizing local knowledge as a way to conceptualize and start thinking about ways of using or harvesting the rich contextual knowledge in the minds, practices, and experiences of professionals such as psychotherapists, social workers, teachers, or physicians (see also Hay, Weisner et al. 2008). Given the push for EBM (also called Evidence-Based Practice), a study that would examine the importance of local experience in physician decision making seemed particularly relevant. And to the extent that physicians reported that they blend EBM guidelines with institutional practice, local clinic evidence, and assessments of the patient at hand, we can ask what information do physicians have on the local clinic part of this blend? This question is the focus of our chapter: what if information were available for systematic evidence about local clinical/ regional treatments and outcomes to complement other kinds of EBM knowledge and clinical experience? If experience is important in clinical decision making, as the literature suggests, we would ask physicians about how evidence farming might facilitate their access to useful decision-making knowledge. Note that the focus is to make local knowledge more shareable, public, and usable, not as a replacement for EBM, but as a complement to it. The spirit is not different from what actually drives EBM: use the best evidence to guide interventions. If this is true for EBM, it should and could be true for local evidence as well.

We came to the study from different backgrounds. Weisner is a psychological and medical anthropologist and human development specialist with extensive experience using mixed methods to understand perspectives and practices within ecocultural settings. Hay, a medical and psychological anthropologist with a strong interest in the anthropology of knowledge—understanding how information moves through communities, changing as individuals reshape it for their needs—was in the midst of analyzing data on how patients with chronic illnesses gather and use online medical information (e.g., Hay, Strathmann et al. 2008; see also Hay, chapter 3). Based on that research, she had a good idea of what patients want from their physicians, but didn't have much of a sense of how physicians go about finding and using information to give patients care. Subramanian, a medical sociologist, had spent several years studying (through in-depth qualitative interviews) the experiences of breast cancer survivors suffering disabling side effects, such as significant cognitive impairment, resulting from their chemotherapy and/or radiation (Boykoff, Moieni, and Subramanian 2009). Based on this research, she produced a feature-length documentary film that has screened extensively as an educational tool for survivors and health care providers alike. When we initially talked as a group about the Evidence Farming project, we were interested in the project primarily as an opportunity to better understand the process by which physicians make treatment decisions, as a complement to other work focusing on patients. But soon it became clear that the Evidence Farming project would provide new perspectives.

How to Study an Idea That People Don't Have Yet?

To study the idea of evidence farming, we first needed to understand how physicians access and use information, and, in particular, what role local contextual information had in their decision-making process. We needed to partner with the physicians, to understand how such information would be useful, and then we needed to test the ideas. Anthropologists have always depended on the collaboration of the peoples we study in order to do research. Yet research in anthropology, as in evidence-based medicine itself, usually follows a research-to-practice model in which the researcher directs the study, expecting that the disseminated results will be read by colleagues, policymakers, and, in the case of medicine, clinicians. While in many ways useful for driving scientific knowledge forward, the research-to-practice model is less useful for acquiring knowledge that can be, readily and with contextual appropriateness, translated into policy or practice. The whole idea of evidence farming was to make local experience and contextual knowledge relevant and accessible for physicians; thus we needed to learn from and partner with physicians from the outset.

The common phrases "research-to-policy" or "research-to-practice" can be fruitfully turned around to suggest another model: "practice-to-research" (Tseng 2013). In the practice-to research model, scientists collaborate with practitioners and clients in a clinic, school, or community program from the beginning, thereby increasing the chances of cultural, institutional and contextual relevance of the study to practitioners (Weisner and Hay 2015). Moreover, few interventions or scientific practices, no matter how well assessed in research studies, will be sustainable unless they can find a place in the daily routines and activities of practitioners (Weisner et al. 2005). Partnering with practitioners facilitates the process of translation by ensuring that the actual practice setting is well understood.

Thus Weisner designed a study to build partnerships with practitioners while enabling us as researchers to gain an understanding of the everyday constraints and possibilities of clinical practice. We conducted a two-phase research project integrating mixed methods of interviews and surveys with the rather innovative methodologies (innovative for anthropologists, at least) of using focus groups and a trigger film. Why did we need these innovations? In large part because the concept of evidence farming was so alien, we needed, with the help of physicians, a way of accessing whether and in what contexts physicians use their experience in making clinical decisions. But we also needed a way to check our findings and verify that the ways physicians could imagine using evidence farming actually made sense and were compelling to a large number of physicians (not just those who dreamed up the concept). Using snowball sampling coupled with targeted sampling, we gained insights from a wide variety of physicians of various ages and levels of experience who were working in various fields of medicine and clinical settings.

Exploring the Idea of Evidence Farming with Physicians

Phase one consisted of exploratory interviews and surveys with a total of thirty-nine physicians, ranging from fourth-year medical students to clinicians with thirty years of clinical experience. Some interesting patterns emerged in the data.

First, while younger physicians tended to be more reliant on EBM summarizing services like Up-to-Date or Cochrane Reviews —"It's almost like all the homework has been done for you," said one—the physicians with more experience in clinical practice were more skeptical of EBM summarizing services. One said, for example: "I am the expert [they call to write the articles in something like Up-to-Date, but] I would take even that with a grain of salt because I realize that lots of times [the author] is just somebody who decided what they thought and wrote it down. But that doesn't mean it's necessarily right." Physicians of all levels of experience relied primarily on their experience (ninety-six percent of the time in our sample) in treating diseases that they had seen many times before. But if faced with a situation in which they didn't have any direct experience, physicians reported that they were likely to consult with trusted others, drawing on the other physicians' experience, and thereby broadening their own, sometimes in combination with specific EBM searches. Indeed physicians reported that a serious drawback of EBM was that it is based on carefully selected patient populations that often didn't match their own patients. For example "Take albuterol. It's not really approved for children under two. But it's used all the time. I mean what else do you do? . . . We do it all the time. You look at what the standard of care is [in the EBM guidelines] and then decide if you're willing to go offline."

Physicians made it quite clear that the best clinical care depended not solely on their knowledge of EBM, but also on their experience, their ability to understand a patient and her living context, their clinical experience watching patient outcomes and responses from one pre-scription or another, their sense of their local patient population and what was relevant to them, and on their ability to consult with trusted colleagues, thereby drawing on colleagues' experiences. In other words, they reported relying on their own gathering of local knowledge, or "farming" for local evidence in combination with the relevant EBM. For physicians, what was important was not merely their scientific knowledge, but their ability to distinguish the most relevant EBM and apply or tailor it to meet the needs of the patient at hand. The physi-cians made clear that good clinicians developed with time, while gain-ing practice integrating multiple kinds of knowledge for the benefit of the patient at hand. Medicine is not merely the application of EBM. Medicine involves the *interpretation* of EBM for its suitability and rel-evance for treating any particular patient and meeting the patient's needs (e.g., Glasziou, Ogrinc, and Good 2011).

Film Making: Using Trigger Film to Verify Phase-One Findings

The concept of evidence farming proved a difficult one to communi-cate to physicians in the early, pilot-phase interviews. They used expe-rience and local knowledge, of course—all the time, actually. But the notion that experience from one's own clinical practice could be aggre-gated, compared, tracked, and legitimated as data was novel for most (though some, mostly younger physicians, it turned out, were doing versions of EF by building spreadsheets of their patients, treatments, and outcomes on their own). So in our interviews, we explored when or in what kinds of clinical contexts physicians really would find it use-ful to be able to mine (or "farm") their own and others' experience, and not rely on memory of their own cases. When or for what kinds of clinical questions would they find it useful to be able to tap into the experience of other clinicians in the area, and how broad an area would they want it to be? The immediate clinic? A geographic area? We took the transcribed interview data, linked it to the individual an-swers to the surveys, and analyzed these together using Dedoose mixed method software.

Our analysis consisted of two coders who independently read all the transcripts, developed a common code tree, and coded all of the in-terviews. One of our goals was to code for ideas and ways physicians thought having access to local knowledge would be useful in their clin-ical practices. These coded data grouped into four basic ideas. Then,

FIGURE 12.1 Educating patients.

FIGURE 12.2 Monitoring local disease outbreaks.

drawing on key examples physicians had given us in the interviews, we worked with a physician doubling as a scriptwriter to draft vignettes of each of the four basic ideas that would bring evidence farming to life on screen. We refined the scripts with a physician on our team, Richard Kravitz, testing to make sure that the language and biological facts were correct and would make sense to a clinical audience. Then we hired a professional film director and editor, Vivian Umino, and a small film crew. Saskia Subramanian from our research team became the producer, and we put out a casting call for actors. The outcome was a trigger film, *Harnessing Clinical Evidence: Four Vignettes*, with each vignette lasting two to three minutes and illustrating a different possible way in which local or cultural contextual data could be useful in clinical practice.

In one vignette (figure 12.1), an African American mother comes in with her ill child and wants antibiotics; the pediatrician shows the mother data from her practice (imagined Evidence Farming data) indicating that ninety-eight of one hundred children in her own practice get better without using them. "Other mothers and children just like you do not need antibiotics—and if your child does not get better in a couple more days, you can give him the antibiotic." The mother is reassured, accepts the prescription, but agrees not to fill it unless her son doesn't improve within a day or two. This vignette offers an example of ways evidence farming could be used to inform patients of disease outcomes of patients like them from their local area. In another vignette (figure 12.2), two physicians are discussing teenagers with sexually transmitted diseases. One physician mentions that it seems like he has seen more cases of sexually transmitted diseases with symptoms that "seem a little worse than usual." The second physician enters variables into an imagined Evidence Farming software program to search for local evidence: a geographic contrast (all clinics in a ten mile radius around the high school) and a time contrast (diagnoses this year compared to last year). The finding in this vignette confirms the first physician's suspicion that more teenagers were diagnosed with sexually transmitted diseases this year (twice as many actually), and then with a click of a button, these physicians can see "what's growing out," that is, what the lab tests on the urethral discharge in the local region have shown. The lab tests showed gonorrhea, and a strain that is resistant to the standard EBM first-line medication, doxycycline. The physicians then know to call the health department to alert them of a potential outbreak and treat their own cases differently: an example of the ways local regional information could be clinically useful. The third vignette (figure 12.3) brought up the complexities physicians face in treating patients with comorbid diagnoses (when most research on medications is conducted among patients with only one disease) and outlines how (imagined) local evidence of similar patients with the same comorbid diagnoses is used to inform the treatment decision.

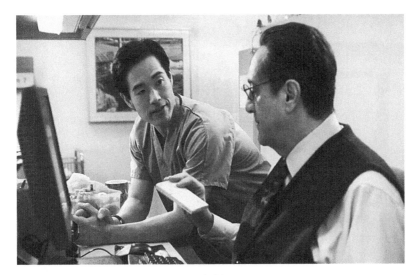

FIGURE 12.3 Treating patients with comorbidities.

And the fourth vignette (figure 12.4) showed an elderly man following a heart attack who needed medication but was resistant and ended up storming out of the physician's office. The physician, frustrated that she couldn't get him to accept the treatment recommended by standard guidelines for care, was also concerned that it would negatively affect her performance evaluation in the clinic, so she sits down with a colleague to look at how her local practice matches up against the national standards for care. All of these vignettes thus illustrated different ways the physicians had told us that they thought the evidence farming idea could positively (or in the last example, potentially negatively for her own evaluations) impact clinical practice.

Phase Two: Screenings and Surprise Findings

With the film in hand, we conducted a pilot study with seventy-two physicians, fifteen of whom had also been in Phase One. These physicians were interviewed individually or as part of twelve focus groups, again representing a range of ages, levels of experience, medical fields, and clinic types. The vignettes were shown one at a time to trigger conversations about whether evidence farming, as illustrated in that particular vignette, would be personally useful in similar clinical situa-

FIGURE 12.4. Self-monitoring performance.

tions. We also stimulated conversation by asking about the reasons for use, the plausibility of the vignette, possible pitfalls in using evidence farming in that way, and barriers to use.

Physicians were uniformly enthusiastic about using film vignettes to verify the communication of the concept of evidence farming as well as to explore the research question on its potential usefulness and relevance. All the physicians coming to the focus groups had been told about the evidence farming concept and had been provided with a description of the concept: farming local evidence as a way of legitimizing and utilizing local clinical experience and outcomes as data for future decision making. Nonetheless, as one physician put it after watching this first vignette: "I didn't really know what I was coming here for today, frankly. I just didn't know what was coming. But when I saw that vignette and I saw what you were getting at, it made the point of what you're getting at, as well as something very useful in the medical community." These trigger films proved an invaluable tool for clarifying the difficult concept of evidence farming for research participants. By partnering with physicians to develop the scripts for trigger films, we were able to verify our initial findings. It is a good thing we did.

Given that the story for each of the vignettes emerged as ideas offered by physicians during our Phase One interviews, we were curious to see which of these four ideas for using evidence farming the physicians would think most useful. Physicians in our study responded positively to the first two vignettes; they thought that an evidence farming system that could be used for educating patients and for monitoring local disease rates would offer a clear advantage in clinical practices. On balance, physicians responded positively to its potential usefulness in treating comorbidities but voiced concerns that finding truly comparable cases to "farm" for evidence in decision making might be a time-consuming or difficult process. Overall, regarding the first three vignettes, physicians responded enthusiastically to the idea that local practice could be used to complement but not replace EBM.

We were surprised at the deep level of concern physicians voiced in response to the fourth vignette that discusses using a local evidence-tracking system to see how well physicians in a group were meeting their guideline goals regarding medication for heart patients. In our initial interviews, physicians thought the system would be a good thing, enabling them internally to track their own patients and improve their own practice or the practice of a local clinic as a whole. However, when it came to the film that shows two physicians discussing their rate of deviation from EBM guidelines in their recent practice, physicians in the focus groups responded very negatively; they worried that insurance companies or other administrators would actually track their own local outcomes and penalize them if they failed to meet the EBM guidelines for all or a certain percentage of their patients. Who would own and have access to Evidence Farming data, and how would it be used? Without the conversations triggered by the film, these concerns would not have emerged as a key finding of our study.

This particular finding actually dovetails with a more pervasive concern about the Accountable Care Movement in medicine. Accountable care is the idea that physicians will be paid not on the services they provide but instead for the quality of their care and the health outcomes of their patients. In a telling editorial in the *New England Journal of Medicine* (Rosenbaum and Shrank 2013), the authors describe the double bind that physicians will increasingly find themselves in as Accountable Care increasingly is used by government health systems such as Medicaid and private insurers. The problem of course is that for doctors who are committed to caring for all patients without discrimination, their pay may be linked to how well their patients fare, which sounds good until we consider that doctors' "willingness to care for patients has never depended on [patients'] willingness to do what we say" (Rosenbaum and Shrank 2013, 694). In other words, a physician could offer the best possible care, but the patient could ignore it—as between thirty and seventy percent of them do (Osterberg and

Blaschke 2005; Scheiman-Elazary et al., n.d.)—and then how would the physician fare?

Showing the vignettes to focus groups of physicians allowed us to test and verify the usefulness of evidence farming as the physicians in the earlier interviews had framed it. It also clarified for physicians what evidence farming could look like and offer them.

This study provided evidence that the best clinical care is care that takes into account *both* EBM and local clinical experience while foregrounding the needs of the patient at hand. Partnering with physicians enabled us to explore a concept that, if carefully designed, would facilitate their abilities to provide better care, because it would give them the means to systematize and draw on their local cultural context of practice as legitimate evidence that could be used in conjunction with EBM. EBM, after all, is massively funded and readily accessible, not just in PubMed but from commercial update summary source firms that medical libraries and doctors subscribe to and download to their PDAs. But nothing like this exists for local, contextualized knowledge as yet.

Interventions That Work

Local cultural contexts of practice are increasingly bracketed in, not out, in global health intervention programs. Well-funded programs based on proven scientific evidence, such as those designed to reduce malaria by providing bed nets in Tanzania, or eradicate polio in Nigeria by vaccinating all infants, failed because the application of scientific logic developed elsewhere did not take into account the cultural assumptions, political ideologies, economics, and histories of the local contexts (e.g., Easterly 2006; Adams, Burke and Whitmarsh 2014). Global health interventions that work are those that show evidence of being based on local partnerships, adapting intervention strategies to fit within the possible accommodations and expectations of the local cultural context (see, e.g., Harkness and Super, chapter 8). As anthropologists have long argued, culture is not just "over there." The best clinical care—whether in Lombok, Indonesia, or Los Angeles, California—is care that draws on the scientific evidence as well as understanding of the local cultural contexts of physicians' practice and of patients' worlds. Physicians use their own experiential and cultural knowledge of their local world regularly in their clinical practice; the best care integrates that local cultural knowledge with exogenous knowledge such as EBM. Even so, the idea of EBM as the gold standard of medical practice is so deeply entrenched in the discourse, teaching, and thinking about medicine, that the idea of evidence farming—that local knowledge could be systematically collected and become relevant to clinical practice—was one that many of the physicians in Phase One of our study found difficult to understand. Thus the iterative development of the trigger film was a method that allowed us to further explore the usefulness and potential threats of systematizing local clinical knowledge.

Even after over two decades of emphasizing EBM, there remain discussions over its relative merits and importance (Devisch and Murray 2009), just as there are discussions in medicine about the importance of culturally competent or culturally informed care in order to best treat the patient at hand (Kirmayer 2012; Weisner and Hay 2015). The Evidence Farming study shows that there is considerable room, albeit within the biomedical world, for incorporating local community, cultural, and personal patient-specific knowledge into treatment, and that many physicians would use such systematically assembled information were it made available. Within nonbiomedical healing and therapeutic traditions, systematizing the use of local evidence and using it alongside available EBM might be useful for these traditions as well.

We combined several methods in this study and could have gone further with quantitative coding of the physician focus groups and interview transcripts, as well as accessing other information from doctors' practices. We could have done a pilot intervention, actually implementing an Evidence Farming study at a clinic and assessing the results. Whatever the next steps might actually be, integrating qualitative and quantitative evidence would optimize the study. Partnering with physicians and patients, and perhaps with hospitals, pharmacies, and others, would also enhance such future work. These are the kinds of designs, methods, and contextual studies that medical anthropology is very well positioned to undertake in the future.

References

Aberegg, S. K., H. Arkes, and P. B. Terry. 2006. "Failure to Adopt Beneficial Therapies Caused by Bias in Medical Evidence Evaluation." *Medical Decision Making* 26 (6): 575–82. Adams, Vincanne, Nancy J. Burke, and Ian Whitmarsh. 2014. "Slow Research: Thoughts for a Movement in Global Health." *Medical Anthropology* 33 (3) (October 29): 179–97.

Bassand, Jean-Pierre, Silvia Priori, and Michal Tendera. 2005. "Evidence-Based vs. 'Impressionist' Medicine: How Best to Implement Guidelines." *European Heart Journal* 26 (12) (June): 1155–58.

Boykoff, Nelli, Mona Moieni, and Saskia Karen Subramanian. 2009. "Confronting Chemobrain: An In-Depth Look at Survivors' Reports of Impact on Work, Social Networks, and Health Care Response." *Journal of Cancer Survivorship : Research and Practice* 3 (4) (December): 223–32.

Cabana, Michael D., Cynthia S. Rand, Neil R. Powe, Albert W. Wu, Modena H. Wilson, Paul-André C. Abboud, and Haya R. Rubin. 1999. "Why Don't Physicians Follow Clinical Practice Guidelines? A Framework for Improvement." *JAMA* 282 (15): 1458–67.

Coderre, S., H. Mandin, P. H. Harasym, and G. H. Fick. 2003. "Diagnostic Reasoning Strategies and Diagnostic Success." *Medical Education* 37 (8) (August): 695–703.

Devisch, Ignaas, and Stuart J. Murray. 2009. "'We Hold These Truths to Be Self-Evident': Deconstructing 'Evidence-Based' Medical Practice." *Journal of Evaluation in Clinical Practice* 15 (6): 950–54.

Duan, Naihua. 2007. "A Quest for Evidence Beyond Evidence-Based Medicine: Unleashing Clinical Experience through Evidence Farming." Unpublished seminar presentation, University of California, Davis.

Easterly, William. 2006. *The White Man's Burden: Why the West's Efforts to Aid the Rest Have Done So Much Ill and So Little Good*. New York: Penguin Books.

Glasziou, Paul, Greg Ogrinc, and Steve Goodman. 2011. "Can Evidence-Based Medicine and Clinical Quality Improvement Learn from Each Other?" *BMJ Quality & Safety* 20, suppl. 1 (April): i13–i17.

Hay, M. Cameron, R. Jean Cadigan, Dinesh Khanna, Cynthia Strathmann, Eli Lieber, Roy Altman, Maureen McMahon, Morris Kokhab, and Daniel E. Furst. 2008. "Prepared Patients : Internet Information Seeking by New Rheumatology Patients." *Arthritis Care and Research* 59 (4): 575–82.

Hay, M. Cameron, Cynthia Strathmann, Eli Lieber, Kimberly Wick, and Barbara Giesser. 2008. "Why Patients Go Online: Multiple Sclerosis, the Internet, and Physician-Patient Communication." *The Neurologist* 14 (6) (November): 374–81.

Hay, M. Cameron, Thomas S. Weisner, Saskia Subramanian, Naihua Duan, Edmund J. Niedzinski, and Richard L. Kravitz. 2008. "Harnessing Experience: Exploring the Gap between Evidence-Based Medicine and Clinical Practice." *Journal of Evaluation of Clinical Practice* 14: 707–13.

Kirmayer, Laurence J. 2012. "Rethinking Cultural Competence." *Transcultural Psychiatry* 49 (2) (April): 149–64.

Lloyd, Farrell J., and Valerie F. Reyna. 2009. "Clinical Gist and Medical Education: Connecting the Dots." *JAMA : The Journal of the American Medical Association* 302 (12) (September 23): 1332–33.

Osterberg, Lars, and Terrence Blaschke. 2005. "Adherence to Medication." *The New England Journal of Medicine* 353 (5) (August 4): 487–97.

Rosenbaum, Lisa, and William H. Shrank. 2013. "Taking Our Medicine—

Improving Adherence in the Accountability Era." *The New England Journal of Medicine* 369 (8) (August 22): 694–95.

Scheiman-Elazary, Anat, Lewei Duan, Courtney A. Shourt, David Elashoff, Harsh Agrawal, M. Cameron Hay, and Daniel Furst. In press. "Rate of Adherence to Medications and Associated Factors among RA Patients: SLR and Meta-Analysis." Journal of Rheumatology.

Sered, S., and E. Tabory. 1999. "'You Are a Number, Not a Human Being': Israeli Breast Cancer Patients' Experiences with the Medical Establishment." *Medical Anthropology Quarterly* 13 (2) (June): 223–52.

Tseng, Vivian. 2013. "Forging Common Ground." In *2012 Annual Report*, 18–25. William T. Grant Foundation.

Weisner, Thomas S., and M. Cameron Hay. 2015. "Practice to Research: Integrating Evidence-Based Practices with Culture and Context." *Transcultural Psychiatry* 52 (2): 222–43.

Weisner, Thomas S., Catherine Matheson, Jennifer Coots, and Lucinda P. Bernheimer. 2005. "Sustainability of Family Routines as a Family Outcome." In *Learning in Cultural Context: Family, Peers and School*, edited by Ashley E. Maynard and Mary I. Martini, 41–73. New York: Kluwer Academic/Plenum Publishers.

PART FIVE

Mixed Methods and the Insights of Longitudinal Research

THIRTEEN

How Siblings Matter in Zinacantec Maya Child Development

ASHLEY E. MAYNARD

Chances are you are a sibling. Have you ever thought about what it means to be a sibling? How influential have your siblings been in your life? Did you teach a younger sibling how to cook, care for others, or ride a bike? Or did your older siblings look after you, helping you understand the goings-on in your household and beyond? How much does it matter whether you are the oldest or the youngest? Does it matter what your respective gender roles are? Do you consult your siblings in your early adult life for advice on how to behave and what is best for your extended family as a whole?

When you think about it, for most people, the sibling relationship is the longest they will ever have. We typically are born into households with our siblings and grow up with them, so we know them before we have friends and spouses. It's also typical to grow old still relating to our siblings, surviving our parents. In some cultural groups, parents raise siblings as peers to each other, but they don't expect the older child or children to provide direct care or be responsible for the safety of the younger ones. In other cultures, care of younger siblings is the norm, and long-standing sibling bonds are forged in childhood and become the foundation for all other relationships in life (Weisner 2005; LeVine et al. 1994). This is different from cultures where the working model of relationships is thought to be the mother-child relationship, as is the dominant pattern in the United States.

A Little Background about My Fieldwork in Mexico

"Siblings always *matter*" (Weisner 1989, 14, emphasis in original). But they matter differently in different cultural places, depending on the practices and values that operate in the cultural setting. I have studied a group of about 200 Zinacantec Maya siblings as they've grown up since 1995, when I first started working in Mexico. The Zinacantecs are a Maya people living in the highlands of Chiapas who have participated in ongoing ethnographic and experimental inquiry for over forty years (e.g., de León 1999, 20021997; Greenfield, Brazelton, and Childs 1989; Haviland 1978; Laughlin 1975; Vogt 1969, 1990). There are about 4,500 people living in the hamlet where I conduct my fieldwork, Nabenchauk. In part because of its proximity to the colonial center of San Cristóbal de las Casas and because of its location on the Pan-American Highway, there has been a shift in Nabenchauk from agricultural subsistence to commercial activity over the past two generations (Greenfield, Maynard, and Childs 2000, 2003). Boys traditionally grew up to spend their lives as subsistence farmers. Girls grew to become mothers and to provide for their families by cooking and weaving. Now these roles are changing, a bit.

Growing up, I had been fascinated by cultural anthropology, and I developed an interest in working with Native Americans in Latin America. I read the early cross-cultural psychology of Patricia Greenfield, who herself had worked closely with anthropologists early in her career. I also began my career working with an anthropologist, Tom Weisner, and I benefited from reading his work, particularly his writings with Ron Gallimore on ecocultural theory and sibling caretaking. I first went to Nabenchauk as a graduate student to learn the language, Tzotzil, and to learn to weave. I ended up learning to do many of the things Zinacantec women do, including making tortillas and carrying firewood from the forest in a tumpline hanging from my head. I was immediately struck by the care among the large groups of siblings. Families typically included six to ten children in the 1990s, and sibling caretaking was normative. Sibling caretaking is one solution to the problem of providing social support for children; older siblings are put in charge of babies at an early age, and the seniority principle that governs all social relations in those groups officially grants older children authority over their younger siblings. Adults support older children in taking an interest in the youngest child and his or her activities, and to make sure the youngster is contented and comfortable.

Traditionally, Zinacantec sibling caretaking has led to lifelong bonds that form the basis of the ideal Zinacantec relationship—that of the sibling. Unlike the Western ideal of the mother-child bond, in Nabenchauk, the sibling bond is a prototype for other relationships. It is an idealized relationship that carries over into other aspects of life and the social organization of the community. In my research, I examine how these idealized notions are evident in children's interactions and how children acquire social and technical skills important in the Zinacantec culture.

Zinacantec Sibling Groups: Going beyond the Dyad as a Research Enterprise

One thing I noticed immediately when I went to Nabenchauk is that Zinacantecs rarely do anything alone—or even in pairs. People are almost always in groups of more than two. Children learn to manage group situations from early in life, and adults respect the skill of managing a group. Yet much psychological research in child development has focused on individuals or dyads, with mother-child dyads or sibling-dyads as the unit of analysis (e.g., Rogoff 1990; Whiting 1986; Youngblade and Dunn 1995). Anthropology, particularly linguistic anthropology, has done much better at studying children as they socialize each other in groups (e.g., Minks 2008; Ochs and Schieffelin 1984; Weisner 2005). Taking the focus off the dyad allows us to look at interactions in diverse, dynamic groups of people (Lave and Wenger 1991). Indeed, in many cultures, the dyad is the exception, whereas the triad or group is the rule (Ochs and Schieffelin 1984). In the triad or group, the actions of each person in the activity setting form the scaffold the young child can use to participate in cultural activities and accomplish new tasks. But this presents a methodological quandary: studying one or two people interacting is hard enough; what is the best way for a social scientist to go about studying children in groups of more than two?

I use mixed methods in my research. My favorite methods to study siblings are ethnographic observations and interviews. Ethnographically, I often act as a participant observer, living with or spending time with families and groups of siblings for a few months at a time. I make spot observations, interview people, take videos of live interactions among children, and write ethnographic descriptions of children's daily activities, the locations of children's activities, and their social companions. I have used these to design more contrived studies, such as quasi-experimental paradigms (e.g., Maynard 2004). For example, when my ethnographic interviews and observations of sibling teaching interactions revealed cross-gender activity with children at age two (teaching toddler boys to cook) but not at age five (boys act as "fathers" when playing "house"), I designed a quasi-experimental study to determine the age at which Zinacantec children understand appropriate gender roles.

I have found it is helpful to have a lens to focus my attention on a particular topic. But at the same time, I don't want to be so focused that I miss the bigger picture. My lens of choice has been the Activity Settings Analysis (ASA) laid out by Weisner and Gallimore (Gallimore, Goldenberg, and Weisner 1993; Weisner and Gallimore 1985). The premise of Weisner and Gallimore's ASA is that the activities making up the routines that comprise people's day-to-day lives provide opportunities for children to learn what is important in their culture and how to behave in culturally appropriate, meaningful ways (Weisner 1989).

ASA examines features of culture within activities and contexts surrounding activities. Features of activity settings include the personnel present, the tasks themselves, scripts for conduct, the motives and emotional experiences of actors in the tasks, and the cultural values being communicated in the activity (Gallimore, Goldenberg, and Weisner 1993). These features are basically the who, what, when, where, why, and how of activities. ASA helps me understand the ethnographic data I get with sibling groups. Understanding how groups function within a particular culture requires specific attention to the cultural models and values and the socialization practices of that place.

The Social Organization of Zinacantec Sibling Interactions

In this section, I describe typical sibling interactions among Zinacantec children, using ASA as our lens. The data come from both video ethnography and field notes I have collected over the years.

Washing Clothes

Valeria (age two) and Manuel (age four) are in the backyard, standing side-by-side at a makeshift bench. Manuel doesn't tell Valeria what to do, but she watches and imitates his actions. Gaby (age nine) enters and places a bucket with a piece of clothing in it between Manuel and Valeria. Then she directs both of them in washing. Manuel expresses that he wants the pants in the bucket. Gaby goes to get something else. She returns with another bucket into the frame. Manuel sees that she has the pants as Gaby is putting the bucket in between the two children. Valeria moves the bucket away from Manuel. He says, "Hand me the pants," as he reaches for them. Valeria protests with a baby sound. Manuel asks for a bucket from Gaby. She says that they are going to do their washing. Gaby then retreats to watch the washing at a distance and says, "Wash! Wash!" Manuel says, "Let's wash!" And he does the washing action with his threads. He says to Valeria, "Hand me a little water." She protests, saying, "Aaaw," as she looks to the water in her bucket and touches her bucket. Gaby enters to help Valeria wash and says, "Wash Vale!" Gaby then narrates her action of removing the pants from the bucket, "Take out—take out the washing here. Wash! Put soap on your washing here," and she shows the washing movement. She then pretends to put soap on the washing. Katal (age six) then enters with a glass of water and says to Gaby, "Look. Look." Gaby tells Katal, "Give to him [so that] he can see it," directing Katal's action. Gaby retreats, to watch the washing from a distance. Gaby then approaches Valeria again to add water to Valeria's bucket, pouring from the big bucket. Manuel continues his washing action, not engaging Valeria. Eventually he knocks over a glass of water, and they all laugh. He asks Manuel to "Draw some water and bring it back!" Katal runs off to get him water. Valeria then looks at what Manuel is doing and imitates the action of washing. Gaby exits the scene completely. Katal notices that Gaby has gone and brings water for Valeria and Manuel. "Look at this!" she says, and gives water in a glass to Manuel. She then pours some out of a glass for Valeria. Manuel and Valeria continue washing. Katal then says, "I am making the foods," as she goes to get leaves off a tree to serve as greens in her cooking.

Three older children (ages nine, six, and four) are involved in a group sibling caregiving interaction. The older children are teaching two-year-old Valeria how to wash clothes, an important everyday task. Each child plays a role in helping Valeria, consistent with that child's developmental capabilities (Maynard 2002). Nine-year-old Gaby provides materials and coordinates the actions of the three younger children; she directs Valeria and Manuel to wash and she directs Katal where to put the water they will use in the washing. Katal, age six, helps out by bringing water for the children to use in the washing. She does so without being asked. Katal provides developmentally sensitive help to Valeria by pouring the water for her. In accord with Manuel's more sophisticated level of development, she merely leaves a glass of water for him to use. After Gaby leaves, Katal shifts the play situation to eating and presents the children with bowls of water with leaves in them. Manuel, the four-year-old, takes no opportunity to teach Valeria verbally. He occasionally looks to the focal child to see what she is doing, and he does engage her by saying, "Let's wash." He never explicitly narrates to her what she should do as he is doing it himself, however. He does the action of washing, but does not engage in attention-getting behaviors. Basically, he serves as an observational model for the two-year-old. A little later we see a shift in frame, from doing washing to making tortillas, but the sibling roles remain similar, with Katal now the oldest and in charge.

Making Tortillas

Katal and Manuel are still in the back yard alone with Valeria. Katal decides to teach Valeria how to make tortillas. Their mother is still inside the house working. Katal says, "Come here Vale! Let's play here!" Valeria walks over to Katal, and Manuel enters to sit with them. He says, "Let's play!" Katal is tearing leaves off a branch to serve as pretend-tortillas as Valeria and Manuel both watch her. Valeria and Manuel both pick up some leaves and imitate Katal. Manuel then quits the tortilla making and exits. Katal says, "Wait then. I'm going . . . I'm going to make it this way—still better," and then goes to pound the leaves and make them better. Katal sees that Valeria is doing nothing and demands from a distance that she pat tortillas. "You pat . . . pat tortillas! Pat tortillas!" Katal herself pounds leaves with a rock on top of a wooden surface, away from Valeria. Katal says, "The tortillas came out thick," and then she comes closer to Valeria and notices that Valeria has taken the wrong leaves off the wrong branch. "Not this," she says, "Just the little ones! Just the little ones! There aren't any . . . (mumbles)." Katal continues, "Where did the stone go?" and looks for the stone. She looks at what Valeria is doing and says, "It's finished already Vale. Wait. Not yet." Katal stops Valeria from making any more tortillas as she prepares little tortillas out of leaves for Valeria. Katal ends the cooking and they play with some glue and paper.

This setting includes three siblings, ages six, four, and two as personnel. The eldest child present, Katal, is teaching the youngest child present, Valeria, how to make tortillas, in the context of sibling caretaking. Katal is keeping Valeria busy so that their mother can work. Katal coordinates the action of Valeria and Manuel, telling them to come play with her. Katal supplies the necessary materials and gives Valeria direct instruction, as well as modeling what to do. However, she does not provide demonstrated narrations for Valeria to tell her what she wants her to do. Valeria watches Katal's behaviors very closely and imitates her. Though Manuel leaves and comes back into the scene at will, Valeria can make use of his cooking behaviors also as he models them. As the older sibling, Katal gives Valeria commands and corrects her behavior when she does something inappropriate. Katal monitors Valeria's behavior and corrects her. Valeria complies with Katal's commands, showing that she has an understanding of authority.

Sibling caretaking interactions are organized by principles of care, and they emphasize social skills, rather than strictly cognitive skills. These two cases are suggestive of the first three principles of what I call the Zinacantec cultural model of social competency.

Social Competency in Zinacantán

Cultural models set the social organization of the community. Three social and organizational principles that govern Zinacantec life emerged from my early analyses of sibling caretaking interactions, forming the foundation of what I call the Zinacantec model of social competency. The first principle is the emphasis on sibling relationships and caretaking. Sibling relationships are encoded in six sibling terms— not just "brother" and "sister." Tzotzil encodes the relative status and gender of each sibling: *bankil*, "older brother of a boy"; *itz'in*, "younger brother of a boy"; *xibnel*, "older brother of a girl"; *ixlel*, "younger sister of a boy"; vix, "older sister of a girl or boy"; and *muk*, "younger sibling (boy or girl) of a girl." Just learning the language, it was easy to see how important sibling relationships were. Parents build up children's skills in sibling caretaking by engaging young children in the care of infants, and by gradually assigning more difficult tasks and parts of tasks. When siblings care for each other, they learn to interact with other children by managing many of their activities and conflicts on their own—without adult intervention.

Second, there is an emphasis on group activities; most activities are organized among groups of three or more, rather than by individuals or by dyads. People rarely do anything alone or even in pairs. Third, older people are given higher status. Elders are the first to be offered a chair or something to eat or drink. Related to this, there is an emphasis on the older-brother/ younger-brother distinction. Consistent with the status of elders, older brothers and older sisters are revered from early childhood through the lifespan. The older-brother/younger-brother distinction remains important throughout life, and it provides a central organizational rule for adult social interactions. For example, who is older than whom is something that is considered when discussing who should go first into a ritual or who should ask someone outside the family for help. When people greet each other on the path, they know how to behave based on who is older. The eldest sister has traditionally been revered as the second mother to all the other children who came along. The next vignette shows how the children continue to follow these principles in their interactions, even as the eldest sister enters adulthood and has her own baby.

Siblings Care for a New Infant

Twenty-one-year-old Loxa, the oldest sister among the children in the three previous examples, had recently given birth to her first child, Erika. She and her husband had moved back into her parents' house so that her mother could help her with her pregnancy. Also, her husband, Palas, was working with Loxa's father, Lol, and living there made the work process run more smoothly. For the first month of the baby's life, Loxa, Palas, and Loxa's mother, Pil, did most of the work in caring for the new baby girl. After the baby was about one month old, Loxa's siblings began to do a lot more to take care of the child. The following is a sample of ethnographic data collected on the topic of child care in Nabenchauk, when Loxa's baby was almost three months old.

The baby began to cry and Manuel, now ten years old, announced to his sister, Gaby, now age fifteen, that the baby was crying. Gaby had been outside the house, within earshot, and came running in to collect the baby from the bed. She immediately began to bounce the baby gently up and down making a "sh" sound to help calm the baby. She asked Katal, her twelve-year-old sister, to bring her the baby's bottle and to make the baby's formula. Katal asked where the bottle was and Palas directed her to the table in the middle of the one-room house. Katal fetched the bottle and then looked for the powdered formula. She put two small scoops of formula in the bottle and added some warm water that had been purchased for the baby and heated up. The warm water is always kept near the fire to keep it warm for the baby throughout the day and night. Katal put her finger over the end of the nipple of the bottle and shook it up to mix it. Gaby told her to hurry up and finally Katal handed her the bottle. Gaby immediately gave the baby the bottle and the baby began to feed. After the baby was calmed, Gaby needed to go outside to do a chore. She gave the baby to Katal by helping her to carry it on her back. The baby slept on Katal's back for about an hour until it began to cry again. This time Manuel was asked to get the baby's bottle ready, and he went about the task of mixing the formula. Katal turned the baby around so that it was resting on her hip and its face was more accessible for feeding. Manuel gave Katal the bottle and Katal fed the baby. Loxa was resting and watched all of this happen.

This is just one incident of many that were recorded over a period of three months of fieldwork. There were many other instances where Loxa fed her baby herself, or when the father, Palas, fed the baby. Loxa's mother, Pil, also fed the baby many times. As the baby got a few weeks older, Manuel, age ten, would hold and feed her.

The personnel in the infant-care scenario are the mother of the baby and three of her six siblings (ages fifteen, twelve, and ten). Other people who might have been present during this child care-episode include the mother's other siblings, her mother and father, and her husband. Loxa's father, brother, and husband work in a transport business together selling fruit and flowers.

The task here is to care for the infant. There is an implicit role for the eldest female present, usually the mother, to take initiative and manage the infant-care situation in the household. The task demands include responding to the infant and getting the necessary materials to soothe the infant's distress. The tools that are required for this infant-care situation include a bottle, warm water, and baby formula.

The organizational script in Zinacantec infant-care routines is for the mother or oldest female present to respond first to the infant and to assign care roles or parts of the task of care to other people present. If the mother is resting or ill, it is often her own mother or her sister who takes the role of primary responder to the infant's distress. Almost everyone in the household will play a part at some point in time in the care of the infant, whether it is to alert a female to respond to the crying child, as a man might do, or whether it is to be a direct provider of care, such as that seen in the example above, when the baby's aunts and uncle provide direct care by feeding and holding her. The sociolinguistic script is for the younger people to follow the directives of the older person in charge. There is no negotiation of what to do for the baby or of who will play what role; roles are assigned by the mother or eldest female in charge and everyone else cooperates. This mirrors the management of sibling caretaking roles and household chores that happens in everyday Zinacantec life.

There are several cultural values and cultural/family goals communicated in this scenario, including the role of females as the primary responders to infants, the role of siblings in the care of infants, sociolinguistic interactional frames of deference to older people, and sensitive guidance. The mother of the infant is nearby, resting, and she does not get involved in the care of her baby in this example. Her siblings are capable of providing the necessary care as she gets some needed rest. Fifteen-year-old Gaby is responsible for engaging her younger siblings in the care of the baby while her own sister rests and her mother works. The children follow her initiative and go along with her directives. The children do not argue over what they will do. This infant-care example highlights the value of help: Gaby is fifteen and can handle the care situation by assigning roles to her younger siblings. She assigns the role of getting the bottle with formula first to Katal, who is now 12 years old. Manuel observes this process. Observation is an important part of cultural learning in Zinacantec life (Childs and Greenfield 1980; Maynard and Greenfield 2005; Maynard, Greenfield, and Childs 1999). The children's discourse reflects the value of more experienced people providing sensitive help to less-experienced individuals. As the younger children observe and show some competence, they are given more elaborate tasks or more responsibility.

The experienced motives and feelings of the participants can be described as focused, collaborative care. The children feel a sense of family as they care for the baby. The oldest child, Gaby, feels a sense of responsibility for the baby's well-being and safety. The younger children feel effective in participating in this important process of infant care.

A fourth principle of the Zinacantec model of social competency emerged from this example: continuity of structures of social life from childhood to adulthood. Children spend much of their time together during the day, interacting with blood siblings and with young aunts and uncles, cousins, and godsiblings, who may be classificatory siblings. They maintain these bonds as they mature, and adult life is organized around these bonds, with siblings, cousins, and godsiblings, who may become compadres (cogodparents). If there was an issue among the adult siblings, the oldest brother was often consulted for his opinion, and what he said was followed, as in childhood. This organization is true in work life and in social and ritual life as well (Vogt 1969).

Reflection on the Ethnographic Examples

The case study of one family shows how each child at a given age interacts with the other children in accord with the Zinacantec model of social competency. They are involved in sibling care, which is almost always a group activity. Each child shows respect for his or her older siblings and the older-brother/younger-brother distinction. And, from the first example to the last, we see continuity across six years of the children's development. Each child demonstrates his or her highest competence in coordinating action of the other children when he or she is the eldest child present.

As we see in the first example, Gaby, age nine, is skilled at coordinating the actions of all three younger children, Katal, Manuel, and Valeria. She is able to tell each child what to do to play "washing." She teaches Valeria how to wash both by giving her commands and by actually demonstrating to her what she wants her to do. When Gaby is present, Katal, age six, helps the episode continue by bringing the necessary items for washing, glasses of water. She does not suggest how the play should go nor does she take the role of teaching Valeria; for that she defers to Gaby.

When we see Katal again as the eldest child present, in the second example, we see that she does indeed know how to structure a play situation. She engages Manuel and Valeria in making tortillas. She calls them to play with her, and again provides the necessary materials for the play. She teaches Valeria how to make tortillas by serving as an observational model and by giving her commands. Katal does not give Valeria any actual demonstrations of making tortillas, the way Gaby gave Valeria a demonstration of washing in the earlier example. Thus Katal's teaching could be called less sophisticated or advanced than Gaby's. Katal does, however, demonstrate knowledge of her status in both situations. When she is the next-oldest child present, she defers to the oldest child to lead the play. When she is the oldest child present, she herself leads and orchestrates the play of making tortillas.

Katal demonstrates adherence to the roles of social organization. She behaves with appropriate deference to Gaby when Gaby is present, and she takes on the appropriate leadership role with the younger children only after Gaby leaves. If one were to consider Katal's behavior only in the episode when Gaby, her older sister, is present, one might conclude that Katal could not lead a play episode herself. This is not the case; as we see in the tortilla episode, she leads by herself. However, the discourse skills she uses across both situations are different. When Gaby is present, Katal does not give commands to Valeria or to Manuel. She also does not begin making assessments of the children's behavior until Gaby is gone.

Manuel, at age four, shows the least sophistication in his interactions, but he does show social competency. He rarely engages Valeria and he never decides what they should play when an older child is present. In another episode not presented here, when he is alone with

Valeria he does not take any opportunity to show her how to do anything with an explicit, intentional demonstration. He serves as the observational model for Valeria throughout the episodes.

In the third example, when the siblings are six years older, they are caring for their older sister's baby, and the Zinacantec models of the sibling relationship, providing care, and respecting those older than you are still in effect. Each person does what he or she can to aid in the care of the infant and contribute to the group harmony and well-being. However, if there were ever a breach in these expectations for social competencies, family relationships, even the tight-knit bond between siblings, could sometimes unravel.

Cracks in Sibling Bonds

Over the years from 2009 to 2012, I observed a breakdown in the sibling relationship. In 2012, Loxa was thirty years of age, Gaby twenty-four, Katal twenty-one, Manuel nineteen, and Valeria seventeen. Loxa had become a widow at the age of twenty-one in 2003. She was raising her daughter, Erika, while living with her parents and siblings. In 2009, she upset her parents by developing a relationship and then marrying a non-Mayan man she met working in the urban market where they sold agricultural products out of warehouse stalls. When the parents got upset, all the siblings began to speak badly of Loxa, and she became socially isolated. She stayed with her husband at the warehouse stall a few doors down and was shunned by her parents and siblings. She had a second daughter, named Katrina. Sadly, Loxa's second husband also died, in a trucking accident, in July, 2012. Devastated, Loxa stayed alone in the small warehouse stall she had shared with her husband, but she could not afford to keep that going. Eventually, her father, Lol, invited her to share part of his large warehouse stall with him, her mother, and the rest of the family. They built a makeshift wall to create a separate space for her and her two-year-old daughter. Her siblings and parents continued to complain and gossip about her as they all sold agricultural products in a large wholesale market area to the south and removed from the tourist center of the colonial city. Loxa's parents maintained the family home in Nabenchauk, but lived five or six days a week in the warehouse.

The reasons Loxa's family gave for shunning her were that she had married a non-Mayan man, and they did not like him. When he died, they thought Loxa "had a bad head" and was very angry. She wanted to live by herself, but she also needed those family ties and limited interactions in order to survive by selling agricultural items in front of the warehouse. She maintained a separate business with the help of her in-laws, the parents of the deceased second husband, who brought her different agricultural products to sell, usually bananas and rambutans. Even though her natal family was a thin wall away, the relations were not smooth. Her father barely talked to her. Loxa's natal family did not share with her the way she did with them. They essentially took Erika and raised her to dislike her mom. And this was all because Loxa had violated the third principle of honoring the desires and opinions of elders by marrying a non-Mayan man whom they didn't like. Loxa wanted to save enough money to buy a plot of land back in Naben-chauk and live there with her daughters. Time will tell.

Having known this family since 1995, and knowing the Zinacan-tec emphasis on sibling relationships and respect for elders, I was quite surprised at the level of gossip and hurtful language about Loxa, some-times within earshot of her side of the warehouse. Sibling relationships in at least one family had changed, significantly. The dissension and conflict occurring in the village and society at large (Cancian 1992) had found its way into what was once a peaceful cradle, the sibling bond. Loxa continued to be gracious, sharing whatever she had with her siblings. She tried to foster a bond between her two daughters, but Erika had been so influenced by the grandmother that she seemed to find it risky to get too close to her own mother. I felt indignant, think-ing, "She raised her siblings! She didn't get to go to school even though she wanted to because she had to raise them! And now they shun her and can't look after her needs for a while to get her through a tough time? A widow twice by the age of thirty? How dare they? Can't they show a little more compassion?"

It was very difficult for me to resolve these issues. I asked the siblings and Pil about the relationships, and got the same answer: she had vio-lated the principle of respect for elders. I tried to be a conduit for mend-ing fences, talking to Loxa's mother about how it hurt Erika's heart to hear bad words about her own mother, Loxa. I would invite them all to join in sharing some food together that I had brought (knowing no one would want to shun my offerings, even if they had to be with Loxa). Over about six months, the relationships appeared to be improving a tiny bit. Loxa was invited to spend a couple of afternoons at her family home back in Nabenchauk. It is especially sad to see the breakdown of family ties in a context where family ties have been so revered and re-lied upon. I am eager to return to see how things have developed, and I continue to hope for the best.

Discussion

The study of Zinacantec sibling caretaking informs us as to the structures of their social relationships, which reflect those of the greater society, especially in the adult world of "cargos" (positions in the religious hierarchy) and interpersonal relationships in families and around the village (Vogt 1969, 1990). In Zinacantán there is a pervasive rule that younger people should respect and follow the authority of older people (Cancian 1964). Respect by younger brothers and sisters for older brothers and sisters is evident in family gatherings and business. Hierarchy and respect for elders exist also in address terms for people older than one's self, even if there is no blood relation; such people are often called "mother" and "father," when passing them on the paths around the village.

This hierarchical system is socialized by Zinacantec parents' and older siblings' use of commands in training younger children (Cancian 1964; Childs and Greenfield 1980; Maynard 2002; Zukow 1989). A good child is an obedient child who does his or her chores to help the family (Blanco and Chodorow 1964). Obedience and respect for authority are aspects of the hierarchical relationships in Nabenchauk (Vogt 1969, 1990) that also appear in children's play. Vogt identifies the older brother-younger brother relationship as the paradigm for all Zinacantec relationships.

During childhood, older siblings direct younger ones in a variety of situations. They see to it that their younger siblings are busy and happy. Their status is recognized by the younger children present. The hierarchical relationships exhibited in children's play are the foundation for later, adult relationships. As children interact together in their own peer culture, they are socializing each other to behave in culturally appropriate ways. The ability of children to interact in a group situation is an important social skill.

Zinacantec children participate in each other's socialization following a model that is reflective of and prepares them for adulthood. This model emphasizes sibling caretaking, status, age hierarchy, and participation in group activities that are socially useful. Zinacantec children's interactions prepare them for the adult social world. In that world, one's siblings are still the most enduring relationships and longest-term support one is likely to find throughout life; this is equally true for women and men. The ideal kinds of relationships one could have are such sibling relationships, and they are mirrored in the compadre "godparent" system. Hence, even in the play of very young children, there is embedded a much more general lesson about the kinds of people, content and contexts of relationships, and emotionally important bonds that Zinacantec society strives to achieve.

Furthermore, the study of children's behavior in the matrix of a group activity highlights the social organization of development itself. Each member of the group participates in the activity setting in accord with his or her developmental status and abilities. The youngest child benefits from each person's input and actions, especially because those actions provide different kinds of information. By shifting the focus from the dyad to the multiage group, this paper has shown how child development may be supported by all others present in the child's environment. In the context of the play of children of multiple ages, ontogeny is recapitulated as each child's behavior forms a rung in the scaffold of help.

These examples show the idea that cultures are not static; they change over time. And the ways that people interact also change over time. In Nabenchauk, sibling relationships and expectations for interaction have changed over the course of my research since 1995. While sibling caretaking is still a dominant pattern, some children are not learning to be sibling caretakers because they are going to school. First-born daughters may go to school now if there aren't a lot of younger siblings to care for or if the mother and daughter want the girl to attend school. And, sibling relationships in adult life do not carry the same weight that they once did. In many families, adult siblings do not work together as much as they used to, and they do not necessarily consult their oldest brother about what to do. And there is a lack of respect for older siblings in some families, as we saw in the example of Loxa and her siblings in adulthood. In short, the cultural model for social competency among the Zinacantec is shifting, as people adapt to shifting ecocultural circumstances.

Methodological Implications: Using Ethnography to Find Out What Matters in Development

I took seriously Weisner's proposal that ethnography should be the first step in the study of human development (Weisner 1996). It made sense to me because I am not Zinacantec. I didn't know how to design research that would be valid or interesting without first getting to know the culture and the community. It wasn't enough to read the excellent ethnographies that had been written. I had to experience the daily routines and everyday interactions on my own. I spent many months living in the village. Going to sleep, I got to see that children have no bedtime or bedtime routines. Getting up in the morning, I got to see who did what and who ate first and how the days unfolded. As part of families in the village, I have participated in curing ceremonies and other rituals, celebrations, and sad losses. Over the years, I've seen how things are changing, making it very clear to me how important long-term ethnography is, and how the insights from long-term ethnography can inform our understanding of the impact of cultural worlds on human development more generally.

My ethnographic experience and mixed methods approach have been critical in helping me understand the cross-cultural psychology of the Zinacantecs. These ethnographic findings are relevant for understanding that human development may not be most strongly defined by dyadic mother-child relations, but by sibling relations, where care is distributed and even longer lasting than parent-child bonds. In the United States, our public school system should understand that family, and the significant relationships within a family that support a child's education, may not just be about parent-child relations, but may be about the care that children learn to give each other. Children's social competencies may be quite developed, and these skills can be harnessed in educational settings where children may serve as peer tutors, or they may work in groups to produce joint projects. Children from cultural groups where distributed care is emphasized may not be comfortable exhibiting their individual skills in front of everyone, but they may be quite comfortable doing so in the context of helping a group succeed. At the very least, educators need to rethink assumptions about family life and what it means for children's social and cognitive development.

Ethnography made it possible for me to study siblings in groups, as they were, doing what they wanted to do, rather than setting up situations and contriving pairs or groups in ways that might not have made any sense to the children themselves (and might have gotten me invalid data). It has been the privilege of my life to be a part of Nabenchauk, and I look forward to many more years together.

Acknowledgment

I am grateful to Tom Weisner for his help in developing the ideas presented in this paper and for his friendship over the years. I also thank the families who participated in the study. Maruch Ch'entik has provided immeasurable help by locating families and assisting me in the field since 1995. Research data presented in this paper were collected with support in part from the Latin American Center and the Center for Culture and Health at UCLA. For some of the data collection, I was supported by a National Science Foundation graduate research fellowship, a fellowship from the Center for the Study of Evolution and the Origin of Life at UCLA, and by dissertation-year and postdoctoral fellowships from the University of California Office of the President. Portions of this research were also supported by the University Research Council at the University of Hawai'i. The ideas in this chapter have simmered over the years and have been shaped by thoughtful feedback and interactions with Tom Weisner, Patricia Greenfield, Geoff Saxe, Mary Gauvain, Ben Bergen, Darnell Cole, Katy Irwin, Su Yeong Kim, Peter Mataira, Lori Yancura, and Cameron Hay. I appreciate their collegiality and their thoughtful reading of various versions of this chapter.

References

Blanco, Merida H., and Nancy Chodorow. 1964. "Children's Work and Obedience in Zinacantan." Manuscript on file, Harvard Chiapas Project, Department of Anthropology, Harvard. University, Cambridge, MA.

Cancian, Francesca M. 1964. "Interaction Patterns in Zinacanteco Families." *American Sociological Review* 29: 540–50.

Cancian, Frank. 1992. *The Decline of Community in Zinacantan: Economy, Public Life, and Social Stratification, 1960–1987.* Stanford, CA: Stanford University Press.

Childs, Carla P., and Patricia M. Greenfield. 1980. "Informal Modes of Teaching and Learning: The Case of Zinacanteco Weaving." In *Studies in Cross-Cultural Psychology*, vol. 2, edited by Neil Warren, 269–316. London: Academic Press.

de León, Lourdes. 1999. "'Mu me majeluk, mu me uteluk' ('Not with Hitting, Not with Scolding'): Socializing Emotion and Moral Agency in Tzotzil (Mayan) Children." Paper presented at the 29th Annual Meetings of the Jean Piaget Society, Mexico City, Mexico.

———.2002. "Body and Domestic Space in Zinacantec Socialization." Paper presented at the 32nd Annual Meetings of the Jean Piaget Society, Philadelphia, PA.

Gallimore, Ronald, Claude Goldenberg, and Thomas S. Weisner. 1993. "The Social Construction and Subjective Reality of Activity Settings: Implications for Community Psychology." *American Journal of Community Psychology* 21 (4): 537–59.

Greenfield, Patricia M., Ashley E. Maynard, and Carla P. Childs. 2000. "History, Culture, Learning, and Development." *Cross-Cultural Research* 34 (4): 351–74.

———2003. "Historical Change, Cultural Learning, and Cognitive Representation in Zinacantec Maya Children." *Cognitive Development* 18 (4): 455–87.

Greenfield, P. M., T. B. Brazelton, and C. P. Childs. 1989. "From Birth to Maturity in Zinacantán: Ontogenesis in Cultural Context." In V. Bricker and G. Gossen, eds., *Ethnographic Encounters in Southern Mesoamerica: Celebratory Essays in Honor of Evon Z. Vogt*, 177–216. Albany: Institute of Mesoamerican Studies, State University of New York.

Haviland, Leslie Knox. 1978. "The Social Relations of Work in a Peasant Community." PhD diss., Harvard University.

Laughlin, Robert M. 1975. *The Great Tzotzil Dictionary of San Lorenzo Zinacantán. Smithsonian Contributions to Anthropology*, no. 19. Washington D.C.: U.S. Government Printing Office.

Lave, Jean, and Etienne Wenger. 1991. *Situated Learning: Legitimate Peripheral Participation.* Cambridge: Cambridge University Press.

LeVine, Robert A., Suzanne Dixon, Sarah LeVine, Amy Richman, P. Herbert Leiderman, Constance H. Keefer, and T. Berry Brazelton. 1994. *Childcare and Culture: Lessons from Africa.* New York: Cambridge University Press.

Maynard, Ashley E. 2002. Cultural Teaching: The Development of Teaching Skills in Zinacantec Maya Sibling Interactions. *Child Development* 73 (3): 969–82.

———. 2004. "Men Don't Make Tortillas: Gender-Role Development in Zinacantec Maya Children." Poster presented at the meetings of the American Psychological Association, Honolulu, Hawai'i, July.

———2015. "Cultural Teaching: The Development of Teaching Skills in Maya Sibling Interactions." *Child Development* 73 (3): 969–82. doi: http://dx.doi.org/10.1111/1467–8624.00450.

Maynard, Ashley E., and Patricia. M. Greenfield. 2005. "Cultural Teaching: Processes, Effects, and Development of Apprenticeship Skills." In *Learning in Places: The Informal Education Reader*, edited by Z. Bekerman, N. C. Burbules, and D. Silberman-Kellers. New York: Peter Lang 139–62.

Maynard, Ashley E., Patricia M. Greenfield, and Carla P. Childs. 1999. "Culture, History, Biology, and Body: Native and Non-Native Acquisition of Technological Skill." *Ethos* 27 (3): 379–402.

Minks, Amanda. 2008. "Performing Gender in Song Games among Nicaraguan Miskitu Children." *Language and Communication* 28 (1): 36–56.

Ochs, Elinor, and Schieffelin, Bambi B. 1984. "Language Acquisition and Socialization: Three Developmental Stories and Their Implications." In *Culture Theory: Essays on Mind, Self, and Emotion*, edited by Richard Shweder and Robert LeVine, 276–320. Cambridge: Cambridge University Press.

Rogoff, Barbara. 1990. *Apprenticeship in Thinking.* New York: Oxford University Press.

Vogt, Evon Z. 1969. *Zinacantán: A Maya Community in the Highlands of Chiapas.* Cambridge, MA: Harvard University Press.

———. 1990. *The Zinacantecos of Mexico: A Modern Maya Way of Life.* 2nd ed. New York: Harcourt, Brace, Jovanovich.

Weisner, Thomas S. 1989. "Comparing Sibling Relationships Across Cultures." In *Sibling Interaction Across Cultures: Theoretical and Methodological Issues,* edited by Patricia Goldring Zukow, New York: Springer-Verlag, 11–25.

———. 1996. "Why Ethnography Should Be the Most Important Method in the Study of Human Development." In *Ethnography and Human Development: Context and Meaning in Social Inquiry,* edited by Richard Jessor, Anne Colby, and Richard A. Shweder, 305–24. Chicago: University of Chicago Press.

———. 2005. "Attachment as a Cultural and Ecological Problem with Pluralistic Solutions." *Human Development* 48 (1–2): 89–94.

Weisner, Thomas S., and Ronald Gallimore. 1977. "My Brother's Keeper: Child and Sibling Caretaking." *Current Anthropology* 18: 169–90.

———. 1985. "The Convergence of Ecocultural and Activity Theory." Paper presented at the Annual Meeting of the American Anthropological Association, Washington, D.C., December.

Whiting, Beatrice B. 1986. "The Effect of Experience on Peer Relationships." In *Process and Outcome in Peer Relationships,* edited by Edward C. Mueller and Catherine C. Cooper, 79–99. Orlando, FL: Academic Press, Inc.

Youngblade, Lisa M., and Judy Dunn. 1995. "Social Pretend with Mother and Sibling: Individual Differences and Social Understanding." In *The Future of Play Theory: A Multidisciplinary Inquiry into the Contributions of Brian Sutton-Smith,* edited by Anthony D. Pellegrini, 221–40. New York: State University of New York Press.

Zukow, Patricia G. 1989. "Siblings as Effective Socializing Agents: Evidence from Central Mexico." In *Sibling Interaction across Cultures. Theoretical and Methodological Issues,* edited by Patricia G. Zukow, 79–105. New York: Springer-Verlag.

FOURTEEN

Why Mixed Methods Matter in Understanding Neighborhood Context and Child Maltreatment

JILL E. KORBIN

Child abuse and neglect occur around the world, affect approximately one million children in the United States, and have been shown to have long-lasting effects on physical and mental health and development. Child abuse and neglect have been discussed and debated for at least fifty years, dating from the landmark paper in the *Journal of the American Medical Association* that drew public and professional attention to "the battered child syndrome" (Kempe et al. 1962) and stimulated action by legislators and policymakers (Nelson 1984). The literature has documented the challenges that child abuse and neglect pose for research, practice, and policy. Recognizing these difficulties, I focus in this paper on the opportunities research in child maltreatment offers for contributing to a broader understanding of human behavior and social problems. I also argue that anthropological theory on culture, context, and human development and a mixed methods approach hold promise for generating findings that matter to an understanding of child maltreatment.

As the vignettes below suggest, child abuse and neglect

occur within broader neighborhood contexts that may be character-ized by social support (the first vignette) or by fear and social distrust (the second and third vignettes). These contexts make a difference.

"If you know a child is being abused, you have to do something or the child could end up being dead. . . . There once was this child whose parents beat him and the neighbors called 866-KIDS." (Adult resident of a Cleveland, Ohio, neighborhood)

"Children are not like they were. It used to be that the parent would punish the child and thank the neighbor [for correcting the child]. . . . One day there was a little boy about four, throwing rocks at my dog. I told him to stop and he turned around and starting yelling swear words at me. The mother did nothing." (Adult resident of a Cleveland, Ohio, neighborhood)

"If you don't know them, I'll get killed probably." (Response from a young child in a Cleveland neighborhood when asked if he/she would accept help from an adult)

Anthropology's initial entry into the world of child maltreatment arose through the discipline's core concept of culture and its use of the ethnographic record to document the remarkable diversity of child-rearing beliefs and practices around the world. The recognition of child abuse and neglect in the United States and European nations stimu-lated questions about whether child maltreatment was universal or cul-turally bound. Disproportionality in child abuse and neglect reports by cultural group within these countries also drew attention to cul-tural influences on child maltreatment. Anthropological efforts were devoted to explaining the parenting beliefs and behaviors of other cul-tures and promoting a cultural-contextual approach (e.g., Fraser and Kilbride 1980; Korbin 1981; Scheper-Hughes 1987; Scheper-Hughes and Sargent 1998) in the face of international efforts to set universal stan-dards for child well-being and child maltreatment (e.g., United Nations Convention on the Rights of the Child). Consistent with anthropologi-cal theory and research on the diversity of child-care beliefs and prac-tices around the world (e.g., LeVine et al. 1996; LeVine and New 2008; Weisner 2009a; Whiting and Whiting 1974; Whiting and Edwards 1992), anthropological perspectives were employed to promote a rec-ognition that definitions of child well-being (e.g., Weisner 1998) and child maltreatment did indeed vary across cultures. For decades, an-thropological research on child rearing and human development had recognized that Western-oriented cultures were often on the far end of the cross-cultural continuum of child-rearing beliefs and practices (e.g., Whiting and Child 1953). In addition, anthropological perspectives on deviance and rule-breaking behavior (Edgerton 1985, 1992) contributed to cross-cultural perspectives on child maltreatment and other social ills.

This initial foray by anthropology confirmed that cultures everywhere had their own rules and ideas about parenting behavior and child treatment as well as conceptions about what constitutes violations of cultural standards and norms. Anthropologists have powerfully argued for the importance of context in efforts to define both child well-being (e.g., Weisner 2009b) and child maltreatment. While there is cross-cultural agreement that certain extreme harms inflicted on children constitute maltreatment, anthropology contributed to the recognition of the importance of context in understanding the definitions, causes, and consequences of child maltreatment. Anthropologists increasingly have been involved in efforts to promote child well-being and prevent child maltreatment, ranging from ethnographic studies of other cultures to advocacy work in international and global arenas.

A related anthropological approach is to employ anthropological theory and mixed methods research to explore the influence of context and specific settings on child maltreatment. In an ecological and ecocultural approach (e.g., Weisner 1997), culture provides the context for settings (people, activities, tasks, routines, scripts, etc.) that shape human behavior and development (e.g., Whiting and Whiting 1974; Whiting and Edwards 1992), including problematic parenting. Since the early 1990s, a multidisciplinary group of colleagues and I have engaged in mixed methods research to study the influence of one such context, neighborhoods, on child maltreatment reports and the conditions that may be linked with those reports. We are embarking now on a National Institute of Child Health and Human Development (NICHD)-supported twenty-year follow-up study of those same neighborhoods and the households within them.

While most prevention and intervention efforts have focused on individuals and families, an ecological/developmental model has been promoted as the best framework in which to understand child maltreatment (National Research Council 1993). Neighborhoods are one important ecological level, and neighborhood factors influencing child maltreatment have received increasing attention (e.g., Ben-Arieh 2010; Coulton et al. 2007; Dodge and Coleman 2009; Drake and Pandey 1996; Garbarino and Sherman1980; Freisthler 2004; Coulton and Korbin

2007; Melton and Holaday 2008; Spilsbury 2002). Our neighborhood-based studies in Cleveland, Ohio, have brought multiple sources of data and multiple perspectives to the task of understanding what it is about neighborhood contexts that may act to prevent child maltreatment or to create conditions making child abuse and neglect more likely. Our project has involved the coordination of aggregate-level analyses and ethnographic research, using samples of individual residents in neighborhoods with differing profiles of child maltreatment reports.

In our work on child maltreatment and neighborhood context in Cleveland, Ohio, we started with the finding that there was unexplained variability in maltreatment reports across Cleveland's neighborhoods. What was it about these neighborhood contexts that explained this variability? High child maltreatment rates, along with many other social problems, are concentrated in high-poverty, disadvantaged neighborhoods. Nevertheless, neighborhood rates of child maltreatment are not explained by poverty rates alone, but by a complex interaction of factors. All poor neighborhoods are not alike, and child maltreatment rates vary across poor neighborhoods. In addition, neighborhoods vary in trends of child abuse reporting. Even as national trends show a decrease in child maltreatment rates (in physical and sexual abuse, but not in neglect or fatal maltreatment), variability is still evident. In some Cleveland neighborhoods, child maltreatment rates have decreased sharply, in some slightly; in others, child maltreatment rates have increased. Again, we want to know what it is about neighborhood contexts that may explain this variability. We have been studying these neighborhoods for more than twenty years.

Let me now turn to our methods, examples of what we have found in our study of neighborhood ecologies, and the potential contribution of our findings to addressing real-world problems.

Methods Mattered

Methods mattered to our research team from the time we began planning this project in the early 1990s (Korbin 2008). The mixed methods approach we selected brought together our different areas of research expertise and interests. We reasoned that this approach would strengthen the credibility of our findings, thereby enhancing the likelihood that our findings could be applied to improve the well-being of children and families. Today the terms "team science" or "transdisciplinary" are used to describe research that brings multiple disciplines and perspectives to the table. This strategy has enabled us to engage in the complex process of bridging research, practice, and policy. More recently, recognizing that offering research findings is only one component in effecting policy change (e.g., Huston 2005; Tseng 2012), my colleagues and I at the Schubert Center for Child Studies at Case Western Reserve University have been working on models that bring what we term "spheres of influence" (different areas of expertise involving researchers, advocates, lobbyists, funders, and policymakers) into play to achieve reform (Celeste 2013).

Our research design was based on the application of complementary methods. We used administrative data from government, health, and economic institutions that can be aggregated to multiple geographic areas. Analyses of these large sets of administrative data are compelling in demonstrating correlations among causal factors. The large number of participants and robust statistical techniques we employed gave credibility to the associations that emerged from our analyses. We also integrated a nested ethnography of individuals from the neighborhoods in our study. A nested ethnography affords an "insider's" perspective on the meanings of the larger correlations and the processes involved—the whys of the associations. Neither the ethnographic approach nor the aggregate analyses tell the whole story alone. Our complementary use of methods and findings has advantages for both the aggregate and the ethnographic data (I will come back to this point in discussing some of the findings below.) The aggregate analyses benefit from ethnography's ability to help explain the meanings and processes behind the larger statistical findings. Similarly, the ethnographic work benefits from having greater generalizability, particularly if nested in the larger study sample.

Because our analysis of administrative data came first, we were able to develop a nested sample that reflected variables of interest to the project. We stratified neighborhoods (using census tracts) based on child maltreatment report rates, poverty rates, and whether neighborhoods had a concentration of African American or European American residents. From this stratification, we randomly selected twenty neighborhoods to represent these strata. We then randomly selected census-defined block groups from within the census tracts, randomly selected streets within the block groups, and randomly selected house addresses as the place to start door-to-door sample recruitment of parents. We then approached every third household from the starting address until we had a sample of twenty parents in each of these twenty neighborhoods. In a later stage of the project, an ethnographic sample of children for a study of their views of neighborhoods was similarly nested within both the neighborhood and ethnographic samples. In our current study, we will be going back to the same house addresses to look at neighborhood change.

The use of mixed methods is receiving increased attention in anthropology (Weisner 2012) and has been promoted as a means to produce meaningful findings that matter (e.g., Yoshikawa et al. 2008). Mixed methods research that includes nested ethnographic samples has been productively employed in policy-relevant research, for example in studying the New Hope project to reduce poverty (Duncan, Huston, and Weisner 2007; Yoshikawa, Weisner, and Lowe 2006). We are examining whether mixed methods are similarly useful in child maltreatment policy-relevant research.

Let me now briefly describe what we mean by child maltreatment/child abuse and neglect and what we mean by neighborhood. Both are critical variables in our work, and both are problematic.

What Do We Mean by Child Maltreatment?

One of the consistent issues in studying child maltreatment has been how to define and identify it. As the dependent variable of interest, this has posed challenges since the beginning of concerted attention to the problem. A large literature has questioned the accuracy of officially reported abuse and neglect rates (and of mandated reporting) and the usefulness of data gleaned from these sources in understanding child maltreatment. Nevertheless, most research (including our own) and major national reports rely on official report data—cases reported to child welfare and child protective services. They do so, in part, because of the difficulty of obtaining a sufficiently large sample for a population-based study, an interest in comparability across studies, and the rationalization that these reports can be used as a measure of distress in a community whether or not they capture all of the incidents. There are, however, some notable exceptions to this practice. For example, Straus, Gelles, and Steinmetz (1980) and Finkelhor (2008) obtained self-report data on family violence and child sexual abuse from randomly selected samples of the population. Although the accuracy of self-reports of socially disapproved behavior is also open to question, these studies have provided an important alternative perspective on the prevalence of interpersonal violence.

Definitions of child maltreatment, and their use in research, are further complicated in several ways. First, research does not always separate types of maltreatment, even though these types may have very different etiologies and consequences. Children may be reported for physical abuse, sexual abuse, psychological abuse, neglect, and a range of subtypes such as educational or medical neglect. In most studies, all of these types are lumped together. Second, children may be multiply victimized, making it difficult to arrive at "clean" categories. Third, there is a deep suspicion that all child maltreatment is not reported (as indicated, for example, by studies of physicians' failure to report). Fourth, official reports generally focus on the consequences (an injury or deficit to the child) rather than on the behavior (striking, pushing) of the responsible parent or caregiver. Because child maltreatment generally occurs in the privacy of the home, the actual behavior is not accessible to direct observation. Instead, we wait for the child to show up at school or a health care setting with injuries or signs of neglect. For the most part, and despite new rubrics for reporting, child abuse data are based on the decisions of child welfare workers and include only those cases that rise to their level of concern.

In keeping with our interest in neighborhood resident perceptions, our ethnographic survey included questions about the definitions and etiology of child maltreatment. Programs aimed at preventing or ameliorating child maltreatment must have at their core an understanding of how the populations being served define child maltreatment and why they believe that it occurs. With respect to definitions, there was congruence across neighborhoods on the catalogue of behaviors that parents defined as abuse and neglect, and these definitions overlapped with the definitions used in agency reports. In addition, because we are interested in the potential of research to provide evidence to support practice and policy interventions to reduce child maltreatment, we asked residents what they thought caused child abuse and neglect. Given the widespread popular and professional literature linking child maltreatment with parents' histories of being abused themselves as children, we were somewhat surprised to find that neighborhood residents placed more emphasis on poverty and family disruption, on substance abuse and stress, and on moral and family values than they did on individual pathology, including parents' own experience of abuse in childhood (Korbin et al. 2000). This is potentially important for practice and policy because child maltreatment prevention and intervention programs generally emphasize individual and family treatment and rarely the larger community or neighborhood context (with notable exceptions; see Dodge and Coleman 2009; Melton and Holaday 2008).

What Do We Mean by Neighborhood?

Census tracts and block groups have many advantages for research because they are the units used for many sources of administrative data, including the census (note that census-tract boundaries can change with significant changes in population from one census to the next, a fact that must be accommodated in the analyses). In addition to actual census boundaries, it is important to know how neighborhood residents define their neighborhoods. Is there a meaningful area for residents? We created a large map that included several adjacent census tracts and asked residents to draw their own census tract boundaries. We entered these boundaries into a mapping program to determine their congruence with census-defined boundaries. What we found was that residents drew areas approximately the size of a census tract, but these did not correspond precisely with their own census tract's boundaries (Coulton et al. 2001). As an anecdotal example, we collected one map that we thought had to be an "outlier" because it was so large, covering many census tracts. When we brought the map back to the ethnographic team, we found that the neighborhood resident who provided it was a plumber who knew hundreds of families in the large "neighborhood" that he drew. In his view, this large area was an accurate reflection of the neighborhood in which he had relationships and provided services. In a subsequent study nesting a sample of children between seven and eleven in the same neighborhoods (Spilsbury, Korbin, and Coulton 2009), we found that parents and children drew different boundaries for their neighborhoods and delineated different areas where children could go unsupervised or with a friend.

While these differences in perspective are not necessarily surprising, they need to be accommodated in analyses and kept in mind when employing "neighborhood" as a meaningful unit. With the software available today, we could have used each individual's self-defined neighborhood. While this approach has some appeal, however, it would have converted "neighborhood" into an individual's "perception of neighborhood," thereby limiting our ability to gather generalizable data that would be meaningful locally and informative for policy. Because we want "neighborhood" to signify something for the group of people living there, we have experimented with ways to identify areas held in common by individuals as the neighborhood unit for analysis. For example, we have begun with the center of the area as residents perceive it and worked outward to encompass areas held in common. We found that in some cases, locally defined neighborhoods map onto indices of social issues (e.g., crime), while in others, they do not. The discrepancies we found suggest that further research is needed to understand what constitutes a neighborhood and why.

Neighborhood Influence on Child Maltreatment

Neighborhood influence on child maltreatment may take multiple pathways that suggest different research strategies and have different practice and policy implications. Since the beginning of research on child maltreatment, there has been controversy as to whether high rates of maltreatment arise from stress (such as that imposed by impoverished neighborhoods) or from greater scrutiny as residents of poor neighborhoods come to the attention of child- and family-serving agencies, making detection of child maltreatment more likely than in wealthier neighborhoods.

In a review of studies on child maltreatment that involved multiple ecological levels, we suggested that there are (at least) three pathways by which neighborhoods exert an influence on child maltreatment (Coulton et al. 2007). These pathways may or may not overlap. The first, which we termed "behavioral influences," suggests that neighborhood structure fosters social processes experienced by families and children in ways that result in maltreating behaviors and child victimization. Interventions to address this problem would emphasize improving neighborhood conditions while also addressing parenting behavior. The second pathway, "definition, recognition, and reporting," suggests that neighborhood conditions are associated with differences in how maltreatment is defined, recognized, and reported (as discussed above), leading to variation in child maltreatment reports, but not necessarily to variation in child maltreatment behaviors. Here, an appropriate intervention would seek to improve how child welfare services recognize and report child maltreatment. It also would promote public awareness, given that neighbors and friends report slightly less than half of all child maltreatment. The third pathway, "selection," suggests that neighborhood patterns of child maltreatment may stem from the characteristics families bring with them when they move into a neighborhood. With rare exceptions, such as research on projects such as Moving to Opportunity, it is not feasible to assign individuals to neighborhoods, thus controlling for these usually unmeasured characteristics of neighborhood residents. However, research, practice, and policy could more fully address influences on residential choice and mobility, such as economic or racial segregation in neighborhoods, to better understand the effects of selection.

Neighborhood Demographics and Cultural Scripts

The study of the demographics of neighborhood settings offers an example of the complementary perspectives provided by aggregate analyses and ethnography. In our analyses of census-based data, we found that child abuse and neglect reports were concentrated in neighborhoods in which there was a preponderance of women and young children, without men or older people (Coulton et al. 1995). This factor, which we termed "child care burden," was the second most important factor in explaining the variance in child maltreatment reports across neighborhoods. To explain this finding, it would be reasonable to assume that in neighborhoods with higher rates of child maltreatment, there are too many overburdened young mothers with too many children, and too few other adults to help. But even though this is certainly the case, there is more to the story.

The nested ethnographic interviews component of our study revealed the dilemmas residents face in some disadvantaged neighborhoods (Korbin and Coulton 1997). Not only were there a lot of children in these neighborhoods, but residents reported that the children were largely unmanageable and, worse, to be feared. Neighborhood residents expressed concern about intervening in other people's children's behavior because the parents would take the child's side. In addition, residents reported that children themselves, even young children, were to be feared. They would throw rocks at dogs, tear out flower beds, and swear at adults who tried to correct them, all with impunity. In the neighborhoods with the highest rates of child maltreatment, residents were the most likely to be fearful of both adults and children should they intervene in response to children's misbehavior. "Neighborly" interventions intended to help guide a child's behavior in socially acceptable directions may be a marker of communities in which individuals look out for one another. Distrusting others' reactions to such well-intentioned interventions may be symptomatic of communities in which no one watches out for the well-being of others, including other people's children. When community members are fearful of intervening in general, they may be less likely to notice or intervene in instances of child maltreatment.

These ethnographic findings did not negate the demographic findings, but elaborated on the processes that may make these demographics more problematic. Cultural scripts about how adults and children interact may compound the impact of demographic profiles (as reflected in the vignettes at the beginning of this chapter). The difficulties plaguing some poor urban neighborhoods (and contributing to child maltreatment) result not only from disadvantage related to population demographics, but also from cultural scripts of nonintervention with other people's children that make help from the few other adults available even less likely. We also saw cultural scripts play out in the nested child ethnography, which suggested that children are reluctant to seek or accept help from unknown adults because of fears that those adults will harm them (Spilsbury and Korbin 2004).

Child Maltreatment and "Race"

Although race is a fraught concept in anthropology, anthropological analyses of administrative data using the static census categories of race offer insight into the variability in child maltreatment rates between neighborhoods. The combination of aggregate analyses with ethnography shed light on differences between neighborhoods that were predominantly African American and those that were predominantly European American. In the total sample, there was a statistical relationship between poverty rates and child maltreatment: the greater the poverty, the more numerous the child maltreatment reports. However, this relationship was significantly less pronounced in African American neighborhoods.

In our ethnographic profiles of these neighborhoods, residents of the African American neighborhoods reported knowing one another longer and having closer ties and helping relationships. In contrast, residents of predominantly European American neighborhoods reported distress at living in neighborhoods where they knew few of their neighbors and where high residential turnover gave them little chance to form social bonds. The administrative data indicate high levels of residential segregation in Cleveland's neighborhoods, and this segregation may help explain the more stable residential patterns in African American neighborhoods. In addition, we found anecdotal reports that young African American professionals and their families were leaving the suburbs and moving into urban neighborhoods. In some cases, they were returning to their parents' homes or neighborhoods; in other cases, they were moving into neighborhoods that had become fashionable. These findings reinforce the notion that neighborhoods have social characteristics far more complex and attractive than can be indicated on census data marking tracts by income.

In terms of policy, however, such findings can be a double-edged sword. If we find that some neighborhoods (in this case, poor African American neighborhoods) have strong social networks that are protective against child maltreatment, we need to be careful to frame this finding in such a way that it does not have unintended policy consequences, such as diminished public investment. After all, neighborhoods with strong social support and trust may still be struggling economically (Korbin et al. 1998).

Concluding Remarks: Poverty and Child Maltreatment

In the early years of research on child maltreatment, several important thinkers proposed that poverty was a core cause (Gil 1973; Pelton 1978). Nonetheless, a model of individual pathology dominated the field and was reflected in the first child abuse and neglect legislation: the Child Abuse Prevention and Treatment Act (CAPTA, PL-97247). Authored by Senator Walter Mondale in the early 1970s and most recently reauthorized in 2010, the law was an effort to address child maltreatment without consideration of poverty as the primary causal factor: "the focus on deviance—and medical deviance at that—turned policymakers away from considering the social-structural and social-psychological underpinnings of abuse and neglect" (Nelson 1984, 3). Instead, child maltreatment was deemed a problem of individuals, originating in large part in an intergenerational cycle of violent parenting. It was also deemed a problem that was democratically distributed across social classes. That not all poor parents abuse their children was taken as "evidence" that poverty and disadvantage were not core causes, though some caveats were added with respect to child neglect. Thus, child abuse was constructed as a social problem separate from all others, and measures to alleviate it were carefully detached from anything resembling an antipoverty agenda.

In fact, research consistently points to the concentration of child maltreatment reports in poor neighborhoods. But the story we have found is far more complex. Our research has pointed to a strong association between cultural and structural factors of disadvantage and child maltreatment reports. We suggest that exploring variability among poor neighborhoods is a way to better understand the causes of child maltreatment and responses to it. Our current mixed methods project will allow us to examine neighborhood structural features, service provision, and neighborhood resident perceptions to further explore their relationships over a twenty-year span.

References[1]

Ben-Arieh, Asher. 2010. "Socioeconomic Correlates of Rates of Child Maltreatment in Small Communities." *American Journal of Orthopsychiatry* 80 (1): 109–14.

Celeste, Gabriella. 2013. *The Bridge to Somewhere: How Research Made Its Way into Legislative Juvenile Justice Reform in Ohio. A Case Study.* Cleveland, OH: Schubert Center for Child Studies, Case Western Reserve University.

Coulton, Claudia J., David S. Crampton, Molly Irwin, James C. Spilsbury, and Jill E. Korbin. 2007. "How Neighborhoods Influence Child Maltreatment: A Review of the Literature and Alternative Pathways." *Child Abuse and Neglect* 31: 1117–42.

Coulton, Claudia J., and Jill E. Korbin. 2007. "Indicators of Child Well-Being: Through a Neighborhood Lens." *Social Indicators Research* 84 (3): 340–61.

Coulton, Claudia J., Jill E. Korbin, and Marilyn Su. 1999. "Neighborhoods and Child Maltreatment: A Multi-Level Study." *Child Abuse and Neglect* 23 (11): 1019–40.

Coulton, Claudia, Jill E. Korbin, Marilyn Su, and Julian Chow. 1995. "Community Level Factors and Child Maltreatment Rates." *Child Development* 66: 1262–76.

Coulton, Claudia J., Jill Korbin, Tsui Chan, and Marilyn Su. 2001. "Mapping Residents' Perceptions of Neighborhood Boundaries: A Methodological Note." *American Journal of Community Psychology* 29 (2): 371–83.

Dodge, Kenneth A., and Dorianne L. Coleman, eds. 2009. *Preventing Child Maltreatment: Community Approaches.* New York: Guilford Press.

Drake, Brett, and Shanta Pandey. 1996. "Understanding the Relationship between Neighborhood Poverty and Specific Types of Child Maltreatment." *Child Abuse & Neglect* 20: 1003–18.

Duncan, Greg, Aletha Huston, and Thomas S. Weisner. 2007. *Higher Ground: New Hope for the Working Poor and their Children.* New York: Russell Sage Foundation.

Edgerton, Robert B. 1985. *Rules, Exceptions, and Social Order*. Berkeley and Los Angeles: University of California Press.

——— 1992. *Sick Societies: Challenging the Myth of Primitive Harmony*. New York: Free Press.

Finkelhor, David. 2008. *Childhood Victimization: Violence, Crime and Abuse in the Lives of Young People*. Oxford: Oxford University Press.

Fraser, Gertrude, and Philip L. Kilbride. 1980. "Child Abuse and Neglect—Rare, but Perhaps Increasing, Phenomena among the Samia of Kenya." *Child Abuse & Neglect* 4 (February 1980): 227–32.

Freisthler, Bridget. 2004. "A Spatial Analysis of Social Disorganization, Alcohol Access, and Rates of Child Maltreatment in Neighborhoods." *Children and Youth Services Review* 26: 807–23.

Garbarino, James, and Deborah Sherman. 1980. "High-Risk Neighborhoods and High-Risk Families: The Human Ecology of Child Maltreatment." *Child Development* 51: 188–98.

Gil, David. 1973. *Violence against Children: Physical Child Abuse in the United States*. Cambridge: Harvard University Press.

Huston, Aletha. 2005. "Connecting the Science of Child Development in Public Policy." *SRCD Social Policy Report* 19 (4): 3–18.

Kempe, C. Henry, Frederic N. Silverman, Brandt F. Steele, William Droegmueller, and Henry K. Silver. 1962. "The Battered Child Syndrome." *Journal of the American Medical Association* 181: 17–24.

Korbin, Jill E. 1981. *Child Abuse and Neglect: Cross-Cultural Perspectives*. Berkeley and Los Angeles: University of California Press.

——— 2008. "Children and Families in Neighborhood Contexts: Ethnography and a Mixed Methods Approach." *Anthropology News* 49 (4): 18–19.

Korbin, Jill E., and Claudia Coulton. 1997. "Understanding the Neighborhood Context for Children and Families: Epidemiological and Ethnographic Approaches." In *Neighborhood Poverty: Context and Consequences for Children*, edited by J. Brooks-Gunn, L. Aber, and G. Duncan, 77–91. New York: Russell Sage Foundation.

Korbin, Jill E., Claudia Coulton, Sarah Chard, Candis Platt-Houston, and Marilyn Su. 1998. "Impoverishment and Child Maltreatment in African American and European American Neighborhoods." *Development and Psychopathology* 10: 215–33.

Korbin, Jill E., Claudia Coulton, Heather Lindstrom-Ufuti, and James Spilsbury. 2000. "Neighborhood Views on the Definition and Etiology of Child Maltreatment." *Child Abuse & Neglect: The International Journal* 24: 1509–27.

LeVine, Robert, and Rebecca New, eds. 2008. *Anthropology and Child Development. A Cross-Cultural Reader*. Malden, MA: Blackwell Publishing.

LeVine, Robert, Sarah LeVine, Suzanne Dixon, Amy Richman, P. Herbert Leiderman, Constance Keefer, and T. Berry Brazelton. 1996. *Child Care and Culture: Lessons from Africa*. Cambridge, UK: Cambridge University Press.

Melton, Gary, and Bonnie Holaday, eds. 2008. "Strong Communities as Safe Havens for Children." *Family and Community Health* 31 (2): 83–186.

National Research Council. 1993. *Understanding Child Abuse and Neglect*. Washington, D.C.: National Academy Press.

Nelson, Barbara. 1984. *Making an Issue of Child Abuse. Political Agenda Setting for Social Problems*. Chicago: University of Chicago Press.

Pelton, Leroy H. 1978. "The Myth of Classlessness." *American Journal of Orthopsychiatry* 48 (4): 608–17.

Scheper-Hughes, Nancy, ed. 1987. *Child Survival. Anthropological Perspectives on the Treatment and Maltreatment of Children*. Dordrecht, Holland: Reidel.

Scheper-Hughes, Nancy, and Carolyn Sargent, eds. 1998. *Small Wars: The Cultural Politics of Childhood*. Berkeley and Los Angeles: University of California Press.

Spilsbury, James. 2002. "'If I Don't Know Them, I'll Get Killed Probably: How Children's Concerns about Safety Shape Help-Seeking Behavior." *Childhood* 9 (1): 101–17.

Spilsbury, James, and Jill Korbin. 2004. "Negotiating the Dance: Social Capital from the Perspective of Neighborhood Children and Adults." In *Rethinking Childhood*, edited by P. Pufall and R. Unsworth, 191–206. New Brunswick, NJ: Rutgers University Press.

Spilsbury, James, Jill Korbin, and Claudia Coulton. 2009. "Mapping Children's Neighborhood Perceptions: Implications for Child Indicators." *Child Indicators Research* 2 (2): 111–31.

Straus, Murray, Richard Gelles, and Suzanne Steinmetz. 1980. *Behind Closed Doors. Violence in the American Family*. Garden City, NY: Anchor Books.

Tseng, Vivian. 2012. "The Uses of Research in Policy and Practice." *SRCD Social Policy Report* 26 (2): 3–16.

United Nations. 1989. United Nations Convention on the Rights of the Child. http://www.unicef.org/crc/.

Weisner, Thomas S. 1997. "The Ecocultural Project of Human Development : Why Ethnography and its Findings Matter." *Ethos* 25 (2): 177–90.

——— 1998. "Human Development, Child Well-Being, and the Cultural Project of Development." *New Directions for Child Development* 81: 69–85.

——— 2009a. "Culture, Development, and Diversity: Expectable Pluralism, Conflict, and Similarity." *Ethos* 37 (2). doi:10.1111/j.1548–1352.2009.01037.x.182.

——— 2009b. "Well-Being and Sustainability of the Daily Routine of Life." In *The Good Life: Well-Being in Anthropological Perspective*, edited by G. Mathews and C. Izquierdo, 228–47. New York: Berghahn Press.

——— 2012. "Mixed Methods Should Be a Valued Practice in Anthropology." *Anthropology News* 53 (5): 3–4.

Whiting, Beatrice, and Carolyn P. Edwards. 1992. *Children of Different Worlds: The Formation of Social Behavior*. Cambridge, MA: Harvard University Press.

Whiting, Beatrice, and John W. M. Whiting. 1974. *Children of Six Cultures: A Psycho-Cultural Analysis.* Cambridge, MA: Harvard University Press.

Whiting, John W. M., and Irvin L. Child. 1953. *Child Training and Personality: A Cross-Cultural Study.* New York: Yale University Press.

Yoshikawa, Hirokazu, Thomas S. Weisner, and Edward Lowe, eds. 2006. *Making It Work: Low-Wage Employment, Family Life and Child Development.* New York: Russell Sage Foundation.

Yoshikawa, Hirokazu, Thomas S. Weisner, Ariel Kalil, and Niobe Way. 2008. "Mixing Qualitative and Quantitative Research in Developmental Science: Uses and Methodological Choices." *Developmental Psychology* 44 (2) (March): 344–54.

FIFTEEN

Multiple Marginality: A Comparative Framework for Understanding Gangs

JAMES DIEGO VIGIL

Poverty is the central reason for the rise of street gangs throughout the contemporary world. Based on over thirty-five years of street-level ethnographic investigations, I have learned that street gangs are the offspring of marginalization. In hierarchical societies, certain groups become relegated to the fringes, where social and economic conditions result in the destabilization and fragmentation of people's lives (Blanc et. al 1995; Hazlehurst and Hazlehurst 1998; Vigil 1987). A sense of powerlessness can develop when these conditions continue over a long period of time (Rodriguez 1991). Some of the gang members that I have known have come from such stressed and unstable circumstances that one wonders how they have survived at all. In this chapter, I will use the framework "multiple marginality" (Vigil 2002) to reflect these strains and their persistence over time. The investigations for this analysis were based on a mixed method strategy that included quantitative and qualitative data, especially intensive interviewing, participant observation, and the collection of life histories.

Multiple Marginality

In its simplest trajectory, multiple marginality can be modeled thus: place/status → street socialization → street subculture → street identity. In short, the power of place and the status of a person or group are the major shapers of gangs, or street subcultures and identities. Many factors are intertwined, and the actions and reactions among them spawn gangs and gang members. With respect to place/status, *barrios* ("neighborhoods") or ethnic enclaves derive both from the external barriers imposed on a people, and from that people's choice to live together in their own community. Living in spatially separate and socially distanced neighborhoods makes for a marginal existence that closes rather than opens doors to social mobility. Race and cultural differences also serve as a rationale for the isolation and denigration of each ethnic group.

The model of multiple marginality helps us to dissect and analyze the ways in which marginal place/status undermines and exacerbates social, cultural, and psychological problems in ethnic minority communities. These forces contribute to the breakdown of social control and the emergence of gangs and gang members. Social dysfunctions especially affect family life, educational trajectories, and interactions with law enforcement. In the absence of these influences, the gang replaces parenting, schooling, and policing to regulate the lives of many youth. Ultimately, a gang subculture arises to set rules and regulations for its members.

Marginalization particularly affects children in the aftermath of massive immigration of ethnically distinct populations, when large numbers of ethnic minorities must find a job for themselves and a place for their families in an urban setting. Immigration affects family structure and stability, school readiness in the context of language and cultural differences, and level of involvement with police and the criminal justice system. These processes occur on many levels as a product of pressures and forces in play over a long period of time. The phrase "multiple marginality" reflects the complexities and persistence of these forces. As a theory-building framework, multiple marginality addresses ecological, economic, sociocultural, and psychological factors that underlie street gangs and youths' participation in them (Vigil 1988a, 1988b, 2002; Covey, Menard, and Franzese 1992).

Gang researchers have emphasized different theoretical or conceptual models in gathering and presenting information on street gang

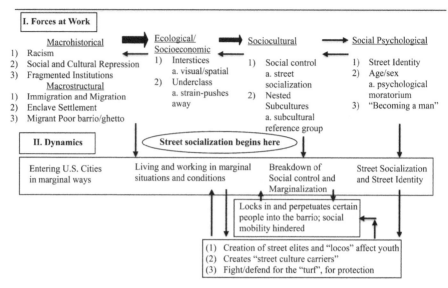

FIGURE 15.1 Framework for multiple marginality (Vigil and Yun 2002).

life (Covey, Menard, and Franzese 1992; Moore 1991; Klein 1995; Miller, Maxson, and Klein 2001; Hazlehurst and Hazlehurst 1998; Vigil 1987). Collectively, such works show that youths from a wide variety of ethnic groups have become involved in gangs and that there are multidimensional facets to the gang phenomenon itself; thus, to unravel these many strands, hard census and archival information must be combined with interviews and observations. A comparative look at other nations' gang dynamics adds to this tradition.

Most researchers are in accord that major macrohistorical and macrostructural forces form the backdrop to street gangs. The causation debate becomes contentious and heated when the focus is on the intermediate and microlevels of analysis. Barring a major overhaul of the social system, a systematic examination of the major socialization agents (i.e., families, schools, and law enforcement) would help our understanding of gangs and gang members and of how a quasi-institutional gang subculture emerged.

A cross-cultural perspective facilitates our examination of the disruptions of social control within families, schools, and law enforcement, and how these disruptions lead to street socialization and gang involvement on the part of some low-income, ethnic minority youth. This approach helps clarify the similarities and differences among groups, while the conceptual model, multiple marginality, specifically identifies the forces that additively and cumulatively shape gangs and gang members. It is a model that gauges the weight and sequence of factors that impinge upon and affect youth that grow up on the streets and aids our understanding of the breakdown of social control and how street socialization transpires. First, some words on greater Los Angeles, a city of diversity and contradictions, generally recognized as the gang capital of the world, and this researcher's fieldwork site.

The Gang Capital of the World

As a growing megalopolis stretching in all directions from the civic center, Los Angeles has become the prototype of urban diversity, with a large immigrant population. It is a city rich with contrasting languages and cultural traditions, but also a place with ethnic and class tensions that threaten to erupt at any moment, as occurred in the King Riots of 1992 (Oliver, Johnson, and Farrell 1993; *Los Angeles Times* 1992). The changes the city has undergone since the 1960s have included white flight and suburbanization, economic restructuring, and large-scale immigration, particularly from Mexico, Central America, and Asia, and most importantly, the entrenchment of street gangs.

Gangs are a stark subset of youth subcultures in a complex society, comprising a dark side of Los Angeles in particular and urban America generally. This is especially the case since the 1980s when diffusion of gang members and gang culture affected other regions and cities (Maxson 1998), and now, of course, other regions of the globe (Hazen and Rodgers, 2014; Flynn 2008; Hagedorn 2006; Hazlehurst and Hazlehurst 1998). In all of them, the mostly poor, struggling communities have produced street gangs, and some seem to be in the process of generating "megagangs." There are similarities in how these subcultural developments unfold across places/statuses and peoples, but there are also instances when historical and cultural factors make each community unique.

Ethnohistorical Considerations

To begin with, there are ethnohistorical nuances and contours to the ways in which gangs have unfolded within each ethnic population. For example, the roots of Chicano gangs in Los Angeles can be traced to the settlement patterns Mexican immigrants typically were required to follow in a city that was ill prepared for their integration. Being forced into isolated and physically substandard neighborhoods (i.e., barrios and colonies) had a series of repercussions, for example, in how Mexicans were socially distanced and made to feel inferior and marginal. Thus the children of the immigrants started off socially and psychologically marginalized, and conventional socialization routines were largely unavailable to them (Vigil and Long 1990). This paper outlines why ecological and socioeconomic factors figure prominently in the segregation and isolation of Mexicans (as of other groups) and examines how the rate and direction of acculturation was undermined under these situations and conditions. Today, Chicano gangs have diffused and generated a symbiotic energy so that even working-class neighborhoods and suburban enclaves have adopted the gang subculture. Because violence has become such a common gang practice, this proliferation, of course, has contributed to an increase in deadly gang incidents and altercations. In the wake of maladaptation from such strains and pressures, a street youth population emerged and evolved into a gang subculture. The power of place and space are noteworthy in these developments.

However, every ethnic group's history (as well as every nation's!) differs in such important areas as time, place, and people—i.e., when and where the people settled, how their communities formed, and what distinguished them from other people in the vicinity. Consideration of the time factor allows for an appreciation of the specific conditions in Los Angeles, for instance, that affected members of the group when they arrived and how they settled.

For the Mexican American and African American groups, the gangs have been around for at least a half century (Chicanos a decade or two longer), and because each group was largely relegated to certain places (East Los Angeles and South Central Los Angeles), territoriality and defense of space became an issue (Vigil, 2014). In addition, both have experienced persistent and concentrated poverty. With major disruptions of social control in these contexts, a rooted gang subculture of age-graded youths (more common among Chicanos) was spawned to dominate the streets of each neighborhood. Older gang veterans became role models to help guide and direct younger street youth in the ways of the street, especially in settling old scores with rival street gangs. This gang subculture born of street socialization eventually had rituals, routines, signs, and symbols to help in the perpetuation of this lifestyle for barrio and ghetto youth, who had no other recourse (Vigil, 2007). In the African American case, there were some major differences, where territoriality meant not just one neighborhood but a collection of enclaves that represented more a confederation, a larger, more-diffused gang. Additionally, drug trafficking became more of a practice, especially during the rock cocaine epidemic in the 1980s. No doubt this turn to money-making enterprises among blacks stemmed from their even lower-income and impoverished backgrounds than the other ethnic groups discussed in this account.

In contrast to the above ethnic groups, the Salvadoran and Vietnamese populations share a more recent migratory background, in both cases from homelands wracked by civil war. Most of the Vietnamese immigrants and a large proportion of those from El Salvador arrived in the United States as political refugees. The unraveling of social control actually began, for both groups, in their home countries, where the United States played a prominent role in volatile military situations sparked by the anti-Communism climate of the era. Thus, Cold War geopolitical considerations have been paramount for both groups.

In contrast to the two older populations' gangs, these two new groups have had a decidedly different experience. Territoriality became a part of the gang identification process, but more so for the Salvadorans, who concentrated in a neighborhood close to the jobs (e.g., janitors, domestics) sought by their parents. For the Vietnamese, a fluid mobility prevailed because of the nature of their secondary migration and settlement, and only recently has gang space (or where certain groups hang out) become important (Vigil and Yun 1990, 1998). Both groups had an accelerated street socialization to speed creation of street gangs and gang members because their neighborhoods and schools were rife with existing Chicano gangs. This was especially the case for the Salvadorans, who resided right in the middle of one of the biggest gangs in Los Angeles, 18th Street. Although older gang veterans are just now becoming a factor, both of these groups have been more likely to develop ties to established criminal elements and activities, as gang members advance from street gang activities to illicit enterprises under the purview of older adults. Coming from civil war backgrounds, gang members sometimes get caught up in the political rivalries and controversies that persist from the home country; graffiti messages or tattoos often reflect these leanings. In the case of the Vietnamese gangs, immigration is near non-existent today, and thus a second generation is not around to join gangs. Gang members from this group are in jail or have matured out to follow more conventional pathways to success. Yet, the lore and style struck by the Vietnamese gangs of yesterday still linger among the younger set looking to the past for inspiration and guidance

(Lam 2015). Salvadorans are different in two important respects. US policy to deport them back to their home countries has backfired in too many ways to detail. Mainly, the deportation involved the exportation of gang culture to the Central America peoples. Whatever street children who resided there became quickly attuned to a formal street gang subculture. Also, as we have learned over the decades from the immigration debacle of the Mexicans, deportees regularly attempt to return back to the United States—more so for many of the Salvadorans who came to the United States when they were children, sometimes at the age of three or four. Further, the returning deportees have travelled to other US places and regions, and now there is a Mara Salvatruchas and 18th Street gang problem that some observers have claimed has reached hemispheric proportions.

A Cross-Cultural Approach and Street Socialization

These four ethnic groups were examined cross-culturally to help identify trends and tendencies found in street youth populations that give rise to participation in gangs (Vigil 2002). This comparative approach is beneficial because it facilitates interdisciplinary analysis and incorporates the multidimensional dynamics (discussed below) that must be considered in understanding the formation and evolution of street gangs. It adds breadth and depth to an appraisal because it helps account for historical, political, and ethnic group differences while examining those differences from a variety of perspectives. Moreover, it facilitates appreciation of each group's experiences as that group understands them. Establishing a cross-cultural research framework helps illuminate most of the forces, events, and circumstances that push gangs to the forefront of contemporary Los Angeles issues and recent history.

Importantly, multiple marginality is a conceptual model, more theory building than a set theory, to help understand why multidimensional strategies and methods are necessary and useful when following this dictum: The more ways we can measure a subject, the wider and deeper our understanding of it.

Methods for Doing Research with Gangs

A general summary of my gang research approach would include: (1) gain rapport and trust by having yourself introduced by a cultural broker, who is also often a key informant; (2) make yourself useful (e.g., functionaries, gofers) in whatever way possible but always with an attitude of volunteerism, making sure you are not manipulated like a puppet; (3) anticipate when to come forward, be proactive but let the gang members set the agenda; it can be a tough balancing act.

A series of steps preceded my fieldwork. Selecting low-income barrios or ghettos (ethnic enclaves) for the study of street gangs was the first goal. First, the barrio/ghetto must contain a large concentration of low-income residents, many of whom have experienced persistent poverty over the span of generations. Second, a high percentage of families there rely on Aid to Families with Dependent Children (AFDC); many of these households are headed by a single parent. Third, the neighborhood features a local established gang, with nearby gangs contending for turf, which brings intragang conflict. Each gang boasts a long history and a self-generating structure in the form of numerous age-graded cliques—a component that makes it possible to examine through retrospective interviews intergenerational change and continuity.

To gain access to the neighborhoods required another method, one that varied from site to site but usually involved contacting a gatekeeper or caregiver of the community. In all instances, I was able to introduce myself to family heads, school officials, police and prison administrators, gang members, and other central contacts in ways where trust and rapport resulted. Simply stated, my research interests were clear and to the point, with no hidden agendas, when I made my presentations— tailored to the age and position of the listeners, of course.

Once a place was identified, a quantitative and qualitative strategy was utilized to gather data at different levels. Statistics from field-derived survey instruments can provide a broad overview of the specified neighborhood. Core anthropological methods, interviews, and participant observation with a sample of residents in the same setting, offered us depth and nuance to the numbers. Interviewing, both closed-ended and open-ended, with selected gang members (note: "jailhouse sociology," or interviewing in prisons, is also acceptable) helped fill the gaps noted in systematic ways, that is, when you can get them to stay put long enough. Participant observation is very difficult to conduct on the streets with a moving, changing cohort of gang members whose activities might be illegal. I learned to observe from a distance and seek ways to capture the rhythms and routines of the street with other information (e.g., key informant, photos, nongang-affiliated youth). As Geertz (1973) pointed out, it is "thick description" that counts.

Where possible, and depending on the study, a further technique was to select and train community researchers, residents who have grown up in the barrio/ghetto. Well informed about the community and connected to the youth population, research assistant trainees conducted many of my interviews. The latter were recruited from the community based on their willingness to gather data and maintain a cultural competence and sensitivity to respondents' concerns. A former male gang member and a female whose brother was a gang member were chosen to act as community researchers, cultural brokers, and key informants; a tall order that greatly facilitated the housing project research.

Another example of this strategy is a project I directed at a California Youth Authority in 1989. I had made several presentations to the counselors and administrators through MACA (Mexican American Correctional Association), and when I asked for approval for our research project it was granted. The Nelles School for Boys had approximately 800 wards of the state, and we sampled over 150 of them. Developing a survey questionnaire in the field, we administered the instrument and then interviewed all 150 wards. The latter interviews were correlated with the survey data, and when we had a range of variations on a number of dimensions, we selected out approximately fifty wards for in-depth interviews or life histories. Using a map of the Los Angeles area, we flagged the neighborhoods where the wards had lived and grown up.

Our "thick" description included where they were born, the name of their gang, family and school life, and with the life histories, we were able to cross-check how the neighborhoods affected their development, when and how they joined the gang, the role of family members in their life, and many other important influences on the role of gangs in their lives. (See *The Projects*, Vigil 2007, on how a similar strategy guided research on a housing project.)

Street Socialization and Wealth Disparity

Generally, the basis for my gang studies stems from the pervasive and overwhelming reality of most neighborhood residents: the often heartbreaking poverty experienced in the face of metropolitan Los Angeles's opulence and opportunity. Just out of reach but always in sight, living in the background of wealth's possibilities brings into sharp focus the structural and functional contrast of such neighborhoods. A nongang member mother once told me: "I always feel like I'm alone and locked in even when I'm outside." Yet for all the physical and symbolic isolation imposed on these enclaves, their residents raise families, are economically engaged in some capacity, and are otherwise interested in the same conditions of stability, personal growth, and self-improvements as their affluent counterparts. Moreover, there is the tacit acknowledgment that the service-oriented labor provided by many immigrant residents is integral to maintaining the status quo of wealth inequity.

It is the street socialization that blurs the ethnic lines among all four groups, because remarkably similar things are learned on the streets, where fear and vulnerability necessitate the need for protection, friendship, loyalty, and other routines and rhythms provided by the gang. The street gang dominates the lives of disconnected youth because other institutions have become undermined, fragmented, fragile, and largely ineffective. Nevertheless, each group has its own uniqueness, such as race being a focal issue for African Americans (Alonso 1999), and the dual-nature relationship of Chicanos with the dominant society as natives (i.e., residents before the Mexican-American War of 1846–1848) and immigrants. Salvadorans and Vietnamese both have global, Cold War political ramifications to their entry into the United States. In large part, marginalization began for them before they entered the country.

All these multiple strains take their toll and strip many people of their coping skills. Being left out of the mainstream of society in so many ways and in so many places relegates urban youth to the margins of society in practically every conceivable area. This positioning leaves them with few traditional options or resources to better their lives. Thus marginalization of all sorts leads to the emergence of street gangs and the generation of gang members.

A macroanalysis sets the stage for other evidence showing how fractured and marginalized a people become, especially children and youth undergoing major developmental changes. From this broad backdrop, a look at the micro events in the life of a gang member will show how social control networks unfold along four dimensions: connections to family and significant others, engagements with avenues of opportunities, involvements with positive and constructive activities, and beliefs associated with the central value system of a society (Conchas and Vigil, 2012). Family organization, schooling experiences, and interactions with law enforcement institutions will surface as sources of problems in the lives of many youth. In assessing the different ethnic gangs along four social-control dimensions (i.e., connections, engagements, involvements, beliefs), a common theme emerges—the weakening of these bonds "frees" the adolescent from the paths of conformity and, with street socialization and the acquisition of a street subculture and identity, ensures that unconventional behavior is likely. Those individuals that desist from this unconventional path struggle and overcome such pressures to chart a new lifestyle.

Social Control Themes

In order to apply social-control theory to the street gangs of southern California, however, modifications are required, as certain elements of traditional social-control theory fail to connect to other forces in the fuller equation of understanding gangs (Wiatrowski, Griswold, and Roberts 1981). We believe, along with Covey, Menard, and Franzese (1992, 173), that social-control theory, "as integrated into ecological and other perspectives [i.e., multiple marginality], appears to be fundamental to understanding the formation and illegal behavior of juvenile gangs" (see also Vigil 1988a; Thrasher 1963[1927]; Shaw and McKay 1942; Merton 1949; Cloward and Ohlin 1960; Moore 1978, 1991; Hagedorn 1988; Spergel and Curry 1998; Klein 1995; Decker and Van Winkle 1996, Conchas and Noguera, 2004).

Families, schools, and law enforcement merit special scrutiny in this regard for two main reasons (Bursik and Grasmick 1995). First, they are the primary agents of social control in society. Second, they are uniquely adaptive and responsive to the concerns of society. Each of these institutions has separately contributed to the gang problem, in terms of what they did and what they failed to do. As a result of their collective failure, street socialization has taken over and rooted the quasi-institution of the street gang (Vigil, 1999).

When street socialization replaces socialization by conventional caretakers, it becomes a key factor in developing not only different social bonds but different aspirations for achievement, levels and intensities of participation, and belief patterns. Whom you associate with, what you strive for, how you spend your time, and why you embrace a belief system are strongly connected to the street subculture.

For female gang members (only five to fifteen percent of gang members), the conflict in gender identification and the need to act out aggressively is considerably more complex. Females are especially hard hit in the street socialization process, for, like males, they must struggle with the same forces that generated their street experience but in addition must contend with their own homeboys, who devalue them. As gender roles continue to change generally, however, the role of females in gangs will likely be transformed. The recent increase in violence among female gang members clearly indicates that these changes are underway. Moreover, of the ninety-four percent of gang females who will have a child in their life, eighty-four percent will themselves become single parents.

The breakdown of social control would not be complete without mention of how street realities, particularly street socialization, become the dominant force in the lives of so many children. Contemporary immigrant children are especially targeted in this regard, as this Salvadoran adolescent so aptly put it in describing how he adapted to Los Angeles:

I came to America in order to become American and leave the killings and sadness that were part of El Salvador behind me. When I first moved in with my aunt I was told to stay away from the Mexican kids in the neighborhood (Pico Union, near the west side of Downtown Los Angeles). They were pandilleros (gang members) and people were always getting shot and kids were getting scared all the time. After school I came home real fast to not talk to anybody, but there was never anyone at home. My mother and aunt always worked real late and had to take the bus home from near the beach, so we (he and his cousins) had to make our own dinner. We were told to stay inside the apartment until they got there. It got boring after a while and we began to go out and play. When some of my friends at school told me to join them, at first I said no. Soon, I was out playing with them. When I got older the playing turned to hanging around with some of the older, tougher guys in the neighborhood. I had come to America to be an American and all there was in my neighborhood was gangbanging, so I became a gangbanger.

Identity and Psychological Issues

Among the many experiences that gang members undergo, none is more crucial than the adolescent psychosocial moratorium. According to Erikson (1956, 1963, 1968), the psychosocial moratorium is the marginal status crisis in the passage from childhood to adulthood. Street socialized males in low-income neighborhoods are especially affected by the transition. During this phase they become tentative and confused about their age and gender identity while learning to cope within an often violent, male-dominated street culture. The personal psychological struggle that occurs in this context is sometimes overwhelming. This "storm and stress" situation triggers in individuals, irrespective of environment, many attitudinal and behavioral shifts that render them unpredictable and ambivalent. Being raised in the streets can make this human development phase even more difficult and problematic, twisting and skewing options and opportunities in detrimental ways.

In gang-ridden neighborhoods, the street gang has become a competitor to other sources of identity formation, often replacing family, school, and other conventional influences. Since their inception more than six decades ago, Chicano street gangs have been made up primarily of groups of male adolescents and youths who have grown up together as children, usually as cohorts in a low-income neighborhood of a city. In Los Angeles today, about 100,000 gang members are spread throughout the metropolitan area, most of them concentrated in Latino neighborhoods. However, only about ten to fifteen percent of youth in most of these neighborhoods join gangs (Vigil 1988a; Short 1996; Esbensen and Winfree 1998); and of this number about seventy percent eventually "mature out" (Vigil 2007). Those who join gangs participate together in both conventional and antisocial behavior (Thornberry 2001). The antisocial behavior, of course, attracts the attention of authorities as well as the general public (Decker and Van Winkle 1996).

The gang, in fulfilling many of the personal needs related to the problems, pressures, and strivings of street socialized youth, has perpetuated itself and has extended its influence over marginally troubled youth. These young males temporarily or sporadically seek the gang as a source of support and identity, especially during junior high school (Goldstein and Kodluboy, 1998). It is this age level of thirteen or fourteen when males in particular undergo the psychosocial moratorium spoken of by Erikson (1956), during the status crisis from childhood to adulthood, when ambiguity and ambivalence reign. It is no coincidence that most aggressive gang behavior is committed by male youths between fourteen and eighteen years of age (Hirschi and Gottfredson 1983).

It is a period of human development in which teens face their new social and sexual identities and roles with uncertainty. As a result, they increasingly rely on peers and slightly older male role models as guides. According to cross-cultural researchers (Burton and Whiting 1961; Bloch and Neideroffer 1958), it is common during this developmental phase to seek older male role models and undergo some sort of initiation ceremony into all male organizations.

One role and role performance especially instrumental in the context of street reality is "locura" (i.e., madness). It is both essential for street survival and for assuaging fear and ambiguity born of the psychosocial moratorium. In street culture, locura is a state of mind where various quasi-controlled actions denoting a type of craziness or wildness occur. A person who is a loco demonstrates this state of mind by alternately displaying fearlessness, toughness, daring, and other unpredictable forms of destructive behavior, such as getting loco on drugs and alcohol or excelling in gangbanging. Such traits are, more or less, considered gang ideals. Some confirmed "vatos locos," as loco actors, can easily and authoritatively manage this role, while others only rise to the occasion when peer pressure or situational circumstances dictate a loco act. This difference reflects the distinction Edgerton (1978) makes between deviant persons and deviant acts.

This psychosocial role has become a requisite for street survival and a behavioral standard for identification and emulation, in addition to providing a quick fix for this developmental phase.

Why the Methods Mattered

Although circumstances have differed for each of the ethnic groups discussed in this chapter, it is clear that a series of breakdowns in adaptation and adjustment to the city has led to the unraveling of social-control institutions within some sectors of these communities. As a result, families, schools—and law enforcement, in particular—have collectively failed to develop the necessary connections, engagements, and involvements to ensure conformity to society's belief and value system. In short, significant numbers of youths from low-income, ethnic minority populations that have been subjected to the combined multiple effects of economic, social, cultural, and ecologic marginalization fall prey to the streets when disruptions in parenting, learning, and sanctioning routines occur. With loosened ties to key social influences and lacking adequate socialization in conventional ways, these youth undergo street socialization in remarkably similar ways. Nevertheless, the street-socialized youth also reflect their own community's unique ethnic histories. In time, as gang members, they become a street fixture. There is an institutionalized street subculture with its own set of rules and regulations affecting both males and females. These patterns and practices are also textured and contextualized by their own ethnic group's subculture and relationship with other ethnic communities. In large part, a street identity is fashioned to aid survival. Understanding why and how this transpired can set the tone and direction for ways to remedy this gang problem.

Comprehending this process and the gang subcultures it has generated is augmented and strengthened by a cross-cultural investigation across groups along similar dimensions, within a social-control framework where conformity, rather than deviancy, is the paramount focus. While this analysis is set in the same time (1990s) and place (Los Angeles), the background times and places of the communities discussed here made for different contrasting macrohistorical and macrostructural experiences. Within these peoples' histories and socioeconomic trajectories, time and place take on a renewed and multidimensional significance, particularly when we look at the connections between the group and individual histories.

It is the life histories that deepen and broaden the historical outlines, however, whether one is studying gangs or other social problems. For example, in conducting evaluations of a Cambodian family preschool prevention and intervention program in Long Beach, California, the team I headed made use of formal testing results, of course, but also observed and interviewed teachers, parents, and children involved in the program. Similarly, in studying the effects of a federally funded drug intervention program in a local public housing development, I gathered official statistics relating to crime and drug use in the neighborhood. More importantly, I met both formally and informally with housing residents of varying social standing to elicit their experiences before and during the implementation of the program. I also spent time simply socializing in the projects and observing everyday events. Included in these ethnographic observations were monitoring the activities of the program-funded extra police surveillance and counseling services and people's reactions to them. In both instances, therefore, the resultant evaluation reports included both emic and etic viewpoints: how the people viewed the program as well as measurable results attained by the program. Overall, the teachers, families, and children had mostly positive feelings and comments on the program, and for many months afterward, parents and program leaders met and kept the intent and spirit of the program going.

Overall, a multimethod analysis sheds more light on a social problem, like street gangs, than do single-method analyses. The individual lives illustrate some features commonly found in their respective communities that, in turn, comprise the background that contributes to the growth of street gangs. In many of the two-parent households in marginalized neighborhoods, moreover, family violence can be even more disrupting in children's lives. In a survey of a thousand seventh and eighth graders, nearly seven in ten children who were exposed to abuse, violence, or neglect in their homes also reported committing "delinquent" acts themselves; and exposure to family violence increased by half the probability of children being involved in violence away from the home (Thornberry 2001; Loeber and Stouthamer-Loeber, 1986). These conditions are often compounded by school problems, reflected in part by school dropout rates: while 7.7 percent of white youths, nationally, drop out of high school, 12.6 percent of blacks and 30 percent of Hispanics do so (National Center for Education 1998; see also Coleman 1990). In California, these circumstances were aggravated for much of the last two decades by declining public funding for family assistance and schooling (see, e.g., Greenwood 1996). Meanwhile, incarceration rates increased, and minority youths disproportionally filled the California Youth Authority's facilities; in 1999, whites made up only 14 percent of the CYA population, while Hispanics and African Americans made up 49 percent and 28 percent, respectively (California Youth Authority 1999; see also Pertersilia, 1992). These statistics tell only part of the story.

In the Nelles California Youth Authority study (above), we discovered that nearly all of those inmates had dropped out of school well before the incidents that led to their incarceration. Most of them indicated they had serious problems with school before dropping out. Four of every five reported they had been raised in single-parent households, and a large majority (as many as ninety-one percent of the Salvadoran inmates) had been exposed to (or experienced) family violence. In short, these youths—almost all of them gang members and all of them convicted of serious, usually violent, crimes—exemplified the marginalized, street-socialized backgrounds that are typical of youth gang participants.

Conclusions: Cross-Cultural Insights into Multiple Marginality

The process of multiple marginalization leads to a breakdown of social control. In turn, this breakdown leads to street socialization and the emergence of a gang subculture and a street identity. To better assess these dynamic developments, a cross-cultural (and cross-methodological) investigation across groups (and nations) along similar dimensions, specifically social-control institutions, will provide more insights and a deeper understanding of the contemporary (and global) gang problem.

Multiple marginality, the framework within which our analysis was conducted, helps us pinpoint and highlight the ways ecological (place) and economic (status) marginalization affect and intersect with social, cultural, and psychological strains and stresses. These forces additively and cumulatively contribute to the breakdown of social control and the emergence of gangs and varieties of gang members. (See Vigil 1988a for varieties of gang members.) It is these broader forces that undermine and create social-control dysfunctions, disrupting family life, undermining education, and leading law enforcement, inevitably, to play a stronger role as society's "conformity" safety net. To fill these gaps (Klein 1971; Moore 1978; Vigil 1988a, 1993; Heath and McLaughlin 1993), the gang replaces the parenting, schooling, and policing to regulate youths' lives to one of a street subculture, where routines and regulations help guide gang members (Conchas and Vigil 2012). The subculture that emerges varies somewhat between males and females, although, as discussed above, there is a remarkable consistency in the major themes among them: multiple marginality, breakdown of social control, and even specific gang routines like initiation, tattoos and graffiti, and gang conflict.

To reiterate, the seeds of the solutions to gangs are found in the root causes. This cross-cultural assessment using multiple methods accounts for the differences in time, place, and peoples (Vigil 2010). Even though larger-than-life historical and structural forces have undermined social-control institutions, such as families, schooling, and law enforcement, there is an opportunity to salvage many of the children who have been marginalized and left to the streets (Rios 2011).

Prevention must begin in the middle childhood years of seven and eight and continue through the ages of fourteen to fifteen. Communities and agencies must take a proactive approach in addressing the primary problems of the general population in low-income areas, as well as factor in secondary prevention for specific youths in need and any related issues. Interventions must be aimed at the crucial preteen years, from about age nine to twelve, and should involve treatment and work with youths who are close to, but not yet deeply connected to, the streets (Rodriguez and Conchas 2009). Dissuading youths early on from the attitudes and behavior that clearly lead to delinquent and criminal paths opens the possibility of a return to more prosocial activities (Conchas and Vigil 2010; Goldstein and Huff 1993).

Lacking in many of these youths' lives are pre-employment experiences that assist human growth and development, such as beliefs and behavioral traits reflecting discipline, obedience, punctuality, responsibility, and the value and honor of work (Conchas 2001, 2006). For this reason, many observers and writers have emphasized that economic concerns matter most in getting youths off the streets (Moore 1998; Noguera 2003; Rothstein 2004). Training, work, and jobs can engage youths in productive, conventional activities and ground them in the skills, knowledge, and attitudes that will stay with them for life and give them a stake in society (Cartwright, Thompson, and Schwartz 1975; Conchas 2001; Rothstein 2004). Successful programs must consider three crucial variables: time management, location modification, and people.

References

Alonso, Alejandro. 1999. "Territoriality among African American Street Gangs in Los Angeles." Master's thesis, Department of Geography, University of Southern California.

Blanc, Cristina S. (with contributors). 1995. *Urban Children in Distress: Global Predicaments and Innovative Strategies*. Florence, Italy: UNICEF.

Bloch, Herbert, and Allan Neideroffer. 1958. *The Gang: A Study in Adolescent Behavior*. New York: The Philosophical Society.

Bursik, Robert J., Jr., and Harold G. Grasmick. 1995. "Defining Gangs and Gang Behavior." In *The Modern Gang Reader*, edited by Malcom W. Klein, Cheryl L. Maxson, and Jody Miller, 8–13. Los Angeles: Roxbury Publishing. Co.

Burton, Roger V., and John W. Whiting. 1961. "The Absent Father and Cross-Sex Identity. *Merrill-Palmer Quarterly* 7: 85–95.

California Youth Authority. 1999. *Report*. California Youth Authority, 1–20.

Cartwright, Desmond S., Barbara Thompson, and Hershey Schwartz, eds. 1975. *Gang Delinquency*. Monterey, CA: Brooks/Cole Publishing.

Cloward, Richard A., and Lloyd E. Ohlin. 1960. *Delinquency and Opportunity: A Theory of Delinquent Gangs*. New York: Free Press.

Coleman, James. 1990. *Equality and Achievement in Education*. Boulder, CO: Westview Press.

Conchas, Gilberto. 2001. "Structuring Failure and Success: Understanding the Variability in Latino School Engagement." *Harvard Educational Review* 71: 475–505.

———. 2006. *The Color of Success: Race and High-Achieving Urban Youth*. New York: Teachers College Press of Columbia University.

Conchas, Gilberto Q. and Pedro A. Noguera. 2004. "Understanding the Exceptions: How Small Schools Support the Achievement of Academically Successful Black Boys." In *Adolescent Boys: Exploring Diverse Culture of Boyhood*, edited by Niobe Way and Judy Y. Chu, 317–37. New York: New York University Press.

Conchas, Gilberto Q., and J. Diego Vigil. 2010. "Multiple Marginality and Education: The Community and School Socialization of Low-Income Mexican-Descent Youth." *Journal of Education for Students Placed At-Risk (JESPAR)* 15 (1–2): 51–65.

———. 2012. *Streetsmart Schoolsmart*. New York: Teachers College Press.

Covey, Herbert C., Scott Menard, and Robert J. Franzese. 1992. *Juvenile Gangs*. Springfield, IL: Charles C. Thomas Publisher.

Decker, Scott H., and Barrik Van Winkle. 1996. *Life in the Gang: Family, Friends, and Violence*. New York: Cambridge University Press.

Edgerton, Robert. 1978. "The Study of Deviance—Marginal Man or Everyman?" In *The Making of Psychological Anthropology*, edited by George Spindler, 442–76. Los Angeles: University of California Press.

Erikson, Erik H. 1956. "Ego Identity and the Psychosocial Moratorium." In *New Perspectives for Research on Juvenile Delinquency*, edited by Helen L. Witmer and Ruth Kotinsky, 1–23. U.S. Children's Bureau: Publication no. 356.

———. 1963. *Childhood and Society*. New York: W. W. Norton and Co.

———.1968. "Psychosocial Identity." In *International Encyclopedia of the Social Sciences*, vol. 7, edited by D. Sills, 61–65. New York: Macmillan and the Free Press.

Esbensen, Finn-Aage, and L. Thomas Winfree. 1998. "Race and Gender Differences between Gang and Nongang Youths: Results from a Multisite Survey." *Justice Quarterly* 15 (3): 505–26.

Flynn, Michael. 2008. *Social Control and Street Gangs in Los Angeles*. New York: Columbia University Press.

Goldstein, Arnold P., and C. Ronald Huff, eds. 1993. *The Gang Intervention Handbook*. Champaign, IL: Research Press.

Goldstein, Arnold P., and Donald W. Kodluboy. 1998. *Gangs in Schools: Signs, Symbols, and Solutions*. Champaign, IL: Research Press.

Greenwood, Peter W., Karyn Model, C. Peter Rydell, and James Chiesa. 1996. *Diverting Children from a Life of Crime: Measuring Costs and Benefits*. Santa Monica CA: Rand.

Hagedorn, John M. 1988. *People and Folks: Gangs, Crime and the Underclass in a Rustbelt City*. Chicago: Lake View.

———. 2006. *Globalization and Gangs*. Champaign: University of Illinois Press.

Hazen, Jennifer, and Dennis Rodgers, eds. 2014. *Global Gangs*. Minneapolis: University of Minnesota Press.

Hazlehurst, Kayleen, and Cameron Hazlehurst, eds. 1998. *Gangs and Youth Subcultures: International Explorations*. New Brunswick, NJ: Transaction Publishers.

Heath, Shirley Brice, and Milbrey McLaughlin, eds. 1993. *Identity and Inner-City Youth: Beyond Ethnicity and Gender*. New York: Teachers College Press, Columbia University Press.

Hirschi, Travis, and Michael Gottfredson. 1983. *Age and the Explanation of Crime. American Journal of Sociology* 89 (3): 552–84.

Klein, Malcolm. 1971. *Street Gangs and Street Workers*. Englewood Cliffs, NJ: Prentice-Hall.

———. 1995. *The American Street Gang*. New York: Oxford University Press.

Loeber, R., and M. Stouthamer-Loeber. 1986. "Family Factors as Correlates and Predictors of Juvenile Conduct Problems and Delinquency." In *Crime and Justice*, vol. 7, edited by Michael Tonry and Norval Morris, 29–150. Chicago: University of Chicago Press.

Los Angeles Times. 1992. "Understanding the Riots: Los Angeles Before and After the Rodney King Case." Special issue, multiple authors, *Los Angeles Times*.

Maxson, Cheryl L. 1998 "Gang Members on the Move." *Bulletin*. Washington, DC: U.S. Department of Justice, OJJDP.

Merton, Robert K. 1949. *Social Theory and Social Structure*. Glencoe, IL: The Free Press.

Miller, Jody, Cheryl L. Maxson, and Malcom W. Klein, eds. 2001. *The Modern Gang Reader*, 2nd ed. Los Angeles: Roxbury Publishing.

Moore, Joan. 1978. *Homeboys*. Philadelphia: Temple University Press.

———. 1991. *Going Down to the Barrio: Homeboys and Homegirls in Change*. Philadelphia: Temple University Press.

———. 1998. "Understanding Youth Street Gangs: Economic Restructuring and the Urban Underclass." In *Cross-Cultural Perspectives on Youth and Violence*, edited by Meredith Watts, 65–78. Stamford, CT: Jai Press.

National Center for Education Statistics. 1998. *Condition of Education 1998*. Washington, DC: US Department of Education.

Noguera, Pedro A. 2003. *City Schools and the American Dream: Reclaiming the Promise of Public Education*. New York: Teachers College Press.

Oliver, Melvin L., James H. Johnson, and Walter C. Farrell. 1993. "Anatomy of a Rebellion: A Political-Economic Analysis." In *Reading Rodney King/Reading Urban Uprising*, edited by R. G. Williams. 117–41. New York: Routledge.

Pertersilia, Joan. 1992. "Crime and Punishment in California: Full Cells, Empty Pockets, and Questionable Benefits." In *Urban America: Policy Choices for Los Angeles and the Nation*, edited by J. B. Steiner, D. W. Lyon, and M. E. Vaiana. 175–206. Santa Monica, CA: The RAND Corporation.

Rios, Victor M. 2011. *Punished: Policing the Lives of Black and Latino Boys*. New York: New York University Press.

Rodriguez, L. 1991. *The Concrete River*. Willimantic, CT: Curbstone Press.

Rodríguez, Louie F., and Gilberto Q. Conchas. 2009. "Action from the Student's Perspective." *Education and Urban Society* 41 (2): 216–47.

Rothstein, Richard. 2004. *Class and Schools: Using Social, Economic and Educational Reform to Close the Black-White Achievement Gap*. Washington, D.C.: Economic Policy Institute.

Sampson, Robert J., and John H. Laub. 1994. "Urban Poverty and the Family Context of Delinquency: A New Look at Structure and Process in a Classic Study." *Child Development* 65: 523–40.

Shaw, Clifford, and Henry D. McKay. 1942. *Juvenile Delinquency and Urban Areas*. Chicago: University of Chicago Press.

Short, James F. 1996. "Gangs and Adolescent Violence." Manuscript on file. Center for the Study and Prevention of Violence, Institute of Behavioral Science. Boulder, CO: University of Colorado.

Spergel, I. A., and G. D. Curry. 1998. "The National Youth Gang Survey: A Research and Development Process." In *The Modern Gang Reader*, edited by Malcom W. Klein, Cheryl L. Maxson, and Jody Miller, 254–65. Los Angeles: Roxbury Publishing.

Thornberry, Terrance P. 2001. "Risk factors for gang membership." In *The Modern Gang Researcher*, 2nd ed., edited by J. Miller, C. L. Maxson, and M. W. Klein, 32–43. Los Angeles: Roxbury Publishing.

Thrasher, Frederic. 1963 (1927). *The Gang*. Chicago: University of Chicago Press.

Vigil, James Diego. 1987. "Youth Gangs and Delinquency: A Cross-Cultural Look at the Children of Immigrants." 47th Annual Meeting, Society for Applied Anthropology, Oaxaca, Mexico, April 8–12. [Organized and chaired session.]

———.1988a. *Barrio Gangs: Street Life and Identity in Southern California*. Austin: University of Texas Press.

———.1988b. "Group Processes and Street Identity: Adolescent Chicano Gang Members." *Ethnos* 16 (4): 421–45.

———.1993. "Gangs, Social Control, and Ethnicity: Ways to Redirect Street Youth." In *Identity and Inner-City Youth: Beyond Ethnicity and Gender*, edited by S. B. Heath and M. W. McLaughlin, 94–119. New York: Teachers College Press, Columbia University Press.

———.1999. *Streets and Schools: How Educators Can Help Chicano Marginalized Gang Youth*. Harvard Educational Review 69 (3): 270–88.

———. 2002. *A Rainbow of Gangs: Street Cultures in the Mega-City*. Austin: University of Texas Press.

———. 2007. *The Projects: Gang and Non-Gang Families in East Los Angeles*. Austin: University of Texas Press.

———. 2014. "Cholo!: The Migratory Origins of Chicano Gangs in Los Angeles." In *Global Gangs*, edited by Jennifer M. Hazen and Dennis Rodgers, 49–64. Minneapolis: University of Minnesota Press.

Vigil, James Diego, and John M. Long. 1990. "Etic and Emic Perspectives on Gang Culture: The Chicano Case." In *Gangs in America: Diffusion, Diversity, and Public Policy*, edited by Robert Huff, 55–68. Beverly Hills, CA: Sage Publications.

Vigil, James Diego, and Steve C. Yun. 1990. "A Cross-Cultural Framework for Understanding Gangs: Multiple Marginality and Los Angeles." In *Gangs in America: Diffusion, Diversity, and Public Policy*, edited by Robert Huff, 161–74. Beverly Hills, CA: Sage Publications.

———"The Vietnamese Youth Gangs in Southern California." In *Gangs in*

America: Diffusion, Diversity, and Public Policy, edited by Robert Huff, 146–62. Beverly Hills, CA: Sage Publications.

———. 1998. "Vietnamese Youth Gangs in the Context of Multiple Marginality and the Los Angeles Youth Gang Phenomenon." In *Gangs and Youth Subcultures: International Explorations,* edited by Kayleen Hazlehurst and Cameron Hazlehurst, 117–39. New Brunswick, NJ: Transaction Publishers.

Wiatrowski, Michael D., David B. Griswold, and Mary K. Roberts. 1981. "Social Control Theory and Delinquency." *American Sociological Review* 46: 525–41.

SIXTEEN

"I Thought Delay Meant She Would Catch Up": Using Mixed Methods to Study Children with Early Developmental Delays and Their Families

LUCINDA P. BERNHEIMER, RONALD GALLIMORE, AND BARBARA K. KEOGH

Olivia was born three years after the Landers's first child, also a girl. Olivia was a healthy, easy baby and her first year passed uneventfully. As she neared her first birthday, however, her mother noticed that "there was something different" about her. She was developing less rapidly than her older sister had. It wasn't small milestone differences. Olivia was slower to sit and to crawl, and was very resistant to eating solid foods. Growing increasingly alarmed, her parents were reassured by the family's pediatrician that all babies developed at different rates, and that Olivia would "grow out of it" by the time she was two.

For the next year, her parents watched anxiously as she continued to lag behind her sister. On her second birthday they took her for an extensive evaluation to a developmental specialist, who determined that she was functioning at fourteen months old—eight months behind a typically developing child. The specialist described her as "developmentally delayed," but expressed optimism that Olivia would eventually "catch up" to her age peers.

The parents were relieved. They had feared she would be labeled mentally retarded.

Developmental Delay, "Catching Up," and Ambiguity

In the late 1970s, the label developmental delay came into fashion as an explanation for children who did not meet milestones at expected ages but who did not fit the usual categories of disabilities. For thousands of parents like Olivia's, the idea that delay meant "catching up" was likely was reassuring. For other parents, the fear their child might not catch up haunted them during preschool years.

These fears often escalated as kindergarten enrollment approached. With the passing years, it seemed to many families that the signs of "delays" grew stronger as they compared their child's growth to older siblings or same-age children of their friends and neighbors. The reassurances of professionals became less comforting, the concerns increased. Many parents began a desperate search for a diagnosis, seeking one specialist after another, hoping to find a reason for the delays— and perhaps a cure, a treatment of some kind to help their child.

Fear and apprehension shifted to panic for those families advised to check school programs for children exhibiting delays. What they found were classes of children who were obviously disabled by physical and behavior problems, speech disorders, and mental retardation.

What they could not find was reliable information about "developmental delay," the odds of catching up, and what families facing similar circumstances had done to adapt. There were anecdotal case studies, such as Olivia's, and the clinical experience of specialists, but little that might confirm or refute prevailing assumptions about children who were slow developing but fit into no obvious or known diagnostic category.

What was needed, what parents and specialists needed, were evidence-based answers to fundamental questions better addressed by a more standardized method: Do children who show early delays catch up? How many? Are children with certain delays more likely to catch up? What kind of delays portend a happier outcome? Which ones don't? Is there a treatment that might help? Do parental child-rearing practices matter?

In this chapter we outline the history of two projects designed to answer these questions for parents of children with early delays, and for the professional communities that try to help them. We believe these longitudinal investigations illustrate the power and benefit of mixing qualitative and quantitative methods. For more than three decades, a team of anthropologists, developmentalists, and psychologists mixed methods in multiple ways we believe produced better results than a monomethod approach might have done.

Project REACH

The Project REACH longitudinal study (Bernheimer and Keogh 1982) was launched in 1977 to answer the question: Do children with developmental delays of unknown etiology eventually catch up? REACH recruited forty-four 25–42-month-old Euro American children with mild to moderate developmental delays of unknown etiology. The principal sources were pediatricians, early intervention programs, regional centers, and preschools. Our focus was on quantitative measurement of each child's development. We conducted standardized developmental assessments in the home at six-month intervals for two years. While we also collected limited information from parents about their use of resources and supports and their search for appropriate programs and therapies, the focus was on child measurement issues over time.

At the end of three years, we knew that children who were delayed at age two–three were likely to be delayed at age four–five. For the group as a whole, cognitive/developmental levels were stable over time. At the same time, the testing provided no basis for predicting the outcome for individual children: some children made developmental gains, others remained stable, and still others declined in developmental level. In addition, the delay was often expressed unevenly in the different areas of development: for example, a two-year-old who was not using language might be at age level in her motor skills. Our findings were useful in showing that children with developmental delays do not typically "catch up" within two years; however, the variability in outcomes and unevenness of delays hinted at a more complicated story and suggested that a wider methodology might be useful.

Ongoing conversations with parents suggested something we had not anticipated investigating when REACH was designed—parents' attempts to come to terms with the ambiguity of the delays. Because the delay was an invisible disability, most REACH children looked like children with typical development. To many families, the term "delay" held out hope that their child would eventually catch up to other children his or her age; as one father commented, "After all, when the train is delayed, it eventually gets to the station."

Much has been written about the stigma associated with labels signifying disability, e.g., Down syndrome, cerebral palsy, autism, etc. While some REACH parents were relieved that their child was not labeled, others struggled with not having a diagnostic and prognostic road map to follow. Still others struggled to understand the multiple diagnoses suggested by professionals, e.g., retarded, not retarded, autistic, language delay, etc., which increased the ambiguity of their child's condition and their own anxieties. One practical problem was finding programs for children given no labels.

Most intervention programs of the 1970s and 1980s addressed well-defined conditions—Down syndrome, cerebral palsy, severe mental retardation, or orthopedic disabilities. Many REACH parents felt their child did not belong in programs for children with these labels and with obvious disabilities, nor did they themselves belong with the parents of such children. Some REACH parents found such groups more stressful than supportive: while other group members were trying to understand why their child had Down syndrome or cerebral palsy, the REACH parents were struggling to discover if their child had a disability.

Philosophical and policy shifts in the last twenty-five years have resulted in today's inclusive programs for young children with disabilities. However, in the early days of REACH, few "regular" preschool programs welcomed children with developmental problems. Several parents who found programs willing to accept their children ended up withdrawing their child as the differences in competencies between their child and the other children became increasingly apparent. Parents were also painfully aware that their child was not included in social activities, and had few if any friends.

One mother lamented the loss of her dream that her youngest would one day be walking to school with her older sister, each carrying a new lunch box, laughing, skipping. As kindergarten approached, she slowly began to realize her daughter would never "catch up" enough to attend their local elementary school. For an American mother dreaming of the opportunities awaiting her daughters in a changing society, it was a devastating blow. Her fears were amplified by a core American value linking early school success to social and economic reproduction. A child unready for kindergarten and first grade is, in this society, a child believed doomed to the lower rungs of the socioeconomic ladder.

At the end of REACH's three-year funding cycle, we confirmed that developmental delay was not a temporary condition. We also realized that the search for a diagnosis and suitable services required enormous parental energy and persistence. Contrary to conventional wisdom, which suggested that a family of a child with disabilities was a family with disabilities, we were impressed by the strengths of our parents.

While parents who investigated a number of programs and therapies were often given the pejorative label of "shoppers," these behaviors were actually adaptive. For example, it was appropriate for parents to be "pushy" in their search for a diagnosis and appropriate treatment. It was adaptive for a mother to withdraw from an early-intervention parent group when she was not sure if her child had a disability. Since the professionals had no idea what their child's problem was, they also had no way to advise what programs might offer some help. "Pushiness" was just parents practicing common sense: the parents were adopting the stance that "if the pros can't help us, then we'll have to get busy and search for answers ourselves."

At the same time, there were many unanswered questions. Why did some children make developmental progress while others remained stable or declined? What was the relationship between the child's functioning level and family adaptation? How do families adjust to the ambiguity of their child's condition over time?

The literature in developmental studies on family coping was of limited help. The bulk of investigations treated children with problems as members of families with problems. Many studies, for instance, compared levels of stress and psychopathology between families with and without handicapped children. Given the "file drawer" problem that only studies with significant results tend to be published, the journals were full of unflattering conclusions about families of children with early disabilities and delays. There were virtually no studies of adaptive behavior of families with delayed children, and the few available were atheoretical or neopsychoanalytic.

Certainly REACH's use of standardized instruments provided valuable quantitative data, systematically documenting the children's development over a twenty-four-month period. REACH had suggested clearly that catching up might not be as common as clinicians had thought. Even without a formal interview protocol focused on family adaptation, contacts with parents had produced a rich array of anecdotes regarding the sometimes remarkable ways they had adapted to their child's delay.

But REACH's limitations needed addressing. The sample size was small, given the variability in child developmental trajectories, and in family adaptation to delay. The information on family adaptation had been collected informally using clinical case methods, so there was reason to believe that many actions of parents had not been recorded. Finally the length of contact with the REACH families had been less than three years, given when data collection began and ended. To get a better picture of child development and family adaptation, we needed a mixed methods, longitudinal study that spanned at least five years, and perhaps ten or more years. At least that was our hope when Project CHILD was launched in 1984 (Gallimore et al. 1983).

Project CHILD: Detailing the Design of a
Twenty-Year Mixed Methods Project

Project CHILD was conducted by a multidisciplinary team of psychologists, developmentalists, psychometricians, sociolinguists, and anthropologists. For the twenty-year life of CHILD, multiple methods of behavioral and social science were used at one time or another.

To begin, the CHILD team turned to methods that have served anthropology long and well—a detailed gathering, summary, and analysis of every scrap of qualitative case material in books, journals, and project files served as an expert informant. To assemble examples and variation of family adaptive response, REACH's primary fieldworker/assessment specialist (Bernheimer) scoured project case notes and summarized her informal clinical observations. She also served as expert informant, enduring long, probing interviews that served to elaborate the adaptive examples she had identified. These materials were supplemented by a review of the existing research and clinical literature. Once assembled, this library of examples was used to develop a standardized protocol.

What transformed this qualitative library from an unorganized—if interesting—pile of information was Ecological/Cultural theory, or Ecocultural theory (Weisner 1984). Weisner and his colleagues and students had been working on a scheme that drew on every available source of data on environmental and cultural effects on child development. A key idea was an ecocultural hierarchy of effects, which provided a theoretically coherent and empirically sound basis for organizing CHILD's library of case materials (see appendix 16.1).

From the unorganized pile of case materials, after a few months we had an interview protocol: the Ecocultural Family Interview or EFI (Weisner, Coots et al. 1997; see also Lieber, chapter 10). The EFI is a focused conversation with parents about how they organize their everyday routine, and plan, create, change, and sustain family activities. Topics covered are based on the original theoretical dimensions described by Weisner (1984). There are numerical ratings from 0–8 for each topic. As example, on the item "Father participation in child care" included in the "domestic workload" dimension, 0–2 indicates little or no participation, 3–5 indicates some participation, and 6–8 indicates much participation. After a conversation with a family, the fieldworker/interviewer wrote qualitative cues for each item, summarizing what data from the interview and family visits led to assigning the score.

Scores on these items were then used to create domain and factor scores (see appendix 16.2 for domains with sample items), so that the meaning of a 3 vs. a 5 was made clear. The EFI introduced a method of interviewing, collecting qualitative information, and scoring interviews that was not available at the time. It provided a description of a daily routine that had meaning to the family, and that fit with the abilities and needs of the family as well as the resources available in the family and the community. The open-ended EFI interviews with parents permitted them to tell in narrative form the "story" of their child from birth to the present, including all the things they had done to find out what was the trouble, what to do, and what they had actually done.

Early on, we described family adaptations as "accommodations." There was an ecocultural theoretical reason for this choice. A key unit analysis in ecocultural theory is the daily routine of family activities. These are mundane, culturally familiar parts of life, such as getting up in the morning, getting ready for school and work, after school child care, mealtimes, after-dinner and bedtime routines. Not only do parents think in these terms, they think about who is present in each setting, what's being done, why it's being done, and the rules of participation that govern interactions.

To construct and sustain the activities of the daily routine, families make accommodations. When a change is introduced that affects the routine, such as the birth of a child, or the emergence of a developmental delay, existing accommodations have to be adjusted, and new ones made. For example, to accommodate getting a child to special therapies or programs, one parent might change shifts to be available for transportation during normal work hours. Sometimes families move to cheaper housing, permitting one parent to give up a job to be home for a child who is difficult to place in day care. These and hundreds of other accommodations were described by the CHILD parents, and most could be reliably classified using the econiche hierarchy we had constructed, drawing on the work of ecocultural theorists (e.g., Weisner 1984; Harkness and Super 1994; see also Worthman, chapter 2).

Although difficult and time-consuming, our approach combined the advantages of open-ended, more qualitative interviewing with a data analysis strategy that yielded findings permitting generalization across a large sample. In addition, we retained the power of interpretive methods because we had the taped and transcribed words of the parents to give meaning to cold statistics.

An interesting but unforeseen variable that emerged from our conversation with REACH families was child "hassle." Earlier research on the relationship between child status and family stress levels defined child status in terms of developmental level (low IQ vs. high IQ) or diagnostic categories (e.g., Down syndrome, cerebral palsy, autism). In general, the data indicated the greater the disability level of the child, the greater stress on the family. But the REACH families did not show this pattern.

To the contrary, some parents of children with severe delays were doing well, while other parents of children with mild delays reported a significant and distressing impact of the child on their daily lives. We realized that parents were responding to something more complex than an IQ score, so for the CHILD study we created a new child status variable. "Hassle," a term used by several of the REACH parents, was defined as the child's impact on the family's daily routine. An example of a high-hassle child was one who required constant monitoring and supervision to be kept from hurting self or siblings. Based on the stories told by Project CHILD parents, we were able to reliably code three types of hassle (behavioral, communication, medical) as high, medium, or low. The hassle variable was a measure of child status that could be examined in the context of family adaptations and used to investigate the direction of effects between child status and family accommodations.

While method development was proceeding, we turned to the daunting task of recruiting one hundred families with a child labeled with early developmental delays of unknown etiology. We chose an age range of thirty-six to forty-eight months, because REACH had shown this was the most likely time the "delay" label begins to be applied by specialists. We began from lists of agencies, organizations, schools, and programs in the greater Los Angeles region. We sought referrals from pediatricians, early intervention programs, teachers, and regional center professionals. It took months, but eventually we successfully recruited and signed up one hundred families whose three- or four-year-old replicated the REACH sample by meeting these criteria: Euro American, mild to moderate delay of unknown etiology (i.e., not related to substance abuse, chromosomal abnormality or genetic condition, anoxia at birth or cerebral hemorrhage shortly after birth). The samples were remarkably similar in other ways: in spite of the ten-year gap between the onset of projects REACH and CHILD, parents reported identical delays in getting their concerns validated and finding programs and therapies for their children.

The same standard developmental and language assessments used in the original Project REACH study were used to establish a baseline in Project CHILD. At the same time, REACH was continuing to use developmental measures appropriate for older children, adding parent and teacher reports of children's behavioral and social competence and parent and child perceived life-satisfaction measures as they reached adolescence and young adulthood. REACH and CHILD continued in tandem for twenty-five years. The final CHILD data collection was conducted when the children were in their early twenties. REACH continued a bit longer, and our last contact with the parents occurred when the REACH subjects were in their mid-thirties.

Mixed Methods, Meaningful Findings

Quantitative methods and psychometric assessment allowed us to provide a detailed description of developmental delay from preschool age to young adulthood in terms of cognitive, behavioral, and social characteristics. Project CHILD's repeated developmental testing results over years confirmed the REACH findings: cognitive functioning for most children is stable over time, the majority of children do not "catch up," and it is difficult to predict individual children's developmental progress over time. In addition, quantitative methods yielded data that alerted us to child characteristics that had the potential to disrupt the family's daily routine. As example, assessments of children's social-behavioral problems and competencies confirmed that the children as a group had higher rates of problems compared to peers who were typically developing, and that over time the frequency of behavior problems remained stable while the types of problems changed.

Indeed, once our study answered the first question parents desperately wanted answered about a young child—"does delay mean catch up?" other parental questions became more pressing. What about the children with early delays who made more developmental gains over time? Was it because their families made more accommodations than those with children who were stable or lost ground? Did family accommodations predict child outcomes? Or did child characteristics predict family accommodation activity?

We were able to answer these questions because CHILD was longitudinal, and multimethod. We assessed child status and family accommodations at ages three, seven, and ten, using quantitative and qualitative methods, respectively. Results indicated that the direction of effects was largely child-driven. Lower child competencies, at younger ages, predicted more frequent and intense family accommodations at later ages. Family accommodations did not predict child cognitive or personal-social competence; families adapt to the child's disabilities and delays, rather than the child adapting or responding to family accommodations. While some might be disappointed there was no evidence that families can affect the trajectory of a developmental delay, there is a compensating finding. Families of children with delays accommodate, but they do not fall apart, they do not succumb to stress, they do not become inert or so troubled they fail to adapt.

With a few exceptions, by child age thirteen, CHILD families were doing relatively well. Like all families, there were ups and downs, but a systematic analysis of case materials suggested that about ninety percent of the CHILD families were managing "good enough" if not as well as they'd like). Except for a troubled few, most families could be described in one of three ways: those with stable daily routines, those who were vulnerable but resilient, and those who were described as "hanging on" (Weisner, Matheson et al. 1997). Some accommodations were predictably related to income, availability of instrumental support, and other resources. These variations aside, whatever their circumstances, families were actively making accommodations to incorporate the child with delays into their daily routine.

Finally, both REACH and CHILD found that—contrary to some literature on families adapting to early-childhood delay—there was no indication that Project CHILD families were suffering from exceptionally high levels of stress, emotional problems, or family difficulties. Most of the major problems families reported were related to death of a grandparent, spouse, or child; loss of a job; or housing. These and other major life events loomed larger than childhood delays in most cases (Weisner, Matheson et al. 1997). We do not mean to minimize the stresses, strains, and problems the families have faced. Indeed some families have carried and some still carry great burdens, but the overall impression is that these families are not that much different from others. We are wise to heed Glidden's challenge of the assumption that a child disability inevitably means the family itself has a disability (Glidden 1993, 426). That is certainly not true of at least ninety percent of the families in the CHILD and REACH cohorts.

Policy and Clinical Implications

Projects CHILD and REACH spanned a thirty-year-plus period during which the political and educational context for children with developmental delays and their families underwent a major shift. Developmental delay is now a category of eligibility for services for children from 0–8, which was not the case in the early years of REACH.

The focus on early intervention has broadened from the child to include the family, and clinicians are now explicitly charged with providing parents the information and education they need to support their child's development. Public Law 99–457, passed almost twenty-five years ago, mandates that parents play a pivotal role in the development of the Individual Family Service Plan (IFSP), a document detailing services that young children with disabilities are entitled to receive. In addition to goals for the child, in developing an IFSP, service providers are expected to discuss with families their goals and priorities, rather than relying on professional protocols. One way to identify these goals and priorities is to have a conversation with parents about their daily routines and the adjustments necessary to make these routines work for all members of the family.

Understanding a family's daily routine addressed the "compliance issue" of concern to pediatricians, psychologists, developmentalists, and other early-childhood specialists. They often complained that parents didn't follow their advice regarding prescribed programs and interventions: e.g., include the child in all family outings, work on speech for thirty minutes a day; bring child to physical therapy twice a week. CHILD findings suggested an interpretation, and a better design strategy.

Many proposed interventions and services ignored the reality that families of children with developmental delays face the same challenges as all families: constructing a sustainable daily routine of life that fits the goals, priorities, and abilities of all family members and matches the available family resources. This task is harder or easier to the extent that the child has an impact on the daily routine. This means interventions and services must take account of more than just the child's assessed level of functioning, her IQ or developmental status. For example, REACH and CHILD parents often described a child who was severely delayed as low hassle, with tolerable impact on the family's routine. In other cases, a child only mildly delayed according to clinical testing had behavior problems or medical problems requiring a complicated regimen of treatments, or medications that significantly impacted the family's daily routine.

To increase the chances that a prescribed program is followed, REACH and CHILD results indicated services need to be sensitive to a family's daily routine and existing accommodations. There has to be a slot in the daily routine in which interventions can fit. Past family research classified families on continua that were not useful in developing interventions (socioeconomic status, maternal education, amount of stimulation in the environment, quality of parent-child interaction). Ecocultural theory tells us not to assume that families located on the same point on any of these continua have the same priorities, values, and goals, or that they would respond to similar interventions.

Perhaps the most obvious REACH and CHILD implication for policymakers and clinicians was that an early developmental delay seldom disappears, and that children who worry their parents at age three are unlikely to ever fully "catch up" to same-age peers. Our follow-up data at ages twenty-plus indicated not only do problems of children with early delays persist, they are enduring. After the youth in our samples left public school, their parents described increasing difficulty finding appropriate programs for their twenty-something offspring. With the end of public school services, both the youth and the parents fell into a service abyss. As young adults, the majority remained at home. There was no ready source of peer groups, and vocational training programs were few and far between, or too costly for most families. Parents expressed concern their children needed to "get a life" but were unsure how to help them find it. For many aging REACH and CHILD parents, yet another new crisis loomed: making arrangements for when they die or can no longer function as advocates and benefactors for an offspring who never "caught up" (see also Daley, chapter 11, for similar concerns among parents of adults with autism). These problems remain, and in a staggering economy are worsened because even those capable of low-skill jobs are facing stiff competition.

Finally, REACH and CHILD results sharply challenged a prevailing American belief—the deeply held assumptions that a child's outcome is substantially determined by parental actions. We found no strong or obvious evidence that parenting in early, middle, and late childhood had a determinant effect on the developmental trajectories of children identified with delays at age three. The "blame the parents" explanation that dominated some twentieth-century clinical theories was dealt a deserving blow by the REACH and CHILD results. And the results indicated that a child with a problem did not inevitably create a problem family, or problems for parents. The divorce rate in both samples was well below the average for the State of California at the time, and most families were managing "well enough" if not as well as they might like. Perhaps the best description of the relationship between child and family outcomes is one suggesting that they are but loosely linked.

Lessons Learned: Working on a Collaborative, Longitudinal, Mixed Methods Research Team

The benefits of multimethods are often lauded, and easy enough to document. The REACH and CHILD projects offer many examples of the benefits:

- Generating fresh and novel hypotheses through qualitative methods that can be tested by quantitative approaches
- Interpreting and describing statistical findings using case materials to illustrate and illuminate
- Using statistical findings as a check on the credibility of anecdotal materials
- Using qualitative materials to question the statistical data that are reliable but perhaps misleading or invalid

The problems encountered by multimethod users in multidisciplinary teams are not so often addressed. Though REACH and CHILD operated successfully for two decades plus, there were challenges. Mix up anthropologists and psychologists, shake vigorously, and from time to time debates arise over methods. Given the importance of disciplines and their apprenticeships for PhD students, it would be surprising if there were no disagreements.

We were lucky to have amiable personalities from all disciplines, but there were at least two reasons the REACH and CHILD team managed to survive so long and produce fifty-plus publications in journals representing a variety of fields, almost all jointly authored. One was an explicit statement of authorship principles, including determining order of authorship. The first principle was "words on paper," meaning authorship is based on authoring, not on status. Secondary considerations were original idea or concept, and original and novel contributions to data analysis. But principles are only as effective as the commitment of collaborators to make discussing authorship an easy topic to bring up—and treat openly as just another issue to systematically analyze.

A second cohesive factor was the shared interest of team members in sustaining the longitudinal sample. Whether an investigator on the team valued the methods of another team member or had some doubts, there was no ambiguity about the value of sustaining the sample. Everyone had a stake in keeping the longitudinal study going, and everyone knew that results and publications were the key to obtaining funding. Because there was enough cohesion in the early project years, everyone eventually saw the value of multimethods. Sooner or later, practitioners of one or another approach found their own study interests aided by the methods of a teammate––even a method that might have been seen as dubious when the project began. An ethnographer eager to claim generality of findings from an intensive examination of a few cases was delighted by confirming statistics. The quantitative-minded psychologist presenting difficult-to-interpret statistics happily and gratefully included rich case descriptions in papers and presentations.

Despite many excellent examples documenting the benefits of mixing methods, "method wars" are likely to continue. Researchers are drawn to the siren call of philosophical debates. Debates are galvanized by academic disciplines treating each other as competitors instead of collaborators. But method disputes are unlikely to be settled in the lifespan of even the youngest investigator, commending the more ecumenical approach taken by REACH and CHILD. Rejecting religious adherence to monomethods in favor of juxtaposing multiple probes using heterogeneous methods is a more promising way to get stable and convergent results across contexts, times, and populations. It is also a better way to get more research done. And if you have amiable colleagues, it's a lot more fun.

Sometimes an ethnographic anecdote provides a project's capstone, an anecdote that even the most committed quantitative researcher is fond of citing. It provides a pithy summary of why certain choices were made and what was learned. For the REACH and CHILD team, if asked why the focus on families' daily routines and the accommo-dations they make to sustain them, we quote this mother from our study: "Professionals keep asking me what I need, I tell them 'just ask me what I do from the time I get up in the morning to the time I go to bed at night.'"

References

Bernheimer, Lucinda P., and Barbara K. Keogh. 1982. *Research on the Early Abilities of Children with Handicaps*. (Final report: longitudinal sample). Los Angeles: University of California.

Gallimore, Ronald, Thomas S. Weisner, Kazuo Nihira, Barbara K. Keogh, Lu-cinda P. Bernheimer, and Iris T. Mink.1983. "Ecocultural Opportunity and Family Accommodation to Developmentally Delayed Children." (Research proposal submitted to the National Institute of Child Health and Human Development). University of California, Los Angeles, Sociobehavioral Research Group, Mental Retardation Research Center.

Glidden, Laraine. M. 1993. "What We Do Not Know about Families with Chil-dren Who Have Developmental Disabilities: Questionnaire on Resources and Stress as a Case Study." *American Journal on Mental Retardation* 97: 481–95.

Harkness, Sara, and Charles M. Super. 1994. "The Developmental Niche: A The-oretical Framework for Analyzing the Household Production of Health." *Social Science and Medicine* 38: 218–26.

Weisner, Thomas, S. 1984. "Ecocultural Niches of Middle Childhood: A Cross-Cultural Perspective." In *Development During Middle Childhood: The Years from Six to Twelve*, edited by W. Andrew Collins, 335–69. Washington, DC: National Academies Press.

Weisner, Thomas S., Jennifer J. Coots, Lucinda P. Bernheimer, and Angela Arzubiaga. 1997. *Ecocultural Family Interview Manual*. Ecocultural Scale Project, University of California, Los Angeles.

Weisner, Thomas S., Catherine Matheson, Jennifer Coots, and Ronald Galli-more. 1997. "Sustainability of Daily Routines as a Family Outcome." Paper presented at Society for Research in Child Development, Washington, DC, April.

REACH and CHILD Key Publications

Bernheimer, Lucinda P., and Barbara K. Keogh. 1986. "Developmental Disabili-ties in Preschool Children." In *Advances in Special Education*, vol. 5, edited by Barbara K. Keogh, 61–93. Greenwich, CT: JAI Press.

———. 1988. "Stability of Cognitive Performance of Children with Developmental Delays." *American Journal on Mental Retardation* 92 (6): 539–42.

———. 1995. "Weaving Interventions into the Fabric of Everyday Life: An Approach to Family Assessment." *Topics in Early Childhood Special Education* 15 (4): 415–33.

Bernheimer, Lucinda P., and Thomas S. Weisner. 2007. "'Let Me Just Tell You What I Do All Day . . .': The Family Story at the Center of Intervention Research and Practice." *Infants and Young Children* 20 (3): 192–201.

Bernheimer, Lucinda P., Barbara K. Keogh, and Jennifer J. Coots. 1993. "From Research to Practice: Support for Developmental Delay as a Preschool Category of Exceptionality." *Journal of Early Intervention* 17 (2): 97–106.

Bernheimer, Lucinda P., Barbara K. Keogh, Donald Guthrie, and Frank Floyd. 2006. "Young Children with Developmental Delays as Young Adults: Predicting Developmental and Personal-Social Outcomes." *American Journal on Mental Retardation* 111 (4), July 1: 263–72.

Bernheimer, Lucinda P., Ronald Gallimore, and Sandra Z. Kaufman. 1993. "Clinical Assessment in a Family Context: A Four-Group Typology of Family Experiences with Young Children with Developmental Delays." *Journal of Early Intervention* 17 (3): 253–69.

Bernheimer, Lucinda P., Ronald Gallimore, and Thomas S. Weisner. 1990. "Ecocultural Theory as a Context for the Individual Family Service Plan." *Journal of Early Intervention* 14 (3): 219–33.

Clare, Lindsay, and Helen Garnier. 2000. "Parents' Goals for Adolescents Diagnosed with Developmental Delays in Early Childhood." *Journal of Early Adolescence* 20 (4): 442–66.

Clare, Lindsay, Helen Garnier, and Ronald Gallimore. 1998. "Parents' Developmental Expectations and Child Characteristics: Longitudinal Study of Children with Developmental Delays and Their Families." *American Journal on Mental Retardation* 103 (2), April 1: 117–29.

Coots, Jennifer J. 1998. "Family Resources and Parent Participation in Schooling Activities for Their Children with Developmental Delays." *The Journal of Special Education* Winter 31 (4): 498–520.

Gallimore, Ronald, Barbara K. Keogh, and Lucinda P. Bernheimer. 1999. "The Nature and Long-Term Implications of Early Developmental Delays: A Summary of Evidence from Two Longitudinal Studies." *International Review of Research in Mental Retardation* 22: 105–35.

Gallimore, Ronald, Jennifer J. Coots, Thomas S. Weisner, Helen E. Garnier, and Donald Guthrie. 1996. "Family Responses to Children with Early Developmental Delays II: Accommodation Intensity and Activity in Early and Middle Childhood." *American Journal on Mental Retardation* 101(3): 215–32.

Gallimore, Ronald, Lucinda P. Bernheimer, and Thomas S. Weisner. 1999. "Family Life Is More Than Managing Crisis: Broadening the Agenda of Research on Families Adapting to Childhood Disability." In *Developmental Perspectives on High Incidence Handicapping Conditions: Papers in Honor* of *Barbara K. Keogh,* edited by Ronald Gallimore, Lucinda P. Bernheimer, Donald L. MacMillan, Deborah L. Speece, and Sharon Vaughn, 55–80. Mahwah, NJ: Erlbaum and Associates.

Gallimore, Ronald, Lucinda P. Bernheimer, Donald L. MacMillan, Deborah L. Speece, and Sharon Vaughn, eds. 1999. *Developmental Perspectives on High Incidence Handicapping Conditions: Papers in Honor of Barbara K. Keogh.* Mahwah, NJ: Erlbaum and Associates.

Gallimore, Ronald, Thomas S. Weisner, Donald Guthrie, Lucinda P. Bernheimer, and Kazuo Nihira. 1993. "Family Responses to Young Children with Developmental Delays: Accommodation Activity in Ecological and Cultural Context." *American Journal on Mental Retardation* 98 (2): 185–206.

Gallimore, Ronald, Thomas S. Weisner, Sandra Z. Kaufman, and Lucinda P. Bernheimer. 1989. "The Social Construction of Ecocultural Niches: Family Accommodation of Developmentally Delayed Children." *American Journal on Mental Retardation* 94 (3): 216–30.

Hecht, Barbara F., Harold G. Levine, and Ann B. Mastergeorge. 1993. "Conversational Roles of Children with Developmental Delays and Their Mothers in Natural and Semi-Structured Situations." *American Journal on Mental Retardation* 27 (4): 419–30.

Juvonen, Jaana, Barbara K. Keogh, Cynthia Ratekin, and Lucinda P. Bernheimer. 1992. "Children's and Teachers' Views of School-Based Competencies and Their Relation to Children's Peer Status." *School Psychology Review* 21 (3): 410–22.

Kaufman, Sandra. 1988. *Retarded Isn't Stupid, Mom!* Baltimore: Paul H. Brookes Publishing Co.

Keogh, Barbara K. 1999. "Reflections on a Research Career: One Thing Leads to Another." *Exceptional Children* 65 (3): 295–300.

Keogh, Barbara K., and Lucinda P. Bernheimer. 1987. "Developmental Delays in Preschool School Children: Assessment over Time." *European Journal of Special Needs Education* 2 (4): 211–220.

———.1995. "Etiologic Conditions as Predictors of Children's Problems and Competencies in Elementary School." *Journal of Child Neurology* 10 (suppl. 1): S100–105.

———.1998. "Concordance between Mothers' and Teachers' Perceptions of Behavior Problems of Children with Developmental Delays." *Journal of Emotional and Behavioral Disorders* 6 (1): 33–41.

———.1998. "Issues and Dilemmas in Longitudinal Research: A Tale of Two Studies." *Thalamus* 16: 5–13.

Keogh, Barbara K., and Nancy D. Burstein. 1988. "Relationship of Preschoolers' Temperament to Interactions with Peers and Teachers." *Exceptional Children* 54 (5): 69–73.

Keogh, Barbara K., Jennifer J. Coots, and Lucinda P. Bernheimer. 1996. "School Placement of Children with Nonspecific Developmental Delays." *Journal of Early Intervention* 20 (1): 65–97.

Keogh, Barbara K., Lucinda P. Bernheimer, and Donald Guthrie. 1997. "Stability and Change over Time in Cognitive Level of Children with Delays." *American Journal on Mental Retardation* 101: 365–73.

———. 2004. "Children with Developmental Delays Twenty Years Later: Where Are They? How Are They?" *American Journal on Mental Retardation* 109 (3): 219–30.

Keogh, Barbara K., Lucinda P. Bernheimer, Ronald Gallimore, and Thomas S. Weisner. 1998. "Child and Family Outcomes over Time: A Longitudinal Perspective on Developmental Delay." In *Families, Risk, and Competence*, edited by Michael Lewis and Candice Feiring, 269–87. Mahwah, NJ: Erlbaum and Associates.

Keogh, Barbara K., Lucinda P. Bernheimer, Steven Daley, and Michele Haney. 1989. "Behaviour and Adjustment Problems of Young Developmentally Delayed Children." *European Journal of Special Needs Education* 4 (2): 79–90.

Nihira, Kazuo, Thomas S. Weisner, and Lucinda P. Bernheimer. 1994. "Ecocultural Assessment in Families of Children with Developmental Delays: Construct and Concurrent Validities." *American Journal on Mental Retardation* 98 (5): 551–66.

Schneider, Phyllis, and Maryl Gearhart. 1988. "The Ecocultural Niche of Families with Mentally Retarded Children: Evidence from Mother-Child Interaction Studies." *Journal of Applied Developmental Psychology* 9 (1), January: 85–106.

Schneider, Phyllis, and Michele Haney. 1992. "Relation of Child Behavior and Activity Type to Maternal Directiveness and Sensitivity in Interactions Involving Preschoolers Who Are Developmentally Delayed." *Developmental Disabilities Bulletin* 20 (2): 13–23.

Schneider, Phyllis, Thomas S. Weisner, and Ronald Gallimore. 1997. "Family and Child Factors Contributing to 'Successful Story Time Interactions' with Children with Developmental Delays." *Developmental Disabilities Bulletin* 250: 33–49.

Weisner, Thomas S. 1993. "Ethnographic and Ecocultural Perspectives on Sibling Relationship." In *The Effects of Mental Retardation, Physical Disabilities and Chronic Illness on Sibling Relationships*, edited by Zolinda Stoneman and Phyllis W. Berman, 51–84. Baltimore: Paul H. Brookes.

Weisner, Thomas S., and Ronald Gallimore. 1989. "Ecocultural Niche of Families with Developmentally Delayed Children." Paper presented at the Society for Research in Child Development, Kansas City, April.

———.1994. "Ecocultural Studies of Families Adapting to Childhood Developmental Delays: Unique Features, Defining Differences, and Applied Implications." In *Family in Focus: New Perspectives on Early Childhood Special Education*, edited by Matti Leskinen, 11–25. Jyväskylä, Finland: University of Jyväskylä, Finland Studies in Education, Psychology, and Social Research 10.

Weisner, Thomas S., Catherine Matheson, and Lucinda Bernheimer. 1996.

"American Cultural Models of Early Influence and Parent Recognition of Developmental Delays: Is Earlier Always Better Than Later?" In *Parents' Cultural Belief Systems: Their Origins, Expressions and Consequences*, edited by Sara Harkness and Charles M. Super, 496–531. New York: Guilford Press.

Weisner, Thomas S., Catherine Matheson, Jennifer Coots, and Lucinda P. Bernheimer. 2004. "Sustainability of Daily Routines as a Family Outcome." In *Learning in Cultural Context: Family, Peers and School*, edited by Ashley Maynard and Mary Martini, 41–73. New York: Kluwer/Plenum.

Weisner, Thomas S., Laura Beizer, and Lori Stolze. 1991. "Religion and Families of Children with Developmental Delays." *American Journal on Mental Retardation* 95 (6): 647–62.

Westerman, Christien, Barbara K. Keogh, and Lucinda P. Bernheimer. 1997. "Factors Related to the Selection and Use of Services for Young Children with Developmental Delays." *European Journal of Special Needs Education* 12 (1), March 1: 30–37.

Appendix 16.1

Ecocultural Dimensions (Weisner 1984)

Work and subsistence
Health and demographic circumstances
Community safety
The divisions of work by gender and age
Children's participation in the routine
Children's and parents' workloads
Organization of child care
Children's friendships, peers, and playgroups
Roles of, and supports for, women
Role of fathers
Diversity and sources of information and cultural influences on children
Parental sources of information
Community heterogeneity and diversity of models for family and child care

Appendix 16.2

Ecocultural Domains with Sample Items (Weisner, Coots et al. 1997)

Socioeconomic status
    Overall resilience of subsistence base
    Family can afford services

Services

    Level of family activity focused on special services

    Amount of action in response to child's diagnosis

Home

    Use of neighborhood places and services

    Safety of neighborhood for child

Domestic workload

    Family arranges schedule around child

    Father participation in child care

Connectedness

    Overall agreement/consistency between parents

    Couple has grown closer because of child

Nondisabled network

    Child's participation in peer groups

    Extent to which child is integrated

Disabled networks

    Family involvement with disability groups

    Child involvement in disability groups

Diversity

    Ethnic diversity of school

    Diversity of family social network

Support

    Support from spouse

    Religion gives meaning to having a child with delays

Information

    Family activity on accessing sources of information

    Information received re: diagnosis and level of functioning

PART SIX

Mixed Methods for Intervention and Policy-Driven Research

Mixed Methods in the Science of Understanding Antipoverty Policies for Families with Children: Four Case Studies

ALETHA C. HUSTON, GREG J. DUNCAN, AND HIROKAZU YOSHIKAWA

Despite a number of successful examples (e.g., Weisner 2005; Yoshikawa, Weisner, and Lowe 2006), mixing quantitative and qualitative methods is not easy. Young children's peer interactions provide a useful metaphor for describing different levels of mixing methods (Huston 2012). The least interactive is parallel play—when children may be side-by-side but their activities are essentially independent of one another; an academic example might be a conference in which both types of data are presented by different investigators. Associative play occurs when children's activities involve the same set of materials but are independent of one another. Research projects with both quantitative and qualitative components may fall in this category if the two approaches are pursued relatively independently, or if the results of ethnographies are used primarily as stories to illustrate quantitative findings.

At the most integrative end of the spectrum is cooperative play, which involves interdependent interactions, for example when children work together with blocks to construct a tower. Reaching truly integrated scholarship at this level involves interactions among methods and investigators in which each builds on and is responsive to the others (Duncan 2012; Huston 2008; Yoshikawa et al. 2008). Overcoming methodological silos with such integrative research is especially important for policy-oriented investigations, both because truly mixed methods offer a more complete understanding of the processes involved and because they can have more impact on policymakers than does either method alone.

In this chapter we illustrate some of the advantages and difficulties of mixing quantitative and qualitative methods, using four large-scale investigations of families in poverty. In the concluding section, we summarize the ways in which integrated methods have contributed to better understanding of the phenomena of interest, and hence to better science. Finally, we discuss the features of research that promote or hinder successful mixed methods research.

Four Mixed Methods Case Studies

Two of our four examples are evaluations of policy interventions, and two are more general studies related to welfare programs and immigration reform in the United States. We first describe the Three City Study, with mixed methods that might best be categorized as associative play. It was developed in the aftermath of the 1996 changes in the federal welfare law. Its quantitative component, directed by Andrew Cherlin, consisted of a longitudinal survey of families living in low-income neighborhoods in three US cities. Linda Burton directed the qualitative component, which drew its participants independently of the survey sample.

A second evaluation study, Moving to Opportunity (MTO), tested for impacts of a residential mobility program in which families living in public housing in five US cities were randomly assigned to three groups, two of which received housing vouchers that enabled them to move to private-market housing in better neighborhoods. Several qualitative studies, coordinated by Susan Popkin at the Urban Institute (in Los Angeles and New York) and Lawrence Katz, Jeffrey Kling, and Jeffrey Liebman (in Boston), were conducted in the early years of the program (Popkin, Leventhal, and Weismann 2010; Kling, Ludwig, and Katz 2005). The one that was most integrated with the quantitative component, directed by Kathryn Edin, selected both treatment and control families at random and gathered extensive, open-ended information about their lives.

The third study is the New Hope Project, which tested the efficacy of a package of work supports for improving the lives of low-income working families and their children, and employed a highly integrated mixed methods design. Thomas Weisner directed the embedded ethnographic study of forty-three families drawn at random from both treatment and control groups.

Finally, the MetroBaby Study is a birth cohort study of citizen children of immigrants. The topic of undocumented status of parents, its relationship to the parents' interactions with policy settings, and the potential effects of the status on children emerged from a three-year ethnography, directed by Hirokazu Yoshikawa, embedded within a larger survey and a developmental study codirected by Catherine Tamis-LeMonda and Yoshikawa.

The Three-City Study

"Welfare, Children and Families, A Three-City Study" was launched in Boston, Chicago, and San Antonio in response to dramatic changes in the federal welfare laws passed in 1996. The major purposes of the study were to "assess the well-being of low-income children and families in the post-welfare reform era" (http://web.jhu.edu/threecitystudy). The study was concentrated on such domains as welfare, health insurance, child care, and employment, all of which were likely to be affected by changes in public policies. It was composed of a longitudinal survey, an embedded developmental study, and an intensive ethnographic study.

The overall study was coordinated by Andrew Cherlin, with PIs (principal investigators) for the surveys and ethnographies in each site. Wave One of the longitudinal survey was conducted in 1999 on a random sample of 2,400 families in low-income neighborhoods who had a focal child age zero to four or ten to fourteen years old. Waves Two and Three were collected approximately eighteen months and five years after Wave One. Surveys, administrative data on parents' employment and welfare histories, school records, and teacher reports were collected for the focal children. For all focal children in the two to four age range, observations of mother-child interactions, observations of nonparental child care settings, and father interviews were obtained.

Between 1999 and 2003, 256 families participated in a longitudinal ethnography led by Linda Burton, with a PI in each city. Most families were selected because they included a child age two to four, but a small sample was recruited because they had a child with a disability. The method of "structured discovery" was used, in which in-depth interviews and observations were focused on specific topics but allowed flexibility to capture unexpected findings and relationships (http://web .jhu.edu/threecitystudy/Study_Design/ethnography.html).

Unlike the other three studies we discuss, the ethnographic sample was not part of the survey sample, but was recruited nonrandomly through institutions in the neighborhoods where survey members lived (e.g., Head Start centers, WIC clinics). Although it may be reasonable to assume that their characteristics were similar to those of the survey sample, these individuals by definition had a connection to at least one institution in their community. This sampling method reduced chances that the survey and ethnographic responses would bias each other, but it also precluded comparing both types of information for the same individuals. Moreover, separate teams collected and analyzed the data from the two substudies. Although most publications from the study drew data from only one of the two sources of data, we describe some examples in which data from the two methods were integrated.

Examples of Mixing Methods in the Three-City Study

In *Poor Families in America's Health Care Crisis* (Angel, Lein, and Henrici 2006), survey and ethnographic data are presented in tandem to document the major theme of instability of families' experiences with the health care system, employment, and social programs. Surveys show, for example, frequent changes in health care coverage; the ethnographies describe the complexity of families' efforts to obtain and maintain insurance for different family members to whom different eligibility criteria often apply. Although some instability of insurance is evident in the survey responses at two time points, the ethnographic accounts show even more instability because they are collected frequently and in depth.

The ethnographies also help to clarify and problematize answers to apparently straightforward survey questions. For example, the answer to "Are you employed?" turns out to be ambiguous; does one count a job that the person thinks she has, but hasn't worked at yet? "Do you/ your child have health insurance? Does your child get Medicaid?" People often are uncertain about their coverage. Parents sometimes believe their child is covered, only to find out that the application never got processed because it lacked one piece of documentation.

Survey analyses were in turn informed by the ethnographic data that suggested the importance of state policy, marital status, and ethnicity. All of these emerged as important predictors of health insurance coverage even with other factors controlled.

Contributions of the Ethnography

The "discovery" mode of the ethnographies allowed topics to arise that were not included in the survey. For example, parents used extensive strategies to obtain insurance and to juggle schedules and resources, yet they felt powerless in the face of the many obstacles they faced. As the authors note, "Quantitative studies provide information on the patterning of social phenomena; qualitative studies provide deeper insights into the forces that give rise to those patterns and the subjective reality that lies behind them" (Angel, Lein, and Henrici 2006, 15).

Ethnographies can elicit sensitive information not readily provided on a survey, and, when the two methods produce similar results, the correspondence between them adds credence to the findings. For example, as repeated ethnographic interviews progressed, more and more respondents talked about physical or sexual abuse in childhood and adulthood. Only 10 percent mentioned it initially in response to semi-structured questions, but the information came out gradually, often in response to apparently unrelated questions about health, employment, and children. Overall, sixty-four percent of the women interviewed reported physical or sexual abuse in childhood or adulthood, and often in both. On the survey, fifty-two percent of respondents reported some abuse on questions asking directly about it (Cherlin et al. 2004). Although the numbers were slightly higher in the ethnography, the overall pattern of high rates of abuse is evident in both types of data, and some of the differences might be attributed to the different ways in which the two groups were selected.

Ethnographies can also identify the salience of survey topics for respondents. In a test of hypotheses about the reasons for low-income women's reluctance to marry, some survey questions addressed women's beliefs that marriages end in divorce. Few women spontaneously mentioned divorce in ethnographic interviews, suggesting that it was not a salient issue for them. When asked directly, about one-quarter of the ethnographic and survey samples thought that divorce or breakups were likely in marriage (Cherlin et al. 2008).

The ethnographic interviews were conducted frequently, providing fine-grained information about the changes that families experienced over time. The quantitative surveys comprised three widely-spaced waves, and many of the survey-based publications report on only two times of measurement, limiting their ability to detect changes. One analysis described the types of union with men. In the ethnography, these were classified a priori as sustained and transitory, but a third category, "abated union" (not in union for a year and don't plan to be) emerged in the ethnographic interviews. The three categories were useful in distinguishing women's attitudes and beliefs about marriage and about men in general. Because only one wave of the survey was available, unions could be classified only on their current status as married, cohabiting, or not in a union (Cherlin et al. 2004).

The Moving to Opportunity Program[1]

The Moving to Opportunity for Fair Housing (MTO) demonstration program was designed to answer the question: What are the long-term effects of moving poor families out of subsidized housing in high-poverty communities and into low-poverty neighborhoods (Orr et al. 2003)? In five cities—Baltimore, Boston, Chicago, Los Angeles, and New York—families were randomly assigned to three groups: experimental, Section 8, and control. The experimental group received housing vouchers to relocate to neighborhoods (census tracts) with poverty rates less than 10 percent, assistance in finding a unit, and housing counseling to help them prepare for the move to the private-rental market. The Section 8 group received conventional Section 8 housing vouchers, counseling, and other assistance, but could relocate to any type of community, regardless of how many low-income residents it had. The control group received no vouchers, only the usual project-based assistance. We concentrate on the contrasts between families in the experimental and control groups.

The MTO quantitative evaluation was based on both survey and administrative data. Surveys were conducted at baseline (just prior to randomization), four to seven years after random assignment (interim), and ten to fifteen years after random assignment (final). Baseline interviews were conducted with parents (usually the mother); interim and final interviews were conducted with both parents and study youth. Administrative data on employment and welfare benefits were collected for the entire study period.

Although several qualitative investigations were conducted, we concentrate on Kathryn Edin's study, which was closely coordinated with the quantitative data collection. It consisted of transcripts and field notes from in-depth, semistructured interviews with a stratified random subsample of families in the Baltimore site. All three program groups were sampled evenly across three household types: (a) children ages eight–thirteen years, (b) children ages eight–thirteen years and fourteen–nineteen years, and (c) children ages fourteen–nineteen years. The interviews were tape recorded, transcribed, coded thematically, and entered into a database by theme. Subsequent coding and analysis allowed the investigators to take the inductive approach that is a hallmark of qualitative work, exploring the relationships of neighborhood characteristics to employment and earnings across the program groups.

How Mixed Methods Helped to Understand the Moving to Opportunity Program

Why didn't MTO boost employment? Boosting employment was expected to be a key potential benefit of offering families living in public housing the chance to move to better neighborhoods (Orr et al. 2003). But both the MTO interim and final evaluations showed that experimental and control families differed little across a range of employment and earnings measures. Qualitative evidence, as well as a consideration of the policy context in which MTO was implemented, helps to illuminate mechanisms that were not initially in the MTO logic model.

Turney et al. (2006) examined employment patterns from the MTO Baltimore site, using data from both the interim quantitative survey and the embedded qualitative study of families in Baltimore. They discovered several reasons why mothers in the experimental-voucher condition might not have benefited from their new communities, relative to the controls, and why the controls might have perceived some advantages.

First, experimental-group women in new neighborhoods perceived their neighbors as working in jobs (e.g., office workers, police officers, lawyers) that required more education than they possessed. Although forty percent of these women had either two- or four-year college degrees or training certificates (e.g., as home health aides, pharmacy technicians), their perceptions about the higher status of their neighbors' employment often made the women reluctant to ask neighbors about job information.

Second, for some movers, ill health interfered with their ability to obtain and/or maintain employment. All of the long-term unemployed movers cited debilitating health issues, often several at the same time, as the causes of their lack of labor-market participation. One woman in the experimental group reported suffering from panic attacks in addition to having HIV, diabetes, and depression; another reported having a nervous breakdown and suffering from depression; and others complained of severe arthritis. Although MTO had positive impacts on mental health, which may have enabled some experimental group members to take jobs, the striking set of health problems undoubtedly limited the scope of MTO's potential employment impacts.

Third, the majorities of both control and experimental families in the qualitative study reported hearing about or getting their jobs through weak ties—ties to people with similar educational levels and jobs as MTO participants. Although women in the control group had lower numbers of employed social ties in their communities, they were more likely to run into these individuals as they went about their daily routines (e.g., work, commuting to work or school, shopping) than experimental movers.

Fourth, in contrast to predictions from theories of "spatial mismatch,"[2] experimental families' new neighborhoods were also farther away from the jobs they would typically apply for, based on their education and skill levels. Some experimental movers reported a lack of adequate public transportation as an employment barrier, and the distance from their original neighborhoods put families farther away from their social support networks, which had been important for providing some of their transportation and child care in the past.

How Housing Choice Relates to School Quality

The first quantitative results from MTO's Baltimore site suggested that moves to better neighborhoods led to improvements in children's test scores and school behaviors (Ludwig, Ladd, and Duncan 2001), but the interim and final data collections showed no educational benefits and surprisingly small improvements in school quality for youth in the experimental group (Orr et al. 2003; Sanbonmatsu et al. 2006; Sanbonmatsu et al. 2011). Although a handful of the Baltimore MTO children attended high-performing, affluent schools in surrounding suburban counties, the vast majority either remained in their original city schools or relocated to other low-performing schools (a result more or less replicated in all five MTO cities). Why did this happen?

Solving these education-related mysteries was an important priority for the Baltimore qualitative team when it entered the field in 2003. Fieldworkers talked to the teachers of children in the MTO families, observed classrooms, and asked parents about homework and school quality. When researchers began to analyze these interviews, the question that arose was not so much "why didn't test scores improve?" but rather, "why didn't school quality improve?" In a mixed methods study, DeLuca and Rosenblatt (2010) combined surveys, data from Geographic Information Systems (GIS) and in-depth interviews to examine one of the main assumptions of the MTO program and the primary mechanism through which educational effects were theorized to occur: that better housing opportunities would lead to access to and attendance at better schools. They discovered that about a third of the parents were resistant to transferring their children because they thought it would be too disruptive for them and too hard for them to be away from familiar faces.

Despite some structural impediments to such moves from reluctant landlords, MTO mothers could have increased the quality of their children's schools more than they did. The most striking explanation was that two-thirds of the parents in the qualitative study believed that school quality mattered less for learning than a child's work effort and "good attitude." Parents like Tisha, an experimental mover and mother of two children, who attended the zone school back in their city neighborhood, explained: "That school is crazy. I have to pray for her, it's like I send my child to hell every day and then I expect her to get good grades and learn. But like I said it's up to the individual 'cause she could separate herself from that and she could get what she needs. And she could keep going or she could fall into that crowd to which she's a follower and she'll mess herself up."

For many poor families, moving priorities began with proximity to transportation, family members, and mothers' jobs—with schools often coming after these, if at all. Even when parents did take school characteristics into account, they sought a sense of comfort and a welcoming atmosphere as well as such nonacademic features as uniforms, security guards, and disciplinary policies. These considerations make sense, given that children were coming from chaotic, violent city schools. School decisions based on these characteristics were unlikely to result in higher academic quality.

The New Hope Program[3]

Our third example, also illustrating mixed methods cooperative play, is New Hope, an employment-based poverty reduction intervention in Milwaukee, Wisconsin, which offered its participants a comprehensive package of benefits. In exchange for work effort of thirty hours a week, participants were eligible for four benefits: (a) a wage supplement that increased family income; (b) subsidized health insurance; (c) a child-care subsidy; and (d) access to a community service job for two renewable periods of up to six months each, if a private sector job could not be found. A final, less tangible, benefit was that New Hope had competent and caring "project representatives," who offered intensive case management as well as emotional and instrumental support to participants who chose to take advantage of it.

Although its designers conceived of New Hope as a permanent package of benefits to which low-income working families should be entitled, budget realities limited its duration to three years and its geographic scope to two low-income neighborhoods. One neighborhood was predominantly African American; the other was primarily Hispanic. Individuals interested in the program attended an orientation session at which benefits were explained as well as the fact that a lottery would be run and half of them would be assigned to a "control" group that did not receive any of the New Hope benefits. Between August 1994 and December 1995, the New Hope project enrolled and assigned 1,357 participants. By all accounts, the program was well implemented (Brock et al. 1997).

The New Hope Evaluation

The evaluation of program impacts on work, family life, and child well-being was based on data gathered from both quantitative and qualitative sources. Thomas Weisner directed the qualitative substudy, while Huston and Duncan, with Robert Granger and other members of the MacArthur Network on Successful Pathways Through Middle Childhood, designed the quantitative Child and Family Survey (CFS) of 743 families, with children from age one to ten years at baseline. Yoshikawa directed an effort that analyzed New Hope's mixed methods data on work and family life (Yoshikawa, Weisner, and Lowe 2006). The quantitative data came from a baseline questionnaire, extensive surveys administered two, five, and eight years after random assignment, questionnaires to teachers of school-age children (five–twelve years old), and administrative data on earnings and receipt of benefits from the state welfare and food stamp programs.

The qualitative data came from the New Hope Ethnographic Study (NHES), a longitudinal study of forty-three families drawn equally from the experimental and control groups in the CFS, who were randomly sampled from the families with children aged one–ten at baseline. Because of funding constraints, the NHES began only in the program's third year of operation. Fieldworkers, in their monthly visits to families, listened to parents tell their stories, conducted participant observation in homes, took families out for lunch and dinner, went with them to church, and visited children's schools.

To guide the topics of these visits, researchers generated a set of topics that explored a family's daily activities and routines as well as beliefs and values (Weisner 2002). Fieldworkers systematically asked every ethnographic sample member about job search and work experiences, household budgets, parenting and child care concerns and decisions, partners and marriage, religion, and many other topics. They learned about families' ecocultural circumstances (Weisner 2002), beliefs, and intentions about these domains. Fieldworkers organized their notes using a template containing main headings (e.g., barriers to employment) and subheadings (e.g., alcohol/substance abuse).

Analysts used the web-based qualitative software Dedoose.com, so that everyone on the research team could use the field notes and interviews, and index and code them online (Lieber, Weisner, and Presley 2003; Lieber and Weisner 2010). Interviews and field notes were indexed and coded, with coding reliabilities averaging Kappa = .83. Several of the fieldwork team members were involved in the analysis of the quantitative data and assisted in the integration of quantitative and qualitative evidence.

Because the qualitative subsample was drawn from the larger set of participants, we were able to draw from the demographic data, New Hope experiences, and child measures for the participants. For each part of the New Hope story, analysts were able to draw on the qualitative data from the forty-three families to help understand the program and how participants experienced New Hope in the contexts of work and family life (Duncan, Huston, and Weisner 2007).

How Mixing Methods Enriched Our Understanding of New Hope

Understanding Program Impacts

One of the most important—and initially puzzling—impacts of New Hope concerned the teacher-reported achievement and behavior of pre-adolescent children. In the experimental group, boys, but not girls, were rated by their teachers as substantially better behaved and higher achieving than their control-group counterparts. Based on the survey data alone, however, we were unable to understand why the New Hope program, focused as it was on the parents' work and income, should have such differential impacts for boys and girls.

The qualitative data suggested that mothers believed that gangs and other neighborhood pressures were much more threatening to their elementary-school boys than to girls. As a response to these pressures, mothers in the experimental group channeled more of the program's resources (e.g., child care subsidies for extended-day programs) to their boys. A thirty-five-year-old African American mother of four, quoted in the field notes, observed: "Not all places have gangs, but [my neighborhood] is infested with gangs and drugs and violence. My son, I worry about him. He may be veering in the wrong direction . . . it's different for girls. For boys, it's dangerous. [Gangs are] full of older men who want these young ones to do their dirty work. And they'll buy them things and give them money."

Similar sentiments appeared consistently in the qualitative data. Further quantitative analyses of both New Hope and national-sample survey data that were stimulated by the qualitative results support the interpretation that parents living in bad neighborhoods do indeed devote differential time and other resources to their boys relative to their girls (Snell et al. 2012). Ethnographic data proved crucial for generating this insight.

In another example, qualitative data served to supplement and explain an unexpected and substantial New Hope impact: increasing marriage among initially never-married mothers (Gassman-Pines, Yoshikawa, and Nay 2006). Unmarried respondents in the ethnographic study often said that they would need to feel more economically independent before they got married, providing an explanation of why a program focused largely on economic household factors might have increased marriage.

Which families benefited the most? Qualitative interviews demonstrated important heterogeneity among the experimental families. Some, perhaps one-fifth, appeared to have so many barriers to employment (e.g., no high school degree, many young children, a criminal record) that New Hope's package of economic benefits was unlikely to be sufficient to overcome all of these barriers. A second group was at the other end of the spectrum: they had none of these barriers and were able to sustain employment on their own. Control families in this group might be expected to do so well in Milwaukee's job-rich environment that it would be difficult for comparable experimental parents to do better.

A third group, however, with only one of the problems of the sort that New Hope might be able to address (e.g., difficulties in arranging for child care, a minor criminal record that experience in a community-service job could overcome) appeared poised to profit from the New Hope package of benefits. Extensive quantitative work on subgroups defined according to the number of potential employment-related barriers at the beginning of the program confirmed the wisdom of these qualitatively derived insights.

Using data gathered from the baseline interviews, Magnuson (1999) constructed an index of potential employment barriers based on past history of employment, completed schooling, arrests, and the presence of either many or very young children. Experimental members who had either no barriers or multiple barriers did not earn a significantly different amount than their control counterparts. Program impacts on the earnings of families with only one barrier, however, were large and statistically significant in both the two- and five-year follow-ups.

The qualitative data were also valuable for subsequent data collection. When the ethnographic work began, we discovered that certain aspects of family functioning were measured poorly in the two-year follow-up survey. Lessons learned in the ongoing qualitative interviews informed the five- and eight-year surveys. By listening to how New Hope families understood their daily routines, we constructed quantitative measures that offered a more complete account of family well-being, including the role of male partners, beliefs about the welfare system, budget questions, and the role of family support. For example, the ethnographic work revealed that the presence of troubled children and inflexible jobs accounted for some of the variance in labor force participation, leading us to expand the measures of job attitudes on the five-year survey to include these content areas.

Iterating Between Quantitative and Qualitative Data

The beauty of ethnographic work is that the data provide detail on topics that cannot be fully explored by survey data. If, however, there is no larger data set on which to test a hypothesis, then qualitative findings are limited in their generalizability and replicability. If both types of data are present, then one can use the qualitative data to explore program dimensions, which can then be analyzed in the larger survey data. An example is the take-up of New Hope benefits by program participants. The intent of New Hope was to centralize assistance for participants, so that they did not have to deal with several different agencies to receive services (Brock et al. 1997). Soon after the qualitative study began, however, fieldworkers noticed that very few families used the program as was intended (as a continuously used bundle of benefits); most used individual benefits selectively and intermittently.

Both New Hope evaluators and designers were puzzled by this disconnect between program intent and use. A systematic qualitative analysis of benefit usage by experimental members of the NHES revealed that participants assessed the advantages of New Hope according to different standards (Gibson and Weisner 2000). Some evaluated it in cost-benefit terms (e.g., the advantages of receiving the supplements versus the demands of working full-time), while others measured its usefulness by how well the program coincided with personal ecological concerns (e.g., not using a community-service job because it was considered too demeaning). Gibson (2003) analyzed the larger survey data and found that heterogeneity of program use was related to sociodemographic characteristics at baseline, as fieldworkers had suspected, but also that it shaped the effect that the program had on individual families. These quantitative analyses, however, were undertaken only after the rich qualitative data revealed their likely potential value.

Increased income was one path through which New Hope was expected to improve children's well-being, but the overall improvement in family income was relatively small. Ethnographic observations and analyses of quantitative data offered insight into some of the ways that small increases in resources translated into both material and psychological changes in family life. In the ethnographies, parents reported using added income in two ways: (a) such basics as food, clothing for children, paying the rent, and utilities and (b) "extras" that went beyond minimal survival—for example, birthday and holiday presents and new rather than used clothes for children. They reported that having money for these extras was highly rewarding, making them feel like members of the mainstream society. Once this distinction was identified in the ethnographies, questions in the survey measuring the two types of expenditures were identified. In the survey sample, the expenditures on extras rather than on basics predicted both positive parenting and children's positive social behavior (Mistry et al. 2008).

The MetroBaby Study

Our final example applies to an earlier stage in the policy process—that of policy conceptualization and development. The MetroBaby Study is an investigation of a birth cohort of children of low-income Dominican, Mexican, and Chinese immigrant and US-born African American mothers. The study was designed to understand how culture intersected with such contextual influences as parenting, child care, parental employment, and contact with such policy-relevant programs as welfare, food stamps, and the Women, Infants, and Children (WIC) program. Surveys were collected at birth, six months, and then each year around the child's birthday for the first six years. Home visits with structured and videotaped observational tasks were conducted at one, two, and three years, and lab visits at four, five, and six. A longitudinal ethnographic study was conducted for a sample of twenty-five families, chosen as a random subsample stratified by child gender and ethnicity. These twenty-five families were engaged in participant observation and semistructured interview visits every ten–twelve weeks for three years (the methods had been determined in a prior pilot ethnographic study of twenty additional families, directed by Ajay Chaudry and Hirokazu Yoshikawa). Field notes were taken on every visit, while on every other visit a semistructured protocol was administered, with responses transcribed, translated, and then content-coded for further, in-depth analysis.

What Mixed Methods Contributed to the Study of Parent Undocumented Status and Its Effects on Children

As the ethnography proceeded, comprehensive narratives emerged of many aspects of these parents' experiences making ends meet while raising very young children in the most expensive city in the United States. As the narratives occurred in the context of trusting relationships with fieldworkers speaking the immigrant mothers' native languages, the experience of raising children while being without papers emerged as a powerful and unexpected theme. This topic was not part of the original design of the study or any of its quantitative elements (survey, structured observation). As a "hidden" but increasingly policy-relevant topic, parent undocumented status and its effects on children ultimately became the focus of a mixed methods book (Yoshikawa 2011), which drew both on the longitudinal ethnographic data and iterative successions of the survey data, in which aspects of the parents' experiences related to undocumented status were assessed. This was the first large-scale study to examine how parent undocumented status might affect children, and thus to draw attention to a population—the 4.5 million citizen-children of the undocumented—who could be affected by comprehensive immigration reform.

The ethnography provided rich information about how being an undocumented parent meant staying "under the radar" in multiple contexts, while the quantitative data provided useful numbers to estimate the prevalence of conditions associated with being under the radar. For example, in work contexts, parents gave heart-wrenching narratives of years and in some cases decades of exploitation at work, particularly around lack of overtime pay in the context of extremely long hours, and the fear of asking for a raise from bosses who knew the worker's status. The workers also experienced very low levels of job autonomy, as defined by Department of Labor occupation codes.

The quantitative data confirmed that between thirty and forty percent of mothers and fathers in the groups most likely to be undocumented were working below the minimum wage, depending on the assessment wave. These workers experienced almost no wage growth, in a context where the documented groups (e.g., the African American mothers, who were US-born and therefore citizens) were experiencing robust wage growth generated by a rapidly growing New York City economy.

The survey did not ask directly about citizenship status. A quantitative measure related to the experience of being undocumented, developed from the ethnographic data, represented lack of household access to resources requiring identification (e.g., checking account, savings account, driver's license). The measure was linked to lower rates of children's cognitive development as early as at twenty-four months, parental psychological distress, lower access to center-based child care, and the lower wages and job autonomy that mothers who lacked these resources experienced.

Potential Interventions

The MetroBaby ethnography also pointed toward interventions that might mitigate the harmful effects of parents' undocumented status on young children. For example, undocumented mothers had such low levels of information about community resources for children that some did not know that public libraries existed in New York City. What information they did possess often came from documented immigrants in their neighborhoods with longer histories in the city, whom they met in playgrounds, workplaces, or other community settings. The potential of these weak ties to provide powerful information was striking. When the parents lived near an organization serving immigrant groups with high rates of undocumented status, it made a powerful difference. These organizations provided access to information about programs for which the citizen children were eligible (e.g., food stamps, child care subsidies, Head Start, and public preschool) that might strengthen the children's cognitive development.

As a study that covered citizen children with at least one undocumented parent in the United States (nearly one in three children of immigrant parents), these data have been relevant to current policy. Both the development, and now outreach and implementation, of a New York City policy that provides $18 million in adult education slots for the undocumented who have not applied to Deferred Action for Childhood Arrivals (DACA) were informed by both the ethnographic and quantitative data concerning this population (DACA is the two-year reprieve from deportation implemented by the Obama Administration, which requires high school graduation or current involvement in formal education, both characteristics that undocumented parents are the least likely to have). In particular, lessons about the organizational and network resources that can mitigate the effects of undocumented status are informing plans for outreach in policy implementation.

What Mixed Methods Contribute to Research on Poverty Policy and Human Development

By definition, mixed methods provide a more comprehensive view of the roles of poverty and policy in the lives of low-income families than does either method alone. They enable researchers to identify processes and outcomes and offer an in-depth understanding of changes over time. Ethnographies typically involve frequent data collection that is well suited to detect and describe the nature of changes over time, which can be tested systematically and further informed with quantitative data on large samples. The most effective mixed methods analyses are iterative (or cooperative, in our play metaphor), with each informing the other. Over time, ethnographies can point to topics that were not part of the original conceptualization, which can then be incorporated into surveys; at the same time, survey results can help to identify areas needing more information in subsequent ethnographic data collection.

Identifying Policy Issues

The in-depth, open-ended qualitative methods allow topics and issues to emerge from the respondents. In the Three Cities study, the ethnographic interviews pointed to the issues of policy implementation, identifying how health care policies operated (or failed to operate) on the ground as well as how different policies (e.g., welfare, child care, health care) intersected in the lives of low-income families. In New Hope, a mixed methods analysis identified families most and least likely to benefit from a comprehensive work-support program. Mixed methods applied to the Moving to Opportunity study identified some of the limits of residential-mobility programs that facilitated moves to better neighborhoods but provided no ongoing services to families who moved. In the MetroBaby study, the interviews identified a set of policy issues concerning undocumented parents and led to a focus on the roles of networks and community organizations in implementation of a pathway to citizenship.

Understanding Processes—How Policies Succeed or Fail

Poverty interventions are typically based on an explicit or implicit theory of change—a set of propositions about the processes through which a policy will affect the lives and behavior of people. Mixed methods offer a powerful means of understanding these processes, helping to explain how predicted effects occur as well as why policies fail to produce expected results. Both MTO and New Hope were interventions based on an explicit set of hypotheses about how policies might affect both adults and children. The quantitative studies were informed by models derived from prior research and theory, and the ethnographic studies helped not only to create those models, but to enrich and modify them through the themes that emerged from the participants. In New Hope, for example, the program impacts on center-based child care were one pathway through which effects on achievement and behavior appeared to occur, and the ethnography led to a rich understanding of how and when center-based child care was integrated into family routines. Similarly, the ethnographic data suggested the importance of being able to buy a few "extras" for both parent and child well-being, and the quantitative data confirmed this insight. The impacts of New Hope on marriage were not expected, but were investigated because of themes emerging in the ethnography.

Mixed methods shed light on policy effects and failures by identifying the match or mismatch between the goals of policymakers and the goals of participants. Both MTO and New Hope were designed by policymakers primarily to increase employment. In initial interviews with potential participants in MTO, however, parents talked about wanting to move to escape the violence and crime in their current housing. Given this context, it makes sense that there were no effects of MTO on employment, but there were positive effects on parents' mental health and on adolescent girls' experiences of violence. Although the benefits offered by New Hope were designed to provide employment supports, the ethnographies made it clear that many participants had obligations and priorities other than employment that helped to explain why they did not take advantage of New Hope or why they used its benefits selectively.

We have presented several examples in which mixed methods helped to understand unexpected results. In MTO, children's school performance was unaffected. Both quantitative and qualitative methods determined that the intervention had little effect on school quality, and the ethnography offered a deeper understanding of why parents made particular school choices. In New Hope, the ethnography provided some hypotheses to explain gender differences in impacts on children, which in turn informed later surveys.

Heterogeneity of Individuals

Because of their in-depth focus on individuals, ethnographies are apt to detect variations among groups of people, whereas surveys are more apt to identify the average patterns across individuals. Policymakers often dislike the idea of targeting services, but it could be helpful to know, for example, that the people who benefited most from New Hope were those with one barrier to employment that New Hope could address. In Three Cities, mixed methods helped to identify different types of unions that might have different implications for parents' well-being.

What Makes Mixed Methods Research Possible

Mixed methods are not easy to implement, especially in policy studies. Our four examples are all "big science"—large-scale studies led by several senior investigators from multiple institutions with multiple funding sources. They were made possible because of questions about major government policy changes. In this final section, we extract from our experience some generalizations about what makes it possible to conduct successful mixed methods research.

In all cases, the investigations in our four case studies received funding from both public and private sources and also had strong administrative supports. With the exception of MTO, they were all initiated by groups of senior investigators. MTO was initiated by the Department of Housing and Urban Development (HUD), a federal agency with a specific goal of evaluating housing policy, but the qualitative studies were funded primarily by private foundations. In many instances, the investigators also had access to NICHD-funded Population Research Centers, which provided infrastructures to support the research. The Mac-Arthur Foundation Research Network on Successful Pathways through Middle Childhood was an important catalyst for the New Hope Child and Family Study.

That said, investigators trying to do this type of work face a number of institutional barriers in universities, publication outlets, and funding agencies. As Duncan (2012) noted, one should probably wait until tenure is assured before embarking on a mixed methods investigation, though New Hope produced a number of young scholars who are exceptions to that rule. Despite lip service to interdisciplinary scholarship, most universities are discipline based; a faculty member is rewarded for professional recognition and publication in her/his own discipline. Many journals and granting agencies are unreceptive to methods outside their core discipline, making it difficult to obtain funding and to identify appropriate publication outlets.

Despite these difficulties, mixed methods research has provided each of us with some of the most exciting and rewarding scholarly experiences in our careers. We have been blessed with funding and administrative support, although, of course, the people doing the research are key to successful mixed methods. We have enjoyed moving out of our usual patterns and biases to think in the lexicons of other disciplines. Successful mixed methods teams are composed of people who play well with others. They are characterized by open interactions, trust, mutual respect, willingness to listen and consider another's point of view, ability to compromise, and willingness to do more than one's share. Over the long haul, these elements constitute the grease that facilitates successful collaborations.

References

Angel, Ronald. J., Laura Lein, and Jane Henrici. 2006. *Poor Families in America's Health Care Crisis*. New York: Cambridge University Press.

Brock, Thomas, Fred Doolittle, Veronica Fellerath, and Michael Wiseman. 1997. *Creating New Hope: Implementation of a Program to Reduce Poverty and Reform Welfare*. New York: MDRC.

Cherlin, Andrew, Caitlin Cross-Barnet, Linda M. Burton, and Raymond Garrett-Peters. 2008. "Promises They Can Keep: Low-Income Women's Attitudes toward Motherhood, Marriage, and Divorce." *Journal of Marriage and the Family* 70 (4): 919–33.

Cherlin, Andrew J., Linda M. Burton, Tera R. Hurt, and Diane M. Purvin. 2004. "The Influence of Physical and Sexual Abuse on Marriage and Cohabitation." *American Sociological Review* 69: 768–89.

DeLuca, Stefanie, and Peter Rosenblatt. 2010. "Does Moving to Better Neighborhoods Lead to Better Schooling Opportunities? Parental School Choice in an Experimental Housing Voucher Program." *Teachers College Record* 112 (5): 1443–49.

DeLuca, Stefanie, Greg J. Duncan, Micere Keels, and Ruby Mendenhall. 2012. "The Notable and the Null: Using Mixed Methods to Understand the Diverse Impacts of Residential Mobility Programs." In *Neighbourhood Effects Research: New Perspectives*, edited by Maarten van Ham, David Manley, Nick Bailey, Ludi Simpson, and Duncan Maclennan, 195–223. Dordrecht: Springer Netherlands.

Duncan, Greg. 2012. "Give Us This Day Our Daily Breadth." *Child Development* 83 (1): 6–15.

Duncan, Greg J., Aletha C. Huston, and Thomas S. Weisner. 2007. *Higher Ground: New Hope for the Working Poor and Their Children*. New York: Russell Sage Foundation.

Gassman-Pines, Anna, Hirokazu Yoshikawa, and Sandra Nay. 2006. "Can Money Buy You Love? Dynamic Employment Characteristics, the New Hope Project, and Entry into Marriage." *Making It Work: Low-Wage Employment, Family Life and Child Development*, edited by Hirokazu Yoshikawa, Thomas S. Weisner, and Edward D. Lowe, 206–32. New York: Russell Sage.

Gibson, Christina M. 2003. "Privileging the Participant: The Importance of Sub-Group Analysis in Social Welfare Evaluations." *American Journal of Evaluation*, 24 (4): 443–69.

Gibson, Christina, and Greg Duncan. 2005. "Qualitative/Quantitative Synergies in a Random-Assignment Program Evaluation." In *Discovering Successful Pathways in Children's Development: New Methods in the Study of Childhood and Family Life*, edited by Thomas S. Weisner, 283–303. Chicago: University of Chicago Press.

Gibson, Christina, and Thomas S. Weisner. 2002. "'Rational' and Ecocultural Circumstances of Program Take-Up among Low-Income Working Parents." *Human Organization* 61 (2): 154–66.

Huston, Aletha C. 2008. "From Research to Policy and Back." *Child Development* 79: 1–12.

———. 2012. "A Path to Interdisciplinary Scholarship." In *Close Relationships*, edited by Lorne Campbell and Timothy Loving, 253–72. Washington, DC: APA Books.

Kling, Jeffrey R., Jens Ludwig, and Lawrence F. Katz. 2005. "Neighborhood Effects on Crime for Female and Male Youth: Evidence from a Randomized Housing Voucher Experiment." *Quarterly Journal of Economics* 120 (1): 87–130.

Lieber, Eli, and Thomas S. Weisner. 2010. "Meeting the Practical Challenges of Mixed Methods Research." In *Methods in Social and Behavioral Research*, 2nd ed., edited by Charles Teddlie and Abbas Tashakkori, 559–79. Thousand Oaks, CA: Sage.

Lieber, Eli, Thomas S. Weisner, and Matthew Presley. 2003. "EthnoNotes: An Internet-Based Fieldnote Management Tool." *Field Methods* 15 (4): 405–25.

Ludwig, Jens, Helen F. Ladd, and Greg J. Duncan. 2001. "Urban Poverty and Educational Outcomes." *Papers on Urban Affairs* (1997): 147–201.

Magnuson, K. 1999. "Appendix K—The Barrier Indicator Index." In Bos, J., Huston, A., Granger, R., Duncan, G. J., Brock, T., and McLoyd, V., *New Hope for People with Low Incomes: Two-Year Results of a Program to Reduce Poverty and Reform Welfare*, edited by Aletha C. Huston, Cynthia Miller, Lashawn Richburg-Hayes, Greg J. Duncan, Carolyn A. Eldred, Thomas S. Weisner, Edward Lowe, Vonnie C. McLoyd, Danielle A. Crosby, Marika N. Ripk, and Cindy Redcross. 346–55. New York: Manpower Demonstration Research Corporation.

Mistry, Rashmita S., Edward D. Lowe, Aprile D. Benner, and Nina Chien. 2008. "Expanding the Family Economic Stress Model: Insights from a Mixed-Methods Approach." *Journal of Marriage and Family* 70 (February): 196–209.

Orr, Larry, Judith D. Feins, Robin Jacob, Erik Beecroft, Lisa Sanbonmatsu, Lawrence Katz, Jeffrey B. Liebman, and Jeffrey R. Kling. 2003. *Moving to Opportunity Interim Impacts Evaluation*. Washington, DC: U.S. Department of Housing and Urban Development, Office of Policy Development and Research.

Popkin, Susan J., Tama Leventhal, and Gretchen Weismann. 2010. "Girls in the 'Hood: How Safety Affects the Life Chances of Low-Income Girls." *Urban Affairs Review* 45 (6): 715–44.

Sanbonmatsu, Lisa, Jeffrey R. Kling, Greg J. Duncan, and Jeanne Brooks-Gunn. 2006. "Neighborhoods and Academic Achievement: Results from the Moving to Opportunity Experiment." *Journal of Human Resources* 41 (4): 649–91.

Sanbonmatsu, Lisa, Jens Ludwig, Lawrence F. Katz, Lisa A. Gennetian, Greg J. Duncan, Ronald C. Kessler, Emma Adam, Thomas W. McDade, and Stacy Tessler Lindau. 2011. *Moving to Opportunity for Fair Housing Demonstration Program: Final Impacts Evaluation.* Washington, DC: US Department of Housing and Urban Development, Office of Policy Development and Research.

Snell, Emily, Nina Castells, Greg J. Duncan, Lisa Gennetian, Katherine Magnuson, and Pamela Morris. 2012. "Promoting the Positive Development of Boys in High-Poverty Neighborhoods: Evidence from Four Anti-Poverty Experiments," *Journal of Research on Adolescence* 13: 357–74.

Turney, Kristin, Susan Clampet-Lundquist, Kathryn Edin, Jeffrey R. Kling, and Greg J. Duncan. 2006. "Neighborhood Effects on Barriers to Employment: Results from a Randomized Housing Mobility Experiment in Baltimore." *Brookings-Wharton Papers on Urban Affairs.* Washington, DC: Brookings.

Weisner, Thomas S. 2002. "Ecocultural Understanding of Children's Developmental Pathways." *Human Development* 45: 275–81.

———, ed. 2005. *Discovering Successful Pathways in Children's Development: Mixed Methods in the Study of Childhood and Family.* Chicago: University of Chicago Press.

Weisner, Thomas S., Hirokazu Yoshikawa, Edward D. Lowe, and Faye Carter. 2006. "'I Want What Everybody Wants': Goals, Values, and Work in the Lives of New Hope Families." In *Making It Work: Low-Wage Employment, Family Life, and Child Development,* edited by Hirokazu Yoshikawa, Thomas S. Weisner, and Edward D. Lowe, 147–72. New York: Russell Sage Foundation.

Yoshikawa, Hirokazu. 2011. *Immigrants Raising Citizens: Undocumented Parents and Their Young Children.* New York: Russell Sage.

Yoshikawa, Hirokazu, Thomas S. Weisner, and Edward D. Lowe. 2006. *Making It Work: Low-Wage Employment, Family Life, and Child Development.* New York: Russell Sage Foundation.

Yoshikawa, Hirokazu, Thomas S. Weisner, Ariel Kalil, and Niobe Way. 2008. "Mixing Qualitative and Quantitative Research in Developmental Science: Uses and Methodological Choices." *Developmental Psychology* 44 (2) (March): 344–54.

Notes

1. Material in this section parallels that presented in DeLuca et al. (2012).
2. See Turney et al. (2006) for a detailed discussion of job mapping in Baltimore County.
3. Material in this section is drawn in part from Gibson and Duncan (2005).

EIGHTEEN

Styles of Mothering, Methods of Engagement: Bridging Anthropology, Psychology, and Education to Inform Policy

CAROLYN POPE EDWARDS

The theme of this volume is mixed methods grounded in psychological anthropology as a tool for understanding important social issues with policy implications. During my own undergraduate and graduate training in anthropology and human development at Harvard University, I learned broad and integrative perspectives, for which the university was renowned. My major advisors, anthropologists Beatrice and John Whiting, imbued their students with interdisciplinary and collaborative approaches to comparative cultural research, and that spirit has stayed with me throughout my academic career. It is important to ground oneself theoretically in a chapter such as this, as the assumptions one holds will potentiate a particular set of possibilities for forging interdisciplinary links in one's work. As a mixed methods researcher with anthropological training, I am grounded in both ethnographic and systematic behavioral methods of observation; and I am a moderate universalist—that is, I would contend there are cultural variations associated with specific cultural practices but at the same time some underlying generalities or universalities in human behavior and functioning. As a developmental psychologist seeking to help create and rigorously test interventions to promote school readiness of young children, my work always involves deep knowledge of the context of research, qualitative and quantitative assessments, and strengths-based strategies of intervention, where the goal is building on competencies rather than remediating profession-ally identified deficits.

The focus of this chapter is parenting styles, and my objective is to show how a background in psychological anthropology and compara-tive cultural psychology is deeply informative for applied work in early childhood education. In fact, I would argue this background provides access to theoretical approaches and data that have assisted us in de-signing parent-professional partnerships more successful than good comparison early childhood programs. I shall first revisit the styles of mothering uncovered in the *Children of Different Worlds* study (Whit-ing and Edwards 1988; Whiting 2003), and turn to a brief compari-son with two major approaches to studying parenting style with cross-cultural or cross-ethnic evidence. Finally, I shall demonstrate how we have applied cultural insights from the *Children of Different Worlds* study in Nebraska, where we are seeking to foster individualized and respectful parent-professional partnerships for children under six—partnerships that depend foremost on open avenues of trust, empathy, and communication.

The *Children of Different Worlds* Study

The *Children of Different Worlds* study, published in 1988 by Beatrice Whiting and me, incorporated and reanalyzed the original Six Cultures Study, running record observations of children aged three–ten plus newer and longer-running record observations collected in: Liberia by Gerald Erchak; India by Susan Seymour; and in various locales in Kenya by Thomas Weisner, Beatrice Whiting, Sara Harkness, and Charles Su-per; and by a team under the leadership of Lee and Ruth Munroe, who made systematic spot observations on children aged five–seven. In designing this and other projects, John and Beatrice Whiting inten-tionally included methods that would provide both qualitative and quantitative findings, in order that direct observations and interview findings would be interpretable in ways that did not simplify and dis-tort their meaning within their cultural frame. The Whitings believed that all cross-cultural observation of children must begin with collection of community and household data and extensive ethnographic background information on cultural practices surrounding family life and child-rearing patterns. They were naturally concerned about how behavioral observations of children in natural settings could be coded reliably and validly, and their solution was to require that the observer/coder be a member of the community who could appropriately interpret the meanings and intentions of social behavior—for example, whether a physically rough act was playful horseplay or intended to hurt, or if a command was intended to serve the household's or commander's welfare, and therefore prosocial versus egoistic. For the first time, researchers had access to worldwide qualitative and quantitative data that could be directly compared on children in natural settings interacting with a full range of social partners available to them.

This observational work was set within a certain definition of culture and a particular theoretical framework. We assumed that "culture" is not something separate from other kinds of environmental effects usually considered by psychologists, but something operating, or instantiated, through them. In Beatrice Whiting's (1976) famous paper on "the problem of the packaged variable," she urged unwrapping, or unveiling the underlying processes by which so much statistical variance is explained by the predictors usually included in developmental studies—e.g., age, gender, culture, ethnicity, education, social class, modernization, urbanization, immigration status. She urged that researchers analyze and explore these packaged predictor variables as deeply and thoroughly as their dependent variables, for example, moving away from cataloging "cultural differences" in specified outcomes, toward looking at the macro- and microdimensions of children's learning environments and recording the details of daily life and socialization experiences, "paying attention to those which have been identified as important predictor variables in studies conducted in the Western world, but being constantly alert for [new] variables which have not been identified because of culturally induced blindness" (1976, 306). Whiting noted that anthropologists have developed strong methodologies for gathering the required descriptive data and should collaborate with other social scientists in conducting these studies (Edwards and Bloch 2010).

Thus, in the *Children of Different Worlds* study, we sought to create causal linkages and get at the underlying processes and mechanisms. Drawing on John Whiting's (1981) Psychocultural Model connecting aspects of history, ideology, and ecology (climate, economic complexity, and maintenance systems) to the micro-environments of child life, we sought to describe and inductively explain significant cultural group differences in the behavior of parents and children. The maintenance systems of a culture include subsistence patterns, means of production, division of labor, social structure, settlement patterns, and systems of defense, law, schooling, and social control. From this perspective, "culture" is not something separate, or "left over," after other variables such as income, religion, education, and urban/rural status have been entered into the equation, but instead encompasses all the dimensions of living associated with the beliefs, values, and customary practices that an individual acquires as a member of society. This psychocultural approach, grounded in qualitative and quantitative methods, served as background for later theoretical work by others. Several such next-generation theoretical frameworks—Harkness and Super's Development Niche approach, Thomas Weisner's Ecocultural Theory, Carol Worthman's Bioecocultural Model, and Heidi Keller's Integrative Model for the Study of Developmental Pathways (see Edwards and Weisner 2010; Worthman, chapter 2)—provide theoretical frameworks for focusing on or incorporating particular data for analysis; each is grounded in what came to be known as mixed methods.

We formulated a key aspect of the parental role as "providing the child with settings of socialization." Adults and children live out their days in normative settings that organize their daily routines, most frequent companions, and work, play, and leisure opportunities; and parents generally control the settings in which their children will spend time. These settings, in turn, facilitate or discourage different kinds of child behavior— for instance, gender roles—just as parents' own settings facilitate or discourage different types of parental behavior. Children are influenced both by their parents' *direct* behavior with them, and by their *indirect* influence that arises from parental control over the children's daily settings, companions, and routines (Whiting and Edwards 1988; Whiting and Whiting 1975).

To look at how a mother's daily context influences her direct interaction with young children, for example, consider the tasks a mother must complete while caring for a nursing baby or a demanding toddler. What cleaning and cooking tasks must be performed? What fuel and water does she have to procure, perhaps carry from afar? Where does food come from? Who cultivates it? Who is available to help her with tasks? We looked closely at our observational data.

We had quantitative data, based on coding the running records and classifying maternal interactions, labeled as maternal *interacts* into the twenty-three social behavior categories. Behavior was recorded as written running records by trained members of the children's culture. In recording the focal child's social acts (event sampling), the observer followed the eyes of the focal child, identifying whenever possible not only the child's social interacts but also the event that invoked it and any response by a social partner, including the mother. Data on maternal behavior was abstracted from the child observations. The records were taken in consecutive English sentences, for later coding. Behavior coding of initiating and responding interacts involved judgment of the apparent intention, which often could be made only when the entire sequence of events was known. Before an observation was started, the date, time of day, exact location, people present, and activities in progress were recorded. Time records were maintained along the left-hand margin of the paper, with notes as to when people entered or left the interactional space. With the exception of Bhubaneswar, India, observations were limited to the daylight hours and were distributed over four or five periods of the day. In the Six Cultures Study, each record was five minutes in length; in the New Samples, they were fifteen–sixty minutes long, depending on the community. Methods of training observers and achieving interrater reliability were roughly the same across communities.

In coding social events, each interact was categorized as a type of *mand*, defined as an attempt on the part of an individual to change the behavior of the social partner (Whiting 1980). There were six major categories of mands, each with subcategories: *ego-dependent* (seeking comfort, physical contact, help, information, approval, food, other material goods, or permission); *ego-dominant* (seeking to injure, annoy, insult, dominate, compete, or escape); *nurturant* (offering comfort, physical contact, help, information, approval, food, other material goods, or permission); *prosocial* (commanding an economic, household, or child-care chore, commanding hygiene or etiquette, reprimanding another's behavior); *sociable* (seeking or offering friendly response, including social play, laughing together, talking together, verbal or physical teasing, or horseplay); and *teaching* (offering general information, abstract knowledge, or information about skills necessary for a chore). After coding the interactions, the frequency totals were converted into proportion scores (proportion of all coded social acts by an actor or category of actors).

Twelve of the twenty-three behaviors occurred with sufficient frequency in mothers to warrant analysis and were combined into four summary categories of material behavior: nurturance, training, control, and sociability. Looking at the rank orders, and poring over the qualitative ethnographic data, three different "profiles" of maternal behavior emerged, which we called the "controlling mother," found in the agricultural communities of north India, Philippines, and Mexico; the "sociable mother," found only in the New England, USA, community; and the "training mother," found in all of the sub-Saharan African agricultural communities.

The "controlling mothers," seen in the North Indian version in the large, extended multigenerational households of Bhubaneswar, Orissa, appeared to encourage an active, insistent, assertive style of dependency in their children through a pattern of inconsistent nurturance in infancy. The caregivers—mothers, grandmothers, aunts, and cousins—responded intermittently and with delay to the children's calls for comfort, care, and attention. These mothers resided in socially dense extended families, where they themselves had to answer to many co-residents. They seemed to respond to the complexity, noise, and movement of the large household through a relatively dominant style of dealing with children; mothers employed frequent task commands and reprimands, to ensure that the work could commence and adults co-exist with numerous children in the vicinity. Bhubaneswar children learned early on to rely on a variety of caretakers other than their mothers for physical caregiving, eating, bathing, and sleeping next to someone (Seymour 1980, 2010).

In contrast, the "sociable" North American mothers, in a suburban middle-class community outside Boston, did not sleep with their babies and used cribs, playpens, chairs, and other furniture to reduce even daytime physical contact. They thus cultivated a vocal style of dependency in their babies and young children, and, in fact, given their own social isolation from other adults in the separate nuclear households, had children as their only available partners for social interaction much of the time. They also knew they wanted to prepare their children to be active initiators of verbal interaction to be successful in school. Thus, these mothers delivered few task demands (their children did by far the fewest household chores) but many "control" commands to their children; and had a much higher percentage of purely "sociable" interacts than the other mothers in our sample (Fischer and Fischer 1963: Whiting and Edwards 1988).

Finally, the "training mothers" of the sub-Saharan African agricultural communities supported yet a third style of dependency in their babies and young children—one that appeared adaptive to their workload and support systems. This is seen in the detailed observational records collected. The Ngecha mothers, in a farming community outside Nairobi, were typical. They slept with their babies at night and carried them in the daytime on their front, back, or hip. They responded immediately to the infant's hunger signals and encouraged a physical rather than verbal style of dependency. Then,

from toddlerhood on, they believe they should train a child to be a competent farmer, herdsman, and child nurse and that a child from age two on should be assigned chores that increase in complexity and arduousness with age. They punish their children for failure to perform these tasks responsibly or for stubbornly refusing to do what their elders request of them. They allow much of their children's learning to occur through observation and imitation; only occasionally do they instruct them explicitly. Moreover, mothers seldom praise their children lest they become proud, a trait that is unacceptable. They allow the major rewards for task performance to be intrinsic, [such as the smiles and love a baby gives back when cared for well]. (Whiting and Edwards 1988, 95).

This was the pervasive style of mothering in the late 1960s and early 1970s. Because culture emerges through the processes and mechanisms that shape particular learning environments, culture is dynamic, not static. In a later book, *Ngecha: A Kenyan Village in a Time of Rapid Social Change* (Edwards and Whiting 2004), based on research from 1968 through 1973, and comparing the data from more traditional households with more rapidly modernizing ones, Beatrice Whiting and I described how many of the training mothers of Ngecha village were changing their goals and expectations for children, wanting them to be successful in school and able to compete in the new nation, a stratified, industrializing, diverse, literate society. They were beginning to add more sociability into their interaction and to encourage their children to ask questions, exchange information, even interrupt adult conversation.

Notice how vivid these composite portraits are. There are not many photos of parent-child interaction in the Whitings' books (instead, photos of children), but I believe that if you were asked to draw the three maternal profiles, you could sketch them, including many contextual details. These drawings would portray the parameters of everyday life, and suggest how mothers' behavior is adaptive or responsive to the children they have. As I will argue, grounding concepts of parental behavior in vivid examples from ethnographic and case-material leads to deeper appreciation of parenting in context, and increases the range of strengths as opposed to deficits that educators can recognize and affirm in the parents they meet.

Our purpose in describing the maternal profiles was not to create a rigid typology of parenting style categories to apply to the world's communities but rather to highlight—bring forward—meaningful connections between the flow of maternal behavior, as it can be observed in natural settings, and children's emerging behavior as they grow from infancy through middle childhood—each stage of childhood with increasing cognitive and social competencies and a widening social world. From Margaret Mead, we got apt labels for this universal course of development: the "lap child" (infant), "knee child" (toddler), "yard child" (preschooler), and "community child" (school child). Beatrice Whiting and I accepted and assumed cultural pathways of child development and mapped onto the stages of childhood the cultural differences we could see arising due to the various routines, settings, and companions that were provided by the different kinds of cultural communities.

Looking back, I would say this was a "strengths-based" approach to understanding culture and parenting—seeing most or at least much of individuals' behavior as reasonable and functional in context, as making sense in terms of prevailing expectations and opportunities.

The Dimensional Models of Parenting Style

The anthropologically grounded, mixed method orientation to maternal styles can be contrasted with two other well-known paradigms for comparing parenting style transculturally. In both cases, the models serve as theoretical frameworks for deductively linking child outcomes to abstract, universalized dimensions of parenting that are assumed to apply in a similar way across all the ages and stages of childhood and both within and between any samples from anywhere.

The first model, Parental Acceptance-Rejection Theory (PARTheory) is a product of the culture-comparative research program of Ronald Rohner and colleagues beginning in 1960 (Rohner 1975), and now including an empirically established set of questionnaire methods leading to a massive body of findings. To summarize this universalized, single-dimensional approach: children throughout development need a specific form of positive response—acceptance—from parents and other primary caregivers, and when this is not met, they tend to become hostile and aggressive, emotionally unstable, and to have a negative worldview. In early formulations, Rohner tended to classify cultures along the dimension of Parental Acceptance-Rejection, and claimed, on the basis of a detailed holocultural study of 101 cultures using the Human Relations Area Files in New Haven, Connecticut, that parents in about 25 percent of the world's societies generally behave in ways that are consistent with the definition of rejection (Rohner 1975,1980). Those groups included the Gusii, one of the sub-Saharan African tribal communities included in the Six Cultures Study, raising questions about this conclusion among others familiar with these cultural communities. Rather than debate cross-cultural variations, Rohner turned his focus onto intracultural rather than cross-cultural variation, noting that, "Even though parents everywhere may express acceptance and rejection, the way they do it is highly variable and saturated with cultural meaning." Contemporary parental acceptance-rejection (PARTheory) research is focused on determining the interpretations or attributions that individuals make of their remembered experiences (including parental coldness/lack of affection, hostility/aggression, indifference/neglect, and general rejection). Adolescents and adults, in any culture, who *perceive themselves to be rejected* are hypothesized to show criminal behavior, conduct disorders, depression, and substance abuse. According to this model, actual context of caregiving can be ignored, as it is the perceptions and interpretations of the individual that are causal.

A second model comes from Diana Baumrind's (1966, 1967) research on the connection between parental behavior and the development of "instrumental competence," as she said, "the ability to manipulate the environment to achieve one's goals." Baumrind laid out two dimensions of parenting style: responsiveness and control—with high responsiveness and firm control providing the optimal combination of authoritative parenting. A contemporary version of this model includes three core dimensions: support, behavioral control, and psychological control (Crockett and Hayes 2011). The theory has received much empirical support, but as the work on North American subcultures expands, increasingly, doubt is growing regarding whether authoritative parenting necessarily produces optimum developmental outcomes for ethnic minorities, such as African Americans, Asian Americans, and Latino Americans. For example, Chao (2001) found that among first-generation Chinese families, youth from authoritarian homes did as well in school as those from authoritative homes. Researchers within this tradition are now seeking the best ways to reformulate or elaborate Baumrind's theory to account for the cultural variations. Stephen Russell says, "We're trying to show that parenting that leads to optimal development for adolescents can differ by culture in important ways" (Van Campen and Russell 2010; see Russell, Crockett, and Chao 2010).

Relevant here is the ongoing cross-national project Parent Behavior and Child Adjustment Across Cultures, led by Jennifer Lansford of Duke University, and involving interviews, on discipline and other aspects of parenting, with children, mothers, and fathers in nine countries.

Notice that these bodies of research focus not on observed behavior in context but instead on symbolic meanings ascribed deductively to parent-child interaction and to the reciprocal relationship between parent and student expectations (Zhang et al. 2011). In general, researchers in these paradigms rely on interview techniques rather than observational or mixed methods research, and they focus on explaining parental deficiencies and/or strengths associated with child outcomes agreed to be desirable or undesirable.

Our Educational Project: Building on Strengths to Promote Child Competence

Finally, recent developments in the field of early childhood education suggests why the ecological and strengths-based approach, coming originally out of psychological anthropology, with its focus on cultural pathways and on parenting in context, may have particular usefulness for applied work. One example is found in projects intended to foster home-school collaborations at preschool and elementary levels on behalf of socioemotional and academic outcomes. In one applied project at the University of Nebraska, Lincoln, led by Sue Sheridan, Lisa Knoche, and me, we sought to foster school readiness of preschool children by promoting the skills of teachers and home visitors to communicate and partner with parents, that is, share expertise and enhance individual parent confidence and competence. Our intervention approach is focused on the triangle of parent-professional-child relationships. The children targeted are those at risk for educational failure due to poverty, household stress, and/or disabilities that make them eligible for early intervention programs such as Early Head Start, Head Start, student- parent high school programs, or early intervention. Their parents' language and cultural differences are aspects of their individual parenting differences that needed careful consideration in designing and implementing the Getting Ready Intervention, not only in assessment but at every phase of the program.

Like Beatrice Whiting, the Getting Ready researchers have found it most constructive to think of "culture" as a variable that needs to be unpackaged, and that is not separable from other background factors.

The members of the project team have learned to be expectant of many patterns and presentations of values, beliefs, and expectations on the part of individual parents in the sample. These families can be described along many lines that are meaningful for data analysis—rural/urban aspects are prominent; also socioeconomic and educational background; language of the home and immigrant status; age and marital status of parents and what kind of social and familial support they have; family stressors; and so on.

The problem for the Getting Ready researchers was how to extract from the anthropological and psychological literature well-supported conclusions that could guide the Getting Ready intervention in sufficiently flexible ways that it would be positive—learning and growth-promoting—for all of the different kinds of parents, professionals, and children. (Note: the term "parents" includes caregiving adults assuming primary or strong secondary responsibility for children, including grandparents or guardians). The research traditions of PARTheory and Baumrind Parental Style Theory may suggest *that* individual variation in parenting competence is to be expected; but they do not provide much assistance for *what* and *how to* observe and listen to parents unlike oneself in the service of respectfully joining agendas with them and affirming and strengthening their best efforts to help their children succeed in school. The Getting Ready team has made some initial steps in that area, though we know we need to go further.

First, as mentioned, we grounded our intervention in a strengths-based vision, that is, aimed at building on family and child competencies rather than remediating professionally identified deficits.

Second, we proposed an outline of child development that we knew would be applicable to diverse families and not be viewed as promoting one "correct" version of good parenting. Reviewing the empirical literature on parental behavior and child outcomes, we concluded, in Sheridan, Marvin, Knoche, and Edwards (2008) that we could lay out components of parent behavior that are beneficial for young children, always including elements of: (a) warmth, sensitivity, and responsiveness; (b) support and guidance for a child's emerging autonomy; and (c) participation in learning. (In a parallel way, Morrison [2009] conceptualizes American parenting as including three dimensions impacting early learning and literacy outcomes: responsivity, management/discipline, and home learning environment; Hindman and Morrison [2012] revise the responsivity dimension as warmth/support/expectations.)

All three dimensions apply throughout infancy and early childhood, but warmth and sensitivity, or nurturance, may be focal during infancy; autonomy and guidance issues arise in toddlerhood; and pro-motion of learning and literacy come to the fore in the preschool pe-riod. We identified many studies, most with US samples, in which each component of parenting can be traced to positive outcomes for young children (reviewed in Edwards, Sheridan, and Knoche 2010; Sheridan et al. 2008), leading to competence in socioemotional and preacademic or early academic outcomes.

Most important for this discussion, we were also able to find world-wide anthropological and cross-cultural evidence that each of these components can be fostered in diverse ways, promoting child well-being in the ways valued by the cultural community (Edwards 2009; Edwards, Sheridan, and Knoche 2010).

Therefore, we introduced into our training of teachers and coaches vivid examples that would help them to notice, recognize, and build on the individual styles of parenting that they might see with their families. These examples (always including photographs, and/or video segments) are drawn from our own project documentary archive of parent-child assessments as well as from my personal research files from studies in many countries. These are intended to create what I would call "memorable instances" in the minds of learners by remind-ing them of instances from their own experience and alerting them to particulars they can look and listen for themselves, suspending evaluative judgment while seeking deeper understanding and trust. In Getting Ready trainings, we illustrate positive examples of parental warmth and responsiveness, promotion of autonomy, and participa-tion in learning, in styles that range from physically sensitive and at-tuned touch, to varied expectations and styles of guidance (household tasks, dressing and hygiene, and mature behavior in social situations), to different styles of reading books to children seen in our Latino ver-sus Anglo families (Cline and Edwards 2013).

As part of the intervention, the practitioners receive professional de-velopment and coaching support for their reflective practice, that is, ongoing training in the skills and dispositions to *intentionally and stra-tegically* implement the triadic and collaborative Getting Ready strat-egies during their home visits, parent-teacher conferences, and other interactions with families. During a typical meeting, for example, the teacher will establish rapport with the parent and child and facilitate an extended period of mutually enjoyable parent-child interaction—which could be around a book, toy, or household routine. The teacher will comment on the interaction to draw the parent's attention to par-ticular competencies in the child, and parent and teacher will share their insights and observations regarding what is going on with the child's development and behavior. The teacher will offer statements that reinforce positive interactions that the parent initiated, and recognize the child's competence as an outcome of effective parenting practices. Developmental information will be inserted as appropriate. At some point, focus will turn to collaborative planning, with parent and teacher discussing ongoing concerns, brainstorming next steps, and selecting what to do at home and in the classroom to support progress in the child's development. The Getting Ready professional strategies are not unique to our project and in fact reflect current notions of best practice, but they are not easy to execute in an intentional and individualized way. In coaching sessions, practitioners see and reflect on many videos of their own work with families.

We have evidence that the Getting Ready strategies are being implemented with fidelity (Knoche et al. 2010), that the training sessions and supervision are experienced as enlightening and supportive by the practitioners (Brown et al. 2009), and that teachers do enrich and improve their home visits and other contacts with parents (Edwards et al. 2009). The findings indicate that the professional development model (including an increased amount of support and supervision tailored to each practitioner's caseload and needs) is helpful to them in implementing the strategies.

Findings suggest that the Getting Ready intervention is effective with a range of families. For example, one report documents the effects of the Getting Ready intervention on the parenting behaviors of families involved in rural Early Head Start home-based programming (Knoche et al. 2012). We hypothesized that parents participating in the treatment group would demonstrate greater levels of warmth and sensitivity, support for autonomy, and participation in learning interactions with their children than parents receiving typical Early Head Start services. The enrolled sample included 234 parents, who represented the primary participant group. They were randomly assigned through their home visitor to treatment versus control conditions. The mean age of parent participants was about twenty-five. Sixty-two percent identified themselves as White/Non-Hispanic, thirty-four percent Hispanic/Latino, and four percent "other." The majority of respondents (94 percent) were mothers, five percent were fathers, and one percent were grandmothers. Forty-one percent did not complete high school, thirty-one percent reported earning a high school diploma or GED, twenty-four percent had some training beyond high school, and four percent reported having a college degree. Twenty-four percent of respondents were born outside of the United States. Thirty percent of families reported speaking primarily Spanish in the home; seventy percent reported speaking primarily English. About two-thirds indicated being married or with a partner. One hundred thirty-nine families were enrolled in the treatment group at baseline, and another ninety-five families were enrolled in the control group. There were no statistically significant differences in demographic composition between treatment and control group participants.

Findings indicated that parents in the treatment group, including English- and Spanish-speakers, experienced maintenance, or slight gains, in positive parenting behaviors over the intervention period, in four out of six parent-infant relationship factors. Specifically, significant differences in favor of the treatment group were identified for the quality of observed warmth/sensitivity and encouragement of autonomy, as well as the appropriateness with which families provided support for learning and offered guidance and directives to the children. Furthermore, data trends indicate not only gains or maintenance of positive parenting behaviors by participants in the treatment condition, but a contrasting decline in quality and appropriateness of certain behaviors by parents in the control condition. For example, on the Encouragement of Autonomy-Quality (figure 18.1) and Support for Learning-Appropriateness scales (figure 18.2), the treatment group increased over time while the control group declined.

On the Warmth and Sensitivity-Quality scale (figure 18.3), the treatment group maintained its level (with minor movement up and down) over the course of the inquiry, while the control group declined rather sharply. Our interpretation of the latter finding is that at baseline, most of the children were infants, and then as the study progressed, they moved into toddlerhood.

In general, infants elicit mostly nurturance (warmth and sensitivity) from adults, whereas toddlers, who are more resistant and demanding at times (harder to control in a structured situation), elicit more controlling and reprimanding behaviors (less warmth and sensitivity). We believe the Getting Ready intervention helped parents sustain their warmth and sensitivity, and not decline over time. In sum, the Getting Ready intervention and strategies proved effective at promoting improved parenting practices for parents of infants and toddlers in rural Early Head Start programs, and the proposed mechanism for these changes was interaction with their home visitors.

Other analyses of data from the Getting Ready intervention to date have yielded effects that indicate this parent-oriented intervention is

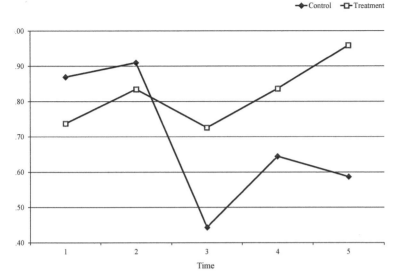

Encouragement of Autonomy – Quality

FIGURE 18.1 Compared to parents in the control condition, *parents who were involved in the Getting Ready intervention demonstrated more skills to support their children's autonomy.* That is, parents involved in the intervention were sensitive to the types of goals they set for their children and used quality approaches to control children's activities (Parent/Caregiver Involvement Scale —P/CIS items: goal setting, control of activities.)

effective at supporting both social-emotional competencies (Sheridan et al. 2010) and language and literacy skills in preschool children (Sheridan et al. 2011). In the latter study, children's primary language also moderated the effects of the Getting Ready intervention, in that children who did not speak English upon entering preschool (according to parents' reports at the time) experienced more gains on the TROLL oral language and reading scores than those who reportedly spoke English.

Why the Methods Mattered

To sum up, findings from psychological anthropology can be deeply informative for work in early childhood education and intervention, by adding a cross-cultural layer to our understanding of three important components of early parenting: (a) warmth and nurturance; (b) support for a child's emerging autonomy and self-control; and (c) participation in learning and literacy. When practitioners are taught an individual-

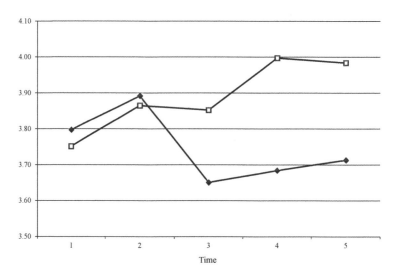

Support for Learning - Appropriateness

FIGURE 18.2 *Parents in the treatment group provided more appropriate supports for their children's learning* than the supports offered by parents in the control group. Parents in the treatment group provided fitting supports for their children, including appropriate teaching behaviors, verbal interactions, and responsiveness. (Parent/Caregiver Involvement Scale—P/CIS items: verbal involvement, responsiveness of caregiver, negative statements, relationship among activities, teaching behavior, play interaction, physical involvement.)

ized, strengths-based approach to listening to parents' goals and directions, and supporting these components in individualized, responsive ways, they can achieve measurable results. Getting Ready's approach to reflective practice requires practitioners to seek attunement with parents and children, to be alert and on the lookout for telling details of behavior in context in order to support emerging competencies. Having a kind of mental "palette" of examples may be useful to this process, and we are finding out more about that. Our project has already published the results of longitudinal interviews with teachers about their perceptions of the intervention (Brown et al. 2009).

As we now undertake phase two of the intervention, with new federal funding from the Institute of Education Studies, we are extending also the qualitative phase of the research to learn in more detail whether, and how, practitioners understand the individuality and cultural variability of the families with whom they work, and what aspects of the training and reflective supervision are enlightening to them as they learn to partner with families. Thus, our data on teachers will include not only quantitative data (assessments of their use of Getting Ready strategies in conferences and home visits; self-reports on instruments such as the Parent-Teaching Rating Scale [PTRS]), but also qualitative, longitudinal data from face-face interviews with a sub-sample selected to represent different partnering agencies and levels of experience. This line of work exemplifies our faith in the unique ability of mixed methods research across different cultural worlds to impact theory with real-world applications for interventions in the local but increasingly diverse cultural worlds in which we all live.

Acknowledgments

This chapter was prepared for the Methods That Matter Conference: Anthropological and Mixed Methods to Understand Contemporary

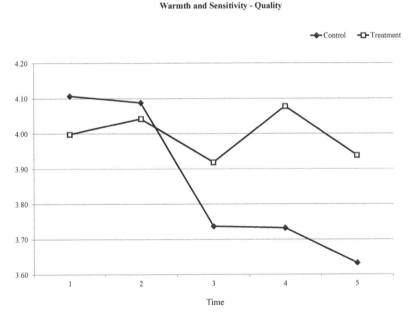

Warmth and Sensitivity - Quality

→ Control □ Treatment

FIGURE 18.3 Parents in the Getting Ready treatment group *interacted with their children using a greater degree of warmth and sensitivity* than their counterparts in the control condition. They demonstrated high-quality, positive, sensitive interactions with their children. (Parent/ Caregiver Involvement Scale—P/CIS items: physical involvement, responsiveness of caregiver, play interaction, directives/demands, positive statements, negative statements.)

Social Issues and Inform Real-World Policy, Miami University (Ohio), September 19–21, 2013. An earlier version was presented as part of an SRCD Invited Symposium (Distinguished Senior Panel) on "Cross-Cultural and Interdisciplinary Research: Studying Diverse Child Development Pathways around the World," Thomas Weisner (chair), April 18, 2013, Seattle. The Children of Different Worlds Project was funded by the Ford Foundation, the Center for Advanced Study in the Behavioral Sciences, the Spencer Foundation, and Radcliffe. The Getting Ready Project, Phase 1, was funded by a grant awarded to Susan Sheridan and Carolyn Pope Edwards from the Department of Health and Human Services (DHHS)— National Institute of Child Health and Human Development (NICHD), Administration for Children and Families (ACF) and Office of the Assistant Secretary for Planning and Evaluation (ASPE); and the Department of Education (ED)—Office of Special Education and Rehabilitative Services (Grant #1R01H00436135).

For critique and suggestions on this paper, the author thanks colleagues and students, including Cameron Hay, Lisa Crockett, Vibeke Grover, Maria de Guzman, Lisa Knoche, Traci Kutaka, Lixin Ren, Susan Sheridan, and Thomas Weisner.

References

Baumrind, Diana. 1966. "Effects of Authoritative Parental Contol on Child Behavior." *Child Development* 37 (4): 887–907.

———. 1967. "Child Care Practices Anteceding Three Patterns of Preschool Behavior." *Genetic Psychology Monographs* 75 (1): 43–88.

Brown, Jill R., Lisa L. Knoche, Carolyn P. Edwards, and Susan M. Sheridan. 2009. "Professional Development to Support Parent Engagement: A Case Study of Early Childhood Practitioners." *Early Education & Development* 20: 482–506.

Chao, Ruth K. 2001. "Extending Expanding Research on the Consequences of Parental Style for Chinese Americans and European Americans." *Child Development* 72: 1832–43.

Cline, Keely Dyan, and Carolyn Pope Edwards. 2013. "The Instructional and Emotional Quality of Parent-Child Book Reading and Early Head Start Children's Learning Outcomes." *Early Education and Development* 24: 1214–31.

Crockett, Lisa, and Rachel Hayes. 2011. "Parenting Practices and Styles." In *Encyclopedia of Adolescence*, vol. 2, edited by Roger J. R. Levesque, 241–48. Waltham, MA: Elsevier.

Edwards, Carolyn Pope. 2009. "An Old Song: Relationship-Based Care in Cultural and Historical Perspective." In *Extending the Dance in Infant and Toddler Caregiving: Enhancing Attachment and Relationships*, edited by Helen H. Raikes and Carolyn Pope Edwards, 45–68. Baltimore, MD: Paul H. Brookes.

Edwards, Carolyn Pope, and Beatrice B. Whiting, eds. 2004. *Ngecha: A Kenyan Village in a Time of Rapid Social Change*. Lincoln, NE: University of Nebraska Press.

Edwards, Carolyn Pope, and Marianne Bloch. 2010. "The Whitings' Concepts of Culture and How They Have Fared in Contemporary Psychology and Anthropology." *Journal of Cross-Cultural Psychology* 41 (4) (July 20): 485–98.

Edwards, Carolyn Pope, and Thomas S. Weisner, eds. 2010. Special Issue: "The Legacy of Beatrice and John Whiting for Cross-Cultural Research." *Journal of Cross- Cultural Psychology* 41 (4).

Edwards, Carolyn Pope, Susan M. Sheridan, and Lisa Knoche. 2010. "Parent-Child Relationships in Early Learning." In *International Encyclopedia of Education*, vol. 5, edited by Penelope Peterson, Eva Baker, and Barry McGaw, 438–43. Oxford, UK: Elsevier.

Edwards, Carolyn Pope, Tara Hart, Kelly Rasmussen, Yang Mei Haw, and Susan M. Sheridan. 2009. "Promoting Parent Partnership in Head Start: A Qualitative Case Study of Teacher Documents from a School Readiness Intervention Project." *Early Childhood Services: An Interdisciplinary Journal of Effectiveness* 3: 301–22.

Farran, Dale Clark, Connie Kasari, Marilee Comfort, and Susan Jay. 1986. *Parent/Caregiver Involvement Scale*. Greensboro: University of North Carolina at Greensboro, Child Development-Family Relations, School of Human Environmental Sciences.

Fischer, John, and Ann Fischer. 1963. "The New Englanders of Orchard Town, U.S.A." *Six Cultures: Studies of Child Rearing*, edited by Beatrice B. Whiting, 869–1010. New York: John Wiley and Sons.

Hindman, Annmarie H., and Frederick J. Morrison. 2012. "Differential Contributions of Three Parenting Dimensions to Preschool Literacy and Social Skills in a Middle-Income Sample." *Merrill-Palmer Quarterly* 58 (2): 191–223.

Kim, Kyoungho, and Ronald P. Rohner. 2002. "Parental Warmth, Control, and Involvement in Schooling: Predicting Academic Achievement." *Journal of Cross-Cultural Psychology* 33 (2): 127–40.

Knoche, Lisa L., Susan M. Sheridan, Brandy L. Clarke, Carolyn Pope Edwards, Christine A. Marvin, Keely D. Cline, and Kevin A. Kupzyk. 2012. "Getting Ready: Results of a Randomized Trial of a Relationship-Focused Intervention on the Parent-Infant Relationship in Rural Early Head Start." *Infant Mental Health Journal* 33 (5): 439–58.

Knoche, Lisa L., Susan M. Sheridan, Carolyn P. Edwards, and Allison Q. Osborn. 2010. "Implementation of a Relationship-Based School Readiness Intervention: A Multidimensional Approach to Fidelity Measurement for Early Childhood." *Early Childhood Research Quarterly* 25: 299–313.

Morrison, Frederick J. 2009. "Parenting and Academic Achievement." *Merrill-Palmer Quarterly* 55 (3): 361–72.

Rohner, Ronald P. 1975. *They Love Me, They Love Me Not: A Worldwide Study of the Effects of Parental Acceptance and Rejection.* New Haven, CT: HRAF Press.

———. 1980. "Worldwide Tests of Parental Acceptance-Rejection Theory: An Overview." *Cross-Cultural Research* 15: 1–21.

Rohner, Ronald P., Abdul Khaleque, and David E. Cournoyer. 2005. "Parental Acceptance-Rejection: Theory, Methods, Cross-Cultural Evidence, and Implications." *Ethos* 33 (3): 299–334.

Russell, Steven T., Lisa J. Crockett, and Ruth K. Chao, eds. 2010. *Asian American Parenting and Parent-Adolescent Relationships.* New York: Springer.

Seymour, Susan, ed. 1980. *The Transformation of a Sacred Town: Bhubaneswar, India.* Boulder, CO: Westview Press.

———. 2010. "Environmental Change, Family Adaptations, and Child Development: Longitudinal Research in India." *Journal of Cross-Cultural Psychology* 41 (4): 578–91.

Sheridan, Susan M., Christine A. Marvin, Lisa L. Knoche, and Carolyn Pope Edwards. 2008. "Getting Ready: Promoting School Readiness through a Relationship-Based Partnership Model." *Early Childhood Services: An Interdisciplinary Journal of Effectiveness* 2: 149–72.

Sheridan, Susan M., Lisa L. Knoche, Carolyn P. Edwards, James A. Bovaird, and Kevin A. Kupzyk. 2010. "Parent Engagement and School Readiness: Effects of the Getting Ready Intervention on Preschool Children's Social-Emotional Competencies." *Early Education & Development* 21: 125–56.

Sheridan, Susan M., Lisa L. Knoche, Kevin A. Kupzyk, Carolyn Pope Edwards, and Christine A. Marvin. 2011. "A Randomized Trial Examining the Effects of Parent Engagement on Early Language and Literacy: The Getting Ready Intervention." *Journal of School Psychology* 49 (3): 361–83.

Van Campen, K. S., and S. T. Russell. 2010. *Cultural Differences in Parenting Practices: What Asian American Families Can Teach Us.* Frances McClelland Institute for Children, Youth, and Families Research Link, vol. 2, no. 1. Tucson, AZ: The University of Arizona.

Whiting, Beatrice B. 1976. "The Problem of the Packaged Variable." In *The Developing Individual in a Changing World*, vol. 1, edited by Klaus F. Riegel and John A. Meacham. 303–09. Chicago: Aldine.

———. 2003. *Ngecha, Kenya, Behavior Observations. Collected by Beatrice Whiting and Research Collaborators in 1968–1972*, edited by Carolyn Pope Edwards, compiled by Maria Rosario Tretasco de Guzman. New Haven, CT: Human Relations Area Files Press, CD Rom format. http://www.yale.edu/hraf/other.htm.

Whiting, Beatrice B., and Carolyn Pope Edwards. 1988. *Children of Different*

Worlds: The Formation of Social Behavior. Cambridge, MA: Harvard University Press.

Whiting, Beatrice B., and John W. M. Whiting. 1975. *Children of Six Cultures: A Psychocultural Analysis.* Cambridge, MA: Harvard University Press.

Whiting, John W. M. 1980. "Environmental Constraints on Infant Care Practices." In *Handbook of Cross-Cultural Human Development*, edited by Ruth H. Munroe, Robert L. Munroe, and Beatrice B. Whiting, 155–79. New York: Garland STPM Press.

Zhang, Yanyan, Eileen Haddad, Bernadeth Torres, and Chuansheng Chen. 2011. "The Reciprocal Relationships among Parents' Expectations, Adolescents' Expectations, and Adolescents' Achievement: A Two-Wave Longitudinal Analysis of the NELS Data." *Journal of Youth and Adolescence* 40: 479–89.

NINETEEN

Intervention Research with Clients of Transgender Sex Workers: Finding Methods That Work with a Virtual Community

BRIAN L. WILCOX

For roughly the past twenty years I have been working with a team of public health professionals and researchers to design, implement, and evaluate interventions intended to reduce the risk of HIV and other sexually transmitted infections (STIs) in high-risk populations in several large urban communities in Brazil, with a primary focus on sex workers and their clients. As with most public health interventions, we began by using quantitative epidemiological research tools to understand the distribution of STIs within our populations of interest, but I focus here on how, as our intervention work proceeded, a blend of qualitative and quantitative methods became essential to understanding the nature of sexual risk behaviors among sex workers and their clients, as well as the impact of our interventions.

From a purely personal perspective, the move to mixed methods represented a significant change. While trained as a community psychologist and intervention researcher whose graduate work included courses in sociology and anthropology, I nonetheless was raised in an almost purely quantitative tradition. We psychologists were all anxious to establish ourselves as "real scientists" and were falsely led to believe that the surest path involved the use of rigorous, psychometrically sound measures and sophisticated statistical analysis. The more arcane, the better. At the same time, we were generally taught to be skeptical of anything in the qualitative realm. While it's true that there have always been qualitative researchers within the field of psychology, they have run counter to the dominant trend of increasing dependence on highly sophisticated quantitative methods.

Consequently, many of us psychologists have traditionally gone into the field with a half-empty bag of methods, and allowed those methods to artificially narrow the scope of our inquiry. It's a case of the Law of the Hammer: give a child a hammer, and suddenly everything looks like a nail. Or perhaps the better analogy is the child with the hammer looking only for nails to pound on. I was that child, looking for problems that seemed to lend themselves readily to quantitative measurement and analysis. Working on the Senior Program Team of the William T. Grant Foundation, which included a mix of qualitative and quantitative researchers, I came to realize that methods need to be subservient to our research questions, and that those questions are almost always more profitably elucidated using a synthesis of qualitative and quantitative data.

Setting the Stage

To set the context for the research described here, my work in Brazil grew out of a sense of frustration with the limitations imposed on similar work on HIV prevention that I had been carrying out in the United States. In the 1980s and 1990s, US social policy had taken a decidedly conservative tilt, and social conservatives in particular were quite successful in imposing ideological viewpoints on social programs and social research. In the area of reproductive health, including human immunodeficiency virus (HIV) and sexually transmitted infection (STI) prevention, this largely took the form of an overwhelming emphasis on abstinence (sexual and substance use) as the preferred prevention strategy. Federal funding was ramped up for what came to be known as "abstinence-only programs" (Wilcox 1999). These programs emphasized abstinence as the only effective means of preventing STIs and either ignored the role of condoms in preventing infections among sexually active individuals or promoted distorted descriptions of condom failure rates in an effort to discourage their use. At the same time, conservatives in Congress and the administration launched a broad attack on research on sexual behavior of all sorts, including studies of abortion, condom effectiveness, sexual risk behaviors, and STI/HIV prevention (Gardner and Wilcox 1993). Organizations receiving Centers for Disease Control (CDC) funds for community-based HIV prevention programs were strongly encouraged to downplay the utility of condoms and to avoid explicit discussions of safer sex practices. In other words, basic researchers experienced a "chilling effect" that led many to put their research studying sexual behaviors associated with risk for HIV infection on hold. Likewise, community interventions intended to serve as the sites for impact studies of promising prevention theories were hamstrung by ideologically inspired funding restrictions on program content. The United States was becoming an inhospitable environment for HIV prevention research.

Two conversations with colleagues led to my moving my work to Brazil. A former program officer at CDC, who had grown frustrated with the ideological restrictions being placed on agency staff working in the HIV prevention area and had left for the World Health Organization, suggested I consider working outside the United States. For whatever reasons, he found that public health officials in many areas of the world facing significant HIV epidemics were far more willing to take a pragmatic, non-ideological, evidence-based approach to addressing those epidemics. He implied that one could try almost anything that seemed grounded in decent research and theory. Shortly thereafter, I related this conversation with a colleague in Brazil. As I described the situation in the United States, she was certain that I was weaving a tall tale, but once I'd convinced her that I was serious, she immediately suggested that Brazil would be a perfect setting for pursuing good prevention research. Despite their country being predominantly Catholic, Brazilians are notoriously open minded about sexuality, and the idea of political or ideological constraints on interventions intended to prevent morbidity and mortality linked to sexual behavior seemed inconceivable to her (hence her initial disbelief of my story). She made a series of introductions, and eighteen years later I am still involved in the most enjoyable work of my professional life in Brazil.

Intervening with an Invisible Population

My intervention studies in Brazil have focused on numerous high-risk populations (sex workers, street children, IV drug users, men who have sex with men) and contexts (organized brothels, sexually oriented night clubs, bath houses, "love" motels, dances in slum communities). The project I describe here is the one that I have found most interesting, for a variety of reasons. It is a project that brought me into contact with a population of individuals about whom I knew almost nothing. Because of the nature of the population, the research and intervention methods we could draw on were more restricted than would normally have been the case. Indeed, the project presented the types of challenges that get a somewhat jaded researcher's juices flowing.

Among the several populations of so-called high-risk populations we had worked with over the years was the community of transgender sex workers. Transgender individuals are generally considered at elevated risk for HIV and other STIs by virtue of their engagement with sexual behaviors—particularly anal sex—that are inherently risky. The risk is magnified significantly for transgender sex workers by virtue of the simple math associated with having many sexual partners (Poteat et al. 2015). Additionally, some survey evidence we collected indicates that transgender sex workers are more likely to engage in higher-risk sexual behaviors, such as unprotected anal sex with a stranger, than is true of the larger transgender population. While little data are available, some studies suggest that rates of HIV infection among transgender sex workers mirror those of male sex workers who have sex with men (Baral et al. 2013).

In the course of our work with transgender sex workers, we had the opportunity to interview many of them at length and over time, and as we did so it became increasingly apparent that with respect to the design of prevention efforts, our singular focus on these sex workers was misplaced. Looking back, it's a bit embarrassing that we homed in on only half of the picture. Generally speaking, sexual behaviors occur within a dyadic context, yet we found ourselves focusing almost exclusively on the transgender individuals. It is very easy, unfortunately, to focus on the more stigmatized member of the dyad, and public health officials and HIV researchers have often been guilty of viewing sex workers, in particular, as "disease hosts or vectors" without acknowledging that their clients are typically individuals who routinely engage in risky sexual behaviors (unprotected sex, high numbers of partners, etc.) that make them likely hosts/vectors as well. The sexual partners of sex workers had not been part of our thinking in any serious way, but after closely reading the transcripts of our interviews, it became clear that the clients of the sex workers were driving much of the high-risk behavior. For example, we repeatedly heard stories of clients who badgered the sex workers to have unprotected sex. Many told us of clients who offered substantial tips for going "sem camisinha" (without a condom). Given the precarious financial condition of many of the sex workers, these offers were often accepted. Others told of clients who surreptitiously removed their condom during sex. A smaller number reported being threatened with violence and forced to have unprotected sex. Part of the underlying narrative that was repeated by many of the transgender sex workers was that they felt particularly vulnerable when clients insisted on unprotected sex. While sex work is legal (or, more technically, decriminalized) in Brazil, transgender sex workers generally feel that if a dispute arises between them and a client, police give far more credence to the clients' reports than they feel is the case for complaints lodged by female sex workers. Occasional reports of police violence against transgender sex workers reinforce this perception. Consequently, many transgender sex workers believe that when clients push them to engage in risky sexual behaviors, resistance may result in more harm than nonresistance.

In light of these insights derived from our qualitative interviews with a select sample of transgender sex workers, we decided to see if we could launch an intervention reaching their clients, who, as noted above, were seemingly driving a good deal of the HIV-risk behaviors occurring during commercial sex transactions. We quickly realized, however, that these are individuals who are not readily identified, and most carefully guard their anonymity.

Reaching out to the sex workers was quite simple: they place ads in newspapers and on escort web sites. Many work on the streets in a small number of locations. Contacting them was a fairly simple process. But we had no straightforward means of reaching their clients, making the delivery of an intervention obviously rather complicated. The transgender sex workers guarded the confidentiality of their clients. We knew almost nothing about these men and had no idea how to make contact with them, let alone deliver some form of HIV prevention intervention. We considered trying to reach out to men as they left the love motels following their trysts, but all agreed this was probably not a workable idea.

Internet Communities

So how does one reach an invisible population that probably strongly desires to remain underground? Men who have sex with transgender sex workers are nearly as stigmatized as the sex workers themselves, a fact exemplified by the ridicule heaped on Brazilian soccer star Ronaldo after he was arrested with two transgender sex workers. We raised this question with one of our program associates who runs a small NGO serving transgender sex workers, and she surprised us by noting that these men actually interact with one another regularly, but in virtual communities. I suppose this should not have surprised us, as there are virtual communities serving every imaginable interest community, especially those representing sexuality-related interests, and as we explored this option, we found that there were multiple virtual communities of clients of transgender sex workers in most of Brazil's larger urban areas.

Thus we began the next stage of our effort by observing the interactions of "members" of two such virtual communities. We downloaded three months of postings to the forum and coded them for communications related to risky sexual behaviors, including statements endorsing high-risk sex (mainly unprotected sexual behaviors) or health-protective behaviors. As suggested by our transgender sex worker interviewees, references to high-risk sex were fairly common, although there were counterexamples in which forum members criticized those boasting about having had unprotected sex. We took careful note to assess the reactions to these posts to see if certain types of responses critical of unsafe sex received more positive reactions from some board members more than others.

The initial analyses of these posts helped the intervention design and research teams with both the design of the intervention and the design of data-collection protocol. The challenges were significant. With most HIV prevention interventions, we are able to interact directly with the intervention recipients, often involving counseling and HIV testing and treatment, and we also typically have a good deal of information about the intervention targets, including profiles of their individual patterns of risk behavior. We are also typically able to individually survey the participants and use standardized measures of some key constructs prior to, during, and after the completion of the intervention. Detailed profiles of the target population are usually essential to shaping the precise nature of the intervention. But, at least initially, we were limited to what we could read on the forum postings, and consequently we still knew almost nothing about whom we were trying to reach.

We rejected the notion of trying to reach out to individual members of the community who expressed support for high-risk sexual activities, and instead opted for a community-wide intervention approach. Our only means for reaching the community was through their web site, so we narrowed our focus to an intervention intended to shift community norms regarding acceptable and unacceptable sexual practices. We asked several transgender sex workers to advise us on the types of messages they thought might be most effective. We also recruited a couple of forum community members, based on posts they'd made in support of safer sex practices, to advise us. All agreed to work with us but insisted on anonymity.

A Community-Wide Intervention for Affecting Values of an Invisible Community

The intervention itself was simple in nature. Members of the intervention team joined the forum, which allowed them to post comments about safe sex and to react to posts describing unsafe sexual behaviors. Based on a careful analysis of forum members' reactions to various comments regarding risky sexual behaviors posted prior to the initiation of the study, we selected two themes to build the norm-focused intervention around: showing respect for the transgender sex workers, and showing respect for the health of fellow community members.

The former theme attempted to counter some messages communicating disrespect for the transgender sex workers as individuals. Such messages often used demeaning slang to refer to the sex workers in ways that depersonalized and dehumanized them. For example, many posters referred to the sex workers as whores, bitches, and much worse. Our thought was that depersonalization and dehumanization contribute to rationalization processes underlying client behaviors putting the sex workers (and themselves) at risk. Changing discourse norms regarding acceptable references to sex workers, we reasoned, might result in sexual interactions showing greater respect for the well-being of the sex workers.

The second theme, respect for the health and well-being of fellow community members, was predicated on the fact that forum members often knew one another, and would interact socially in the real world.

We reasoned that a theme of consideration for the potential consequences of one's own behavior for other members of the community
might encourage safer sexual practices. Ironically, it seemed that even
men who showed little regard for their own well-being would respond
positively to appeals to respect the integrity and health of other community members.

Delivering the intervention was fairly straightforward. Intervention
team members joined the forum and posted a variety of messages, usually but not always in response to posts by other forum members, reflecting these two themes. For example, one forum member wrote a
long description of an interaction with a sex worker in which she had
resisted his (the client's) request for unprotected anal sex until he convinced her that he would never see her again unless she agreed to forgo
using a condom. The post was laced with disparaging terms for transgender sex workers. In response, an intervention team member wrote
the following (translated and paraphrased, given the use of street slang
and crude sexual terminology):

Dude, is it really necessary to be so harsh and so disrespectful of [sex worker's
name]? Let's think about this. All of us see these girls because they bring pleasure
into our lives. Without them our lives are duller and less enjoyable. The girl you
have treated with such disrespect is someone who is just trying to make a living,
and she's trying to take care of herself at the same time. Barebacking her against
her wishes is disrespectful to her as a unique person, and shows disregard for her
health. You may not care if you pick up some nasty disease from her, but in fact
she's just as likely to get something from you as you are from her. Take a minute and
think about how you'd feel if someone coerced you to [engage in receptive bareback anal sex] against your wishes. Imagine how it feels to be manipulated because
you're poor or can't find another job. [Name] and the other [sex workers] we write
about here are not just playthings to be used and tossed away. They have lives,
families, friends, and feelings, and are easily hurt when one of us treats them so
disrespectfully. There's no need for this. Just because you are paying for sex doesn't
mean you can demand that [name] do whatever you wish. She made it clear she
wanted you to use a condom. She does this for many reasons, including protecting herself and protecting her clients, and that includes many of us here on [board
name]. You say you don't like sex with a condom. Brother, in an ideal world we
wouldn't need to use them, but we don't live in such a fantasy world. If you can't
enjoy sex with a condom, perhaps you should find someone who will be your one
and only partner. But [name] is a professional who sees lots of men, and we need to
look after her and respect her so that she will do the same for us. I think you'll also
find that if you respect these girls, they will treat you with more respect and affec-

381

tion. I don't personally know [name], but I am certain that sex is always better when there's some chemistry, and disrespect is the quickest way to poison any chemistry. Try thinking of her as a person and not only as a receptacle for your orgasms.

At the outset, these posts received mixed responses from forum members, as we expected, given that prior to the onset of the intervention most posts mentioning unsafe sex practices received neutral or minimally positive responses from other members. The question we were most interested in was whether seeding the forum with statements and responses supportive of the norm of respect, along with pro–safe sex practices, might shift community norms around these behaviors, with the hope that changing the norms of discourse on the forum might change behaviors as well.

The intervention, once fully implemented, ran for twelve months, as the intervention design team felt that this would give them ample opportunity to populate the message board with statements supportive of pro–safe sex norms.

Assessing Interventions with an Invisible Community

The research team was confronted with problems similar to those of the intervention team: how do you assess changes in norms around safe sex behaviors when you can't directly query those people subject to the intervention? I'd never conducted intervention research with a virtual community, particularly one where anonymity was carefully protected. In all of our other studies, we were able to question participants directly about beliefs, attitudes, perceptions, intentions, and self-reported behavior, and we often used measures with known psychometric characteristics to assess those constructs. In this instance, at least through the first two years of the project, we were unable to contact members of the community, per an agreement with the web board administrators. Hence we had to set aside all of our usual assessment approaches and worked with the only source of information available to us—the discussions among members of the board.

Once the intervention was put into place, the research team returned to the transcripts of postings, this time downloading six months of discussions occurring prior to the intervention for qualitative analysis, with the goal of establishing a baseline measure of forum community norms around safe sex practices. We set aside the codes from the pilot analyses that were used to help design the intervention and began with a blank slate. Graduate students experienced in qualitative coding and discourse analysis reviewed the transcripts of all discussions dealing with the use or nonuse of condoms during sex, as well as discussions touching on attitudes toward the transgender sex workers. Qualitative software (Dedoose) was used to manage the data and assist with coding and analysis.

For purposes of comparison with a control population, we downloaded and transcribed six months of discussions from a nearly identical Internet forum serving men who have sex with transgender sex workers but that was focused on a large urban community in another Brazilian state. This forum did not receive the community norm intervention. While a sample size of two does not lend itself to strong causal inference, we felt the comparison would be useful on a purely descriptive level. Thus we were able to look at change over time within our intervention community along with a comparison to a nonintervention community.

The baseline data gave us three main insights into the sexual behaviors and attitudes of the clients of transgender sex workers. First, in the majority of instances in which forum members described their "sessions" with sex workers, they referenced using condoms. Typical of such posts was the following: "So with the preliminaries out of the way, I slipped on a condom and began the fight (slang for sex)." By counting posts with particular codes or themes, we were able to quantify forum norms about interacting with sex workers. At baseline, fifty-three percent of posts describing anal sex acts in the intervention community and fifty-eight percent in the comparison forum mentioned the use of condoms. Twenty-two percent of comments in the intervention community and twenty percent in the comparison community made no mention of condom use or nonuse. Twenty-five percent of the intervention community comments explicitly mentioned condom nonuse compared to twenty-two percent in the comparison community.

Second, these more detailed analyses of the baseline data supported our earlier findings regarding the themes discussed with respect to condom use and nonuse. Every "debate" around condom use occurred in response to a forum member's posting describing unprotected anal sex. Not once did anyone criticize a member for mentioning that he'd used a condom for anal sex. On the other hand, positive responses to the mention of condom use were also rare. Instances of nonuse typically triggered discussion, and these debates often featured appeals to the twin themes of respect for the sex worker and respect for the members of the client community. Occasionally someone would also appeal to the wisdom of caring for one's own health and well-being, but this was a minor theme, although this focus on self-protection was raised more indirectly in the many discussions of the risks of unprotected sex. At least three forum members claimed to be physicians, and two of the three regularly posted references to studies on the relative risks of protected and unprotected sex with transgender sex workers. These posts tended to be more fact-based appeals to rationality ("Look at the numbers! What kind of an idiot would have bareback sex with any prostitute, but especially anal sex with a transgender one") than appeals to norms of respect for self and others.

Third, mutual oral sex was ubiquitous, and almost always carried out without protection. Only four percent and seven percent of the descriptions of sex by Internet board members mentioned condom use for oral sex, while about seventy-five percent in both communities mentioned condom nonuse for oral sex. Moreover, in the very few instances where a community member criticized another for engaging in unprotected oral sex, he was routinely dismissed as a crank or alarmist. Appeals to data on the risks of unprotected oral sex were seemingly simply ignored. Our hope was that appeals to respect for others might alter this equation.

These baseline data from the two communities were then used to assess changes in safe sex-related discourse over the course of the intervention. The research team captured all conversations and posts on the two boards on a weekly basis. All posts related to condom use or nonuse were transcribed and coded as per the protocol used during the baseline analyses. This was done for eighteen months: twelve months during the intervention and six months following the termination of the intervention, resulting in a massive amount of data.

We had not anticipated that the intervention would lead to a significant increase in board discussions around the themes central to the intervention. This occurred slowly at first, but within six months our intervention team found that they were frequently beaten to the punch by forum members quick to weigh in on the issue, and that these comments regularly reflected the respect themes. Indeed, we found increased commentary reflecting both of the expected respect themes: respect for the personhood of the sex worker and respect for the general well-being of the other community members.

Health issues were secondary, if they were mentioned at all. We did not find any increase in discourse around protection of one's own health; community members focused more on general welfare of community members than specifically on their health (although health is certainly a central component of well-being). Respondents did not put forth the concern that those engaging in unprotected sex should be concerned about their own health. They focused more on the overall well-being of the community members, and only occasionally focused primarily on health as the central component of that well-being. The comments were mostly of the "show respect for the rest of us even if you're not concerned about yourself" variety, which can be taken to imply a concern with health. But responders rarely went so far as to explicitly say, Hey, you're putting my health at risk with your behavior." This is interesting because the intervention also placed more emphasis on how unsafe sex affects the community and shows disrespect for the community rather than on an individual level. This was done because it was clear that most members really thought of this virtual community as an identity community.

Our supposition, supported by interviews conducted later with a non-representative and small sample of clients, is that health issues were too uncomfortable to raise, given that even those members of the forum who were relatively committed to safe sex practices were also clients of transgendered sex workers, were largely continuing to engage in unprotected oral sex, and therefore were engaging in behaviors that elevated their risk for a variety of STIs.

Because we were figuratively drowning in data, we randomly sampled "threads" for analysis. Most Internet forums are designed around threads (content responding to an initial post on a topic), so we chose to protect the integrity of threaded conversations. Over the course of the eighteen months of data collection, we randomly sampled 285 conversations (about one-third of the full sample of conversations) for full analysis, with two-thirds drawn during the intervention period and one-third during the post-intervention period, for each of the two communities. Our analyses focused on several key questions. Did the frequency of discussions of safe sex practices not triggered by an intervention team member post increase over time? Did these same themes increase in the intervention forum relative to the comparison forum? Did the themes of respect for sex workers, community members, and self appear with greater frequency over time? Were discussions of these themes more common in the intervention-forum community relative to the comparison-forum community? Did the ratio of mentions of condom use relative to mentions of nonuse increase over time? Was this same ratio more positive in the intervention than the comparison forum? These final two questions were analyzed separately for mentions of condom use and nonuse for anal and oral sex.

The power of this fairly simple intervention surprised us. Overall, as mentioned before, the discussion of safe sex-related topics increased significantly (speaking not in the statistical sense, but in the practical and meaningful sense) over time within the intervention community. There was no corresponding change in the comparison community. During the preintervention phase, most discussions stemming from a report of condom nonuse focused on health risks, with the discussion generally revolving around the tradeoffs between risk and pleasure. This remained the case in the comparison community across the data collection period, while in the intervention community the respect themes dominated discussions within six months of the intervention's onset. Within eight months of the intervention's onset, only seven percent of discussions of anal sex within the intervention community mentioned nonuse of condoms, compared with twenty-five percent at baseline. In contrast, there was no meaningful change in the rate of mentions of condom nonuse within the comparison community over the eighteen-month course of the study (twenty-two percent versus eighteen percent).

Our one disappointment was that the intervention had absolutely no discernible impact on mentions of condom use/nonuse for oral sex. The intervention and comparison communities looked remarkably similar on this outcome variable. This failure was not entirely unexpected, given the high baseline rates of nonuse for oral sex, and given the discourse around condom use for oral sex we saw in the baseline data. Later conversations with both transgender sex workers and the small sample of clients we interviewed suggested that both groups found the risk/reward ratio for unprotected oral sex significantly less daunting than the same ratio for unprotected anal sex. The sex workers, in separate conversations, acknowledged that they, too, disliked giving or receiving oral sex with condoms. From an actuarial and epidemiological standpoint, both groups are correct with respect to the relative risks associated with unprotected oral and anal sex, but a lower risk/reward ratio does not imply insignificant risk. Nevertheless, our informants assured us that unprotected oral sex was deeply ingrained in Brazilian sexual culture, and neither our intervention nor anyone else's was likely to change this.

We were somewhat surprised by the staying power of the intervention. After twelve months, the intervention team stopped their posts to the forum, but discussions of safe sex behaviors framed around the respect themes continued, as forum-community members appeared to have adopted these themes as personal and community norms. One forum member started a thread on the "ethics of commercial sex," and the most common theme repeated in this thread was that, absent mutual respect between client and provider, commercial sex takes on coercive properties that undermine both pleasure and well-being. Mutual respect was exhibited through consistent mutual consent on what took place between provider and client. Board members continued to speak of "sex with respect" and to harshly criticize those expressing support for unsafe behaviors or making demeaning remarks about the sex workers.

We remain somewhat in the dark about many issues, because our primary source of data was Internet forum discussions. It is difficult to determine, for example, whether individual community members whose statements in support of unsafe sex actually changed their attitudes over the course of the study, as we were unable to track change at the individual level. It is conceivable that members holding such attitudes simply stopped expressing them in order to avoid criticism, although the expression of unpopular views seems common on most Internet forums, where members communicate anonymously. And we have no idea whether the changes in expressed norms around respect and safe sex translated into genuine behavioral change. We did find that self-reports of unprotected sex declined significantly over time within the intervention-forum community but not within the comparison community, but this too may reflect reporting bias stemming from perceived pressure to offer socially desirable responses on the part of forum members. Finally, we have no way of knowing whether the intervention might have reduced rates of HIV and STIs within the target community. Mention of exposure to STIs was very rare, and self-reports of such matters are untrustworthy for a variety of reasons.

Nevertheless, the state and federal ministries of health found the results encouraging enough to adopt the "Let's Respect One Another" theme for a variety of interventions intended to reduce HIV and STIs. In addition to expanding the model to other Internet communities serving clients of sex workers (including transgender, male, and female sex workers), the ministries mounted a large public information campaign around the respect theme, featuring TV ads, billboards, signage on public transportation, and a variety of other actions focused on large public events such as Carnival and music festivals.

Methods and Questions Revisited

Necessity is often the driving force behind the selection of research methods used in a study. By virtue of the fact that we were working with an invisible, virtual, and somewhat stigmatized population, we felt that it was best to make use of the qualitative "data" provided by forum members through their web site conversations. The anonymity of the site seemed to provide members with a certain freedom to speak on topics and describe interactions with transgender sex workers that they might well have been reluctant to address in other ways. The conversations on the forum were seemingly candid and extremely explicit, providing the research team with a glimpse into this community that probably could not have been accomplished in any other manner. Conversely, during the early stages of our work, we felt it would be disruptive to try to enter the community and solicit participation in quantitative data collection.

We were able to contact and survey some community members as the study wound down, but we are quite certain that those who were willing to respond to our requests for interviews and online surveys using quantitative measures were atypical. Reliance on the quantitative data alone would have been a mistake, and given the selection bias resulting from relying on volunteers, we placed little weight on our quantitative findings in this instance. Looking back, we probably should have forgone this part of the data collection, but given that most of the research team came from primarily quantitative disciplines (public health, psychology), we found it hard to set aside old habits.

Questions should drive methods, and not vice versa. In this intervention study, both the questions asked and the nature of the population being served dictated that we rely primarily on qualitative data sources. In some of our other studies with other high-risk populations, the questions and the nature of the population allowed for a different balance of methods. This is as it should be.

References

Baral, Stefan D., Tonia Poteat, Susanne Strömdahl, Andrea L. Wirtz, Thomas E. Guadamuz, and Chris Beyrer. 2013. "Worldwide Burden of HIV in Transgender Women: A Systematic Review and Meta-Analysis." *The Lancet Infectious Diseases* 13 (3): 214–22.

Gardner, William, and Brian L. Wilcox. 1993. "Political Intervention in Scientific Peer Review. Research on Adolescent Sexual Behavior." *American Psychologist* 48 (9): 972–83.

Poteat, Tonia, Andrea L. Wirtz, Anita Radix, Annick Borquez, Alfonso Silva-Santisteban, Madeline B. Deutsch, Sharful Islam Khan, Sam Winter, and Don Operario. 2015. "HIV Risk and Preventive Interventions in Transgender Women Sex Workers." *The Lancet* 385: 274–86.

Wilcox, Brian L. 1999. "Sexual Obsessions: Public Policy and Adolescent Girls." In *Beyond Appearance: A New Look at Adolescent Girls*, edited by Norine Johnson, Michael Roberts, and Judith Worrell, 333–54. Washington, DC: American Psychological Association.

PART SEVEN

Why Mixed Methods?

TWENTY

Findings That Matter: A Commentary

THOMAS S. WEISNER

Our purpose for research and scholarship is to discover findings that matter. Methods matter to the extent that they provide tools, ways of working, that lead to findings about the world that matter. In this commentary on the papers and the theme of the volume, I will describe how a commitment to integrating a wider range of qualitative and quantitative research methods can matter—matter for what goals and for whom—and use the papers in our volume, and some of my own research and others', as examples. Integrating a wide range of qualitative and quantitative methods in research, a theme for this volume, greatly increases the likelihood of producing findings that matter, as does strong research design and incorporating context and experience into our work. I also will describe how our professional practices as researchers can contribute to this goal for the fields of anthropology and more broadly in the social sciences.

Research and Findings That Matter

Research that is primarily focused on findings that matter extends beyond what is usually considered applied, policy, clinical, evaluation, or intervention studies. Research can influence policy, practice, and well-being through basic social science, not necessarily through work specifically focused on a policy or applied issue. Similarly, research specifically focused on practical benefit feeds back to basic knowledge in social science. So "public anthropology" at its best speaks to anthropology and social science generally, not only what focuses only on current social issues. Research that improves a core theory, or improves research methods, or discovers mechanisms that influence society and behavior is the basis for research explicitly contributing to policy, practice, or current issues. Findings that matter for current policy and practice issues always will have implications for basic knowledge as well.

Research that discovers findings that matter can make a difference—can matter—in many ways, and the studies in this volume illustrate this beautifully. For example, we can discover findings that matter when they add to the empirical, descriptive *evidence base* for how people and communities behave, think, and feel around the world: How do gang members experience their participation and then "age out" of their world? How do physicians and neurology patients communicate and use the Internet? What are the experiences of parents of adults with autism in India? Findings can matter for discovering the *mechanisms* in the social and biosocial world that produce the outcomes that we are studying (the role of explanatory models for illness identification and treatment; multiple caretaking of children and the effects on social behavior development; neighborhood poverty concentration and child maltreatment). Findings matter to the extent that they will improve *theory and conceptual frameworks* and can increase the use of *international and cultural-comparative evidence* (attachment theory placed in the context of the world's differences in child socialization; family understanding and accommodation to children with mental illness and disability; predictive logic models for reducing family poverty).

Findings matter for *integrating our work across the social sciences* by framing work in a way that moves beyond a particular discipline or subfield and speaks to wider questions. Our research findings also can matter to the extent that they are *in the service of improving the well-being of those whom we study*. The conceptualization of outcomes in this volume includes both standardized, normed scales and indicators, as well as contextual understanding of well-being—that is, the ability of a child to competently engage in the activities deemed desirable by the family and communities he or she lives in, and the experiences produced by that active engagement (Weisner 2014).

Many of the studies in our book identified a gap in understanding and then framed this as a puzzle to solve through empirical research.

The implicit question is: "it is currently unknown if" something was true, or why something was true, or what the mechanisms are that contribute to behaviors. Bernheimer, Gallimore, and Keogh frame their work on disability and educational achievement in this way (how do families accommodate to their children with disabilities, and what outcomes for parents and children result?), as do Huston, Duncan, and Yoshikawa in their review of experimental studies using mixed methods (can an antipoverty program tied to work and supports for children reduce poverty and improve child well-being; how and for whom might such programs work?).

Many of these papers contribute to theory through their richness, inclusiveness, and holism, and by mobilizing conceptual frameworks from a wide range of disciplines in the social and biological sciences (the chapters by Bernheimer, Gallimore, and Keogh; Duncan, Huston, and Yoshikawa; Edwards; Fuligni; Harkness and Super; Worthman; Keller; Korbin; Lowe, and others all do this). Nine (forty percent) of our twenty-three contributors are anthropologists, with other contributors from education or psychology—most with strong cultural and international emphasis—and economics. These interdisciplinary studies bring biological, ecological, cultural, and psychological theory and concepts into their work. Of course, interdisciplinary research and integrating a range of methods very often go together. The papers do more than mention these theoretical concepts but then ignore them; the papers often are embedded in a richly described local context, with complex daily processes and constraints, and thus more likely will produce findings that matter because the local context and meaning systems are bracketed in. Harkness and Super illustrate this in their chapter on mixed methods and the importance of analysis of the developmental context, as does Maynard's deep knowledge of the Mayan cultural community. Daley's chapter on the daily concerns of parents of adults with autism in India is explicitly about that daily routine, for example, as is the disability research with families from Bernheimer, Gallimore, and Keogh's chapter, and Hay's observations of actual clinical interviews and patient care in Los Angeles.

Research that uses "mixed methods" or "integrated qualitative and quantitative" methods, as these studies do, also seeks to understand a problem holistically and communicate across the methodological boundaries that unfortunately can divide disciplines (Weisner 1996). LeVine provides a rich history and argues for the contemporary relevance of this mixed methods tradition across the social sciences. Interdisciplinary work and mixed methods were expected, the default, in the development of the social sciences until the recent era of increasing specialization! Lieber illustrates this in his paper, as well as the added value of mixed methods software as research tools to make integrating qualitative and quantitative data easier.

Several chapters present research focused on interventions for the purpose of improving well-being. Many of these studies involve research that uses "practice to research" or "partnership" models, in which communities and practitioners and researchers work together from the first moments of research conceptualization; these types of studies by design are meant to make a difference for practices or policy that hopefully can improve the well-being of children and families. There are many examples of this kind of collaboration throughout the book, including Daley, Edwards, Gallimore, Hay, Korbin, Vigil, Wilcox, and others.

The research programs in this book show how valuable integration of methods and interdisciplinary work can be. But have no doubt: it is neither easy nor the default today. Our rather expansive approach to both qualitative methods and the integration of qualitative with quantitative methods in interdisciplinary research in our book is certainly not universally agreed upon nor widely practiced (as yet). In principle yes, such work may be valorized, but in practice (in teaching, training, funding, publishing, disseminating) not as much. There are "paradigm wars," closed-off schools of thought, and derogatory reviews. Even within qualitative and ethnographic fields, there is a great deal of critique, ambiguity, and interpretive debate about methods. In anthropology, for example, qualitative methods, ethnography, and fieldwork seemingly are continually in a "crisis" of representation, practice, and interpretation. Any research encounter involving fieldwork and a personal relationship with participants will be fraught with reflexivity, contingencies, unknown effects, and situational influences. But nonetheless, "being there" in the field, in the community, in the classrooms and living rooms of those we study, matters greatly (Borneman and Hammoudi 2009).

Basic Science Remains Close to Practice and Intervention Research

Findings that can matter for policy, practice, or public impact do not have to be explicitly guided by a policy or practice question, or by a social concern or problem. Findings that matter for policy or practice can come from basic social science knowledge, knowledge transfer from other fields, and from making contributions to general community understanding of a topic or problem. Public understanding, or the "enlightenment function" of research, has inherent value and in turn provides the basis for support for more specific public anthropology work.

Heidi Keller's chapter on prototypical socioecological environments (interdependent and independent) has led to a wide range of studies on family functioning and developmental theory in infancy and later childhood stages. Her current work with Hiltrud Otto and others on attachment theory and early emotional socialization for calmness, social intelligence, and awareness of context (a widespread pattern around the world) is a particularly strong example (Otto and Keller 2014). The mixed method and contextual framework described by Harkness and Super, Keller, and Worthman, and many others in the book suggests that global developments in policy and interventions for children and families will not be helpful for local communities if based exclusively on a middle-class Western development model.

Richard Shweder is an exemplar of this kind of crossover from basic theory (culture theory and psychological/cognitive theory) to applications that matter for contemporary social issues, including the remarkable collection *The Child: An Encyclopedic Companion* (Shweder et al. 2009). Shweder also co-organized a conference in the mid-1990s on the use of ethnography in human development research (Jessor, Colby, and Shweder 1996), for example. Taking local beliefs and practices and their meanings seriously has led to papers debating practices such as cosleeping, gender, initiation ceremonies, female and male genital surgery, food preferences, immigration, and many other contested "hot" topics of current policy relevance (e.g., Minow, Shweder, and Markus 2008).

Worthman's chapter on ecocultural theory illustrates the vital pathways between basic theory and her decades of work in Kenya and around the world on biosocial mechanisms for wellness and well-being, often in a public health and community health context. Harkness and Super also have done ground-breaking research in several international projects, including their comparative infancy studies across Europe and in the United States, international public health work in Southeast Asia, their studies in Kenya with the Kipsigis, and much more. Their developmental niche model ("the physical and social settings of development, the customary methods of child care, and the psychology of the caretakers") (Harkness and Super 1996, 449) has been widely taken up as a conceptual framework for contextual studies of development.

Carolyn Edwards has contributed seminal books and papers from the *Children of Different Worlds* studies with Beatrice Whiting (Whiting and Edwards 1988), which found basic patterns in children's and caregivers' social behaviors across fourteen communities around the world. These are basic science studies in comparative human development research, not initially pointed toward policy or intervention. At the same time, Edwards has described Reggio Emilia in Italy, and worked with Half the Sky Foundation and preschool programs in Nebraska. Edwards develops general, basic developmental science findings, discovered through mixed methods work on maternal care and contexts of care, which in turn are used to describe and improve the quality of early education and girls' opportunities. Jill Korbin similarly has combined an internationally recognized career in the field of child maltreatment and cultural variations in parenting and child care, with her leadership in the field of policy studies as director of the Schubert Center at Case Western and her experience as a Congressional Fellow in the US Senate with Bill Bradley. Her work on maltreatment is contextual, emphasizing the roles of neighborhood and culturally accepted practices in diverse local communities. Brian Wilcox has a parallel career trajectory working as a fellow and then for the American Psychological Association, and directs the Center on Children, Families and the Law, a major policy research center at the University of Nebraska, all the while continuing research on adolescent sex education and policy, HIV/AIDS interventions around the world, and other topics.

Ashley Maynard's work presents three-plus generations of longitudinal research with a Mayan community in Southern Mexico, including path-breaking work on intergenerational change in parenting, children's work and schooling, and the effects of economic, demographic, and gender role changes. At the same time, she has brought these insights into her teaching, a major new textbook in human development that highlights cultural and international children and families, and a wide-ranging research, lecturing, and teaching career. Cameron Hay also built her research, methods, and theoretical base from her intensive ethnographic fieldwork in Lombok in Indonesia on health, well-being, and health practices in an impoverished community there, and now is working with patients and physicians in Los Angeles and the US Midwest on doctor-patient communication to improve patient health outcomes.

Ted Lowe's research on suicide and adolescence in Chuuk, Micronesia, not only has contributed to the general theory of suicide and the particular context and economic era found in Chuuk, but he also has worked with local communities on the issue to find ways to improve the circumstances there. His work on poverty has a similar crossover in poverty and globalization theory, mixed methods, and applied relevance. Tamara Daley also has devoted her professional career to applied, policy, and intervention research at the large national research firm Westat. Daley also has made contributions to cross-cultural findings as well while a student and clinical postdoctoral fellow at UCLA with her research on Cambodian immigrant families and adolescent mental health issues, collaborative work done at UCLA on nutrition and schooling outcomes in Kenya, and on the beliefs of teens with disabilities in Los Angeles regarding self and identity.

Greg Duncan, Aletha Huston, and Hiro Yoshikawa are international leaders exemplifying this tradition of research that adds to basic scientific understanding of human development, is interdisciplinary, and provides high-impact policy and intervention research findings on both national and international issues, including interventions for policy reduction; Head Start; effects of media, gender, immigration processes, and policies; and many others. Andrew Fuligni also has pioneered research in immigrant communities in the United States to examine their family dynamics and educational outcomes. Diego Vigil has written both on the Latino/Chicano experience in the United States, and the worlds of gangs and lives of gang members in the United States and internationally, and has consulted in many settings based on this work.

Last but not least, Cindy Bernheimer, Ron Gallimore, and Barbara Keogh describe the CHILD Project, a longitudinal research program on the study of families with children with developmental disabilities. These studies of families with children with developmental disabilities focused on family daily routines and accommodations parents provided for children. This work shows that more stable, sustainable family routines predicted long-term family outcomes as well or better than child diagnoses or standard parental stress scales. In addition, Gallimore's chapter lays down the "first law" of both the theory and the practice of educational intervention research: "It depends"! A successful intervention research program begins with an understanding of the ecology and culture of the schools and classrooms or families. What interventions will fit within and survive and be sustainable in the local school, classroom, and community context? He illustrates a sequential approach, a model of continuous improvement, and an institutional learning model for lasting change, using mixed methods throughout. Gallimore and many colleagues combine basic research on classroom learning and behavior change theory with long-term intervention and educational development work with Native Hawai'ian, Latino, and other children.

I have had similar research experiences in which basic research findings using mixed methods led to further policy and applied studies that were informed by the basic research, which (I hope) also produced findings that mattered. A series of early research studies in Kenya beginning in 1968 illustrate this wonderfully virtuous—and quite unpredictable—research circle. The research began as a project to understand the effects of rural-urban migration on children and parents; at that time, the modernization framework was the standard model for theorizing this process and the rural-urban migration that went with it. This theory proposed that as new nations emerged from colonial control (Kenya did so formally in 1963), the growing wage-labor economy and new political and educational opportunities would lead to new sets of beliefs and values. These would in turn lead to changes in parenting strategies and beliefs more similar to those of the Western middle class.

I was a fortunate participant in the collaborative *Children of Different Worlds* studies, created by John and Beatrice Whiting as part of the Child Development Research Unit in Kenya, which used a wide range of fieldwork methods. I assembled a sample of low-income Nairobi households with young and middle-childhood-age children to track these changes in parenting and children's social behavior. But the urban family sample I started with in order to study change in children's behavior and parenting kept shifting and disappearing; forty percent had left my Nairobi site after four months!—but later, some of them returned from their rural homes. The truly appropriate sample design—which best fit the social situation for families and children—was a matched comparison, because it would capture the fluid commuting and migration back and forth. The sample finally selected for these studies was composed of two groups: a sample of urban families from a single low-income housing estate in Nairobi, and a matched sample of families related to those urban families from the same lineage and clan locations they came from in Western Kenya, Kisa Location. Following these families for two years, talking with parents, observing and assessing children, and understanding the contexts of care in a complicated economic and family setting led to many important findings, including the importance of multiple caregiving of children by other children.

Sibling caretaking remained an important form of care but was disrupted due to urban-rural migration; for example, older children might remain in the rural area while younger children came to Nairobi with their mothers. The multiple-care system was partly disrupted, putting pressures on mothers and younger children in the city especially. Sociable, nurturant, and responsible social interactions were more frequent in the rural homes in part because the sibling care system was more intact. Disruptive, aggressive mother-child interactions increased in Nairobi when the socially distributed care system, with its multi-age, multisex group, was less available. The original attribution of the mechanisms causing changes in children's social behavior due to urban migration or modernization current at the time (change in parent values and beliefs) simply had not considered the effect of changes in sibcare or socially distributed care into this model, because the conceptual framework had not included this important caregiving system, and research methods up to then largely had missed it (Weisner 1982; Weisner, Bradley, and Kilbride 1997).

The work on multiple caretaking, migration, and global change in turn raised new questions; what was originally "basic research" in culture and human development led to practice, policy, and public research in unexpected ways (Weisner and Gallimore 1977). The surprising research findings on socially distributed caregiving influencing the effects of migration on children and parenting in turn led to a series of papers on sibling care and other forms of socially distributed care that have had influence in the child development and cross-cultural research field certainly not anticipated at the time. For example, how should siblings be participating in care for children whose parents have died due to HIV/AIDS? —the circumstances of drastically reduced resources, supervision, and support are very different; what are the implications for dyadic attachment theory models?—plural attachment to multiple caregivers is the more common and more likely evolutionary adaptation (Weisner 2015); what of the role of sibling care among Native Hawai'ians and implications for classroom practices?—it occurs but not uniformly across all households; aspects of the practice can be useful in classroom management and mixed-age tutoring (Weisner, Gallimore, and Jordan 1988). If children work for the family, or do child care, does that come under efforts to regulate and eliminate child labor? If girls are more likely to be child caretakers, and so be held out of school, should the practice be changed or accommodated? If child care is seen as preparation for motherhood and parenting, and girls do it more often, what are the implications for early marriage, arranged marriage, and family cycles of early marriage? Patricia East (East, Weisner, and Reyes 2006) extended sibcare questions into her studies of teen Latina mothers (who in turn have their younger siblings and cousins caring for their children around twenty-five percent of the time). These research questions and findings mattered because the conversations between basic research and policy or practice studies are fluid, closely connected, and can influence one another in unexpected ways, and because a wide range of methods and research designs helped to frame and to answer some of these questions. But without mixed methods that included fieldwork ("being there" in close personal and community contact), ethnography, and context-relevant samples, many of the original findings regarding sibling and socially distributed care and their effects would have been missed.

Research That Invites Conversations across Disciplines and across Methods

Findings matter when they can *integrate our work across the social sciences* so that what anthropology finds with ethnography or person-centered interviews can be used, for example, with what psychology finds with questionnaires or fMRI, and public health finds with quantitative epidemiology. Mixed methods and the best research designs available make this goal easier and reduce methodocentrism, as so many of these chapters demonstrate (Weisner 2011a, Weisner 2012). Pluralism in the methods we use increases the likelihood that we will discover new information about the topics, people and places we are studying. It can persuade more readers of our work that our descriptions and findings are believable (valid, reliable, veridical, captures local context and experience, coherent, in conversation with other points of view). Integration of methods often goes along with richer descriptions and understanding of the context and the mechanisms leading to the behavior we are interested in, and is often essential for including evidence across levels of analysis (e.g., biological, social, cultural, psychological, ecological) (Weisner 2005). In the chapters in our volume, methods are not simply added separately, or in parallel. They are integrated in a coordinated, intentional way to help test a theory, discover new evidence, or systematically add value and validity through different voices and perspectives.

Every chapter in this volume, and every contributor, integrates a range of methods. For example, Huston, Duncan, and Yoshikawa describe some of the improvements in the intervention and policy research field made possible through the integration of qualitative and quantitative methods: (1) understanding mechanisms of program or policy impact; (2) understanding the implementation of the program or policy and relating implementation to impacts; (3) interpreting null findings; (4) interpreting treatment impact heterogeneity; (5) informing further improvement of the program or policy. Robert LeVine's chapter makes the historical case that integration across methods and disciplines was the default practice throughout the rise of the social sciences and has always been a touchstone for many in the field. It is only in more recent decades that silos have been established, journals and publication venues become more restrictive, and training more specialized and exclusive.

This volume exemplifies ways to counter this trend. Many contributors did not start out with specialized training and expertise in mixed methods or research designs. Many partnered with colleagues who have the other skills in collaborative research groups. Funders and journals may have asked in the past, "why are you using qualitative methods?" or "why are you using a questionnaire or survey with this cultural group?" Perhaps in the future the question will be, "why are mixed methods not incorporated into this study?" The gold standard for social science research should be a thoughtfully designed, integrated multimethod study to the extent possible (Yoshikawa et al. 2008). For most programs of research, mixed methods should be the default expectation, the unmarked strategy.

Expertise in particular methods is of course important and desirable; but expertise and specialization should not lead to excluding the consideration of other methods. Research studies using only one or a small set of particular methods of course are valuable; a research *program* intended to explore a topic more broadly, however, should normally have diverse methods incorporated. Other ways to counter the methodocentric or silo trends are to explicitly include mixed methods as among the criteria favored in research proposals, as well as offering support for mixed methods in other ways. Providing workshops, and connecting scholars in diverse fields who are doing mixed methods research but perhaps are unaware of others also doing so, are useful ways that senior scholars, funding agencies, and others can encourage mixed methods. Explicitly including the rich description of context and social settings in criteria for publication and funding also can have a positive effect on the reporting of research findings in ways that make them more useful for comparative analysis. One way to put pressure in this direction, of course, is to direct funding toward such work! Workshops at meetings with funders and grantees—as many of these authors in this volume have done with groups of NIH K awardees, NIH Institutes,

Foundations (The W. T. Grant Foundation, led by Robert Granger, initiated a mixed methods program, for example, which continues), and other venues—provide hands-on training in skills and techniques for integrating mixed methods.

Tools for doing qualitative analysis of text, photos, and video also have improved and make it easier to use mixed methods; they are now easier and cheaper to use. Consider how relatively easy it is to use statistical analysis software now available for instant use on a laptop; there are online tutorials, workshops, and other taken-for-granted training opportunities for undergraduates and graduate students alike. Qualitative and mixed-methods software is moving in this direction; training and routine use in teaching should also become more common. Eli Lieber, Jason Taylor, and I developed such software, Dedoose (Dedoose .com), initially for our own use when we could not find other software that met our needs. It is now spun off as a commercial software tool with tens of thousands of users.

Research That Focuses on a Policy or Social Problem

Research that matters can of course explicitly aim to produce results that directly claim to improve the well-being of families and children. I've pointed out the many chapters in this volume where this is the goal and the result. The study of poverty reduction and child well-being among working poor families and children (Lowe; Huston, Duncan, and Yoshikawa) illustrates research demonstrating potential gains in well-being for children as well as for their parents and other adults. Children and parents can benefit from anti-poverty programs that combine wage work with income supplements, child care, health care, and other benefits, although not all families participate and not all children benefit equally.

New Hope, for example, included a random experimental design with ethnographic, qualitative, child assessment, classroom teacher ratings, administrative, questionnaire, and survey research methods, as described by Duncan, et al. New Hope did reduce poverty and resulted in many other positive outcomes for children and adults. However, the theory or logic model for how New Hope would reduce poverty did not always work as expected, leading to proposed revisions of the theory more generally as a conceptual model of change for future interventions. The model proposed that a change in resources through work supports and child-care supports could change parenting practices and/or parental investment in children; the combination of resource supports and parenting in turn could produce gains in academic achievement, child health, and other well-being outcomes in children. The results of the experiment and mixed methods analyses showed that some of these pathways made a difference and some did not. Gallimore's work in education and classrooms also combines basic theory for learning, teaching, and behavior change on the one hand, with rich contextual understanding in the service of improving reading, math, and academic achievement on the other. Similarly, Lieber's Head Start example is related to an assessment of an early literacy curriculum program intended to improve preparation of low-income children for school.

Findings matter *for those we study* through improving well-being and through engaging and participating with the community as part of the research—seeing their world through their experiences. I believe that our research stance in this respect should be a collaborative one, based on the stance of a *committed fair witness* (Weisner 2011b). That is, we should be committed to research that might improve the well-being of families and communities, which characterizes all of the studies in this volume. We must aim to be fair in the sense of having the strongest conceptual framework, research design, measures, analyses, and so forth that are possible to bring to the research. Being fair involves being truly open to many possibilities in our findings, not only those we favor or that might support our advocacy of a certain kind of change, or our own beliefs. That is, being fair means being open to the possibility that our prior expectations may be wrong or need revision, and that outcomes hoped for may not have happened. And finally, our methods should ultimately ensure that we are witnessing what we want to study, most likely through including at least some ethnography, fieldwork, contextual and cultural understanding, and direct, personal connection to the experiences of the participants in our research. Many of the chapters in this volume reflect the authors' own versions of this kind of committed fair witness approach.

Findings That Matter for Researchers and Their Careers

Finally, we would be missing an important part of the story of research findings and methods that matter if we do not consider our own careers and how we best can approach work using mixed methods. Academic researchers' work is typically divided up into three categories: teaching, research, and administration/service to the university and to the community. Work for a research firm such as Daley does with Westat is largely research and management; for Lieber it also means developing Dedoose as a business. The contributors to this book not only take on the usual tasks, but exemplify how to combine even more roles than research, teaching, and administration. There are at least five more kinds of tasks or professional roles that add value to producing and making use of findings that matter reflected in many of the chapters and the careers of the authors contributing to this book.

First, several authors are involved in frank activism and public advocacy through political action, op-ed writing, and serving with organizations that do this; Edwards, Korbin, Wilcox, Vigil, and others have done these types of activities, for example. Second, several have served in legislative or executive branches of government, or in NGO and intermediary organizations. Korbin directs a policy center, served as an aide in the US Senate and has taken on similar roles; Harkness has been a State Department Fellow; Wilcox served as an aide in Congress, worked for the American Psychological Association, and has been an advisor to a variety of agencies; Wilcox, Korbin, and I serve on the board of ChildFund International; Daley's work at Westat is often directly used by government in policy, and the work is contracted for that purpose; Vigil consults for LAPD and other departments; Yoshikawa, Duncan, Huston, and others have served in policy-advisory roles of many kinds, and I am sure there are other examples among the contributors. Third, many contributors give lectures and talks outside of our professional worlds and disciplines. They are bringing their work to other fields, and write for popular magazines and blogs (Shweder writes for *Psychology Today*, for example). Fourth, several authors are involved with foundations, federal funding agencies such as NSF or NIH, and are involved in policy decisions regarding how research funds should be allocated (for example, Weisner, Wilcox, Duncan, Yoshikawa, Worthman, and Huston have done this with the W. T. Grant Foundation and other foundations, LeVine for the Spencer Foundation, and no doubt there are others). And finally, the development and dissemination of new tools and research methods can improve research that contributes findings that matter (Lieber is the president of Dedoose, for example, as well as holding a research position at UCLA). These, then, are scholars who not only are leaders in their research fields, but are taking research findings and following through to attempt to make them matter in the world in many ways. Their research mattered to them personally. Grounded in their disciplines, they also were able to reach out to other fields, use diverse methods and tools, and do so in many roles and settings.

In summary, the chapters in this volume are terrific examples of mixed methods work (including creative research designs and uses of theory across disciplines) that produced many findings that mattered (in the many senses of this term). They discovered new findings about the world and the mechanisms that produced those results. They are very often international and cross-cultural/comparative in scope and evidence, and are interdisciplinary. They integrate a wide range of methods; they reflect many versions of the "committed fair witness" orientation to research on policy and public issues; they contribute to both general theory, methods, and mechanisms in the social sciences, as well as focusing on community and policy issues and producing results that could improve the well-being of families and communities.

References

Borneman, J., and A. Hammoudi, eds. (2009). *Being There: The Fieldwork Encounter and the Making of Truth*. Berkeley: University of California Press.

Duncan, Greg J., Aletha C. Huston, and Thomas S. Weisner. 2007. *Higher Ground: New Hope for the Working Poor and Their Children*. New York: Russell Sage Foundation.

East, Patricia L., Thomas S.Weisner, and Barbara T. Reyes. 2006. "Youths' Caretaking of Their Adolescent Sisters' Children: Its Costs and Benefits for Youths' Development." *Applied Developmental Science* 10 (2): 86–95.

Harkness, Sara, and Charles M. Super, eds. 1996. *Parents' Cultural Belief Systems*. New York: Guilford Press.

Jessor, Richard, Anne Colby, and Richard A. Shweder, eds. 1996. *Ethnography and Human Development: Context and Meaning in Social Inquiry*. Chicago: University of Chicago Press.

Minow, Martha, Richard A. Shweder, and Hazel Rose Markus. 2008. *Just Schools: Pursuing Equality in Societies of Difference*. New York: Russell Sage Foundation.

Otto, Hiltrud, and Heidi Keller. 2014. *Different Faces of Attachment: Cultural Variations on a Universal Human Need*. Cambridge: Cambridge University Press.

Shweder, Richard A., Thomas R. Bidell, Anne C. Dailey, Suzanne D. Dixon, Peggy J. Miller, and John Modell, eds. 2009. *The Child: An Encyclopedic Companion*. Chicago: University of Chicago Press.

Weisner, Thomas S. 1982. "Sibling Interdependence and Child Caretaking: A Cross-Cultural View." In *Sibling Relationships: Their Nature and Significance across the Lifespan*, edited by M. Lamb and B. Sutton-Smith, 305–27. Hillsdale, NJ: Erlbaum.

———. 1996. "Why Ethnography Should Be the Most Important Method in the Study of Human Development." In *Ethnography and Human Development: Context and Meaning in Social Inquiry*, edited by Richard Jessor, Anne Colby, and Richard A. Shweder, 305–24. Chicago: University of Chicago Press.

———, ed. 2005. *Discovering Successful Pathways in Children's Development: Mixed Methods in the Study of Childhood and Family Life*, The John D. and Catherine T. MacArthur Foundation Series on Mental Health and Human Development. Chicago: University of Chicago Press.

———. 2011a. "Culture." In *Social Development: Relationships in Infancy, Childhood and Adolescence*, edited by Marion K. Underwood and Lisa H. Rosen, 372–99. New York: Guilford.

———. 2011b. "'If You Work in This Country You Should Not Be Poor, and Your Kids Should Be Doing Better': Bringing Mixed Methods and Theory in Psychological Anthropology to Improve Research in Policy and Practice." *Ethos* 39 (4): 455–76.

———. 2012. "Mixed Methods Should Be a Valued Practice in Anthropology." *Anthropology News* 53 (5): 3–4.

———. 2014. "Culture, Context, and Child Well-Being." In *Handbook of Child Well-Being*, edited by Asher Ben-Arieh, Ferran Casas, Ivar Frones, and Jill E. Korbin, 87–103. Dordrecht, The Netherlands: Springer Reference.

Weisner, T.S. 2015. The Socialization of Trust: Plural Caretaking and Plural Pathways in Human Development across Cultures. In Otto, H. and H. Keller, eds. *Different Faces of Attachment*. Cambridge, UK: Oxford Univ. Press, 263–277.

Weisner, Thomas S., and Ronald Gallimore. 1977. "My Brother's Keeper: Child and Sibling Caretaking." *Current Anthropology* 18: 169–90.

Weisner, Thomas S., Candace Bradley, and Philip L. Kilbride, eds. 1997. *African Families and the Crisis of Social Change*. Westport, CT: Bergin & Garvey.

Weisner, Thomas S., Ronald Gallimore, and Cathie Jordan. 1988. "Unpackaging Cultural Effects on Classroom Learning: Hawaiian Peer Assistance and Child-Generated Activity." *Anthropology and Education Quarterly* 19: 327–53.

Whiting, Beatrice, and Carolyn Pope Edwards. 1988. *Children of Different Worlds: The Formation of Social Behavior*. Cambridge, MA: Harvard University Press.

Yoshikawa, Hirokazu, Thomas S. Weisner, Ariel Kalil, and Niobe Way. 2008. "Mixing Qualitative and Quantitative Research in Developmental Science: Uses and Methodological Choices." *Developmental Psychology* 44 (2) (March): 344–54.

Contributors

LUCINDA P. BERNHEIMER, PHD Lucinda Bernheimer has spent thirty years in the field of early childhood special education. Her research has focused on children with disabilities and their families. With Barbara Keogh she served as a codirector of Project REACH within the UCLA Department of Psychiatry's Sociobehavioral Group from 1985 to 2004. This longitudinal study followed young children with developmental delays and their families for thirty years. She was also a member of the multidisciplinary team that followed children similar to those in the REACH sample for a twenty-year period (Project CHILD). With Tom Weisner she conducted ethnographic research with counter-cultural families, and with families making the transition from welfare to work. Bernheimer has been involved in program and systems evaluations at the local, state, and national levels and has served as evaluator for the Chartwell Education Group, the Hilton/Early Head Start training program, the California Early Intervention Distance Learning Project, and the California Early Intervention Evaluation: Implementation of Part H and the Family Resource Centers. Currently, she is a senior research associate at the WestEd Center for Child and Family Studies.

TAMARA COHEN DALEY, PHD Tamara Daley is a Westat senior study director with seventeen years' experience conducting research and evaluation on educational, health, and mental health issues. She has led or contributed to the design of evaluations of varying complexity, including single-site national and international programs and multisite longitudinal studies. She is well versed in conducting ethnographic fieldwork and is able to analyze large-scale data sets. Topically, Daley's work has spanned programs serving a range of vulnerable populations, including children with disabilities and their families, at-risk young men and boys of color, refugee populations in the United States, and individuals who have been trafficked internationally. Her work on autism in India dates to 1995, and includes the first national study of parents of children with autism in India; a national survey of diagnostic practices and beliefs among pediatricians, psychiatrists, and psychologists; a comparison of pediatrician practices and beliefs about autism over a ten-year period; a comprehensive review of published literature on autism; the effect of the popular media on awareness of autism among the general public; an evaluation of a parent training program; and a study of adults with autism in New Delhi. She is also involved in ongoing evaluation of the implementation of the US federal special education law through studies collecting data from nationally representative samples of children and districts and census surveys of states.

GREG J. DUNCAN, PHD Greg Duncan is distinguished professor in the School of Education at the University of California, Irvine, and previously served as the Edwina S. Tarry professor in the School of Education and Social Policy and faculty affiliate in the Institute for Policy Research. He spent the first twenty-five years of his career at the University of Michigan working on and ultimately directing the Panel Study of Income Dynamics (PSID) data collection project. He has published extensively on issues of income distribution, child poverty, and welfare dependence. He is co-author with Aletha Huston and Tom Weisner of *Higher Ground: New Hope for the Working Poor and Their Children* (2007). With Richard Murnane, Duncan coedited *Whither Opportunity* (2011) and coauthored *Restoring Opportunity* (2014). The focus of his recent research has shifted from these environmental influences to the comparative importance of the skills and behaviors developed during childhood. Duncan was elected president of the Population Association of America for 2007–08 and president of the Society for Research in Child Development for 2009–2011. He was elected to the American Academy of Arts and Sciences in 2001 and to the National Academy of Sciences in 2010. In 2013 he was awarded the Klaus J. Jacobs Research Prize.

CAROLYN POPE EDWARDS, EDD Carolyn Edwards is the Willa Cather Professor and professor of psychology and Child, Youth, and Family Studies at the University of Nebraska–Lincoln. She received her EdD in Human Development from Harvard University, and she teaches courses in developmental psychology and early childhood education. Beginning with research in East Africa, she has studied cultural influences on children's development around the world. In the field of early childhood education, she is best known for her studies of the innovative public early childhood services of Reggio Emilia and Pistoia, Italy. She is also part of federally funded research projects at the University of Nebraska seeking to evaluate and improve the quality of children's services, to strengthen parent-child-teacher relationships to help children get ready for school, and to improve PK–3 mathematics education throughout the state of Nebraska. She is author or editor of seventeen volumes and 130 scholarly articles and chapters.

She is a recipient of the Outstanding Research and Creativity Award (ORCA) from the University of Nebraska system, in honor of outstanding research or creative activity of national or international significance in 2012. Her work emphasizes interdisciplinary and cross-cultural collaboration. In making contributions to anthropology, psychology, and early childhood education, she has brought the methods and thinking of each of these disciplines to the others.

ANDREW FULIGNI, PHD Andrew Fuligni is professor in the Department of Psychiatry and Biobehavioral Sciences and the Department of Psychology at the University of California, Los Angeles. His research focuses on family relationships and adolescent development among culturally and ethnically diverse populations, with particular attention to teenagers from Asian and Latin American backgrounds. Much of his work has examined the adaptation of immigrant families to American society, and how that adaptation process ultimately influences the development and adjustment of adolescents in those families. In several studies, he has employed multiple methods to examine the extent to which the cultural beliefs and values of adolescents in immigrant families shape their family relationships, peer relationships, educational adjustment, and psychological well-being. Fuligni was a recipient of the American Psychological Association's Boyd McCandless Award for Early Career Contribution to Developmental Psychology, a William T. Grant Faculty Scholars Award, and a FIRST award from NICHD, and he is a fellow in the American Psychological Association and the Association for Psychological Science.

RONALD GALLIMORE, PHD Ronald Gallimore is distinguished professor emeritus, Department of Psychiatry & Biobehavioral Sciences, University of California, Los Angeles. Gallimore's research focuses on culture, education, teaching, and behavior change, and currently concentrates on improvement of teaching, training, and coaching. He was cofounder of Kamehameha Elementary Education Project (KEEP), a laboratory school for Native Hawai'ians; cofounder of LessonLab Research Institute, an education research organization; and codirector of the TIMSS Video Study of Mathematics and Science Teaching in seven countries. He collaborated with Barbara Keogh, Tom Weisner, and Cindy Bernheimer on Project CHILD (1984–1999, a multimethod, longitudinal study of children with developmental delays and their families). He was principal investigator of the Latino Home School Project (1988–2005, a longitudinal study of immigrant Latino children and their families). He is the author of four books and 140 journal articles and chapters. He observed and published a description of the teaching practices of UCLA's Coach John Wooden (ESPN's Coach of the Twentieth Century). He conducted numerous interviews with Coach Wooden, the results of which were published in four articles and the book *You Haven't Taught Until They Have Learned*. His book *Rousing Minds to Life*, recognized with the 1993 Grawemeyer Award, was described by the awarding committee as an "outstanding educational achievement with potential for worldwide impact." He also received the University of California Presidential Award for research contributing to improvement of public schools (1992), the International Reading Association's Harris Award for best research article (1993), and the National Staff Development Council Best Research of the Year Award (2010).

SARA HARKNESS, PHD, MPH Sara Harkness is professor of human development, pediatrics, and public health at the University of Connecticut, where she also serves as director of the Center for the Study of Culture, Health, and Human Development. In 2012–2013, she was a Jefferson Science Fellow, serving in Washington, DC, as a senior advisor to programs in education and health at USAID. Her research focuses on how the culturally structured environments of children and families, in interaction with biological factors, shape children's health and development. She has been editor of *Ethos* (the journal of the Society for Psychological Anthropology) and is currently on the editorial boards of the *International Journal of Behavioral Development*. In 2009, she received (jointly with Charles Super) an award from the Society for Research in Child Development for Distinguished Contributions to Cultural and Contextual Factors in Child Development. She continues to consult with USAID on issues in global health, and recently gave an invited address to a national conference in Botswana on early childhood education. Harkness's research has been supported by, among others, the NIMH, the NICHD, the National Science Foundation, the Spencer Foundation, and the Carnegie Corporation; she also collaborates on state-funded intervention research related to parenting and child development in Connecticut. She has served on federal review panels for the National Institutes for Child Health and Development, the National Science Foundation, the Maternal and Child Health Bureau, and the Agency for Health Research and Quality. She is an editor of four books, including (with Charles Super) *Parents' Cultural Belief Systems: Their Origins, Expressions, and Consequences*, as well as author of many journal articles and chapters. She has lectured worldwide on her research, and her work has been widely featured in the media.

M. CAMERON HAY, PHD Cameron Hay is an associate professor of anthropology at Miami University, where she also serves as coordinator of Global Health Studies and director of the Global Health Research Innovation Center and is an associate research anthropologist in the Center for Culture and Health at the University of California, Los Angeles. She has over twenty years' experience conducting research on how people identify, understand, cope with, and manage illness and death, with significant funding from the National Science Foundation. As a medical and psychological anthropologist, she conducted ethnographic research in rural Indonesia resulting in *Remembering to Live: Illness at the Intersection of Anxiety and Knowledge in Rural Indonesia* (University of Michigan Press, 2001). Her research has since become more collaborative and transdisciplinary, and she is currently working on multiple research partnership projects with physicians, psychologists, gerontologists, midwives, public health officials, community members, and, of course, other anthropologists. Her work is published in anthropology, medical, and health policy journals.

ALETHA C. HUSTON, PHD Aletha C. Huston is the Priscilla Pond Flawn Regents Professor Emerita of Child Development at the University of Texas at Austin. She specializes in understanding the effects of poverty on children and the impact of child care and income support policies on children's development She was principal investigator of the assessment of child and family impacts of parents' participation in the New Hope Project, a work-based program to reduce poverty, coauthoring a book with Greg Duncan and Tom Weisner, *Higher Ground: New Hope for the Working Poor and Their Children* (2007). She was an investigator in the ten-site NICHD Study of Early Child Care and Youth Development, and codirector of the Center for Research on the Influences of Television on Children at the University of Texas. Her other books include *Developmental Contexts of Middle Childhood: Bridges to Adolescence and Adulthood* (2006), and *Children in Poverty: Child Development and Public Policy* (1991). She is past president of the Society for Research in Child Development, the Developmental Psychology Division of the American Psychological Association, and the Consortium of Social Science Associations, and is the recipient of the Urie Bronfenbrenner Award for Lifetime Contributions to Developmental Psychology in the Service of Science and Society.

HEIDI KELLER, PHD Heidi Keller is a professor emeritus of psychology in the Department of Human Sciences of the University of Osnabrueck and a codirector of Nevet, a greenhouse for context-informed research and training at the Hebrew University of Jerusalem. Her main interest concerns the conception of development as the interface between biology and culture. Her research program consists of cultural analyses of infants' early socialization contexts and their developmental consequences in different cultural environments. She is also interested in the development of dysfunctional pathways in different cultural environments and the application of culture-informed research to educational contexts in multicultural societies. She has published textbooks and handbooks of child development and is on the editorial board of several developmental and cross-cultural journals. Awarded the Nehru chair professorship at the MS University of Baroda, she taught there and at the University of Costa Rica in San Jose and the University of California–Los Angeles. She was also a fellow in residence of the Netherlands Institute of Advanced Sciences. In 2014, she was awarded the ISSBD Distinguished Scientific Contribution Award for the Applications of Behavioral Development Theory and Research and the award for career achievement from the German Society of Psychology.

BARBARA KEOGH, PHD Barbara Keogh is an emerita professor in the UCLA Graduate School of Education and Information Sciences, and a professor in the Sociobehavioral Group in the UCLA Department of Psychiatry. Her primary interests are in children with developmental and learning problems and their families, and in research issues in learning disabilities. She has authored or coauthored a number of books and many articles focused on children with learning disabilities. She is a licensed clinical psychologist in California and has experience in school, juvenile court, and medical/psychiatric settings. She was a member of the National Advisory Committee on the Handicapped and continues to serve as a consultant to a number of governmental and private agencies including the US Department of State Office of Overseas Schools. She was the recipient of the 1992 Research Award from the Council for Exceptional Children.

JILL E. KORBIN, PHD Jill Korbin is the Lucy Adams Leffingwell Professor in the Department of Anthropology, associate dean, director of the Schubert Center for Child Studies, and codirector of the Childhood Studies Program at Case Western Reserve University. Her research interests include culture and human development; cultural, medical, and psychological anthropology; and the effects of context on child maltreatment and child well-being. Her awards include the Margaret Mead Award (1986) from the American Anthropological Association and the Society for Applied Anthropology; a Congressional Science Fellowship (1985–86) through the American Association for the Advancement of Science and the Society for Research in Child Development; and the Wittke Award for Excellence in Undergraduate Teaching at Case Western Reserve University. Korbin served on the National Research Council's Panel on Research on Child Abuse and Neglect, and is currently a member of the board of ChildFund International. Korbin has published on culture and child maltreatment, including her edited book *Child Abuse and Neglect: Cross-Cultural Perspectives* (1981). She coedited the five-volume *Handbook of Child Well-Being: Theories, Methods and Policies in Global Perspective* (2014, with Asher Ben-Arieh, Ferran Casas, and Ivar Frones), *C. Henry Kempe: A 50 Year Legacy to the Field of Child Abuse and Neglect* (2013, with Richard Krugman), and the *Handbook of Child Maltreatment* (2014, with Richard Krugman).

ELI LIEBER, PHD Eli Lieber is associate research psychologist in the UCLA-NPI Center for Culture and Health and president and CEO of SocioCultural Research Consultants (Dedoose.com). His scholarly work focuses on the development and application of methodological strategies for integrated (mixed methods) research in the social sciences. He has worked on collaborative projects such as an experimental mixed method study of the impacts on families and children of early literacy interventions for Head Start programs, an intervention research project seeking to prevent the transmission of HIV/STDs in China, and the study of Mexican immigrant women's reproductive medical decision making following genetic counseling. Other research interests center on the adaptation of Asian and Asian immigrant families with children and youth with Type 1 diabetes and their families. Many of these interests have grown from his nearly five years of work in Taiwan and his continued collaboration with investigators in Taiwan, Hong Kong, and China in the study of social cognition, social cognitive development, parenting styles and practices, and the general adaptation of families to the challenges of immigration and a modernizing world. Initially trained as a quantitative psychologist specializing in social-cognitive development and measurement, his postdoctoral training and subsequent collaborations and work have focused on the development and implementation of mixed methods research methods, design, and data analysis. He has earned a reputation for developing creative strategies to maximize the use of technologies in social science research—his contributions to the development of Dedoose being a primary outcome. He has published broadly in both the general area of mixed method research as well as a range of substantive areas where qualitative and mixed method research has been applied. He also works with the W. T. Grant Foundation and other groups in promoting the use of mixed method approaches.

ROBERT A. LEVINE, PHD Robert LeVine is the Roy E. Larsen Professor of Education and Human Development, Emeritus, in the Graduate School of Education at Harvard University. He is an anthropologist who has studied parenting and child development in Kenya, Nigeria, Mexico, and Nepal and investigated the effects of schooling on maternal behavior in diverse cultural contexts. His most recent book is *Literacy and Mothering: How Women's Schooling Changes the Lives of the World's Children* (2012, Oxford University Press), which won the 2013 Eleanor E. Maccoby Book Award of the American Psychological Association. LeVine has, with his collaborators, published eleven books and more than one hundred articles contributing to psychological anthropology and comparative education as well as the cross-cultural study of parenting, child care, and enculturation. He has also written on comparative personality research, person-centered ethnography, and the relationship of psychoanalysis to anthropology. The awards received by LeVine include the Career Contribution Award of the Society for Psychological Anthropology (1997), the Distinguished Contributions Award of the American Educational Research Association (2001), and fellowships from the Center for Advanced Study in the Behavioral Sciences (1971–72) and the John Simon Guggenheim Memorial Foundation (2004–2005). He was chairman of the Social Science Research Council (1980–83) and distinguished visiting professor of the University of Hong Kong (2001–02).

EDWARD LOWE, PHD Edward Lowe is associate professor of anthropology, Soka University of America. As an applied anthropologist, he uses the methods and theories of anthropology to study and help solve human problems. His research interests focus on the mental health of young people in cultural contexts, family life in local and global contexts, and poverty and inequity. He has worked with children, youth, and their parents in the islands of Micronesia, studying issues of identity, well-being and suicide. He has also worked with a large consortium of researchers and policy advocates that has studied the impact of welfare reform on American families who live in inner-city neighborhoods. He is current editor of *Ethos*, the international journal of the Society for Psychological Anthropology.

ASHLEY MAYNARD, PHD Ashley Maynard is professor and chair in the Department of Psychology at the University of Hawaii. Her research program is concerned with the interrelationships of culture and the contexts of child development, and the healthy cognitive and social development of children. Based in the sociocultural paradigm, the overarching developmental and theoretical question that lies at the heart of her research program is the ways in which a variety of culturally based activity settings influence pathways of development for children. Maynard is interested in cultural settings at nested levels of development: from cultural values and economics in the macrosystem down to children's microsystem interactions. She conducts studies in Hawaii and at her international field site, Nabenchauk, a Zinacantec Maya hamlet located in the highlands of Chiapas, Mexico. The domains of her research cover: the developmental trajectory of children's teaching abilities; the interacting roles of culture and cognitive tools (e.g., books, media, or weaving tools) in the development of thinking; the impact of historical change and changing cultural models on child socialization; and the role of siblings in cognitive and social development. She is coauthor, with Jeffrey Jensen Arnett, of the textbook *Child Development: A Cultural Approach*. She has held several offices in national organizations, including secretary-treasurer of the Society for Psychological Anthropology, treasurer of the Jean Piaget Society, and secretary of the Council of Graduate Departments of Psychology. She is a member of the American Psychological Association's Commission on Accreditation.

RICHARD A. SHWEDER, PHD Shweder is a cultural anthropologist and the Harold H. Swift Distinguished Service Professor of Human Development in the Department of Comparative Human Development at the University of Chicago. For the past forty-seven years, Professor Shweder has been conducting research in cultural psychology on moral reasoning, emotional functioning, gender roles, explanations of illness, ideas about the causes suffering, and the moral foundations of family life practices in the Hindu temple town of Bhubaneswar on the East Coast of India. His recent research examines the scopes and limits of pluralism and the multicultural challenge in Western liberal democracies, particularly focusing on the norm conflicts that arise when people migrate from Africa, Asia, and Latin America to countries in the "North." He is author of *Thinking Through Cultures: Expeditions in Cultural Psychology and Why Do Men Barbecue? Recipes for Cultural Psychology*, editor-in-chief of *The Child: An Encyclopedic Companion*, and editor or coeditor of numerous books in the areas cultural psychology, psychological anthropology, and comparative human development. Shweder has been a fellow at the Wissenschaftskolleg zu Berlin (The Institute for Advanced Study in Berlin), and, twice, at the Center for Advanced

Study in the Behavioral Sciences at Palo Alto. He has also been a Carnegie Scholar, and at separate times, has been a visiting scholar at the Russell Sage Foundation, at the Stanford University Research Institute for the Comparative Study of Race and Ethnicity, and at the Stanford University Hoover Institution as well as a member of the School of Social Science at the Institute for Advanced Study in Princeton, New Jersey. He has also been a member of the MacArthur Foundation Research Network on Successful Midlife Development (MICMAC), and has served as president of the Society for Psychological Anthropology. He is a Fellow of the American Academy of Arts and Sciences.

SASKIA SUBRAMANIAN, PHD Saskia Subramanian is an associate research sociologist in the UCLA Center for Culture and Health at the David Geffen School of Medicine and served as a lecturer in the UCLA Gender Studies Department for over a decade. She is the past recipient of two major grants from the Susan G. Komen Foundation for psychosocial research on breast cancer survivors. She co-authored *After the Cure: The Untold Stories of Breast Cancer Survivors* (NYU Press, November 2008) and produced the feature-length documentary film *Beyond Breast Cancer: Stories of Survivors*, which has been shown at numerous film festivals and invited screenings, including the Baltimore Women's Film Festival, the Reel Women International Film Festival, the Pan-African Film Festival, and the Katharine Houghton Hepburn Center. Subramanian's research centers on women's health issues and disparities as well as the social construction of medicine.

CHARLES M. SUPER, PHD Charles M. Super is professor of human development and pediatrics at the University of Connecticut and is codirector of the Center for the Study of Culture, Health, and Human Development. He has been listed in the Registry of Health Providers in Psychology. He served as field director of the Child Development Research Unit at the University of Nairobi, department head for Human Development and Family Studies at the Pennsylvania State University, and dean of the School of Human Development and Family Studies at the University of Connecticut. Super's research focuses on the cultural regulation of development in infancy and childhood, and on interventions to promote the health and well-being of young children. He has participated in research and interventions in more than a dozen countries and is editor (with Pia Rebello Britto and Patrice Engle) of the *Handbook of Early Childhood Development Research and Its Impact on Global Policy* (Oxford University Press, 2013, published with support from UNICEF and the Society for Research in Child Development). In 2009, he received (jointly with Sara Harkness) the Society for Research in Child Development's Award for Distinguished Contributions to Cultural and Contextual Factors in Child Development. He is author or coauthor of numerous articles and chapters in psychology, anthropology, and pediatrics. He is currently associate editor of the journal *Child Development* and serves on the US National Committee for Psychological Science of the National Research Council, National Academy of Sciences.

DIEGO VIGIL, PHD Diego Vigil is professor emeritus in the School of Social Ecology at the University of California, Irvine. He received his degrees from Long Beach State (BA, 1962) and Sacramento State (MA, 1969) in history. Graduate studies were at UCLA in anthropology (MA, 1973; PhD, 1976). His teaching career spans fifty-one years and includes elementary (three years), middle school (one year), high school (two years), and community college (ten years). After the publication of his first book, *From Indians to Chicanos* (1980, 1998, 2012), he spent the subsequent decades at USC, UW–Madison, UCLA, Harvard, and, finally, UC Irvine. Known for his work and publications on urban adolescents and youth, he has written *Barrio Gangs* (1988), *Personas Mexicanas* (1997), *A Rainbow of Gangs* (2002), *The Projects* (2007), *Gang Redux* (2010), and *Streetsmart Schoolsmart* (2012). His expertise is in urban anthropology; psychology, socialization, and education in Mexico and the United States; and Southwest ethnohistory. While he continues to write for academia, in his retirement he has begun to devote time to fictional writing (novels/screenplays, children's books), oil painting, and his ubiquitous tenor saxophone (he now plays pachuco hop).

THOMAS S. WEISNER, PHD Thomas Weisner is distinguished professor of anthropology emeritus, Departments of Psychiatry (Semel Institute, Center for Culture and Health) and Anthropology at UCLA. His research and teaching interests are in culture and human development, families and children at risk, mixed methods, and evidence-informed policy. His current research includes work with Mexican American teens and parents in Los Angeles (with Andrew Fuligni and Nancy Gonzalez); a research and fieldwork training program with the Culture, Brain, Development, and Mental Health program at UCLA, including a partnership with an NGO in India, Action for Autism; and a qualitative follow-up study of 185 young adults diagnosed as children with ADHD from the MTA study. He participated in a longitudinal study over eight years of a successful random-assignment experimental support program for working-poor parents (with Greg Duncan, Aletha Huston, Hiro Yoshikawa, and Bob Granger). He has collaborated in a longitudinal study of families with children with developmental disabilities (with Ron Gallimore and Barbara Keogh). He has done longitudinal field research in Western Kenya and Nairobi on sibling caretaking of children and on the long-term consequences of urban migration for children and families, as well as studies of sibling caretaking and school competence among Native Hawai'ians (with Ron Gallimore). He collaborated in a twenty-year longitudinal study of nonconventional, countercultural family lifestyles in California and effects on children and youth. He has developed tools for mixed methods, including Dedoose web-based software (with Eli Lieber and Jason Taylor) and the Ecocultural Family Interview (the EFI). Weisner has been a fellow at the Center for Advanced Study in the Behavioral Sciences, a member of the MacArthur Foundation research network on successful pathways in middle childhood, is past president of the Society for Psychological Anthropology, has been a senior program advisor to the William T. Grant Foundation, and is on the board of ChildFund International as well as the Governing Council of the Society for Research in Child Development. He is the coauthor of *Higher Ground: New Hope for the Working Poor and Their Children* (2007, with Greg Duncan and Aletha Huston); *Making It Work: Low-Wage Employment, Family Life, and Child Development* (with Hirokazu Yoshikawa and Edward Lowe, 2006); and *African Families and the Crisis of Social Change* (with Candice Bradley and Phil Kilbride, 1997); and editor of *Discovering Successful Pathways in Children's Development: New Methods in the Study of Childhood and Family Life* (2005). His BA in anthropology is from Reed College (1965) and his PhD from Harvard University (1973) in anthropology and social relations.

BRIAN WILCOX, PHD Brian Wilcox is the director of the Center on Children, Families, and the Law, and professor of Psychology at the University of Nebraska–Lincoln. Trained in community psychology at the University of Texas in 1979, prior to coming to Nebraska he taught at the University of Virginia, served as a legislative assistant to Senator Bill Bradley, and was director of public policy for the American Psychological Association. In addition to his intervention research on HIV prevention, his teaching and research interests focus broadly on the linkages between human development and public policy, including adolescent sexual behavior, child welfare, child care, and children and the media. All of his work is geared toward directly connecting research with social policy and/or practice. Wilcox is a fellow of the American Psychological Association, and is a past president of APA's Division of Child, Youth and Family Services. He is on numerous editorial boards, including the *Journal of Adolescent Health*, *Psicologia: Reflexão e Crítica*, and *Acta de Investigación Psicológica*. During the 2004–2005 year he was a visiting professor at the Pontifícia Universidade Católica in Rio de Janeiro and a Senior Fulbright Scholar at the Universidade Federal do Rio Grande do Sul in Porto Alegre, Brazil.

CAROL WORTHMAN, PHD Carol Worthman is the Samuel Candler Dobbs Professor, Department of Anthropology, and directs the Laboratory for Comparative Human Biology at Emory University. She takes a biocultural approach to the pursuit of comparative interdisciplinary research on human development, reproductive ecology, and biocultural bases of differential mental and physical health. Worthman has conducted cross-cultural ethnographic and biosocial research in twelve countries, including Kenya, Tibet, Nepal, Egypt, Japan, Papua New Guinea, and South Africa, as well as in rural, urban, and semiurban areas of the United States. For the past twenty years, she has collaborated with Jane Costello and Adrian Angold in the Great Smoky Mountains Study, a large, longitudinal, population-based developmental epidemiological project in western North Carolina, and is currently conducting research in Vietnam. Her research aims to contribute to intelligent human being-in-the-world, based on a conviction that how we understand human nature and culture influences and legitimates our behavior, values, and decisions. Hence, her goals are as much practical as intellectual, aimed to illuminate the pathways to differential human well-being and thereby to both critique existing social conditions and point the way toward redressing and forestalling distress and inequity. Unlike many human biologists, then, she is concerned as much with psychological as physical development and health. Like many biological anthropologists, she also sees biology as a lens through which we can gain fresh insight into culture and its large but bounded roles in human behavior and experience.

HIROKAZU YOSHIKAWA, PHD Hirokazu Yoshikawa is the Courtney Sale Ross Professor of Globalization and Education at NYU Steinhardt. Previously he served as the Walter H. Gale Professor of Education at the Harvard Graduate School of Education and as its academic dean. He is a developmental and community psychologist who conducts research on the development of young children in immigrant families and the effects of public policies and early childhood intervention on children's development. His currently funded work examines how public policies, parental employment, and transnational contexts influence very young children's development in Chinese, Mexican, Dominican, and African American families. This work combines longitudinal survey, observational, and ethnographic methods. He has conducted extensive research on the effects on children of public policies related to welfare, employment, and early childhood intervention. Recent books include *Immigrants Raising Citizens: Undocumented Parents and Their Children* (Russell Sage, 2011); *Making It Work: Low-Wage Employment, Family Life, and Child Development*, with Thomas S. Weisner and Edward Lowe (Russell Sage, 2006), and *Toward Positive Youth Development: Transforming Schools and Community Programs* (coedited with Marybeth Shinn, Oxford, 2008). He currently serves on the Leadership Council and as the cochair of the early childhood development and education workgroup of the U.N. Sustainable Development Solutions Network, the research and technical group advising the Secretary-General on the post-2015 global development goals. He has served on the Board on Children, Youth, and Families of the National Academy of Sciences, the Early Childhood Advisory Committee of the Inter-American Development Bank, and the DHHS Advisory Committee on Head Start Research and Evaluation for the Clinton and Obama administrations. In 2012 he was nominated by President Obama and confirmed by the Senate as a member of the National Board for Education Sciences. In 2014 he was elected to the National Academy of Education. He currently serves on the National Academy of Sciences Committee on the Integration of Immigrants into American Society, the National Academy of Sciences Forum on Investing in Young Children Globally, and the boards of the Foundation for Child Development and the Russell Sage Foundation.

Index